Qualitative Research Interviewing

Biographic Narrative and
Semi-Structured Methods

TOM WENGRAF

SAGE Publications
London • Thousand Oaks • New Delhi

© Tom Wengraf, 2001
First published 2001
Reprinted 2002, 2004

Apart from any fair dealing for the purposes of research or private study,
or criticism or review, as permitted under the Copyright, Designs and
Patents Act, 1988, this publication may be reproduced, stored or
transmitted in any form, or by any means, only with the prior permission
in writing of the publishers, or in the case of reprographic reproduction,
in accordance with the terms of licences issued by the Copyright
Licensing Agency. Inquiries concerning reproduction outside those
terms should be sent to the publishers.

SAGE Publications Ltd
1 Oliver's Yard, 55 City Road
London EC1Y 1SP

SAGE Publications Inc
2455 Teller Road
Thousand Oaks, California 91320

SAGE Publications India Pvt Ltd
B–42 Panchsheel Enclave
PO Box 4109
New Delhi 110 017

British Library Cataloguing in Publication data

A catalogue record for this book is available from the British Library

ISBN 0-8039-7500-7 (hbk)
ISBN 0-8039-7501-5 (pbk)

Typeset by SIVA Maths Setters, Chennai, India
Printed and bound in Great Britain by
Cromwell Press Limited, Trowbridge, Wiltshire

Summary of Contents

Contents

Figures

Exercises

Abbreviations

Some people react badly to acronyms and special scientific terms, which they experience as unnecessary jargon; but special terms are inherent to any relatively developed craft, and I find that, provided that they are properly introduced and make sense, they make communication and thinking easier. Nobody complains that motor engineers have a specialized and sophisticated vocabulary for the parts and processes of motor cars, nor that chefs have a complex vocabulary for their expertise. A social research text has no less need for an expert vocabulary (or theory-language). I hope that the terminology below shows its value in use, and apologize to the extent to which it does not.

Relevant terms are introduced and made meaningful within the text. This list provides a quick reference in case of uncertainty.

ACRQ	answer to a Central Research Question
ATQ	answer to a Theory-Question
BDA	Biographical Data Analysis
BDC	Biographical Data Chronology
BIM	Biographic-Interpretive Method[1]
BNIM	Biographic-Narrative-Interpretive Method
CF	conceptual framework
CH	counter-hypothesis (to one previously put forward)
CLS	critical linguistics/semiotics
CRQ	Central Research Question
DARNE	description – argumentation – report – narrative – evaluation
EH	experiential hypothesis
EI	empirical indicator/indication
FFSI	fairly-fully structured interviewing
FH	following hypothesis (a predictive hypothesis about what will be found next or later in a lived-life chronology or in a told-story text)
II	interviewer intervention
IL	informant language (or folk-language)
IM	interview material

---

1 In previous publications, including Chamberlayne et al. (2000), I referred to the German QUATEXT approach as 'BIM'. Upon reflection, to stress the key role of narrative in the method, I refer to it in this text as 'BNIM'.

IQ	informant question
LSDI	lightly-structured depth interview
NVC	non-verbal communication
PL	paralinguistics
QUATEXT	Institute for Qualitative Social Research
RP	Research Purposes (the purposes which determine the objectives of your research and your Central Research Question)
sH	shaping hypothesis (about how an event might shape the future of a life)
SH	structural hypothesis (a hypothesis about what might be the structural principle of a biographical chronology [BDC] or of a told story [TSS] or of a case history)
SHEIOT	situation – happening – event – incident – occasion/occurrence – time
SOSTRIS	Social Strategies in Risk Society
SQUIN	Single Question aimed at Inducing Narrative
SQUIN-B	Single Question aimed at Inducing Narrative of a Biographical nature
SSDI	semi-structured depth interview
TC–EI	theoretical concept/empirical indicator
TFA	thematic field analysis
TL	theory-language
TQ	theory-question
TQUIN	Topic Question aimed at Inducing Narrative
TSS	Text Structure Sequentialization (the structure of the sequential development of a [narrative] interview)

Preface

I wrote this book because, over the past 15 years, I have not been able to find one text that dealt in a coherent way with the *full* range of issues and practices involved in doing semi-structured interviews. Constantly moving from conceptual works such as Briggs (1986) and Mishler (1986) and even more general conceptual texts on qualitative methodology as such (e.g. Mason, 1996), on the one hand, to severely practical 'how-to-do-it' books such as Spradley (1979) and Dillon (1990), on the other, was confusing since their implicit concepts and philosophies were often quite discordant. Then, to help analyse the materials, there were books like Strauss (1987) and Coffey and Atkinson (1997) but they didn't deal with the task of writing-up reports and more complex texts for different audiences, on which I found material in yet other places such as Clifford and Marcus (1986) and Hammersley (1990). Again, the implicit concepts and philosophies differed, leading to considerable difficulties and confusion both for myself and my students. The more books, the less they added up (except in cash terms!).

As a result, I decided to attempt a synthesis for advanced undergraduates, and for postgraduates and professional researchers, that would be conceptually coherent but severely practical at the same time, covering the full gamut of practice from the conceptualization of topics to structures of writing-up. It would have to provide a conceptual-philosophical approach that was compatible with – and might even serve as an introduction to – key questions of qualitative and even quantitative social research methodology in general, but one which provided a solution compatible with a moderate position in the excesses of 'paradigm wrangles'. It was to be full of examples, because it is only by working through examples (of bad and good practice) that the generalities would make more than trivial sense, and clear guidance could be given.

I made progress in providing such a 'one-stop-shop' text for myself and my students and then came across the *Quatext* practice of doing and interpreting biographical-narrative research interviews. Since it exemplified much of what I wanted to put across, and is a powerful and enjoyable paradigm to work with, I have integrated my use of it into the book. My debt to *Quatext* is acknowledged in the relevant chapters.

I am grateful to all those researchers and writers whose contributions I have brought together and built upon, though, needless to say, I alone am responsible for the result. I also thank 'Harold' whose case will be met in the following pages, my students, the production team and my readers at Sage (especially Bob Miller) and Colin Macnee who struggled with my drafts as I searched for both sufficient detail and conceptual clarity across a widening and proliferating universe. My love and gratitude go to my parents, Paul and Dada, and to Prue Chamberlayne, both professionally and personally, for the support she has given me. For the love, challenge and excitement they bring to my life I dedicate the book to her and – though they are unlikely to read it – to my children Maya, Joe and Katia.

I also dedicate the book to its eventual readers, users and critics; reports of experiences of using it, comments and suggestions as to how to improve it, would be welcomed at <tom.wengraf@cheerful.com>

Introduction

PURPOSE OF THE BOOK

This book is designed to address a number of questions: what is meant by a 'depth' or 'in depth' interview? How do you prepare to do such interviews; how do you do them; and how do you analyse and present the results? How do you present, compare and theorize the results from a number of such interviews?

The concept of a 'semi-structured depth interview' covers a great range of interview strategies, all counterposed to the concepts of a 'fully structured' interview and (less strongly perhaps) of a haphazard or unstructured one. This text is concerned in particular to look at the difference between, on the one hand, narrative – and especially biographic-narrative – interviews with minimal interviewer-structuring and, on the other, more classical semi-structured depth interviews with partially prepared questions that are fully structured by the researcher/interviewer's concerns and initial theoretical framework. It puts forward a model of sequencing such different interview experiences and strategies so that the advantages of both can be maximized.

Those interested in a detailed exploration of the currently increasing interest in biographical methods within social science should consult *The Turn to Biographical Methods in Social Science*, edited by Prue Chamberlayne, Joanna Bornat and the author, in some senses a companion volume to this one, or, for those concerned more with oral history's uses of such interviews, *The Oral History Reader*, edited by Perks and Thomson. The substantive findings of the SOSTRIS project frequently referred to in this book will be found in *Contemporary Europe: biographical approaches to social exclusion* (edited by Prue Chamberlayne, Mike Rustin and Tom Wengraf) to be published by Policy Press. Two relevant email addresses are <biog-methods@mailbase.ac.uk> and <psych-narrative@massey.ac.nz>. A more general qualitative one is <qualrs-l@listserv.uga.edu>.

STRUCTURE OF THE BOOK AS A WHOLE

The book comprises six parts:

- I: Concepts and approaches to depth interviewing
- II: Up to the interview: strategies for getting the right material
- III: Around the interview
- IV: After the interview: strategies for working the materials
- V: Comparison of cases: from contingencies to typologies
- VI: Writing up: strategies of re/presentation

I use the language of 'concepts and approaches' and of 'procedures and strategies' in order to stress the amount of *decision-making* in which researchers are constantly involved: research is as much a question of inventing a practice as it is a question of understanding the point of rules.

The devil and his friend were out walking, and saw a man ahead of them stoop down and pick something off the ground.
'What did the man find?' asked the friend.
'A piece of truth', replied the devil.
'Doesn't that worry you?', asked the friend.
'No', replied the devil. 'I shall let him make a belief about it.'
(A. de Mello, 1984)

[The goal is] the development of generalisations of ever increasing scope, so that greater and greater varieties of phenomena can be explained by them, larger and larger questions answered by them, and broader and broader reaching predictions and decisions based upon them
(Leon Levy, 1970)

To Generalise is to be an Idiot
(An annotation by William Blake to Joshua Reynolds's *Discourses*)

Understanding individual life histories requires not only the employment of general conceptual frameworks and theories but also methods for understanding what is particular, distinctive or unique about the individual.
(W.M. Runyan, 1982, who also cited the above three quotations)

CONCEPTS AND APPROACHES TO DEPTH INTERVIEWING

OVERVIEW

'Qualitative' research interviewing tends to under-theorize its data (see, e.g., Frisch, 1998). It assumes too easily that an interview is an unproblematic window on psychological or social realities, and that the 'information' that the interviewee gives about themself and their world can be simply extracted and quoted, as the word of an ominiscient and disinterested witness might be accepted at face-value in a law-court.

I start from a particular position about interview data – namely that, in themselves, they are data only about a particular research conversation that occurred at a particular time and place. If we wish to use such data as evidence to support assertions about extra-interview realities (as we nearly always do), then this requires assumptions and contextual knowledge and argument.

Starting from this deliberately narrow position, I then go on to show the problematic nature of interviews and suggest some models put forward for interpreting the facts of interview interaction. I compare interactional models with anthropological ones, to show that both narrow and broad concerns need to be addressed.

Finally, I look at models of research design in general and interview research in particular to suggest the issues that must be borne in mind.

In this context, I then put forward a case for an approach to semi-structured depth interviewing in which the purposes and theory of the interviewer are always strategically crucial but in which that theory requires the interviewer to combine – but not necessarily in the same session – sometimes fairly-fully or heavily structured and sometimes very lightly structured sessions and questions.

Unlike many who argue for 'qualitative interviewing', I believe that great attention must be paid by the researcher to his or her own conceptual frameworks and to clarifying the research questions. In addition, proper design and analysis calls for a full acceptance of a distinction usually summed up as 'operationalization', a term normalized in quantitative social research but usually ignored or underplayed by so-called qualitative researchers. Making inferences from interview data is no less problematical than making inferences from quantitative data, as we shall see. However, I personally find it more fun.

Interview 'Facts' as Evidence to Support Inferences to Eventual Theorization/ Representation Models

DATA-COLLECTION (UP TO AND INCLUDING THE INTERVIEW) AND DATA-INTERPRETATION (FROM INTERVIEW TO RESEARCHER PRODUCT)

In social research methodology we typically distinguish the collection of data from the interpretation of data. How these are to be related can then be seen in two different ways: by a common-sense hypothetico-inductivist model and by a hypothetico-deductivist model.

Common-sense Hypothetico-inductivist Model

In a fairly common-sensical model, the researcher collects 'all the relevant facts' and then examines them to see what theory is suggested by this set of 'all the relevant facts'. The theory thus 'emerges' from the data. This is the original 'grounded theory' tradition (Glaser and Strauss, 1968) in which theory emerges by a process of 'induction'. The facts are believed to suggest – or even 'require' or 'dictate' – the theorization.

Anti-common-sense Hypothetico-deductivist Model

The counter-model is anti-inductivist. It declares that there is no thing as 'all the relevant facts', there are only 'hypothesis-relevant facts', and that research must always start with a body of prior theory, if only to decide which set of 'collectable facts' should be collected or generated. It is this prior body of theory from which the researcher generates a particular hypothesis whose truth or falsity could be 'tested' by a particular selection of 'hypothesis-relevant facts'. The hypothesis-relevant facts are then collected, and the hypothesis is either supported by the evidence of those facts or it is refuted by them.

Inductivist and Deductivist 'Moments' in Doing Research

Both the 'inductivist' and the 'deductivist' models correspond to styles of doing research; both have philosophical flaws which enable them to be criticized for ever. In order to have survived their innumerable critics for so long (see, for example, Layder, 1998) each model must correspond to some real experience of researchers.

I would argue that both are appropriate as descriptions of what researchers experience as happening at different moments of the research cycle and that another relationship between the inductivist and deductivist models may be that of *level*.

I would regard myself as strategically being largely a 'deductivist' or a theoreticist while fully appreciating the need for particular moments of inductive working. For many of the purposes for which I do research, my general 'deductivist' strategic theory dictates 'giving up control' at a tactical level to the person being interviewed. For other purposes, my same theoretical model – which will be elaborated later – dictates 'control being taken back' by the interviewer. However, other researchers may be strategically inductivist while at certain moments using deductivist tactics. To understand why one can feel both an inductivist and a deductivist at different times or even in the same moment of research, I find the concepts of different levels, or of the difference between strategy and tactics, to be helpful. Gregory Bateson's argument for a combination of 'loose' and 'tight' thinking is similar.

SOME FEATURES OF DEPTH INTERVIEWING AS DESIGNED PRACTICE

If these are features of the approach being taken, what are the main points that I wish to stress about the style of interview that I am talking about?

- The interview is a research interview, designed for the purpose of improving knowledge.
- It is a special type of conversational interaction: in some ways it is like other conversations, but it has special features which need to be understood.
- It has to be planned and prepared for like other forms of research activity but what is planned is a deliberate half-scripted or quarter-scripted interview: its questions are only partially prepared in advance (semi-structured) and will therefore be largely improvised by you as interviewer. But only largely: the interview as a whole is a joint production, a co-production, by you and your interviewee.
- It is to go into matters 'in depth'.

I shall deal with these briefly in turn.

The Interview is a Research Interview

The 'form' of an interview – questioning by one person, answering by another – can be used for a variety of purposes (Dillon, 1990: 2, and below, p. 154). Teachers use questions in order to help students learn; psychotherapists use questions to heal; secret police use brainwashing questioning to break down the interviewee's grip on reality.

In future, when I refer to 'interviewing' in this book – unless it is clear from context that I am using it differently – I shall mean 'research interviewing'. To me – and in this book – scientific research has to do with 'getting a better understanding of reality'.[1] The ethics of the research interview are that, at minimum, the informant should not be changed for the worse: against certain objections, I maintain that the research interview is not designed to 'help' or 'empower', or 'change' the informant at all. In my interviews, I collect information with the purpose of

1 developing/constructing a 'model' of some aspect of reality that I hope will be found to be in accordance with 'the facts' about that reality,
   or
2 testing a constructed model to see whether it is confirmed or falsified by 'the facts',
   and, more usually,
3 doing both the above.

I shall argue in Part II that the 'semi-structured depth interview' normally involves the interviewer in a process of both model-building and model-testing, both theory-construction and theory-verification, within the same session or series of sessions.[2] I shall explore further the considerable difficulties that arise with the concept of 'the facts', the concept of 'being in accordance with the interview facts' so easily (but only provisionally) assumed in statements 1 and 2 in the list above.

The Interview is a Type of Conversational Face-to-face Interaction

Psychologists, social psychologists, sociologists, anthropologists all study human interaction in general and face-to-face interaction in particular. People work together, live together, make love together: there are co-operative aspects to (interview) interactions, and conflictual ones. Interactions can be between people of similar statuses or those of different statuses. They can be ritualized, heavily formatted by custom, or they can be more exploratory, uncertain and potentially innovative. They can leave people feeling positive, negative, or nothing. They can involve expensive material resources, or none at all. They can be remembered, they can be forgotten. They can be 'typical of the time and place and of their type', they can be 'different'.

When you come to study and plan interviewing, bear fully in mind all the knowledge derived from your discipline (sociology, psychology, cultural studies, history, etc.) about face-to-face interaction and about the specificity of the society and the setting and the types of people involved, especially yourself. Don't put on a set of blinkers marked 'research methodology' to exclude other considerations!

The interviews that you do or that you study are not asocial, ahistorical, events. You do not leave behind your anxieties, your hopes, your blindspots, your prejudices, your class, race or gender, your location in global social structure, your age and historical positions, your emotions, your past and your sense of possible

---

1 This philosophical position has been called a 'realist' one, and there are other philosophies: for example, those that hold that there is no such thing as a 'reality' out there but only an inter-subjective agreement to pretend to the existence of such an independent-seeming reality. *Strategically* I work with the axiom that there is a historically occurring reality out there; *tactically*, methodologically, we should always suspect that our most recent account is a fiction requiring further rectification.

2 It also is liable to involve *the informant in such a process as well* as they struggle to make sense of the interviewee's responses and non-responses and how to respond and not-respond to the interviewer. The interviewer is as engaged in hypothesis-formation and theory-rectification as you are.

futures when you set up an interview, and nor does your interviewee when he or she agrees to an interview and you both come nervously into the same room. Nor do you do so when you sit down to analyse the material you have produced.

It has to be Particularly Well-prepared (Designed) to Allow it to be Semi-Structured

Semi-structured interviews are designed to have a number of interviewer questions prepared in advance but such prepared questions are designed to be sufficiently open that the subsequent questions of the interviewer cannot be planned in advance but must be improvised in a careful and theorized way. As regards such *semi-structured interviews*, they are ones where research and planning produce a session in which most of the informant's responses can't be predicted in advance and where you as interviewer therefore have to *improvise* probably half – and maybe 80% or more – of your responses to what they say in response to your *initial prepared* question or questions.

In particular, I am concerned with semi-structured interviews where the interviewee is asked to tell a story, produce a narrative of some sort regarding all or part of their own life-experience. These biographic-narrative interviews are of considerable interest in their own right, and they also illustrate rather well more general principles of semi-structured interviewing.

Very often, semi-structured interviewing is seen as 'easier' in some not very clear way. Novice researchers often feel that, with interviews that are only semi-structured, they do not have to do as much preparation, they do not have to work each question out in advance. This is a *terrible* mistake. Semi-structured interviews are not 'easier' to prepare and implement than fully structured interviews; they might be seen as more difficult. They are *semi*-structured, but they must be *fully* planned and prepared. Improvisation requires more training and more mental preparation before each interview than simply delivering lines prepared and rote-learned in advance. Compared with fully structured interviews, *semi-structured interviews* to be successful require

- *as much preparation* before the session, probably, and certainly
- *more discipline and more creativity in* the session, and certainly
- *more time for analysis and interpretation after* the session.

Given an equivalent amount of time and money, you can 'do' (prepare, do and analyse) *far fewer* semi-structured interviews than you can do fully structured ones. They may yield much more than fully structured ones can, under the right conditions. Under the wrong conditions, they may yield nothing at all. They are high-preparation, high-risk, high-gain, and high-analysis operations.

Thinking clearly about the right conditions for being successful in such skilled interviewing and analysis is what this book is about.

It is an Interview 'in Depth'

What is meant by 'depth' will be discussed in more detail in Part II (see, however, Rorty, 2000 for a recasting of the concept of 'depth' into one of 'width'). To attempt to 'formalize' the concept and give it a bogus rigidity and precision at this point would not be helpful. There are two meanings for 'depth' which are useful to distinguish.

1 To go into something 'in depth' is to get a more detailed knowledge about it.
2 To go into something in depth is to get a sense of how the apparently straight-forward is actually more complicated, of how the 'surface appearances' may be quite misleading about 'depth realities'.

Perhaps this second is more in tune with the approach in this book. To go into something in depth means to get a deep understanding of how little you knew about it, and how provisional one's 'formulations of truth' have to be – even by, or about, depth-interviewing.

Let us try to see how these generalities might work in a particular analysis.

THE 'HARD AND ONLY FACTS' OF INTERVIEW INTERACTION, AND INFERENCES

As said above, for the purposes of this section, I have assumed the relatively inductivist position that, if properly recorded by tape-recorder and properly transcribed, the words spoken in the interview are relatively non-controversial 'facts'.[3] From the words of the interview, what sort of inferences to extra-interview realities can I make? More importantly: *how* do I make and question such inferences?

Old Wu: Knowledge of Discourse, Referents, Subjectivity

What follows is an extract from an interview conducted with an elderly Chinese lady. I have chosen this text partly because most readers of this book will, like me, be unfamiliar with the cultural context. At this point in the interview, she is talking about her experience of the Maoist period in China.

'The Anti-Rightist campaign started. My ex-husband was accused of vilifying the Party and was labelled a rightist. In China, the Communist Party exercises leadership in everything. My ex-husband was jailed for being a counter-revolutionary and a suspected spy for speaking out and having overseas relatives.

For the future of the family, and especially for the children, he thought it would be better that I divorced him. The Party secretary from my workplace had discussed my case at a mass-meeting and suggested that I get a divorce. He told me that love was not just for love's sake; love must have a political basis. My husband was an enemy of the people and did not deserve my love; if I didn't divorce him, then I supported the enemy. The Party secretary told me not to be afraid, as the masses would support and help me to divorce my husband [a doctor at a hospital]. It seems inconceivable and ridiculous to young people nowadays, but this kind of propaganda beguiled our generation for several decades. I thought my children would suffer for ever if I did not divorce him. Furthermore, because my husband was in prison, he could not get any salary. I was a nurse and did not earn much. In the end, I decided to get a divorce and I married another man who was a worker.

continued

---

3 Later on, when dealing with the task of transcription (p. 212–23 onwards) this model will be moderately questioned; here it is used as a basis for further argument.

continued

My son was only a teen-ager and was strongly against my divorce. After five years of prison life, my ex-husband died of some illness in prison. When my son heard the news of his death, he could not control himself and went mad. It was a great tragedy for my family. I am very fond of my son, and his mental illness has led me to study spirituality ever since.

My ex-husband was not pardoned until 1981. I am not fully satisfied with my second marriage. I don't think I have enough courage to divorce again. Divorce belongs to the young. I am too old to divorce, I do not want to catch the vogue. I love my children more than myself. That is the great love of Chinese women.' (Farmer, 1993: 91–2)

Let us assume that this transcript 'is' or contains the data of the interview – as we shall see later, it is not 'raw' but 'processed' data, not only because it is a translation but also because it is a transcription – and consider what inferences might be made. What can we learn from this piece of data, this datum?

At the moment, and only for the moment, I shall set aside the interview interaction as an 'object of research' in its own right (reserving this for Chapter 3). Just for the moment, I shall assume we are only interested in it as a means to study other things. What extra-interview objects of study can this material be used for studying?

There is no end to the list of possible 'objects of study' for which I might wish to gather information by way of depth interviews. For convenience's sake, I shall create three categories, and then apply them to the Old Wu text.

We can use our interviews to know more about

1　discourse
2　objective referents
3　subjectivity.

Discourse

The *discourse* is the mode of talk spontaneously chosen by the subject. A 'linguistic performance' occurs (carefully registered by the tape-recorder) and this can be analysed in a number of ways. One mode of analysis, that associated with the work of Foucault and of Chomsky, is where you attempt to identify a 'deep structure' which underlies or (as some would argue) generates the 'surface performance' of the things actually said. This is like a system of rules that creates 'patterned productions' of things likely to be said ('sayables') and things unlikely or impossible to be said ('unsayables') within that particular 'regime of discourse'.

- For example, Hollway (1989: 53–7) identified four discourses around sexuality: (i) the discourse of male sexual drive; (ii) the 'have-hold' discourse; (iii) the permissive discourse; and (iv) feminist discourse. She describes this identification of types of discourse as being 'tools to help in organizing … accounts'.
- For example, in economics, we can distinguish the 'neo-liberal discourse' promoting unregulated world free trade, from various 'social and ecological discourses' concerned to protect humans, animals and the environment from the ravages of the search for corporate profit.

- For example, Pierret (1993) has identified four different discourses about health and illness in France and compared them to the distribution of English ways of talking about health.

In general, researchers attempt to identify the systemic nature of discourses which enable certain sorts of things to be said and make other sorts of things difficult to say. I might wish to explore the 'structure of discourse' underlying the flow of utterances of Old Wu in this segment of text. What are the organizing principles of her flow of talk?

There are serious problems in exploring this, since all I do have as raw material is the mode of talk, the joint performance, in which two particular people engaged on the special occasion of this particular interview. In the Old Wu text, I do not have any idea as to what the interviewer said to prompt the flow of talk: the interviewer's contribution, their questioning, is absent. Was the original interview question about 'the great love of Chinese women' (the final sentence in the extract)? Was it 'What happened to your family in the Maoist period?' Was it 'How did Maoism work out in practice?' The significance of the interviewee's response cannot be gauged without understanding the implications of the questioning for the production of that response.

I may wish to 'infer', from this co-produced joint mode of talk, what one of them (the interviewee; Old Wu, in our example above) would produce 'spontaneously' (on his or her own? to themselves in internal speech?) but this is an inference, not a fact. Some 'discourse analysts', as we shall see (for example, Potter and Weatherell, 1987), argue that all speaking (discoursing) is bound to the contexts and especially to the other people for whom it is produced, and so I can only say that somebody is capable of producing the 'discourse' that they did produce, that they have that particular discourse within their repertoire of discursive performances. They argue that I cannot be sure that one has a more privileged, or 'authentic', status – always more preferred – than any other.

Nonetheless, whether I see people as having an 'authentic discourse' and a number of 'socially constrained' ones, or whether I think of all modes of talk as being equally constrained and equally (in)authentic, I can use interview material to learn more about discursive productions and performances (see e.g. Squire, 2000).

However, if I wish to make inferences from the discourse in the interview to other realities, I can move in either or both of two directions. One direction is towards knowledge of that which is being talked about (the topic, the referent); the other is towards knowledge of the time-and-place located subjectivities who are doing the talking. We shall deal with these in turn.

Objective Referents

One such set of other realities may be that of the objective referents: those things that are referred to (hence 'referent', that to which reference is made) in the talk, or about which information can be gleaned 'through' the talk (excluding from the latter the 'subjectivity' of the individual informant, to be discussed later). See Figure 1.1. These are sometimes called the 'topics'.

If a policeman interviews a witness about a scene in a supermarket that led to an act of violence, he is interested in the 'objective facts' to which the individual informant was a witness: who did what, said what, what happened next? ... The

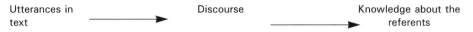

FIGURE 1.1   **From Utterances, to Discourse, to Knowledge of Referents**

policeman is interested in the 'discourse' or the 'subjectivity' of the witnessing subject only to the extent that he must evaluate the reliability of the witness in order to make up his own mind about what inferences about 'what really happened' he is justified in drawing from the witness's statements.

The individual subject is being asked to talk so that some information, not about him or her, but about a present or past 'context' which happens to be 'carried' by him or her, can be obtained. 'Interviewing for the facts', analysing interview material for 'factual content', for information about certain referents, is a very frequent, and obviously important, use of interview material. For an interesting discussion of knowledge-elicitation, see Firlej and Hellens (1993).

In the case of the Old Wu extract, I can ask what knowledge about the relationships of Old Wu's family, her local Communist Party and its officials, the treatment of family members inside and outside the family, etc. can be gained from this account and what knowledge about such relations more generally can also be inferred.

Subjectivity

Or I may wish to interview and use interview material because of my interest in making inferences about subjectivity (Figure 1.2).

FIGURE 1.2   **From Utterances, to Discourse, to Knowledge about Subjectivity(ies)**

Subjectivity is a term for a model I construct of what I see as some of the permanent or transient characteristics of the subject who is acting as informant in the interview. Our research may be concerned with them as a unique person, or as a 'representative' of a certain 'social type', or in some other way. Though our hypothetical policeman is only interested in subjectivity of the witness as a possible 'contaminating factor', I may be interested in the subjectivity of the interviewee as a clue to 'witness psychology', for example. In a more therapeutic situation, I might suggest that the interviewee talk about any number of subjects (e.g. what happened to them the day before) not because I am interested in that objective referent but because I am interested in how he or she talks about it, thus revealing their subjectivity. The topics themselves would be of subsidiary interest. What can I gather about Old Wu's (changing) subjectivity and the subjectivities of those inside and outside the family with whom she had a complex of voluntary or forced relationships?

The 'subjectivity of Old Wu within the interview' may be different from that which she exhibits or possesses or is subject to in other practical and relational contexts of her life. The interplay between my and your subjectivity in an interview interaction is a matter for research. It can be argued (see e.g. Hollway, 1989;

Henriques et al., 1984) that subjectivity should be more fully understood as not just a predisposition within the individual but also as a complex interplay between people – for example, between the interviewer and the interviewee. I refer to this as being interested in the *inter/subjectivity* of the interaction.

Inferring the Three Types of Knowledge from the Transcript Data

Given a research focus on discourse, the referents, and subjectivity, what points can I infer about each from the raw data of the interview transcript?

The 'Old Wu' 'case-narrative' is rich, and Figure 1.3 represents a 'first run through' of attempting to 'fill the columns, with appropriate material. Bear in mind, though, as the overlapping nature of the material suggests, the answers to these questions are inter-related, and that inter-relation will need to be explored. If I am to understand any one of the domains (discourse, the referent, subjectivity), I have to understand more about the other two, since all are imbricated in any one understanding.

The assertions in Figure 1.3 should be regarded as hypotheses which are inferred from, and supported by, or at least not disconfirmed by, the transcript data. They are hypotheses about different types of knowledge that I as researcher might be interested in: knowledge about the way she talks about things, knowledge about the changing social and cultural contexts she has lived through, knowledge about Old Wu herself: discourse, referents, subjectivity.

It may be useful to have a model of the relation of these three types of inferences from the interview interaction data to knowledge about discourse, about objective referents and about subjectivity see Figure 1.4.[4]

The diagram of how inferences can be made from utterances recorded in interview texts has certain implications:

- It suggests that, as a researcher working towards a particular research project, I might be finally more interested in subjectivity – in which case, *knowledge about the referents is a means* to that end – or I might be more interested in the referents – in which case, in its turn, *knowledge about subjectivity is regarded as the means* to that other end. I might of course be spontaneously interested in both. Whether I am or whether I'm not, I am arguing that I *must* be interested in all the aspects in order to be relatively objective about any one of them.
- It also – at the bottom of Figure 1.4 – points out the importance of our existing contextual expertise and misinformation. Such prior expertise and misinformation strongly influences the way that I make inferences (from left to right, in the diagram) from the hard facts of interview interaction to the relatively low level of inferences – but still inferences – about discourse used in the interaction, and then to the more assumption-rich inferences about subjectivity and about referents and the objective context. I refer to 'misinformation' rather polemically so as to help me keep in mind that *I should expect myself to be carrying misinformation as well as information, prejudice as well as knowledge*, and that

---

4 In Figure 1.4, I have extended the concept of 'hard facts of interview interaction' to include non-verbal as well as verbal interaction, as well as the experience of the interviewer of that interaction as recorded on paper or tape by him or her in debriefing 'session notes' immediately after the interview session.

Interview interaction	Discourse	Objective referent (evolving context)	Subjectivity (recounting subject)
	Fluent in recounting narrative of her divorce and re-marriage – Generalizations about self and husbands and children – Fluent in the 'politicized' speech of Communist China of her generation – Discourse about 'love' of husbands, of children, of chairman Mao, of self – Discourse about generational differences – Discourse about 'self-control' ('my son could not control himself and went mad') – Apparent general fluency of discourse: no recorded hesitations, non-grammatical sentences, etc.	CCP exercises 'leadership' in everything (now and at time of divorce) and there is no sense in resisting it – Workplaces had Party secretaries who discussed 'cases' at 'mass meetings' and gave strong advice about courses of action – She divorced her husband who died in prison, but was 'pardoned' in 1981 – She thinks her son 'went mad' because of this – she has other children but no information about them except that she loves them – The 1950s marriage law of free choice in marriage and divorce 'became hollow and meaningless' – Young people now see what was 'inconceivable and ridiculous' in earlier periods but can't understand how it was 'believed in' at the time	Remembers past mode of decision-making ('this kind of propaganda') and can contrast it with current mode of 'being less beguiled by propaganda' – Now very cynical about 'propaganda' and 'catching the vogue' – Is concerned to study 'spirituality' and does so ever since her son's mental illness started – Love is very important for her and she loves her children more than herself – Is not fully satisfied with her second marriage – Explains her non-divorcing by 'lacking the courage' given that she is 'too old'

FIGURE 1.3 **Old Wu – Hypotheses about Three Types of Knowledge Gained or to be Gained through the Raw Data**

this should increase my (and your) caution as I 'infer and interpret' the interview data I collect.

While strategically my prior contextual knowledge and misinformation 'governs' the process of 'making inferences from the data', prior knowledge, expertise, ignorance and prejudice luckily need not be all-powerful. As I struggle to make sense of (make sensible inferences from) the data, I hope to find that my previous body of knowledge and misinformation gets disturbed and enriched: i.e. I 'learn' from the process.

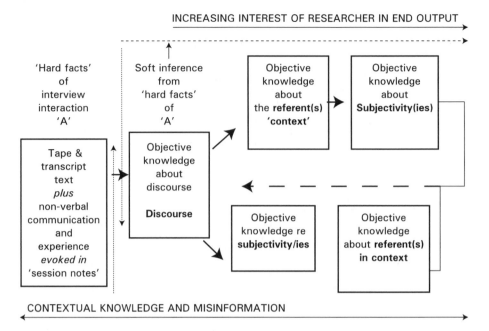

FIGURE 1.4   **Reading Interview Interaction 'Facts' for Discourse, Objectivity, Subjectivity in the Light of Contextual Knowledge and Misinformation**

In Figure 1.4, the first set of inferences are from the 'hard facts of that particular interview' to a model of the interviewee's discourse. There is then a second set of inferences which can either take a *top-line movement* from inferences, knowledge and misinformation about objectivity towards a model of subjectivity, or take *a middle-line movement* from inferences, knowledge and misinformation about subjectivity towards a model of objective context and the referents. In either case, the models developed then have to be rendered coherent with each other in the light of the mutual inspection of models of discourse, objectivity and subjectivity, and of the *diagram's bottom line*: the resources and handicaps with which I start: my existing prior knowledge and assumptions, prejudice and ignorance. The process is iterative.

Inference = Assumptions + Evidence-handling Argument Against Counter-arguments

Assuming (for the moment) that our record of the 'hard and only verbal facts of an interview interaction' is correct, I then put forward hypotheses (or knowledge-claims) on the basis of those facts about discourse and/or objective referents and/or subjectivity. These are put forward on the basis of inference-drawing about the significance of the interview interaction data. Inferences require assumptions and an argument. The arguments take the form of bringing evidence for and against various alternative accounts that might be considered, each of which takes 'the facts' into account in a different way to different inferred conclusions (knowledge-claims) about discourse, objective referents, or subjectivity. Such quasi-judicial arguing *for* certain inferences and *against* rival inferences depends to a considerable extent on *making and questioning assumptions*. These assumptions may be based on general cultural common-sense or on specialized knowledge and expertise, on information prejudice and misinformation, or usually on a mixture of all these.

One assumption that I make is that of intended truthfulness. One assumption that I make in coming to the provisional inferences collected on p. 6 about Old Wu is that she is a real person recounting her own experience. If I were to have further information, identifying the speaker of the transcript words as an accomplished actress with a quite different personal history, then many of the inferences made in the diagram above would be undermined.

> One interviewer I know has never been able to decide whether a particular inter-
> viewee of his was involved with the IRA in the 1970s in the frightening way he
> described or whether he wasn't. As the transcript was re-examined, the researcher
> became increasingly unhappy about making the assumption of intended truthfulness
> and, in the end, decided that the interview could not be used.

Even if I make the assumption that the interviewee is trying to be as truthful as they can, I may have to consider what errors they may be making. For example, people may make mistakes about dates: perhaps Old Wu's husband was only pardoned in 1982? *Myths We Live By* (Samuel and Thompson, 1990) has useful discussions and examples of how our 'accounting for the past' may not be as true to the facts as we like to think, since such accounting is subject to a myth-making propensity both at the individual and at the collective level (see also papers in Perks and Thomson, 1998).

Similarly, I may make assumptions which question the significance of the assertions in the interview. For example, in the text on page 7, Old Wu explains the madness of her son by his hearing of the death of his father in prison; it may be that this madness was also (or instead) the result of other factors of which she was unaware. It might also be the case that his 'madness' might be better described in other words: 'madness' is a cultural category, a historical 'label', and other terms might be more appropriate for the Chinese concept or for her son's reality, or both. I might assume that she is knowledgeable about the circumstances of her husband's life but less knowledgeable about the nature of her son's disturbance.

I might make a further general assumption. I might make the assumption that people attempt to minimize information about their history that puts them in a worse light than they are comfortable with. Making that assumption, I might entertain the speculative hypothesis that Old Wu might be aware that her son became disturbed partly as a result of her remarrying (in itself, or how it turned out), but might not wish to acknowledge this to herself or to the interviewer. *This 'further general assumption' changes the inferences that I might make* from her data and *provides me with further research questions*: Was the son even more against the remarriage than he was against the divorce? If she loves her children more than she loves herself, as she now presents herself as doing, why did she divorce, and remarry? What other children does she have and why are their responses to the situation not presented? These questions arise from changing the assumptions that I make to generate inferences from the datum of the transcript.

A further assumption may be in order, based on knowledge about Chinese society. Classically, sons were valued more than daughters. I might speculate about inferring that, since she refers to one son, the rest of the category 'children' are made up of one or more daughters.

I have argued, using the case of Old Wu as an example, that it is convenient to think of the interview interaction as a single 'event' that occurs at a particular moment in social history, that I attempt to use 'interview material' as evidence for making inferences from 'the facts of the interview' to possible truths about extra-interview realities (whether they be about the person being interviewed, the society and culture they inhabit, the sequence of events they have lived through, or any other subjective and non-subjective realities). I have argued that, in such arguments about extra-interview realities, I use not just evidence to question or argue cases but also assumptions, contextual expertise and misinformation with which I question or buttress those arguments. I shall return to these matters in some detail, particularly in Part IV dealing with the analysis of interview materials.

FINAL PROPOSED RE/PRESENTATION PRODUCT/ PURPOSE DETERMINES APPROPRIATE DESIGN OF DATA-GENERATION/PROCESSING

'Fitness for purpose' is the criterion by which I design and choose instruments and procedures for my social research. How can I use this idea in respect of the instruments of semi-structured depth-interviewing and of the procedures for collecting and analysing such interview data?

I need to be clear about the intended use of such analyses, about what 'product of interview analysis' I wish to provide for myself and others. Once I know what the shape of the desired product should be, then I can be more specific about what needs to be done in order to produce such a product.

This involves thinking very precisely about the type of text that I wish to produce, or that our sponsors or market will wish, or allow, us to produce. However, to attempt to define all the possible purposes/products that might be developed on the basis of semi-structured depth-interviewing practices would be impossible.

In this book, I shall take up a particular position about social research products using depth interview material: other positions are perfectly possible and legitimate. This position will be argued for below. Very broadly, I shall argue, following the work of Kuhn (1970), that all social research work and production is largely determined by the norms and exemplars of professional practice characteristic of the research community to which the researcher belongs or wishes to belong. Consequently, to know what your research community wishes to see, you need to study examples of 'very good, very recognized practice' within your discipline. Your training has or will provide you with an experience of the intensive study of 'the classics' (different in each discipline, changing with the society in question), each of which serves to convey to you a model of what is recognized as good practice within the discipline in the society or university at the time. This is known as the 'paradigm' or as an/the 'exemplar'. A collection of such exemplary texts is sometimes called the 'canon' – as in the 'canonical works of English Literature'. Obviously, learning a paradigm is more than just reading texts: it is 'working the tools' and 'interpreting the product' (making inferences from the data) produced by that proficient working of the tools.

One of the directions for any system of social knowledge hoping to be accepted as (relatively) 'scientific' is that existing 'theory' must always be 'critiqued' and 'better theory' must be argued for. In this theory-focused model, *material from interview research is used to develop better theory than that which existed before*; what counts as 'better' is of course always a matter of intense argument.

In the next subsection, such an orientation to theory-development and improvement is taken on board as a way of thinking about the uses of interview material in social research.

There is another approach to that focused upon critique. It is concerned with 'adequacy of representation', and it is not solely focused upon 'representation as theory'. A painting of a person may be criticized as a bad likeness or representation, but such a critique will not criticize the 'theory' of the painting or of the painter. Instead, the painting will be asserted to be a *bad description or model* of that which it is attempting to describe or model. In the next subsection, such a concern to use interview materials to provide improved representations, models, or descriptions will also be located.

This book, therefore, attempts to be useful both to social researchers who believe that the object of research is that of advancing theory and to those who believe it is that of advancing (verbal/discursive) description. Both groups place great emphasis, consciously or unconsciously, upon the conceptual frameworks we have to use in any assertion of theory and any modelling of reality. I therefore now go on to consider conceptual frameworks used in the study of the practice of interview interaction, and to clarify the notion of 'conceptual framework' itself as it relates to different uses of the term 'theory'. The need for such frameworks needs to be first established, though: I shall attempt to do this by first indicating the 'problematic' nature of interview interaction, in a rather more 'applied' way than I have done so far, and then by suggesting that certain conceptual frameworks can help us to handle this problematic nature.

2

Conceptual Frameworks for Studying and Inferring from (Research) Interview Interaction Practice

INTERVIEWS AS PROBLEMATIC

Interview Interaction as Located Practice

Introductory texts on depth interviewing can tend towards a 'social unrealism' in which the real histories and the real social identities of those involved are in some ways ignored. Social research, however, invariably considers people to be characterized – either by themselves or others, or by the social researcher, or both – by such 'statuses' (sociological word) or 'characteristics' (neutral word) as class, gender, race, marital status, age, family position, occupational status, citizen status, tax/welfare status, religious status, neighbourhood status, educational status, prospective 'serious relationship status', sexual preference and any number of others.

What happens when I think about the 'interview cycle interaction' of people about whom I only know some of the 'statuses' or 'aspects' of who they are, but not their proper names: 'social typifications' (of persons, of contexts, of interactions) as discussed originally by Schutz (1970: 111–23)?

Vignette A: Lorna and John

Supposing that you are a black single mother on social security (Lorna) who, without any basic qualifications, has come to college as a mature student. You do some 'no questions asked' work on the side and you have an occasional boy-friend who is not at college, who is married to someone else and with whom your relationship is quite difficult. Among your fellow-students is a younger white part-time student (John) who is a professional social worker and has got good qualifications. He is hoping to do the course and be promoted. John is unattached, and student gossip has it that he is on the look out for a girl-friend. You have both been asked to practise research interviewing as part of your course. John says he is 'interested in the problems of social welfare clients' and asks you to agree to be researched – confidentially of course – as part of the course (NOT, he stresses, as part of his job) on 'the life-experiences of single mothers with special reference to the courts and the welfare services'. What do you do? If you refuse, what will this do to your further relations as fellow-students?

What do you think about, when wondering whether to agree to John's request? What do you think about in terms of planning your responses to anticipated 'difficult questions'? When your 'planned responses' (strategy) don't completely work, what do you think and feel? What do you do? How do you and John feel about each other the day after the interview as fellow students in a class room?

The above 'mental experiment' can also be thought about from the point of view of John. Take his role.

What misapprehensions do you, as John, think 'Lorna' might have about you and the interview, and how could you deal with them? Are there any fears and apprehensions she might have about you and your suggestion, which you might have to admit are legitimate and maybe well-grounded, and what does this mean for your thinking about the issue? What uses of any interview material might you need (reluctantly) to rule out, given the sensitivity of the situation? Is it fair to ask a fellow-student for such an interview? What areas will you go for and what will you avoid? What will it do to your relationship after the interview, if the interview does not go well? How will other students regard you? What would you do 'next time'?

Supposing you are the 'ethics vetting committee' for such an interview proposal. What would your thinking be about the issue? What conditions or alterations (if any) would you make in respect of the proposed research interview?

The above vignette is designed to help you think about the present and future contexts of the real relationships of real people who may or may not agree to play their respective roles.[1] In the next section, I deal with an aspect of the important 'hidden dimension' of the two people concerned: namely their individual and collective respective interview pasts.

Past Interview Experiences for both Parties

The Impact of 'Past Interview Experiences' Real and Imagined in Two-person Interviews

I like to think that I am not liable to do any harm, as interviewer. Kvale (1996) argues eloquently – as do many qualitative research evangelists – for the democratic 'inter-view' in which two 'people' wish for existential closeness and mutual knowledge and come to view each other more closely. It is true that, as you become more proficient in depth interviewing, you are likely to have good experiences of real 'personal encounters'. But in order for anything remotely like that to happen, you need to focus on the 'down side' of interviewing.

Dillon (1990) has usefully identified a large number of types of social interviews and interpersonal communicative encounters in our type of society. I might suggest educational, medical, police, judicial, immigration, occupational, promotional, devotional, journalistic, 'celebrity self-promotional', welfare, jobstart, charity, disciplinary, university entrance, PhD 'oral', etc.

Though being interviewed for research purposes is rare, most adults have a lot of experience of being interviewed or of imagining being interviewed for other

---

1 If you found this helpful as a 'device to think with', you might consider constructing such vignettes for your own interviews. You don't have to use questions alone to get reflective responses. Vignettes are reviewed briefly in Barker and Renold, 1999.

purposes. Usually, there have been strong inequalities of power and vulnerability between the interviewer and the person who has either 'requested and obtained' an interview or has 'been requested and required to come for interview'. Most of us have had some (some of us have had many) involuntary interviews with head teachers, with suspicious police, with people who 'call you in for an interview'. There are individual but also collective 'histories' that circulate between people and through the media about the resource-holding/withdrawing power of the 'official' of the State or some other organization interviewing a would-be immigrant, a would-be worker, a would-be social rights claimant, somebody applying for a 'post', for 'social support', for 'promotion', for an 'award', trying to get 'clearance' from doctors, from parents, from friends. I am likely to have had, or at least to have envisaged if only in a nightmare or a novel, punitive and disciplinary encounters with authorities such as bullies, parents, head-teachers, police, social welfare officers, higher-ups in powerful organizations.

To paint the 'worst case scenario', all of us have 'secret personal histories' of being interviewed by 'superiors' (societal and institutional), at our request or at their requirement, who have something to reward and something to punish us with. It might be safest to assume that we have all been in vulnerable, one-down, positions, wishing we didn't have to be there, thinking it was a great mistake to have come, struggling to make the best case we can, pleading a 'less than watertight' case, hoping the other has no information with which to ask us difficult questions or puncture our self-presentation, as we try to hide, underplay, or explain away 'facts' which are not helpful to the 'interpretation' we want others to accept.

These are routinized stressful and fraught experiences in a bureaucratized and hierarchical society. So what happens to both you and your interviewee as you 'psych yourselves up' and 'get ready' for interviewing?

As a *would-be interviewer*, your experience of being interviewed may lead you to behave and 'come across' in your interviewing improvisations like a policeman, or a parent, a teacher or academic, or any 'authority' by whom you have been interviewed and from whom you learnt a way of handling stress and ambiguity. Similarly past experiences of formal or informal 'interviewing' (as a parent, in a profession, as somebody allowing somebody to join something, as a jealous lover) will also be there helping to shape and colour what you do.

You are likely to respond by 'playing particular interview scenes' or the whole cycle in terms of your unconscious repertoire. In the same interview, both informant and interviewer may be constantly switching roles through a medley of historic 'interview identities' without ever realizing what they are doing.

There is an up-side, too. There are *positive* experiences of real, vicarious and hallucinated, formal and informal 'interview' experience, and these also form part of most people's secret unwritten history and potential 'interview identities'. Emancipatory and self-expressive encounters with relatives, friends, lovers, clergy, counsellors, therapists, and other supportive people are also experiences which occur with less routinized regularity. They provide a basis for more positive evocations in ourselves and others, and the possibility of more positive responses to the conscious or unconscious evocations of others. People who have had a lot of positive experiences of 'deep friendly talk' will be better placed to participate in depth interviews than those who have none.

I am only likely to provide 'relatively safe research interview experiences' for myself and my informants if I am fully aware both of the current social positioning of myself and my interviewee – as described in the 'Lorna and John' vignette – and ready to detect the impact of any collective and individual past experiences and 'potential interview identities' which I and they ineluctably bring to our interviews.

In looking at the interview extract in Figure 2.1, we know rather little of the past experiences and current identities of the interacting participants and how they bear upon the interaction. The interviewer is an attractive young woman in her late 20s; the man is somewhat older. For the interviewer, this is her first semi-structured interview (on her research topic about the effects on men of having their father disappear at an early age from their life).

Interpreting Interview Data: Interview with 'W'

The Transcript Segment

The extract given in Figure 2.1 is derived from a first interview by an undergraduate student. The three-column format and the numbering of speaker turns and units of meaning will be discussed later in Chapter 10.

'Reading' the Transcript in Four Different Ways

In the light of our earlier discussion, I will now explore its relevance in four different ways: (i) about the informant's relation to his father; (ii) about the interview as an interactive process; (iii) about the 'discourse' of the informant; and (iv) about the subjective world and the strategy of the informant.

1. What Inferences does the Transcript Allow You to Hypothesize about the Informant's Relation with his Father?   The formal focus of the inquiry was into 'the effects on the adult of paternal deprivation when the child was young'. This very precise focus needs to be constantly borne in mind when thinking about the interview process.

In terms of events in a life story, after 69 lines of interview, the *only hard datum about events* obtained so far is that W was six years old when his father left (line 31).

In terms of the *quality of his early relationship* with his father, W says that he 'was afraid of him', 'didn't really know him' and was 'kind of glad when he left' (lines 35–7). It is certainly hard data that W said this in the particular interview: can I infer that *this account now* is an adequate description of *his feelings then*? As a basis for inference to long-past periods of feeling, it may be seen as much less reliable information. Perhaps W was very disappointed when his father left but decided, later, to 'be glad' in order to avoid feeling loss and anger? He starts by warning the interviewer that 'I don't remember much about him from those days', and this may indicate that he does not think that his memory of the past relationship should be given too much weight.

He gives information about his theory of the three-way relationship with his father and mother by indicating that he thinks he (the informant) was 'probably really jealous and possessive of my mother, she was always the one I felt emotionally close to, very very much so' and 'one senses that he was in the way of that' (lines 38–42). The strength of this statement – 'always ... very very much so' – makes this appear more convincing to the reader and gives credence to the earlier proposition (by explaining it) about his 'fear' of his father and being 'kind of glad when he went'.

There are 'gradients' of the information from 'hard' to 'soft': Different approaches to interviewing have different theories of the relative 'hardness/softness'

Ref. no	Space for one type of notes	Transcript	Space for other type of notes
001		Isobel: OK. Now I've switched on the tape I can start talking. Thanks for the tea and biscuits, they are wonderful	
002		W: You're welcome.	
003		Thank you for giving up this time for me.	
004		W: Well, I don't see it as giving up the time, more as contributing ...	
005		I: Well, for giving me the time, contributing the time, thank you very much	
006		W: If it furthers someone's psychological understanding even a tiny little snippet, it can be of value to me and maybe someone else	
007		I: Lovely, thank you	
008		Anyway, as I said, I'm doing research into paternal deprivation and different people's experience of it	
009		Anyone who has had an absent father is an expert in this field, mostly without being aware of it.	
010		Of course, like all the others, you are totally anonymous,	
011		when I write up the report	
012		everything you say that I write down or record, with your permission, is totally anonymous.	
013		W: So you won't tell anyone	
014		that I'm Prince Charles?	
015		I: No.	
016		OK, so you're anonymous, so you can say what you like.	
017		It is necessary to say that just to make sure that you know	
018		First of all, briefly, a general question:	
019		I would like to ask you	
020		what you think about the role of the father today.	
021		W: 'The role of the father today' is very wide	
022		I guess, it's difficult.	

continued

Figure 2.1 continued

Ref. no	Space for one type of notes	Transcript	Space for other type of notes
023		It's tough	
024		In terms of roles	
025		being the breadwinner, responsibility, financial, classical role	
026		Myself as a father	
027		er ...	
028		I'm not sure.	
029		*I: Perhaps you could tell me a little*	
030		*about your own father*	
031		*W:* Well, I was six when he left.	
032		I don't remember much about him from those days,	
033		I know him now as a man,	
034		but my relationship with him when I was younger seems to be	
035		that I was afraid of him,	
036		didn't really know him,	
037		yes I was kind of glad when he went.	
038		I think I was probably	
039		really jealous and possessive of my mother.	
040		She was always the one I felt emotionally close to	
041		very very much so.	
042		And one senses that he was in the way of that.	
043		*I: Well, you've anticipated my next question,*	
044		*which was going to be:*	
045		*'are you aware of having any particular feelings about him?'*	
046		*W:* Well, I've just told you ...	
047		do you want any more?	
048		*I: No,*	

continued

Figure 2.1 continued

Ref. no	Space for one type of notes	Transcript	Space for other type of notes
049		that's OK.	
050		Can you describe to me	
051		if it is possible	
052		a typical day in your home	
053		when you were a boy of less than fourteen?	
054		W: I can remember hot summers.	
055		One particular summer	
056		there was a swarm of flies	
057		that were enormous.	
058		I can remember	
059		treading on them	

FIGURE 2.1 **Interview with W**

of different 'interview facts'. Different assumptions, as we saw with Old Wu, change the apparent 'hardness/softness' of the transcript evidence.

2. What does the Transcript Tell You (the Reader) about the Interview as an Interactive Process?   It is possible to segment the interaction into an 'introduction' (lines 1–17), a first question which is not answered (18–28), a second question which is given an answer (29–42), a slightly confusing passage (43–9) in which a question is first offered and then withdrawn, and finally the asking of another question to which we have the beginnings of an answer (50–9) which is not completed by the end of the extract.

There are two moments in which the interaction appears to be 'uneasy'. The first is that of the introduction (lines 1–17); the second is that of the awkward passage of lines 43–9. What is the quality of that unease (the two moments may of course produce different 'sorts' of unease for different reasons)?

This is difficult to answer, since I do not have any material (such as field-notes) to help us determine the 'feeling' of the interaction. Nonetheless, I can generate some provisional hypotheses, some ideas as to what might be going on.

Let us start with the introduction (lines 1–17): the uneasy movement which is ended by the 'general question, I would like to ask you about the role of the father today'.

Some rather different alternative hypotheses suggest themselves, none of which can be 'decided' by the transcript that we have.

These exchanges could be read as merely normal courtesy on both sides with a mutually enjoyed joke (lines 13–15).

Alternatively, they could be read as an attempt by W to assure the interviewer that he doesn't see the interview as 'giving up the time, more as contributing' coming up against the interviewer's slight disinterest (line 5) in the distinction which the informant W felt it important to himself to make. W then insists upon it by insisting on his interest in 'the furthering of someone's psychological understanding even a tiny little snippet' which she then counters by a not very responsive 'lovely, thank you' which again puts W in the position of needing to be thanked. She then concludes with a deliberately unspecific appreciation 'lovely' which again keeps him somewhat away from the position of being recognized as a co-contributor to psychological understanding for which he seems to have been angling quite determinedly.

W at line 6 might possibly be being a little ironical by implying that 'someone' may have their 'psychological understanding' furthered 'even a tiny little snippet'? Certainly, his joke about Prince Charles (13–14) suggests a slight lack of reverence for the dignified assurance given by the interviewer of his 'total anonymity' (perhaps experienced by W as laboured pomposity). The lack of any obvious sharing of the joke by her (15–16) and her rather over-serious 'it is necessary to say that just to make sure that you know' (17) suggests a slight 'edge' by line 13 even if there was none by line 6.

It is not clear what we or the informant are to make of the posing of the first question 'a general question … about the role of the father today' (18–20) except to note that it doesn't seem to work as a question that gets a flow of answering response. By line 28, after some floundering, W has given up with 'I'm not sure'.

The shift to the more personal question (lines 29–30) gets much more of a response, a flow of a definite account or analysis by W who goes firmly to an account of the 'early dynamics' between himself and his father and mother in a way that is both very expressive and also not very open to further questioning. Whether this is a definitive overcoming of the early unease by plunging into a complete 'self-account' or whether that 'self-account' (he was asked to say 'a little about your own father') is a way of handling that unease by giving a 'quick final analysis or self-theory not to be questioned' is difficult to say. His 'one senses that he was in the way of that' (42) suggests a sudden distancing from the previous 'I-talk' (31–41) which suggests another moment of unease.

For whatever reason, perhaps her own unease, the interviewer does not probe at all into any of the rich potential offered (lines 33–42). She could have asked about the unexplained 'being afraid' (35) or the qualified 'kind of glad' (37); she could have asked for the 'not much' that he implied that he *did* remember (32); she could have asked of any examples or instances of *how* his father was 'in the way' of the boy's closeness to his mother.

Her practice at this point seems marked by a lack of flexibility (difficult to avoid in a novice interviewer) in handling the 'planned sequence of questions' written down on her piece of paper. Instead of taking up any of the material, and asking a question that goes deeper, she remarks 'Well, you've anticipated my next question' thereby implying that she does not need to ask any more questions in relation to either the one she did ask (line 29) or the one she 'was going to ask' (44–5).

W might well feel that his 'self-revelation' (if that is what it was) of lines 31–42 has not really sparked off any desire by the interviewer to probe him further in this area, and has fallen a bit flat. Perhaps the 'one senses' was him starting to feel her non-responsiveness. Alternatively, it was his self-induced self-distancing by the 'one senses' which led the interviewer to feel that he really did not want to talk any more about this (at least at this time) and so to rush to help him close the vein of self exploration – that he had plunged into, and led her to plunge into – but that he now regretted? I don't know which.

In either case, lines 43–5 seem partly to offer the opportunity to say more but mostly to indicate that the material necessary to answer the proposed next question has already been provided.

W then accepts her definition that she has already had this 'my next question' answered and offers her the opportunity to probe any further if she so wishes. By saying 'do you want any more?', W responds to the implied message of her taking the trouble to tell him that he had 'anticipated her next question'. He may well be assuming that, if his answer had *fully* answered that next question, then the neatest tactic by the interviewer would have been to move smoothly on to the next unanswered question. He may well be thinking as follows:

1 If I had fully answered her next question, she would just have moved on to the question after that.
2 By mentioning that I have answered her next question, she is implying perhaps that I have answered in part but not in full.
3 She is leaving open a possibility that I could provide more information to provide her with a full or fuller answer.
4 I will indicate that I am sensitive to this possible wish of hers.
5 'Do you want any more?'

Actually, I don't know if he says this 'Do you want any more?'[2] in a spirit of would-be co-operation ('I'm happy either way'); or in a mood of reluctant co-operation ('my "one senses that" should have told you that I don't really want to say more, but I will if you push me'); or in a tone of grumpy politeness ('please don't ask!'). Stage directions about the tone of voice, which would have been inserted within the transcript in one or other side-column, or session notes by the interviewer as to how she was feeling at the time, would resolve some at least of these questions; but I don't have these.

For whatever reason, the interviewer says 'No, that's OK' and switches to a quite different question (line 53) with an odd framing about the time ('a typical day … when you were a boy of less than 14'), and W starts to produce a 'story' in what appears to be an easy flow of memory. Is the interviewer responding to pressure from W? Or, instead, is she refusing to follow W down a path of exploring an early emotional triangle along which he wishes to go? If the latter, *why* is she refusing? Is she shifting from 'asking for feelings' to 'asking for story'? What implications will this have for the way in which the rest of the interview will unfold and for the use to which she will subsequently put the material?

So what can I say about their respective possibly very different interview experiences?

---

2 Rather like a parent at table asking a child whether they 'want any more?' 'Is there anything more about this that you would like to know?' would be more inviting.

First, is there some way of summing up a version of *his* interview experience?

> He starts by 'promising all' with (lines 4–6) even rather an evangelist note, but, perhaps as a result of her over-general first question, ends with a 'failure' by line 20. He then takes the next question as an opportunity to say much more, but may be regarded (it certainly seems as if she regards him) as having 'said too much' because one or both of them do not want to 'go further' into the 'deep water' that he was rushing into. So, in effect, another 'failure' by lines 42–3.
>
> After the 'confused exchange' of lines 43–9, he is given another rather general prompt – What is a 'typical day'? Is 'less than 14' a useful way asking somebody to think about a specific historical period or moment in their life? Is the point of the question clear? – and he produces another rush to co-operate by a story (started at the end of the segment quoted) which may or may not be helpful to the interviewer's conscious purposes.

Is there a way of summing up *her* experience of the interview segment?

> She starts off by trying to express thanks for his provision of food and to maintain control of the interviewer role and the interview. She tries a gentle 'general question' as a lead-in which manifestly gets nowhere. She then tries a very personal question which seems to get somewhere fairly deep fairly fast. Either because of the un-cued self-distancing of W at the end of his answer (line 42) or because of her mounting sense of an inability to know what to do with such an unexpectedly personal answer, followed by his to-her-unprovoked aggressive response in lines 46–7, she rushes off – in perhaps a rather awkward and abrupt fashion (lines 48–9) – to another question which may be less awkward, less deep, and gives her time to think what to do next.

The above analysis of questions about the 'interaction' in the interview suggests that, if I am to resolve some of the questions and confirm or deny some of the hypotheses which the words of the transcript suggest about what is going on between the interviewer and the informant in the interview, it will be very important to know more than the words on the page tell us about the interview interaction.[3] Just exploring the problems suggested by the bare transcript is of value in itself, however.

3. What does the Transcript Tell You about the 'Discourse' of the Informant? Any conversation – and an interview is just a (special type of) conversation – is more or less a co-production of the participants. Each is taking cues and ideas from each other and giving off cues and ideas for the other to take note of in their turn. I both respond to what has been said (and not said) so far in the conversation, but also act in the present in anticipation of possible futures of the conversation which I wish to move towards (or to avoid).

Consequently, disentangling the preferred mode of talk (discourse) of one of the participants from the joint production of both is particularly problematic as an activity.

Let us look at a number of points where it is plausible to think that the spontaneous mode of talk of W had most chances of 'coming out'.

---

3 In Parts II–IV, I shall argue that more information can be provided for analysis through better transcripts, through session-notes written after the interview and through memos to self written during the analysis of the interview material.

1   On line 4, it is clear that W distinguishes 'giving up time' and 'contributing … to psychological understanding'.
2   On lines 21–7, he is trying to guess at some official discourse about 'the role of the father' and not finding a way of making much sense of the interviewer's broad sociological question. I can guess that he is mouthing fragments of a discourse he feels he is being expected to use but does not in fact find a way of guessing or using it.
3   Lines 31–42 are much more likely to be his own discourse about his own concerns. Asked (29) for 'a little about your father', he develops a discussion of the three-way dynamics of the family in terms of a discourse about being 'emotionally close (and distant)' from people, being 'possessive (and non-possessive) about people', about being 'jealous' (and not), about 'really knowing' somebody or not, and about 'being (un)afraid of somebody', and finally about being 'glad (or not)'. How this discourse is put together, how it has developed, are different sorts of questions, but it seems plausible to infer that he already possesses quite a complex and articulate set of concepts (discourse) around family dynamics. He has put this forward without any 'conceptual constraint' from the interviewer, who shows no special signs of wanting precisely this discourse or of wishing to stay with it either.
4   Lines 54–9 are also not constrained particularly by the discourse of the interviewer; they do not at first glance present any very special features but they are worth thinking about. The opening has a rather 'dream-like quality' characteristic of an 'image' which initiates the production of a narrative. It is not clear what link this narrative will have to the research focus of the interview any more than it is clear what the link to that purpose was of the interviewer's third question that prompted it. Expecting to talk about his experience of paternal deprivation, he might be non-plussed by being at this point being asked to talk about 'typical days in his life as a boy [not as a "son"]'.

It might be a rather frantic 'free association' ('remember *something! answer at least one question satisfactorily*') – flailing around rather like he did in his answer to the first general question about 'the role of the father today' – but this time landing on a particular memory as a basis for talking.

It might, rather speculatively, have some connection to the experience of the current interview situation. He has a strong image of 'treading' on some irritating thing or things; it may be that, at some level, the questions are seen as 'enormous flies' or maybe an 'enormous swarm' (in lines 21–3 he is dealing ineffectively with something 'very wide', 'tough', 'difficult') and he would like to cope with the questions (or even the questioner?) by an effective 'treading'. Alternatively, it might be that he found himself unwillingly 'treading on the flies' just by walking along and so wanted nothing better than to be somewhere else?

So can I come to *any conclusions about the 'discourse' of the informant*? I can say that he seems happier with a psychological discourse around (his personal) family dynamics than he does with a sociological discourse about 'the role of the father today'. I can suggest that perhaps he sees emotions as an expression of social relations and struggles rather than as an expression of psyches irrespective of situation: he distinguishes his relationships now from his relationships then, and talks about his relationship with his father when the request has been to talk about his father. I can say that he is happier to remember particular events (the summer's day) and to give an account in generalized terms of his own 'family dynamics' than to make general points about 'the role of the father today'.

Having made some preliminary inferences from the transcript to points about the discursive repertoire and practice of 'W', let us now look at the two areas or domains to which inferences from transcript material can be made. We have already noted the 'age at which the father left', the strongest candidate for an uncontroversial real-world/real-history referent in the extract: we now turn to look at inferences to an end-output about subjectivity, the uppermost broken line in Figure 1.4.

4. What does the Transcript Tell us about the Subjective World and Strategy of the Informant? Provisional partial answers to this question can be derived from the reading of the 'discourse' suggested in the previous section.

> I say 'provisional' because it is important to bear in mind that the way people talk on a particular occasion may be part of their 'presentation of self' in a very specific context. Consequently, the interview needs to be 'read' to check that the hypothesis that the 'self and world presented in the discourse' is the 'real' subjective world and self of the interviewee. Should I as researcher feel that the 'self-presentation' should be considered with any caution?

> *Some caution always.* On occasion, a lot of fencing and self-promotion may go on in interviews involving sensitive subjects. Any analysis of interview material which assumes (rather than questions) a straight-forward automatic correspondence between the 'presented world' and the 'actual world' may be considered to be variably naive and potentially worthless. Ruthrof (1981) has a useful table which is reproduced in Appendix A.

> Germans who lived through the Nazi period tend to represent themselves as 'naive and ill-informed and ignorant' of the inhumane activities of the Nazi regime'; only certain aspects of Britain's colonial past and present (e.g. on the island of Ireland) are well-remembered by the British; ex-President Nixon was as 'economical with the truth' as any other interviewed government official is likely to be.

The transcript may convey an official story about the subjective world and the strategy of the informant (as expressed in discourse); however, if analysed in context, it may reveal a much more complex and possibly opposed one.

> In W's case, one's general knowledge about the attachment of children to both parents might lead one to question whether 'kind of glad when he went' (line 37), which is firmly there in his discourse, should be taken at face value in the analysis of subjective meanings *behind* the discourse. Is it not more likely that he felt glad *and* sad when his father left, perhaps that his fear of his father was of some imagined 'retribution' and perhaps came after the father left rather than before, that the wealth of qualifiers in lines 34–42 – 'seems to be', 'didn't really know him', 'kind of glad', 'I think that I was probably' – reflect a much greater uncertainty of the adequacy of 'that version as told then' than a quick reading of the 'face value of the words' would suggest?

These suggestions are put forward as currently purely speculative hypotheses that one might wish to think about, as bases for actual or possible later questions or explorations during the interview, as ideas that might be checked against interviews with other people in or close to the family, as a base for looking through letters and other documents. Their function here is to suggest the way in which the 'stories as presented' may not be the same as the 'realities as were', and the 'reader' of an interview text should always be alert for suggestions of difference between the two.

Semi-structured interviewing is very often concerned to explore the subjective world of the interviewee, but this does not mean that what they say is treated uncritically, accepted at face value. I have tried to suggest this through the analysis of segments of interview with Old Wu and with 'W', and will develop this further. We must not be more naive about deception and self-deception in research interaction than we are in interaction with our friends, our lovers, our superiors, our partners, our children, our parents.

Making Decisions in the Interview

In the analysis that I have made above, I have frequently suggested how the interviewer might have made different decisions within the interview, and these might have produced different 'effects'. When learning a craft, such as that of interviewing, it is particularly important to constantly review what you did and the way you did it so as to see how you might have done it differently and better.

To suggest something of the constant decision-making that the interviewer has to make in the interview, a skill that can only be developed by practice and the careful review of practice, I give below (Figure 2.2) a suggestion as to how, in the interview with W, the interviewer might have proceeded better by making different decisions in the interview segment. Clearly, they are based on some ideas about interviewer and informant which might be wrong. You may have different ones, and it would be a useful experiment for you to explore other possibilities.

Decisions to Interview Differently: Alternative Interview Decisions

	Comment		Alternative interviewer interventions
001		Isobel: OK. Now I've switched on the tape I can start talking. Thanks for the tea and biscuits, they are wonderful	
002		W: You're welcome.	
003		Thank you for giving up this time for me.	
004		W: Well, I don't see it as giving up the time, more as contributing . . .	
005	Stay silent, let him clarify whatever the point is he wishes to make	I: ~~Well, for giving me the time, contributing the time, thank you very much~~	
006		W: If it furthers someone's psychological understanding even a tiny little snippet, it can be of value to me and maybe someone else	

continued

Figure 2.2 continued

	Comment		Alternative interviewer interventions
007		I : ~~Lovely, thank you~~	I'm certainly expecting that it is going to help *me*. So, thank you.
008		*Anyway, as I said, I'm doing research into paternal deprivation and different people's experience of it*	
009		*Anyone who has had an absent father is an expert in this field, mostly without being aware of it.*	
010	This gives the impression that he is being seen as part of a mass–best not said	*Of course, ~~like all the others~~, you are totally anonymous,*	
011		*When I write up the report*	
012		*everything you say that I write down or record, with your permission, is totally anonymous'.*	
013		*W:* So you won't tell anyone	
014		that I'm Prince Charles?	
015		*I: No.*	
016		*OK, so you're anonymous, so you can say what you like.*	
017	Formally redundant. Don't imply that he is slow on the uptake – it might be better to cut the whole sentence. Alternatively	~~It is necessary to say that just to make sure that you know~~	I felt I wanted to say that.
018	General questions are rarely helpful, especially this early on	*~~First of all, briefly, a general question:~~*	

continued

Figure 2.2   continued

	Comment		Alternative interviewer interventions
019		~~I would like to ask you~~	
020		~~what you think about the role of the father today.~~	
021		W: ~~'The role of the father today' is very wide~~	
022		~~I guess, it's difficult.~~	
023		~~It's tough~~	
024		~~In terms of roles~~	
025		~~being the breadwinner, responsibility, financial, classical role~~	
026		~~Myself as a father~~	
027		~~er ...~~	
028		~~I'm not sure.~~	
029		*I: Perhaps you could tell me a little*	
030		*about your own father*	
031		W: Well, I was six when he left.	
032		I don't remember much about him from those days,	
033		I know him now as a man,	
034		but my relationship with him when I was younger seems to be	
035		that I was afraid of him,	
036		didn't really know him,	
037		yes I was kind of glad when he went.	
038		I think I was probably	
039		really jealous and possessive of my mother.	
040		She was always the one I felt emotionally close to	
041		very very much so.	

continued

Figure 2.2   continued

	Comment		Alternative interviewer interventions
042		And one senses that he was in the way of that.	
043	Stay with what he wants to talk about, since it is relevant to 'effect of paternal deprivation'. The 'all that' is non-directive.	I: Well, you've anticipated my next question, ⟶	'Could you tell me a bit more about all that?'
044		which was going to be:	
045		'are you aware of having any particular feelings about him?'.	
046		W: Well, I've just told you …	
047		do you want any more?	
048		I: No,	
049		that's OK.	
050	After he finishes talking about the dynamics from his point of view, might it be helpful for him to think about the changing role of 'the father' for him at different times, not just at the age of 6?	Can you describe to me	'Can you remember an early point in your life when your image of your father changed from what it was before?'
051		if it is possible	
052		a typical day in your home	
053		when you were a boy of less than fourteen?	
054		W: I can remember hot summers.	
055		One particular summer	

continued

Figure 2.2   continued

	Comment		Alternative interviewer interventions
056		~~there was a swarm of flies~~	
057		~~that were enormous.~~	
058		~~I can remember~~	
059		~~treading on them ....~~	

* This is unclear. Does she mean 'everything that you say that I use when I write up the report'? Does she mean 'any material of yours that I use will be completely anonymized' so that nobody else (not even you?) could recognize it or you through it'?

FIGURE 2.2   **Interview with W – Alternative Interview Decisions**

Discussion

One particular point:

> The third question at lines 52–3 – 'a typical day when you were under 14' – seems to me to be the wrong question at the wrong time, given that the central research focus of the interview is on the effects of paternal deprivation of boys under 10, and that the informant has just started to talk about his emotional situation at the time when he was deprived of his father at the age of 6. Perhaps, at some other point and in some other context, it might have been a theoretically useful question, but at this point it just seems to lead away from a fruitful vein of response.

In general, if I think about the excerpt as a whole, its difficulties may lie in

- a bad sequencing of prepared questions, or of
- a failure to follow-up on a good answer, or of
- a prepared informant-question that was not sufficiently rooted in and related to the research problem of the impacts of paternal deprivation.

The interviewer may not have

- prepared her questions well enough (so that they were likely to produce the most relevant material for the research problem), or (though probably and)
- she may not have prepared the best sequence of such questions, or (though probably and)
- she may not have focused on listening to the answer such as to grasp what best to do next (e.g. line 50) irrespective of her (over?)-prepared list of questions.

Empathy, close listening, close attentiveness to what is said and not said, is the most important quality that can (sometimes, not always) save a not-too-well-prepared – or in this case, a perhaps over-prepared – interviewer from disaster.

It is perhaps worth noting that, after this difficult start, in fact the interview was not a disaster, it was a very productive one, partly because there was a lot of learning by both parties during the early course of the interview. She *learnt to be a better interviewer for him* and he learnt *to be a better informant for her* as the interview session developed. They could have done with a second follow-up interview, but this did not happen.

Imagining the Original Interview Differently: the Importance of 'Going Beyond Written-down Words'

In my earlier discussion of the 'interview interaction' of Isobel and W in respect of her interview with him on paternal deprivation, I found that lack of information about the way the words are said (often called 'paralinguistics', PL) and about non-verbal communication (NVC) by way of body posture, clothes, setting and the like was peculiarly aggravating. For good inferences in the eventual analysis, I needed more data.

In Figure 2.3 I have imagined two different ways the words might have got said in the way they did. They might be considered as 'stage directions' in the manner of the early 20th century playwright George Bernard Shaw. The two alternative 'versions' are given either side of the transcript. First read the transcript using ONE as a guide; then TWO. You may wish to consider how they suggest quite different 'personalities' for the two participants.

It is important to see how the same flow of words can be interpreted quite differently *after* the interview. You might also want to think how each party *in* the interview as it develops might be responding and interpreting their own and the other's behaviour in quite different ways. Certain points might be said in ONE way but heard as if they had been TWO, and so on. My particular 'ONE' and 'TWO' by no means exhaust the possibilities.

> 'Everything that is said must be said in some way – in some tone of voice, at some rate of speed, with some intonation or loudness. We may or may not consciously consider *what* to say before speaking. Rarely do we consciously consider *how* to say it, unless the situation is obviously loaded: for example, a job interview, a public address, firing someone, or breaking off a personal relationship. And we almost never make deliberate decisions about whether to raise or lower our voice and pitch, whether to speed up or slow down. But *these are the signals by which we interpret each other's meaning*, and decide what we think of each other's comments – and each other.' (Tannen, 1992: 27, final italics added)

Having raised some of the dimensions of doing, transcribing, and analysing semi-structured depth interviews that will be explored later, I now turn to the key question: what conceptual frameworks exist for research into the scientific practice of depth interviewing?

CONCEPTUAL FRAMEWORKS FOR THE STUDY OF SEMI-STRUCTURED DEPTH INTERVIEWS

An Under-researched, Historically Infrequent Social Practice[4]

From our exploration so far, it should be clear that the 'scientific research interview' is a very complex process. Given its importance in the practice of social

---

4 Scientific interviewing might be thought of as having some aspects of the 'sacred'. Durkheim's analysis of 'religion' as involving 'special time and place' and imagined equality between a community of believers through religion's 'special officers' and the 'sacred' might be thought of as occurring between interview partners in a 'sacred time' outside ordinary life, time and space, statuses and personal histories. It is a sacred time between a truth-searcher and a truth-sayer, both part of the 'community of believers' in the 'sacred of scientific truth' and of 'research'. Religious experience has been explored in terms of its profane side – but most social researchers do not wish to look sceptically at their own practice as 'believers in science' though they are happy to subject other institutional practices (such as religion) to such a view. Consequently, 'research interview experience' is not so well explored by social researchers and anthropologists.

	ONE		TWO
001	slightly gushy	*Isobel: OK. Now I've switched on the tape I can start talking. Thanks for the tea and biscuits, they are wonderful*	genuinely grateful
002	a bit reserved	W: You're welcome.	a bit reserved
003	even more gushy	*Thank you for giving up this time for me.*	trying to get her thankfulness across
004	suddenly eager	W: Well, I don't see it as giving up the time, more as contributing ...	a bit stiffly
005	interrupting – formal and disinterested – asserting control	*I: Well, for giving me the time, contributing the time, thank you very much*	rushing to repair a mistake she perceives she's made
006	continuing eager, but faltering	W: If it furthers someone's psychological understanding even a tiny little snippet, it can be of value to me and maybe someone else	refuses repair, stiffly and slowly
007	formal + discouraging	*I: Lovely, thank you*	quickly to cover up awkwardness
008	bored and a bit formal and quick	*Anyway, as I said, I'm doing research into paternal deprivation and different people's experience of it*	eagerly
009	ditto	*Anyone who has had an absent father is an expert in this field, mostly without being aware of it.*	
010	said in a 'kindly' tone	*Of course, like all the others, you are totally anonymous,*	
011	formal	*when I write up the report*	
012	formal	*everything you say that I write down or record, with your permission, is totally anonymous.*	
013	attempts to make a 'joke' to humanize the situation	W: So you won't tell anyone	makes 'joke' to indicate that he finds her remarks slightly silly
014		*that I'm Prince Charles?*	
015	flat – discouraging,	*I: No.*	taken aback

continued

Figure 2.3   continued

	ONE		TWO
016	a bit patronizing	*OK, so you're anonymous, so you can say what you like.*	Re-states anxiously, because she feels she must have not put her message across well before
017	ditto	*It is necessary to say that just to make sure that you know*	
018	rather formal	*First of all, briefly, a general question:*	
019	ditto	*I would like to ask you*	a bit uncertain of reception
020	ditto	*what you think about the role of the father today.*	
021	taken aback – was expecting something more personal	*W:* 'The role of the father today' is very wide	a bit censorious
022		I guess, it's difficult.	pompous
023		It's tough	
024		In terms of roles	
025	throws out words to please her	being the breadwinner, responsibility, financial, classical role	
026		Myself as a father	slightly more personal
027		er ...	uncertain
028		I'm not sure.	hoping to be asked some more about 'being a father himself today'
029	starts again, slightly desperately	*I:* *Perhaps you could tell me a little*	ignores implied request but moves eagerly on to her intended focus on him as a son

continued

Figure 2.3   continued

	ONE		TWO
030		*about your own father*	
031	high levels of intensity throughout	W: Well, I was six when he left.	moderate intensity
032		I don't remember much about him from those days,	
033		I know him now as a man,	
034		but my relationship with him when I was younger seems to be	starts to give his worked-out 'official position' as developed over the years
035		that I was afraid of him,	
036		didn't really know him,	
037		yes I was kind of glad when he went.	
038		I think I was probably	
039		really jealous and possessive of my mother.	
040		She was always the one I felt emotionally close to	
041		very very much so.	
042	doesn't feel listened to – wraps it up finally and quickly	And one senses that he was in the way of that.	formality matches earlier formality of 'stating official position'
043	'congratulatory' if a bit patronizing	I: Well, you've anticipated my next question,	taken aback
044		which was going to be:	
045		'are you aware of having any particular feelings about him?'	
046	uncertainly	W: Well, I've just told you ...	very aggressively
047	genuine offer	do you want any more?	very aggressively
048	hastily	I: No,	hastily, afraid of hostility
049	definitively	that's OK.	reassuring

continued

Figure 2.3 continued

	ONE		TWO
050	rather bored inquiry plucked out of the air	*Can you describe to me*	moves away from 'dangerous topic', hoping to come back to it later
051		*if it is possible*	
052		*a typical day in your home*	
053		*when you were a boy of less than fourteen?*	
054	not particularly interested but still trying to co-operate: doesn't see the point of the question	*W:* I can remember hot summers.	reassured by shift away from any discussion of 'official position'; happy to co-operate by remembering an unimportant memory about much later period
055		One particular summer	
056		there was a swarm of flies	
057		that were enormous.	
058		I can remember	
059		treading on them	

FIGURE 2.3 **Interview with W – Alternative Attributed Personalities ONE and TWO – Informal Paralinguistics**

research – Briggs (1986: 1) cites Brenner (1981: 15) as asserting that 90% of all social science research involves interviews – one would imagine that it would itself be the object of much research, if only to improve the practice of professional depth interviewers.

One would expect the normal social research questions to be applied: who does what, when do they do it, how do they do it, what do they do, with what do they do it, with whom, for what purposes and with what effects? Sadly, this is not the case.

There has been very little social research into 'semi-structured research interviewing' as a historically produced and socially proliferating practice. Briggs in his review (1986: 27) found that things had not moved on much since the depressed and depressing findings of Dexter in 1970:

'Professional interviewers have for the most part assumed without analysis the nature of the process in which they are engaged. Until that process itself is seen as problematic, something to be analysed and explored, we will not be ready to determine what it records and measures, let alone how it can be used to draw valid inferences .... ' (Dexter, 1970: 157)

Twenty-three years after Dexter, Foddy remarked (1993: ix–x) that

'although a number of studies have been carried out to increase our understanding of question-answer processes, there are few signs that social researchers have made major improvements in their ways'.

Although I cannot explore that research here (Briggs, 1986: 1–30 provides an excellent start to such a discussion), in what follows, I shall attempt to be sensitive to its implications.

Frameworks: Interactional and Anthropological-historical

Objectives

In analysing the practices of ourselves and others (as in the 'W' transcript segment and in looking at our own transcripts of our own interviews), we have to search unendingly for 'communicative' and 'interpretive' blunders and naiveté[5], for ways of doing things better. You need to 'analyse' your interviews (as soon as they happen) as a 'researcher of interviews' would research it, in order to improve your practice for your next interview. Schon's (1983) model of the 'reflective practitioner' is appropriate here.

I now provide conceptual frameworks which enable such exploration of the practice of research interviewing. I shall start with relatively narrow interactionist speech-event models (Foddy, Markova), and then shift to a more anthropological 'historical situation' model developed from Charles Briggs's synthesis. This latter model is spelled out at some length to function as a checklist of issues for you to think about when reflecting in or after the interview you conduct.

Interactional Frameworks: Adjacent and Non-adjacent Units of Meaning

Foddy's Symbolic Interactionist Model   An initial framework for the analysis of the 'unique' time–space event of every interview is provided by Foddy (1993: 22). His framework is one of symbolic interactionism, and he suggests the way in which meanings of questions and answers have to be negotiated between the participants. Typically, like the participants in the interview with W, interviewer and interviewee are variably successful in doing this and variably aware of their success or lack of it. His conceptual framework is based upon the Communication Studies/semiology concept of encoding and decoding of messages. Meaning is not transferred, only messages (consisting of bundles of signs, like this book) into which meanings have been subtly or grossly encoded that may be decoded by the recipient in ways that are subtly or grossly different from those intended by the sender.

---

5 Compare the question of 'consciously controlling for potentially confounding variables'.

Interviewer (her)	Respondent (him)
Encodes her question, taking into account her own purposes, and presumptions/knowledge about the respondent, and perceptions of the respondent's presumptions/knowledge about her ⟶	Decodes her question, taking into account his own purposes and presumptions/knowledge about the interviewer, and perceptions of the interviewer's presumptions/ knowledge about him
	↓
Decodes his answer, taking into account her own presumptions/ knowledge about the respondent and perceptions of the respondent's presumptions/ knowledge about herself ⟵	Encodes his answer, taking into account his own presumptions/knowledge about the interviewer and perceptions of the interviewer's presumptions/ knowledge about him

FIGURE 2.4 **Foddy's Symbolic Interactionist Model of a Question–answer Sequence, Modified**

In the conversational shuffling between W and his interviewer, we can see a whole variety of a less-than-full meeting of minds. Foddy's model can help us explore the interview with W in this way.

The key philosophy behind the above formulation is that it is unlikely that the meaning of any utterance as 'decoded' by the recipient will be identical to that 'encoded' by the questioner. The struggle to recognize and minimize subtle erroneous 'decoding' in oneself and in the other person is the mark of the sophisticated communicator: it is characteristic of the naive communicator that he or she can only recognize very obvious cases of breakdown and does not have a variety of techniques for doing repair-work.

However I want to suggest a further development. The general concept of encoding and decoding of messages embodied in signs (semiotics, semiology) does not have to be restricted to the question–answer pair embodied in Figure 2.4 above.

The 'question–answer' model of the 'unit of speech analysis' is dangerously akin, as Mishler (1986) points out, to the 'stimulus–response model' of the 'unit of behavioural analysis' as used, for example, by the dominant mainstream school devoted to fully structured questionnaires. Let us attempt to weaken the 'magical hold' of the question–answer model over our imaginations first by looking at a three-step model which suggests a much more processual flow of interview interaction and then by considering a more 'jumpy' model.

Linell–Markova's Three-step Interactional Model   Markova (1990) asks 'What is the best model for understanding interview processes?' Though the 'obvious' answer in an interview would appear to be the two-step unit, Question+Answer, she argues convincingly for a minimum of a 'three-step unit' which may all be completed within a single utterance (1990: 136–40) or which may cut across an utterance (1990: 140–2).

She points out that 'a single utterance or a single turn' can be seen as a 'natural unit of understanding'. Working on the primary conceptual axiom that each turn is a combination of some degree of initiative and of response, and on the basis of another chapter on interactional dominance by Linell in the same book, Markova writes as follows:

> 'By looking at each initiative and response in each turn in terms of maintenance and changing of topic by the interlocutors, the researcher's problem is to identify the features of interactional dominance. Each turn has the characteristics of a three-step process, each turn being the result of some initiative and some response. As Linell claims, each turn or utterance is Janus-like, i.e. it is potentially directed simultaneously towards the past and towards the future.
>
> The retroactive feature of the turn or utterance is internally related to the proactive feature. Take for example, the health visitor's turn ...:
>
>> "That's very good. That's very good. And did he lose on his birth weight at all while you were in hospital or ...?"
>
> The health visitor's contribution is *retroactive*, i.e. it is a response to the mother, confirming that the health visitor has understood and confirmed the mother's previous turn about her baby's birthweight.
>
> However the health visitor's turn is also *proactive*, i.e. it initiates further exploration of the discussed subject-matter by asking whether the baby has lost any weight while in hospital ...
>
> In this case the *response* to the mother [i.e. "That's very good. That's very good"] and the *initiative* [i.e. "And did he lose", etc.] are both clearly identifiable parts ....
>
> In reality, though, many dialogical turns may only be responses while others may only be initiatives [and in many cases] one cannot meaningfully physically separate the retroactive and the proactive [aspects] of the participants' turns.' (Markova, 1990: 137, modified)

I can apply this conceptual framework to the 'W' interview and see how each utterance might be seen as pointing both towards the past and towards the future of the conversational interaction. Looking at just one segment, it might come out something like that shown in Figure 2.5.

The research tradition of Conversational Analysis (CA) looks for adjacent natural units: with Markova's three-step analysis being perhaps better than the normal stimulus–response two-step one.

However, tracing intelligible units may engulf looking at *non-adjacent* speech.

Discussion of Models Focusing on Non-adjacent Speech   Even Markova's version of the traditional 'question+answer' segmentation of the text underplays the point that at some points either the interviewer or the informants inevitably decide (not necessarily in harmony with each other) not to ask or answer further questions or points on a given topic. Similarly, the decision by one participant *not*

		Initiatives for conversational future	Responses to conversational past
1	I	are you aware of having had any particular feelings about him?	
2	W	do you want any more?	Well, I've just told you ...
3	I	Can you describe to me if it is possible a typical day in your home when ...	No, that's OK.
4	W		I can remember hot summers ...

FIGURE 2.5 **Interview with W Analysed in Markova's Three-step Model**

to follow-up a certain 'lead' offered by another – or to not follow it up at the time but to return to it *much later* – is a decision that may not be as visible as some other speech decisions, but may be just as important.

Markova argues for units that are not characterized by physical togetherness in the text but 'that are primarily conceptual and epistemological in character' (Markova, 1990: 131). I strongly agree. The 'unit of analysis' should not be *merely* the utterances of the informant (thus ignoring the question, as in the Old Wu extract) nor even the 'question plus answer plus follow-up question plus follow-up answer' (as in the interview with W).

For example, in a way that will be shown to be important later on, the 'thematic analysis' of narrative accounts may look, quite rightly and very productively, at 'units of analysis' that have been carefully separated into non-adjacent spaces. A person may start an argument, break off into a story, half-tell the story, start another argument, go back to the first argument, complete the final half of the first story. Identifying segments of the same argument interrupted by a half-told story and the start of another argument; identifying when argumentative speech appears to be part of one argument but actually functions as part of another: these are all skills dependent on the understanding that adjacent phrases may be part of separate units of meaning and that a single unit of meaning may be spread in a variety of speech locations (and therefore in the transcript text) (Casement, 1985).

Similarly, the interviewee may drop hints while telling one story, which are not noticed by the interviewer at that moment but 'puzzle' him or her so that the interviewer goes back to the 'dropped hint' at a much later point and gets at a different dimension that was present but not observed at the time. Conversation is much more *artful* than is suggested by turn-by-turn analysis or question+answer models. That artfulness is hardly ever fully conscious, in the way that a hypnotist or a propagandist consciously 'embeds' significant units in such a non-adjacent way that their hypnotic or functional connection is not perceptible. More usually, the separation is that of half-conscious mental functioning.

I hope the above argument has convinced you that units of meaning may not consist only of adjacent speech, and that adjacent speech may be part of different units of meaning.

An Anthropological-historical Approach
to Interview Interaction based on Briggs

In the discussion thus far of the contribution of Foddy, Markova and Linell, I have been working with interactional models which tend to abstract from the 'whole-person relations and context' in which the communication is embodied.

I now present a model which asks you to take more account of the real-life context: a more anthropological and historical account which, while providing space for the analysis of verbal interaction developed by the CA-school and others, goes beyond it to a more inclusive synthesis.

Such a model is provided by Charles Briggs in his *Learning How to Ask* (1986: 41). I have modified it below in order to take account of insights and terminology developed by Muriel Saville-Troike (1982) and to include other items and dimensions I consider important, such as Foddy's interactional material.

In Figure 2.6, the centre of the diagram is *the relationship and communication between the interviewer and the informant*, as represented by the solid black horizontal line. My understanding of that relationship and that communication will be determined by the *particular model of human inter/subjectivity* with which I understand all relationships and communications. In particular, the process will be one involving constant *emotion* and constant *evaluation* on both sides.

Looking first at the bottom right of the diagram, the fact that this communicative event occurs within a given and historically evolving *social setting* is stressed, and that this *communicative event* is of a certain *type*, one with its own norms of what should or shouldn't happen during and after the event, its own *norms of propriety*. Obviously, it is quite possible for those involved to disagree about what the social setting is and about what the appropriate norms are.

If I then move from the social setting and the cultural definitions of the type of event and its norms of propriety to the scene within the 'black box' of the interview interaction, I find useful the image of a see-saw which represents *the evolving power-balance* between those involved. This power-balance is strongly affected by the items at the top of the black box, namely the *histories and social roles* of those involved and their goals in general which determine their particular *goals and strategies for the interview interaction* itself. In the process of interview interaction, existing power resources may be mobilized and new ones created or lost. The power-balance of interviewer and interviewee when they end the interview may be the same or may be different from that with which they started. Even if it remains the same, this may only be the result of a frustrated attempt by one or both parties to increase their own power or that of both parties together. *The fact that a dimension of power is always present doesn't mean that a power-interaction is always on a win–lose basis.* Both interviewer and interviewee may struggle for power within an interview and both may emerge from the interview more powerful than when they started.

If I then look at the communication itself, the material below the central black bar, I find the models of Foddy and of the semiologists relevant in their discussion of the codes which determined *the encoding and the decoding of the messages as communicated through the channels*, mostly of sound but also involving non-verbal

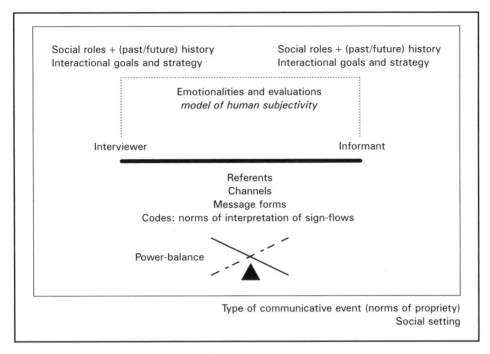

FIGURE 2.6   **Briggs–Wengraf Model of Components of the Interview Situation**

communication channels and codes as well. Much of the message-exchange will be about the *referents* to which the verbal exchange is oriented, but much of it will not.

Let us look at the components already discussed and represented in the figure.

Social Setting[6]   Here such factors as location, type of day, time of day, social-constraints, physical and social arrangements and interruptions need to be considered. These physical and temporal arrangements are always of considerable importance. Is the interview in a private space of one of the participants, or in a public one? Most 'private spaces' are liable to overhearing interruption by flat-mates, family members, assorted others, the telephone or just distracting sights or sounds. It is important to try to avoid these. Public spaces also have their distractions. A 'neutral space' may be the best to aim for, unless you want to get clues from the surroundings that your informant wishes to present himself or herself in. What might be the effects of a social setting on you and the interviewee?

Type of Communicative Event with Norms of Propriety   Here the constructions of the two parties may be very different. For the researcher, this is a semi-structured depth interview run as a professional operation. For the informant, it may be a favour of a not very clear sort that they are doing for the friend of a friend or a local power-figure.

---

6 I have here relied on Saville-Troike's (1982) reworking of Hymes, replacing Briggs's original 'social situation'.

Briggs, early in his career, went to 'interview' as a youthful anthropologist two elderly Mexican-Americans. In his enjoyable and insightful study of his own communicational blunders (1986), he stresses the way his notion that he was 'doing an interview' did not relate to any concept in the conceptual framework of his informants. It took him a while – coming from an 'interview' discipline in an 'interview society' – to realize that the two elderly Mexican-American respondents did not have such a 'speech event' as 'an interview' in their culture and saw him merely as a young White Anglo asking rather intimate questions of 'his elders' without having earned the legitimacy to do so.

As I have already argued, even within societies where 'interviews' are more current as a genre of social event, very different personal and collective constructions can be put on the term 'interview', not all of them pleasant or auguring well for 'the next interview'.

Obviously, each participant may have to adjust their sense of 'the norms' to how the other is behaving, and at times the strategy of either party may be to 'depart' from the expected norms. The norms of any given interview are partly given in anticipation before and are partly subject to negotiation and mutation within the interview interaction itself.

Social Roles + (Past/Future)History   The question of 'social roles'was raised in the discussion of the Lorna and John vignette (p. 16). It is important to note that you do not just inhabit one social role ('research interviewer'). In fact we all carry around a bundle of roles with us – as was discussed in the discussion of multiple statuses characteristics we all possess – and the fore-grounded interviewer–interviewee roles are not the only ones to be operative. Indeed, they may just be an area in which other roles come into play.

The 'social roles *and (past/future) history*' in the diagram above is designed to stress the way both you and your interviewee come towards this interview carrying all the positive and negative 'personal history' that each of you have. These may be similar in surprising ways and very different in surprising ways: they may form what you do and how you interpret it in ways that are very difficult to detect. You need at least to get clear for yourself the collective history which you share and the histories which you imagine that you might well not share, prior to designing the interview.

'History' as a dimension includes feared and desired and expected 'futures' which may be affected by the interview interaction in the present: Lorna's reflection on her post-interview 'future history' as it might be affected by her present decisions about the interview is a case in point. The same is true of John.

Our sense of what to do (in respect of the present moment of the present interview) can be seen as determined by our current sense of the past and our strategy for our future. Alternative 'future histories' we carry in our heads (as a result of our past histories) affect our present-time deciding. I have therefore referred, in the diagram, to 'past/future history'.

Interactional Goals + Strategies   'Interactional goals' may vary a lot. People's 'official purposes' may be one thing, but there may be real or suspected unofficial purposes which may also affect the outcome. You and your interviewee have separate goals of various sorts (expressed in hopes and fears for its process and its outcomes) and prepared or emergent strategies for achieving them.

The interviewer may be determined not to 'lose control of the interview' and the interviewee equally determined to have his or her say as they want to say it. The informant may wish to avoid giving the interviewer information that might upset the interviewer, and be either quite right or quite wrong in their estimate of what questions or answers would cause pain.[7] Bear in mind the case of W and the way the talk was moved away – by one or both of them – from the topic of his closeness to his mother and his belief in his father's jealousy, etc.

You need to stay sensitive to unavowed and unofficial goals and purposes! Especially your own.

For example: if you are determined to 'prove' a pre-existing theory when you go into an interview, you will behave quite differently than you would if your 'unofficial goal' was to find ideas for 'new interesting theory'. If your goal is to 'impress' the informant, your behaviour will be different than if you want to 'listen to' them.

- What might be different interactional goals that John and Lorna (p. 16) might have had for 'their interview'?
- What might the goals have been in the interview with W (p. 20) or with Old Wu (p. 6)?

Bear in mind that 'interactional goals' may change as the 'interview interaction' is co-steered by both of you. Do not assume that goals or strategies are fixed.

In the phrase 'interactional goals and strategy', the *'and* strategy' is important. Even assuming they have common goals, people may have different 'strategies' for the interview. One person's strategy may be to avoid being too passive at the start – perhaps this was the case for W? Another person may allow the 'other' to dictate the depth and pace of answering for at least a while. Again, people may change their tactics within a given strategy as the interview develops. They may also – if their current strategy seems not to be working – shift to a quite different strategy which they think has a better chance. If you feel that your 'polite non-pushy' strategy of eliciting responses hasn't worked at all for the first 10 minutes of a 30 minute interview, you are likely to shift to a 'more pushy' alternative, or to a quite different alternative.

Power–knowledge, Domination and Resistance   The question of the politics of interview interaction and the conditions and outcomes of interviews have been raised particularly by feminist writers, sometimes simply inspired by the exploitation of interviewees in a weak power position and sometimes with their sensitivity enhanced by such writers as Foucault, concerned for the relationship between power and knowledge. For whatever reason, concern for the micro-politics of researched interview work has been higher in Britain and Anglo-Saxon countries than on the European continent (see the introduction to Chamberlayne et al., 2000 for a further discussion; also Perks and Thomson, 1998). It is not possible to develop a general theory or account of power at this point. I wish only to stress that power is a dimension of interview interaction dangerously likely to be overlooked or ignored or denied by the well-intentioned and good-natured interviewer.

---

7 See Figure 2.4 on this symbolic calculation.

At any given moment, there is an overall fluctuating 'power-balance' as the attempts to co-operate and pursue interactional goals 'register'. This is indicated by the little power see-saw drawing at the bottom of the diagram.

The 'Referent'   The question of the 'referent' is a crucial one. People may imagine that the topic (or referent, that which is being referred to) is commonly understood by both parties, but in fact there may be a greater or lesser degree of unperceived discrepancy between the imagined referents.

When you refer in your questions to racism, and ask me whether I think 'racism is increased or reduced by certain legislation', I may be thinking that the word 'racism' in your question refers to what I call 'institutionalized racism' but you may have a quite different concept of the referent from me. The word 'racism' is conjuring up two different referents in our mind. When this is obvious, it's easy to deal with or make allowances for.

> In our vignette about John and Lorna, what different 'referents' might be the real focus of the would-be interviewer? In the interview with W, what was or were the referents in that case?

There may be more than one referent, of which only one is explicit. You may be talking about 'wrongdoing in general in society' but I may be thinking of some specific act of wrongdoing about which I feel guilty and perhaps of which I think maybe you too are very aware, and so my referent may be double while your's may only be single.

Tannen (1990) suggests that in the society and milieux she was studying, there can be a contradiction between talk which is 'report-talk' (reporting on one or more referents) and talk which is 'rapport-talk' (in which the referents are merely pegs on which to hang other speech functions, such as getting a better sense of the other person, deepening the relationship, etc.). In the interview design, what proportion of referent-report talk you wish to elicit (and when) and what sort of other talk (e.g. rapport-relationship) you wish to elicit (and when) are important questions. For many purposes, rapport needs to be developed before reports on some referents are likely to be of the highest quality.

Emotionalities and Evaluations   At a given moment, both you and your inform-ant will be experiencing more- or less-strong emotions, and you will be express-ing such emotions anywhere on a spectrum from 'imperceptible' to 'over the top'. You will be doing all this experiencing and evaluating more or less consciously and unconsciously; you will be sharing some emotions and evaluations, not shar-ing others, and perhaps denying the rest. As a result, this fluctuating emotional experience and exchange will be the context in which you will be 'evaluating' what you are doing and what the other person is doing and how the whole inter-view is going in terms of your interactional goals and the working out of your interactional strategies and tactics. Think of the 'interview with W' and the implied complex questions of emotional inter/subjectivity as suggested in the two alterna-tive readings, ONE and TWO (p. 34).

Researcher's Model of Human Subjectivity and Intersubjectivity   Summing up much of the above, I may say that understanding the interview interaction between two people will depend on our model of human inter/subjectivity in general and our evolving model of these two subjectivities in particular. A clarification by Hollway and Jefferson of two contrasting models can be found on pages 158–9, where the implications of such models of human subjectivity for the preparation and design of interviews are discussed.

Channel   The question of 'channel' is of great importance. It is easy to believe that in interviews, messages are being conveyed acoustically through voice, that there is one channel and that is auditory. Or our conception may be even more narrowly conceived: that meaning is just conveyed through the words spoken and heard on that vocal-auditory channel.

If I just pay attention to the words spoken, I have a very impoverished idea of the communication. However, since it is 'words only' that can be most easily loaded into a transcript, there is a terrible temptation just to analyse the words. It would be a great mistake to do so. Think back to the interview with 'W' and the importance of 'stage directions' in determining what meaning was being conveyed. The 'stage directions' have to do with 'how the words are said': this is known more technically as 'paralinguistics' (p. 216 onwards, for analyses of interviews with a strong emphasis on paralinguistics and procedures for registering and displaying them).

Actually the paralinguistics in how I say the words may (as in an 'ironical' tone) completely subvert the meaning of the words. One has only to think of excessive politeness by a teacher or a pupil in a school context. One of Elliot Mishler's chapters in his excellent *Research Interviewing: Context and Narrative* is entitled 'research interviews as speech events'. They are; but they are, of course, much more. In speech, the tone of voice and the speed of delivery, the silences, the hesitations, the mode of delivery of the words can be as important in determining meaning and reception as the actual words themselves. Fritz Perls, the founder of Gestalt Therapy, stressed the importance of listening to the emotions of the voice rather than getting confused by the words actually being said: 'Forget what your words are saying; what is your voice saying?' There is much more to speech interaction (say on the telephone) than just the words of the transcript.

Just adding the paralinguistics to the auditory channel is not enough. Other channels are involved. A depth interview is normally carried out in a face-to-face setting with multiple extra channels of communication. The eye perceiving the body is another channel. Our face moves as we talk, our whole body shifts position, we fidget, make notes or not, adjust the tape-recorder, move our chairs around and move in our chair, our bodies do a number of things, often out of our own awareness, but within the awareness of an anxious interviewee. *And you as interviewer are similarly affected by the non-verbal communication (NVC) of the interviewee.*

Most communication analysts stress the way that non-verbal communication occurs through non-auditory channels. There is the smell or perfume of the people involved; their clothes; their body-language and body-styles; there is the arrangement of objects and space between and around the participants. There is the interface between the tape-recorder, microphones and the participants; perhaps the question-schedule on the knee of the interviewer and their pen and papers. There are movements of impatience, slightly blank gazes, sudden leaning-forwards in the seats; raising of the energy and alertness levels of the participants, a sense of what some might call the constantly mutating 'vibrations' or 'feel' of the interaction. In addition, there are the 'messages' conveyed by the 'choice of setting' for the interview, the part of town, the implied income-level, the type of decoration.

Interviews are not merely speech-events, they are NVC and whole-body/whole-context events.

To start to approximate to this rich inter-personal reality, video-taping would be a great help. But nothing replaces the self-monitoring sensitive interviewer making detailed session-notes immediately after the session on all outer realities and all inner experiences that they can remember. Even if I cannot for normal purposes articulate anything but a fraction of this richness, the more that can be articulated the better for my future understanding of the interaction.

Codes: the Interpretation of Sign-flows Through the Channels   The interaction will normally take place in one language. However, for certain interviews, you may find yourself using a professional or an amateur translator – for example, with an elderly immigrant who does not speak your own language. This will raise additional questions of how well the 'translation' is being done. I raised this question in respect of the 'narrative' in English of Old Wu, the Chinese woman reported in Chapter 1. Does the English term 'madness' convey the nuance of the Chinese original? In addition, the elderly immigrant may say different things if her (say) school-age daughter is acting as translator (bear in mind that the translator has the other permanent social role of being the school-age daughter!); and, irrespective of what she says, the school-age daughter – not being a professional translator – is likely to 'edit' what she reports her mother as having said so as to fit what the daughter thinks of as being 'the proprieties'.

Even given a common language code (say English), there is an immense amount of variation in the 'encoding of subtle meanings' even if the same words are used. The 'meanings' of words are held in a dictionary, and changes and varieties of meaning of words are to some (weak and decontextualized) extent caught there. However, for languages and sign forms other than verbal ones, we do not have 'explicit common code books' with anything like the power of a 'dictionary of words'. There are constant attempts to produce 'code-books' for signs sent through different non-verbal channels. There are books on body-postures, for example, which attempt to lay down the 'meaning' of this or that way of 'holding' or 'moving' the face and the body; there are books on 'the language of clothes' (fast changing sign-forms and fast-changing meanings) which indicate meanings that can be 'read' from particular combinations of clothing items and ways of wearing them. There are books on the language of smells and scents. Gestures for example, have different meanings in different gesture codes: one person's 'smile' may be decoded differently by two different people. Dress codes vary between generations, between subcultures, over time and in all sorts of ways. Body-posture codes are also liable to misinterpretation: the same posture might be interpreted as 'deep interest' by one decoder and as 'passive waiting' by another.

Bear in mind that codes are always being invented, mutated, and rendered obsolete by human intervention: people switch between existing codes in mid-communication. Norms of propriety are brought into being and broken for 'artistic' or strategic effect, and so forth. All attempts to render codes explicit are of value; none of the attempts is likely to catch more than a fraction of our tacit receptivity to subtle nuances of meaning in our multi-channel, multi-code, multi-cultural exchanging of messages within and outside consciousness.

The interviewer needs to be as conscious as possible of how the 'effects' of messages encoded and transmitted through such non-verbal channels are impinging on the interviewer and the interviewee.

Message-form   The message form concerns the 'sign systems' through which meaning is conveyed. I may convey dislike by saying 'I dislike you' in a 'sincere' tone of voice, or by 'I like you' using an 'insincere' voice. In both cases, you recognize the message-form of the words and the message-form of a 'tone of voice', and the total message comes through both 'message forms' being used simultaneously. I may indicate non-welcome through the 'message form' of making you wait a long time in an uncomfortable room while I ostentatiously have a long trivial phone call with somebody at the time I agreed to have an interview with you. I may 'say it with flowers'.

Within a given sign-system (English words), the message form and the content may be different in another respect. A request may be put in the form of a 'question' – 'would you like to open the window?' – or a question may be put in the form of an assertion – imagine the voice going up towards the end of the following set of words: 'it is a nice day'.

Some of the complexities of understanding 'the interview with W' transcript lay in attempting to understand the relation between message-form and the message-function.

Multiple-channel Encoding and Decoding, and 'Communicative Blunders'   And in each of the many channels through which messages are exchanged in face-to-face interviews, encoding and decoding is always in question. My attempt at politeness may be experienced by you as an 'impersonal push-away'; your attempt to break the ice may be seen by me as dangerous aggression. My attempt to be precise may be experienced by you as nit-picking. The speed at which I speak may indicate laid-backness to one person and excessive speediness to another, depending on the subculture that they come from. When the English talk of mountains with the Tibetans, the two groups may have quite different categories of size in mind.

In Briggs's (1986) Chapter 3 'On communicative blunders' he explores how there may be a mismatch of any of the components of the research interview interaction identified in the model above. The US sociologist Jessie Barnard is supposed to have said that in any marriage, there were two marriages: 'his marriage' and 'her marriage'. The same is true of any given interview: remember how Isobel and W might have interpreted 'their interview' quite differently. There is W's interview and his interviewer's interview. There is the 'informant's interview' and there is 'your interview'.

The above discussion could not be conclusive and does not attempt to be so. The function of the conceptual framework and the summary discussion of each concept is to suggest the sort of consideration that you might give to what you plan to go on in your future interviews and how you make sense of what did go on in past ones.

Sequencing in the Interview   Saville-Troike (1982) stresses the interaction-sequence within the communicative exchange. A question posed at the beginning of an interview may get a quite different response than the same question posed at the end. Alternatively, the answer may be identical in phrasing but quite different in meaning. Mishler (1986: 52–3) argues that

> 'an adequate understanding of interviews depends on recognizing how interviewers reformulate questions and respondents frame answers in terms of their reciprocal understandings as meanings emerge during the course of the interview ... the internal history of the developing discourse. ... Within the perspectives of interviews as speech events and speech activities, variation in how particular questions are asked as well as variation in the overall course of interviews become objects of inquiry. Because I cannot ascertain the meaning of a question simply by referring to the interview schedule and interviewer's notes, the research question is transformed from a search for "errors" into an analysis of the interview process in order to determine the meaning of questions and answers ... through mutual reformulation and specification ...'

Summary

This chapter has presented the case 'and a technical language' for becoming sensitive to, and analysing for, a number of different dimensions in the interview. The case is not just technical, however.

I have tried to show that interviews are culturally and historically specific phenomena, to be studied as a practice or set of practices just like any other set of socio-historical practices. I have argued that without such research into interviews as a located socio-historical practice, any inferences about the 'functions for gaining and changing knowledge' through any particular interview interaction is likely to be naive.

I have provided a number of frameworks in terms of which some of the 'features' of interaction of the interview before-and-after can be analysed. These should sensitize you to the potential for 'communicative blunders' that may emerge in your interviewing and, I hope, to some of the ways these can be 'repaired'. Or at least, not repeated.

I shall now go on to consider models of social research design in general and then apply them to develop a model of interview evidence research design applicable particularly to semi-structured depth interviewing.

3

Models of Research Design and their Application to Semi-Structured Depth Interviewing

MODEL-BUILDING, MODEL-TESTING SEQUENCE

In social research I am concerned with building and testing descriptive and explanatory models of the realities with which I am concerned. Any particular model is a simplified version of a more complex social reality. Just as no map can include everything about the territory of which it is a representation – a map that excluded nothing would be an identical full-size reduplication of the original – so no model can include everything about the reality it represents.

In general, social research moves from model-building to testing the model that was built. Sometimes, this is described as the move from exploratory research where an unknown area is given a preliminary mapping to theory-testing research where the current provisional map is tested against reality. Whether the metaphor is of *mapping* or of *modelling*, the argument about sequence is the same.

At any given moment of *an overall research cycle*, particular types of interviews may be used for model-building or model-testing; in any *given round of interviews*, particular types of interview session may be used for model-building or for model-testing; in a *given interview*, the interviewer may shift between model-building and model-testing activity. However, given that you cannot test a model until you have built one, the general sequence is from model-building to model-testing at all these levels.

How to Think the Relation of Models to Evidence: Questions, Concepts and Indicators, the Problem of Operationalization/Instrumentation

Collingwood and the Language of Theory-questions and Theory-answers

A theory, or a particular theoretical proposition, is an assertion about reality. Such an assertion is an answer to a question. The question and the answer need to be taken together.

The historian and philosopher R.G. Collingwood just before World War II wrote rather clearly about this in his *Autobiography* as follows:

'I began by observing that you cannot find out what a man means by simply studying his spoken or written statements, even though he has spoken or written with perfect command of language and perfectly truthful intention. In order to find out his meaning, you must also know what the question was (a question in his own mind and presumed by him to be in yours) to which the thing he has said or written was meant as an answer ....

A highly detailed and generalized proposition must be the answer, not to a vague and generalized question, but to a question as detailed and particularized as itself.

For example, if my car will not go, I may spend an hour searching for the cause of its failure. If, during this hour, I take out number one plug, lay it on the engine, turn the starting handle, and watch for a spark, my observation "number one plug is all right" is an answer not to the question "Why won't my car go?" but to the question "Is it because number one plug is not sparking that my car won't go?" Any one of the various experiments I make during the hour will be the finding of an answer to some such detailed and particularized question.

The question "Why won't my car go?" is only a kind of summary of all these taken together. It is not a separate question asked at a separate time, nor is it a sustained question which I continue to ask for the whole hour altogether. Consequently, when I say "Number one plug is all right", this observation does not record one more failure to answer the hour-long question, "What is wrong with my car?" It records a success in answering the three-minute long question, "Is the stoppage due to failure in the number one plug?"....[1]

It seemed to me that truth, if that meant the kind of thing which I was accustomed to pursue in my ordinary work as a philosopher or historian – truth in the sense of which a philosophical theory or a historical narrative is called true, which seemed to me the proper use of the word – was something that belonged not to a single proposition, nor even as the coherence theorists maintained to a complex of propositions taken together, *but to a complex consisting of questions and answers* ....

I could hazard a few statements about it ...

- Each question and each answer in a given complex had to be relevant or appropriate, had to "belong" both to the whole and to the place it occupied in the whole.
- Each question had to "arise"; there must be that about it whose absence I condemn when I refuse to answer a question on the grounds that it "doesn't arise".
- Each "answer" must be the "right" answer to the question it professes to answer: by "right", I do not mean "true". The "right" answer to a question is the answer which enables us to get ahead with the process of questioning and answering.'

(Collingwood, 1939: 31–2, 37, paragraphing modified)

Collingwood's final paragraph seems very important, and can be commented upon as it affects *research questioning* and *the answering of research questions by the researcher* (the context of Collingwood's discussion above). (Later on, we will see how it affects *interview questioning* and *the answering of interview questions by interviewees*, to which Collingwood's discussion can be cautiously extended.)

---

1 I would argue that it is both.

I wish to argue that the conceptual framework in terms of which research-questions are posed and in terms of which research-answers have to be given is provided by a theory-language (theoretical discourse). Few are likely to argue with such a proposition, but often its implications are underestimated.

Social research devoted to theoretical development rests upon a number of distinctions which are not obvious to common-sense and often neglected by qualitative researchers. Perhaps the crucial distinction is between *a (social science) concept* and *its indicators*.

> Consider the relation between a theory-language in which 'social class' is a crucial characteristic to be established about a person, and interview evidence. What interview evidence would help to establish the person's 'social class'?
>
> You might decide that social class cannot be determined from somebody's talk, and only a document indicating source of income would be a relevant indicator. Consequently no verbal statements by an interviewee would be indicators of social class, if the concept was defined in this way.
>
> Alternatively, you might decide that the indicator of social class was the capacity or otherwise to engage in 'middle-class talk' (Bernstein's elaborated code). In this case, documentary evidence about source of income or anything else would be useless as an indicator of social class; only an interview or an overheard spontaneous conversation would provide evidence about the capacity to engage in 'middle-class talk in a middle-class accent'.
>
> Alternatively, your concept of social class might involve both source and level of income, customary mode of talking, and type of occupational activity. This would mean that the concept had three indicators, and that interview evidence might be a strong indicator for one of them (mode of talk) and a weaker indicator for others.
>
> The researcher who decides to use multiple indicators for any particular theoretical concept in their conceptual framework has a problem: what happens if the indicators point in different directions? The person talks with a public-school accent; they present documentary evidence of living on minimum welfare benefits; they say that their work involves driving expensive cars and negotiating prices. Can this person be simply ascribed to a single social-class position? If so, which and why? If not, what can be inferred from the interview material? 'Interpreting evidence' involves exploring issues like these.

Theories in social science are couched in a 'theory-language' made up of a body of concepts, for which the indicators are often typically indirect and non-obvious.

> If you wished to investigate whether a given organization was suffering from 'information overload', or a particular group of workers from 'alienation', or a particular empire from 'imperial overstretch', or a society from 'accelerated social polarization', you would need to define the key conceptual terms, and you would need to define what 'indicators' you would collect for each of the terms in order to determine whether the hypothesized condition or change of condition was actually occurring, and, if so, to what extent?

An 'empirical indicator' (EI) is a measurement, an observation, a datum, which is taken to be 'evidence' for a particular theoretical concept (TC) being in one 'state' or another (such as information overload or its opposite, high medium or low alienation, increasing or decreasing rates of social polarization, etc.).

Since Lazarsfeld, in social research the custom has often been that the more abstract the theoretical concept, the greater the number of 'indicators' that need to be examined. To establish somebody's 'address' or 'gender' is relatively easy and might normally be quickly established with rather few EIs; to establish somebody's 'sexuality' or their 'social class' or their 'ideology' might require rather more EIs and rather more complex argument.

In sociology, the principle of 'triangulation' has been put forward which suggests that you should consider looking for at least three empirical indicators for any particular moderately complex theoretical concept (Denzin, 1970).

How does this discussion of concepts and their difficult relation to different indicators relate to interviews? Our discussion of the conceptual framework needed to understand interviews seen as problematic should suggest the answer. The entire interview contains evidence for answering a variety of theory questions, but *problematic* evidence. The evidence is problematic *because the relation between theoretical concepts and their empirical indicators is always across a gap, which one always has to be prepared to argue over.* There is a gap which has to be filled by a justification of why this particular evidence should justify certain claims that a particular hypothesis or theorization has been supported or disconfirmed by a particular pattern of interview evidence. I need to argue a case as to why a pattern of data should be taken as indicating at the level of my theoretical discourse (in my theory-language) a particular 'reality'. Inferences from data-indicators to conceptual significance cannot be assumed: they must be argued for.

It may be useful to look at a model of sociological research in which the distinctions raised above are embodied.

CLASSIC MODEL OF PRE-CONCEPTUALIZATION, PRE-THEORIZATION AND STAGES OF THEORY-TESTING: ROSE–WENGRAF

Classical models of research design in general and social research design in particular assume that the 'conceptual structure and the theories couched in terms of that conceptual structure' have arrived *en bloc* from somewhere else, that in some sense they are 'given', and that the task that remains is that of testing such a pre-given theory by deriving from it testable hypotheses (all of which are couched in terms of the given, the received, conceptual structure). Formulated in terms of a received conceptual structure, the model assumes a pre-theorization and is only concerned with theory-testing/model-testing.

If you are going to start with a theorization-*testing* model, then it is important to work the theorizations out very well in advance, as the 'model of the research cycle' set out below suggests.

Rose (1982: 14) developed and used to good effect a diagram which I have revised as Figure 3.1.[2]

---

2 I have added the items on the CF and the CRQ, and also added the words 'a descriptive or' to the description of what a 'Theory' is. First point: Very briefly, earlier writers tended not to distinguish between conceptual frameworks and assertions about reality (theories, propositions) couched in terms of them: both were called 'theory', and Rose's original formulation follows this tradition. I consider it to be very important to distinguish the two, both in relation to the conceptual frameworks of the researcher (Kuhn, 1970; Bachelard, 1999) and – though this is not our concern at the moment – in relation to the conceptual framework of the interviewee. Second point: Researchers are concerned to develop better accounts of reality, better models of entities and processes. Against positivist orthodoxy, I see no absolute distinction between description and explanation and I do not privilege causal explanation over understanding.

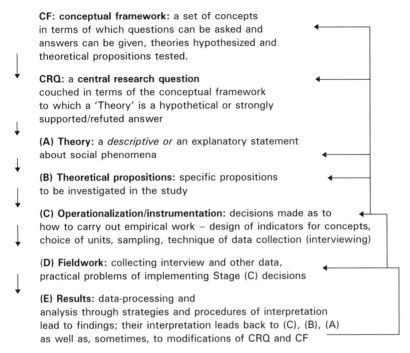

CF: conceptual framework: a set of concepts in terms of which questions can be asked and answers can be given, theories hypothesized and theoretical propositions tested.

CRQ: a central research question couched in terms of the conceptual framework to which a 'Theory' is a hypothetical or strongly supported/refuted answer

(A) Theory: a *descriptive or* an explanatory statement about social phenomena

(B) Theoretical propositions: specific propositions to be investigated in the study

(C) Operationalization/instrumentation: decisions made as to how to carry out empirical work – design of indicators for concepts, choice of units, sampling, technique of data collection (interviewing)

(D) Fieldwork: collecting interview and other data, practical problems of implementing Stage (C) decisions

(E) Results: data-processing and analysis through strategies and procedures of interpretation lead to findings; their interpretation leads back to (C), (B), (A) as well as, sometimes, to modifications of CRQ and CF

FIGURE 3.1   **Rose–Wengraf Model of the Research Process**

The model involves a 'stages element' in that one proceeds down the arrows on the left-hand side of the diagram, but the 'return arrows' going back up the page on the right indicate that the researcher may have to 'return' to 'earlier stages' if the situation at 'later stages' requires it. In this version, it is problems with the 'results' that lead to a 'return' to the 'fieldwork' or other elements of the research design.

For other models of the research process, see de Vaus (1996), Black (1993: 5, 10), Evertson and Green (reprinted in Rossmann and Marshall 1995: 20–1), Maykut and Morehouse (1994: 84).

The classic model of research involves *a conceptual framework* – which, once established, is normally not modified during the process of theory-testing – and, couched in terms of that conceptual framework, *a theory* composed of *theoretical propositions* which are also normally not modified during the process of theory-testing. Very often, the choice of *samples* is also not modified after the original selection has been made.

This is by no means the only model, however, of how research is done, because models, and the conceptual frameworks in terms of which models and theorizations are couched, get revised, rectified and improved.

Research which is concerned for model-*building* and model-*rectification* very frequently changes its sampling strategy as the research proceeds; it puts forward theories not originally envisaged at the start of the research; it accounts itself particularly successful and important if it manages to contribute to a better conceptual framework than the one with which it started off. This can be called the 'romantic' model of social research. For various reasons it is ideologically and often empirically associated with qualitative work.

The linkage of theoretical concepts with empirical indicators through an explicit operation is a crucial insight associated with quantitative research, but one underestimated, ignored or even denied by researchers declaring themselves to be 'qualitative'.

> This is a serious error, but it can to some extent be understood. It should be stressed that the terms of 'operationalization' and even of 'instrumentation' have the hidden premise of a fixed prior theory, a premise which is characteristic of theory-testing quantitative research. In this model, the theory-language composed of agreed received theoretical concepts is already fixed, and intellectual ingenuity is confined to finding, at the level of empirical indicators, different operationalizations for those fixed theoretical concepts. Given such a fixity, the only conceptual design research question left open appears to be the identification of empirical indicators and their mutual relationship.
>
> Qualitative researchers are more typically interested in *the generation and rectification of theoretical concepts*, and therefore reject the top-down assumption behind 'operationalizing pre-fixed theoretical concepts'. Where, as in all theory-building, model-building research, the theory is *emergent* from the research, then we have a reverse process upwards, the 'upwards inferring' of theorizations and even of theoretical concepts on the basis of examined evidence. This contrasts with the 'downwards' metaphysic of the term 'operationalization'. Such upwards inferences, such 'instrumentation/ interpretation', such invention and rectification of appropriate concepts, will be further discussed below.

To sum up: in this text, I argue for the existence of a gap between the level of theoretical concepts and theory-language and the level of empirical indicators and evidence, but I reject both any notion that the theoretical concepts are more fixed than the empirical indicators and any notion that the practice of 'interpreting evidence' can ever be fully reduced to an explicit mechanical operation that can be summed up in a verbal formulation called a 'theory'. Our practice of inter-level movement between concepts and material, between theory-language and empirical indications, is always more complex than any theorization I produce about it.

The second model I shall present as background to the discussion of semi-structured depth interviewing is Joseph Maxwell's model of design components and his useful conception of a well-designed research programme.

MAXWELL'S MODEL OF DESIGN COMPONENTS

A 'well-designed' object is an object whose component parts have been designed to be able to work together and in sequence such that the functions, or purposes, for which the object was designed are most likely to be served. The same functions, or purposes, can be carried out by different (well-designed) objects. What are the characteristics of a good, as opposed to a poor, 'research design'? I shall quote at length (and with permission) from Maxwell's account:

'Design in qualitative research is an iterative process that involves 'tacking'[3] back and forth between the different components of the design, assessing the implications of purposes, theory, research questions, and validity threats for one another .... The model I present here has five components. These components are characterized by the issues that each is intended to address:

1 *Purposes*. What are the ultimate goals of this study? What issues is it intended to illuminate, and what practices will it influence? Why do you want to conduct it, and why should we care about the results? Why is the study worth doing?

2 *Conceptual Context*. What do you think is going on with the phenomena you plan to study? What theories, findings and conceptual frameworks relating to these phenomena will guide or inform your study, and what literature, preliminary research and personal experience will you draw on? This component of the design contains the *theory* that you already have or are developing about the setting or the issues that you are studying. There are four main sources for this theory: your own experience, existing theory and research, the results of any pilot studies or preliminary research that you've done, and thought experiments.

3 *Research Questions*. What, specifically, do you want to understand by doing this study? What do you *not* know about the phenomena you are studying that you want to learn? What questions will your research attempt to answer, and how are these questions related to each other?

4 *Methods*. What will you actually do in conducting this study? What approaches and techniques will you use to collect and analyse your data, and how do these constitute an integrated strategy? This component of your design consists of four main parts: your research relationship with the people you study, your site selection and sampling decisions, your data collection methods, and the data analysis techniques you use.

5 *Validity*. How might you be wrong? What are the plausible alternative explanations and validity threats to the potential conclusions of your study, and how will you deal with these? How do the data that you have, or that you could collect, support or challenge your ideas about what's going on? Why should I believe your results?'
(Maxwell, 1996: 4–5)

See also Figure 3.2.

BRIEF NOTE ON ASSUMPTIONS BEHIND INFERENCES AND INTERPRETATIONS: INSTRUMENTALISTS vs REALISTS

Maxwell distinguishes a debate among interpreters of interview evidence. This is between what he calls 'instrumentalists' and 'realists'.

'Interviewing someone can only tell you what that person thinks or feels or values about what they think is real. It can never tell you what is actually real now or was actually real in the past.'

---

3 For a similar concept, see 'double-fitting' between theory and data as discussed by Baldamus (1982).

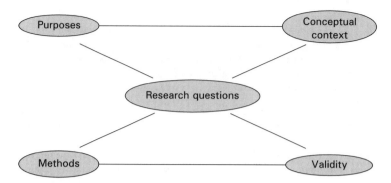

FIGURE 3.2   **Maxwell's Interactive Model of Research Design (Maxwell, 1965: 5)**

Maxwell (1996: 56) identifies the type of assertion above as being 'instrumental-ist'. He recounts the following history:

'Gail Lenehan, for her dissertation, proposed to interview nurses who specialize in treating sexual assault victims about their cognitive, behavioural, and emotional reaction to this work .... Her research questions included the following:

1   What, if any, are the effects on nurses of working with rape victims?
2   Are there cognitive, psychological and behavioural responses to having experiences of rape "shared" with them, as witnessing victims' suffering after the assault?

Her proposal was not accepted [Maxwell continues the story], and the reviewers, in explaining their decision, argued (among other concerns) that

"the study relies solely on self-report data, but your questions do not reflect this limitation. Each question needs to be reframed in terms that reflect this limitation. Some examples might be: 'how do nurses perceive and report ... the effects of working with rape victims?' or 'what specific cognitive, psychological (emotional?) and behavioural responses do nurses report?'"'

Maxwell discusses the point:

'... Instrumentalists ... prefer to stick to what they can directly verify. Realists in contrast do not assume that research questions and conclusions about feelings, beliefs, intentions prior behaviour, effects and so on need to be reduced to, or reframed as, questions and conclusions about the actual data that one uses. Instead, they treat their data as fallible *evidence* about these phenomena, to be used critically to develop and test ideas about the existence and nature of the phenomena .... Each approach has its risks .... The main risk with realist questions ... is that your increased reliance on inference may lead you to draw unwarranted conclusions or to allow your assumptions or desires to influence your results. My own preference is to use realist questions and to address as systematically as possible the validity threats that this approach involves ....

continued

continued

What John Tukey (1962) said about precision is also true of certainty: "Far better an approximate answer to the right question, which is often vague, than an exact answer to the wrong question, which can always be made precise".' (Maxwell, 1996: 56–7)

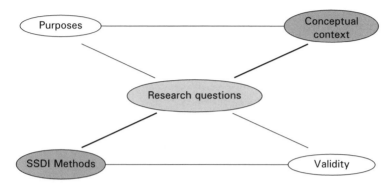

FIGURE 3.3 **Maxwell's Interactive Model of Research Design – Modified for Semi-structured Depth Interviewing (SSDI) Method**

It is because I am interested in going beyond people's interview self-report (truthful, partly deceptive, often self-deceptive, etc.) that I need to be aware that anything that is said, done, or apparently expressed in an interview is, as Maxwell points out, *fallible evidence of extra-interview realities*.

When you want to use the evidence in an argument about non-interview realities, your final research design and data analysis will need to address the validity threats that interview-evidence has to confront. Questions of validity are about the arguments in which you justify inferences from interview data (empirical indicators EI) to theorizations couched in terms of theoretical concepts (TC). However, validity questions will not be dealt with separately in this text in general terms, for reasons of space. Therefore, the key areas addressed in this book are on the diagonal from top right to bottom left in Figure 3.3. It means, in particular, unpacking the concept of 'methods' in respect of semi-structured depth interviews. This axis is therefore highlighted in the figure.

4

Lightly and Heavily Structured Depth Interviewing: Theory-Questions and Interviewer-Questions

SEQUENCE AND SPECTRUM: BRIEF OVERVIEW

This text is concerned particularly for semi-structured depth interviewing as a practice, locating such a practice, of model-building and model-testing, within the spectrum of depth interviewing practices.

The degree of 'structuring' is taken to refer to the degree to which the questions and other interventions made by the interviewer are in fact pre-prepared by the researcher. On the spectrum of interviewing, from the point of view of the interviewer designing the session, interviews vary from lightly structured to heavily structured; even more extremely, from the completely unstructured to the fully structured.

There is an argument that, as I move from model-building to model-testing, I also move from lightly structured to more heavily structured types of depth interviewing.[1] The research focus at the start of the research cycle is that of building a theory or model of a particular reality typically requiring an unstructured or lightly structured interview. Once the model or theory has been built, it is then tested by a more heavily structured or fully structured interview. Such a view might be expressed as shown in Figure 4.1.

My own opinion, however, is that lightly structured interviews are also perfectly appropriate for testing highly developed theories, if those theories require data that a heavily structured interview schedule discourages. Much clinical work might be rather of this order. Consequently, the correlation suggested above is at most an empirical correlation and not a logical necessity.

Earlier, I identified a basic distinction in general research talk between theoretical concepts (TC) and empirical indicators (EI). I shall now distinguish between research/theoretical questions (TQs) and answers to such questions (ATQs).

---

1 Such an argument needs to be considered critically. Under certain circumstances, building a model of the particular situation of a particular person can be economically achieved by asking certain standard questions derived from a more general model of the logically possible situations of all persons. It is when we lack a general model that would warrant strongly-structured questioning that our questioning – by which we hope to develop a general model we don't yet have – becomes more tentative, less heavily structured, more oriented to learning from our informant.

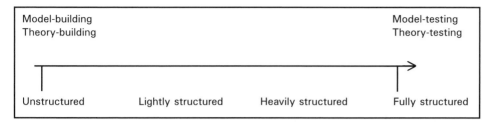

FIGURE 4.1 **Spectrum from Unstructured to Fully Structured Interviewing, and Possible Relationship to Phases in the Development of a Theory**

On the basis of the discussion of approaches, I shall now put forward the algorithm that will be used in this book for designing interview research.

THEORY-QUESTIONS MUST BE DISTINGUISHED FROM INTERVIEWER-QUESTIONS

I am concerned to collect semi-structured depth interviewing (SSDI) material as 'indications' for the concepts in particular research questions. Interview material may provide valid indicators under certain conditions for some theoretical concepts and very invalid evidence for other theoretical concepts. What 'collection-conditions' and what 'analysis-conditions' destroy, or ensure, the potential value of SSDI material for the same concepts?

I stressed with Rose the need for 'operationalization', the work of linking theoretical concepts to possible empirical indicators, a process that might also be called 'instrumentation' or 'interpretation'. This is a problematic question, both working downwards from the level of theory-concepts in a theory-language to develop indicators and then, also, working upwards from 'collected evidence' to decide what inferences can be drawn about appropriate general and particular models, what revisions of existing conceptual structure and theory-language would be appropriate at the TC level to make most sense of the data.

Research questions need to be distinguished from research answers, and the conceptual framework in terms of which research questions and answers are both couched needs itself to be identified *separately*. The conceptual framework – roughly equivalent to Maxwell's 'conceptual context' – is not the same as any theorization dependent upon it and formulated in terms of it.

In addition, *research questions (which I call 'theory-questions')* need to be clearly distinguished from any *interview-questions/prompts* that you might design or use. Theory-questions are not interview-questions.[2]

The general rule I would suggest – to which there are exceptions – is that you do not normally ask your theory-questions to your interviewees. A *TQ is not*

---

2 It would be possible in many contexts to exchange the term 'research question' for that used in this book of 'theory-question'. Insisting on the theory-laden, theory-using, theory-testing function of questions seems to require a term that, using the 'theory/data' dichotomy familiar in social science, makes more salient the question of '*which* theory?' Hence the use of the term 'theory-question' and the initials 'TQ' to refer to it. See Cooper (2000) for a recent discussion of how international comparison forces an awareness of the theory-ladenness of the apparently most neutral descriptive terms.

Just as a theoretical concept must not be identified with an empirical indication:
TC ≠ EI
so a theory-question couched in the theory-concepts of your research language must not be identified with the interview-questions (couched in terms of the language of your informant) which seek to generate the appropriate data, the appropriate empirical indicators:
TQ ≠ IQ

FIGURE 4.2   **A Theory-question is not an Interview-question**

an interview question (IQ).[3] The theory-questions 'govern' the production of the interviewer-questions, but the TQs are formulated in the theory-language of the research community, and the IQs are formulated in the language of the interviewee.

Distinguishing research/theory-questions (and the concepts in terms of which they are couched) from the interview-questions (indicative-material-seeking) is crucially necessary to create a space for the problematic indicator–concept relationship filled by instrumentation theory and assumptions (see prior discussion of the Rose–Wengraf diagram, Figure 3.1). I shall now unpack this statement.

TQ and IQ Linked by Instrumentation Theory and Assumptions

Putting an IQ to an informant is supposed to help produce the interview material that is relevant to a particular TQ. I can say that the relationship between IQ and the TQ is governed by *our instrumentation theory* which tells us how the interviewer should intervene (or avoid intervening wrongly) in each interview if they wish to get material relevant to a TQ or set of TQs.

There is no single instrumentation theory that I can simply outline, adopt and forget about. Decades of research into the positivist model of the survey questionnaire and the instrumentation theory on which that practice of fully structured questioning depends have produced numerous insights and many oversights (Mishler, 1986; Briggs, 1986) suggesting that, instead of a single and coherent universal instrumentation theory, all that we can have is a constant reflection upon the successes and failures, the strengths and weaknesses, of particular instrumentation practices (see the earlier discussion of the interview with W). Such theorizing about past interviews should help us design our next interview and help us direct that interview as it develops (Schon's reflective practitioner). The always-uncertain relationship between our research questions and our interview interventions provides a permanent flow of material for examining the instrumentation assumptions and practice in each act of intervention.

One act of intervention is the design of sessions. The term 'semi-structured' suggests a certain degree of standardization of interview questions, and a certain degree of openness of response by the interviewer.

It may be that the whole interview is conceived of as being a simple unity with a fairly fixed proportion of standardized to follow-up interview questions. Take an imaginary one-hour interview. I may decide to have four standard interview questions and want to spend about 15 minutes on each, getting and following up the initial answer to each, making an hour in total.

---

3 I shall consider apparent exceptions to this rule later, as well as Pawson's (1996) opposed theoretical position.

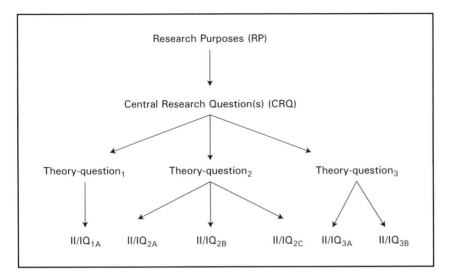

FIGURE 4.3 **CRQ → TQ → IQ/II: Pyramid Model**

Alternatively, I may design the interview to be in quite different segments: for example, a completely unstandardized half-hour starting off from a very general initial interview question, to be followed by a fully structured half-hour of prepared interview questions in a given sequence.

Inasmuch as the interviewer is in charge of the development of the interview, then it will be particular research purposes and a particular instrumentation theory that will govern your attempt to create this or that type of session with its pattern of (non)interventions.

The CRQ–TQ–IQ(II) Algorithm

The algorithm which will be used in our practice of designing interviews and analysing interview material is given as Figure 4.3. It is based upon the primacy of the research question and upon the distinction between the theory-language used in research questions and the interview-language used in interview interventions.

I refer to interview interventions (II) more often than to interview questions (IQ), partly because 'interview questions' are only one of the types of intervention that interviews make; see Dillon (1990: 176–207) and on pp. 199–200 for an excellent discussion of the need to limit one's use of questions in interview. Indirect questions are often better than direct questions, and non-questions can often be better than indirect questions.

I do this also to stress that the interview material may not always be a useful answer to a specific interview question, but may still provide very good indicative material for a research question. A failure to answer an interviewer's interview questions may herald more useful material for a research question; in semi-structured depth interviewing, an interviewer who uses too many questions and an interviewee who insists only on replying precisely to precise questions may both help to frustrate the generation of material relevant to theory-questions.

Finally, 'intervention' suggests that the interviewee would give a certain direction and pattern to what they are saying, and the 'intervention' of the interviewer must be calculated as either changing or as reinforcing the pattern that the interviewee would spontaneously give to the flow of speech. Even not-saying-something when something might be said is a form of 'intervention'.

What is the sequence of activities?

- You need to define your Research Purposes (these can be spelled out, if you wish, into a number of 'objectives') and Central Research Question(s)[4]
- Your Central Research Question needs to be spelled out into several (I suggest between three and seven) Theory (Research)-questions[5] which you want your interviews to help answer. (Another way of saying this is that you need to 'group' your various Theory-questions in such a way that they can all be seen as aspects of the Central Research Question.)
- For each of your Theory-questions, you need to develop suitable sets of Interview-question/interventions (IQ/IIs) appropriate for a type of informant.
- You need to define your type of intended informants.

In the diagram below, I have not included the specification by the CRQ and the TQs of the target informant(s); this is dealt with separately on p. 95 and onwards on sampling.

THEORY-LANGUAGE AND IDIOLECT

Learning the Language (Idiolect) of the Interviewee

This is a key area of difficulty, precisely because it appears to the novice as though there is no special difficulty. You may need to overcome resistance in yourself. If you don't, you will be tempted to skip over it.

However well prepared you feel yourself to be, however well you have tried to design the interview questions in a style that your informants would not be put off by, in the actual interview, you will need to rapidly learn the specific way this unique informant speaks to you on this unique occasion: you will need to learn their 'idiolect' (discursive practices).

A 'dialect' is a shared mode of discourse, but just as everybody has a close-to-unique fingerprint, it is useful to think of everybody having a close-to-unique mode of talk which can be called an 'idiolect', the mode of speech at a given time of a given individual for given social encounters. Failure to learn this can lead to considerable clumsiness.

> One interviewer interviewing somebody in relation to eating disorders, had an interview which included the following passage:

> *'How do you differentiate between your ideal self (how you'd like to be) and your actual self?*
> *What do you mean?*
>
> continued

---

4 I will assume from now on you are dealing with only one CRQ.

5 I will refer in future to research questions (RQs) usually as Theory Questions (TQs). If I wish to refer only to the Central Research Question, I shall refer to it in full or as CRQ, to distinguish it from the other research-questions.

continued

Well, do you sometimes wish that, as you stated earlier on, you'd like to be smaller on
the bottom but you know that can't be achieved to the extent that you would like. So
how do you really rationalize that, come to terms with this?
Make the most of what I can, really.
What, do you think, are the current influences that affect the way you think at the
moment ... '

The interviewer quickly attempted to re-phrase her initial prepared question, but,
judging by the banality of the informant's response, failed to do so in a way that
generated anything like useful data for her 'how do you differentiate ... ?' question.[6]
Given the uninformative response to her re-phrased follow-up question, she might
have tried to re-phrase again to get an answer to the original question but, rightly or
wrongly, she cuts her losses and goes on to a different question. Had she realized that
this 'psychological theory-language' of *ideal self* and *actual self* and *differentiation* produced
a so-called interview question posed in Psychology-speak, rather than in a language
'ordinary-enough' for her interviewee's idiolect, she might have prepared a better initial
question and/or improvised a better replacement.

Even if you and your informants have been brought up with the same natural language, they may have a style of speaking that is not natural for you. You will have
to work to design informant questions in the style and the language that *they* feel
happy with.

This might require a fair amount of informal research, some pilot work with
helpful associates more used than you are to the style of speech of your expected
informants.

- For example, if you are investigating emotional violence in the home, it is no
  good asking a 4-year-old 'Do your parents or siblings engage in verbal abuse?'
  Their 13-year-old old sister will need a different language again.
- If you are interviewing criminals and police about 'violence', to get answers for
  the same theory-question, you will probably formulate informant-questions
  differently to fit the ordinary-language of each type of informant.

The Theory-language of a Particular Research Community

The language of research purposes and research questions is the language of one
or more research communities; it is the language of research in the academic or
practical disciplines in which you have been or are being trained, in which as a
researcher you think, and in which as a researcher you are likely to communicate
with your research peers and to many of the users of your eventual research.

This research-language, this theory-language, is *not* likely to be the language in
which your interview questions and your talk with your interviewees will be held,

---

6 In fact, the second question assumes she has already 'differentiated[?]' in the way the researcher
is looking for; has told the researcher what the differences are; and focuses on how she rationalizes
(comes to terms with in her head?) and comes to terms with (in real life behaviour?) 'that'. Given such
a complex question with far more presuppositions than the first question, it is not surprising that the
informant gives up!

as the example of the Psychology student asking her interviewee about 'differentiating the real and the ideal self' shows. *If you find that many of your basic theoretical concepts in your research conceptual framework pop up into your interview questions, the chances are that your designed interview questions will fail badly.*

One student had a set of IQs in which he insisted on his informants working with his own (Marxist) theoretical concepts. If the *informant* did not have the, or at least a, concept of 'capitalist' society, of 'the division of labour' or of 'social pressures', then the informant-questions in the following example would have produced pretty certainly no useful material at all.

'TQ1: How does the respondent understand the role of higher education in a capitalist society?

    1.1. How would you define a *capitalist society*?

    1.2. Do you see yourself living in a capitalist society?

    1.3. For you, what is the role of higher education in this type of society you've described?

    1.4. In this society you have described, what would you feel if higher education were not available?

TQ2: What does the respondent gain from higher education within a capitalist society that applies division of labour [sic]

    2.1. How would you define *division of labour*?

    2.2. Did your understanding of division of labour influence your decision to return to higher education?

    2.3. Tell me, appreciating your definition of division of labour, what new employable skills do you think you will now have, having returned to higher education?

    2.4. What do you think is going to happen to your employable skills in ten years time?

TQ3: In a capitalist society, what social pressures exist, influencing a respondent's decision to return to higher education?

    3.1. Tell me, how would you define *social pressures*?

    3.2. To what extent was your decision to return to higher education influenced by social pressures?

    3.3. Tell me what you feel higher education can give you in order to deal with social pressure?

    3.4. How much social pressure do you think there is in today's capitalist society which you described earlier?'

It is clear that the informant is being required to join the interviewer's language-community and pass a test in it. It proved counter-productive.

Here is another example.

One scholar, Karen Sacks (1989), noted that she achieved a flat lack of success when she put her sociological research questions directly and abstractly to her informants. When she asked them to give sociological answers, they gave her sociological answers – which helped her not at all:

'In the spirit of feminist collectivity, though naively, I put my [research] problem to as many of the women I knew who were willing to discuss it: I had a strong hunch that women learned the values and skills to resist oppression at work from their families. Did they share that feeling? If so, could they figure out what they had learned and how they had learned it?

The questions I posed to the women were sociological, and women responded in that mode, giving me answers that linked sociological variables to personal militancy. At first there was no definitive pattern: maybe birth order was important, maybe race, or working mothers, marital status, and so on. Their answers were as abstract and uninformative as my own thinking ....'

Chase (1995: 4–5) remarks that 'Sacks then dropped her sociological questions'. This is misleading: Sacks did not drop her sociological research questions *as research questions*. She dropped them as interview questions. She took these 'theory-questions' and completely re-designed new interview-questions for them. These tended to become interview-questions eliciting narratives. As Chase puts it,

'[Sacks] began to ask for life stories – something she had no idea of doing when she started the study – when she realized that the general processes she sought to understand are embedded in women's lives.'

She then continues her citation of Sacks:

'There were a few women whose constructions of their life narratives and analyses became exemplars of how family learning empowered women to rebel, and whose experiences became central for developing that [theoretical] model. *This happened when I finally asked them how they learned about work and what it meant to them.* That generated narratives about work – childhood chores and a progress report about the kinds of tasks and responsibilities each woman had at different ages' [italics added].

Her theory-questions did not change: what she stopped doing was to ask them directly as interview questions, a strategy that had such poor results. She decided to ask an IQ about life-stories and about 'how they learnt about work and what it meant to them' and so obtained narrative accounts that gave her the material that her TQs needed.

A clearer construction of the difference between TQs and IQs is given in Figure 4.4.
There is a clear distinction between the theory-terms used in the three TQ research questions in the central column, and language of the six IQs on the right that gather useful material for them. We can also see how the same IQs can be designed to gather information for different TQs.
The point is that it is almost always harmful to couch informant questions in researcher language; informants have their own language which the interviewer must learn in order to be effective. IQs should rarely, if ever, be simple 'echoes' of TQs.

IQ no.		Theory-question	IQ formulation
1			Do you find the subjects you learn important?
2		A. Which form of learning motivation dominates in high school?	Do you find learning interesting in itself?
3			What is your main purpose in going to high school?
4		B. Do the grades promote an external instrumental motivation at the expense of an intrinsic interest motivation for learning?	Have you experienced a conflict between what you wanted to read (study) and what you had to read to obtain a good grade?
5			Have you been rewarded with money for getting good grades?
6		C. Does learning for grades socialize to working for wages?	Do you see any connection between money and grades?

FIGURE 4.4   **Examples of TQs and IQs, Constructed from Kvale (1996: 131)**

DEPTH-INTERVIEWING DESIGNS AND THE FREE-ASSOCIATIVE / FULLY STRUCTURED INTERVIEWING SPECTRUM

Introduction

From the point of view of the interviewer, heavily structured means heavily structured by the interviewer; lightly structured (from the point of view of the interviewer) means the informant influences the structuring of the content and form of their material.

I distinguished above between two extreme points on the interviewing spectrum: at one end, the fully structured question-schedule where all interviewer interventions (II) are specified in a required sequence and where no new ones and no variants may be invented; and, at the other, the free-associative interview as developed by Freud as a component of psychoanalysis. We shall now look at these in turn.

Heavily Structured Interviewing

Pawson (1996) has put forward a strong argument for what he calls a 'theory-driven interview'. In such an interview, the interviewee is enlisted as a collaborator in the researcher's project. The researcher teaches the interviewee the theory-language, the conceptual framework, of the theorist, identifies for the interviewee the research problem that the researcher is struggling with, and then asks the interviewee to provide 'answers' in terms of the theory-language and the problem that the researcher has defined and in which the interviewee has (at least temporarily) been enrolled.

This approach appears in extreme and unskilful form in the schedule, cited in the previous section, about capitalism and higher education. In terms of our model of the CRQ–TQ–IQ, Pawson attempts to solve the perennial gap between the theory language of the researcher and the informant-language of the interviewee by making the informant learn the language (the conceptual framework) of the researcher.[7]

As we shall see, such an imposition of the conceptual world of the researcher onto the responses of the interviewee stands in complete opposition to the more traditional ethnographic depth interview concern for the interviewing researcher who attempts (literally for those learning a native language which is not their own) to acquire and be socialized into the *language and concerns of the informant* (Geertz, 1983). The TQ–IQ model that I am putting forward adopts the latter model with depth-interviewers adapting to the informant's language and concepts.

Questioning in the language of the informant can be just as theory-driven as Pawson would wish, but I think with more chance of success. It is the TQs that drive the interviewer-questioning and interventions, but it is the researcher who attempts to anticipate and rapidly improve his or her understanding of the language code of the informant, so as to 'intervene well' in the informant's own ordinary-language, their idiolect.

Free Associative and SQUIN Interviews

Freud, the founder of psychoanalysis, believed – as did many gestalt psychologists – that the observation of 'free behaviour' would reveal to the researcher the current 'structuring principle' (gestalt) of all the particular behaviours being expressed. The more free the behaviour was from external constraint, the more completely the internal dynamic could be expressed, and the more intelligible to the researcher that internal dynamic would then become.

In interviewing terms, this means, for those who wish to allow the gestalt of the interviewee to become observable, adopting an interview strategy that minimizes (for as long as possible) the interview*er's* concerns (system of values and significance) to allow fullest possible expression of the concerns, the systems of value and significance, the life-world, of the interview*ee*.

---

7 In his revised 1997 version, Pawson's position is modified slightly.

CONCLUSION

In this part I have tried to show the value of proceeding from a narrow conception of what interview material can directly provide – namely evidence of a single research conversation – in order to show the necessity of using assumptions, argument and evidence to draw inferences about extra-interview realities, such as the subjectivities of interviewer or interviewee or the realities of the topics or referents referred to. As we saw in the case of 'the interview with W', such inferring of meaning – even with a lot of information about the way the words are said, paralinguistics and session notes – is complex and problematic.

In order to understand this complex and problematic process of inferring from interview material to extra-interview realities, I looked at explicit models of communication: first at the speech-act models of Foddy and Markova and then at the broader historical-anthropologically-sensitive model of Briggs which would enable us to understand the 'located' nature of any interviewer interaction in a hierarchical society where power/knowledge issues and past and future histories are always in play – as, for example, in the case of 'John' and 'Lorna', and indeed ourselves when we come to interview.

Distinguishing between lightly structured, free-associative, interviewing and strongly structured, prior-theory, interviewing, I suggested that just as theory-building and theory-testing needed appropriate interview design strategies for their different purposes, so, very often – as in the case of biographic-interpretive narrative interviewing (to be raised in Part II) – what is needed are combinations of both lightly structured and strongly structured designs in different proportions in a planned sequence.

Using models derived from Rose and from Maxwell (the hour-glass figure), I stressed the importance of the gap between the 'theoretical level' of theory-language and theory-concepts and the 'empirical level' of interview evidence. This was the basis of the CRQ–TQ–IQ/II model which was then presented, in terms of which theory-language the arguments of the rest of this book will be presented.

II

UP TO THE INTERVIEW: STRATEGIES FOR GETTING THE RIGHT MATERIALS

This Part is divided into three chapters. Chapter 5 relates to all depth interviewing, whether lightly (LSDI) or fairly-fully (FFSSI) structured; Chapter 6 relates only to lightly structured depth interviewing, especially biographic-narrative interviewing; Chapter 7 relates particularly to fairly-fully structured depth interviewing.

5

Preparing for any Interviewing Sequence

In this chapter, I start by discussing the design of all semi-structured depth interviews. I do this with respect to the concept of constantly combining lightly and fairly-fully structured sessions with the same person. It is true that occasionally you may wish to have a 'pure' rather than a combined strategy (using only LSDI or FFSDI), but this is comparatively rare; in any case, a discussion of pure types must come before any discussion of how to combine them.

I then go on to consider how to prepare for both first contact with possible interviewees and for problems of interview interpretation that may later arise. Then follows the question of sampling and identifying possible informants, and the problem of managing contact with them, both theoretically and practically.

CRQ–TQ–II DESIGN AND SEQUENCED COMBINATIONS OF TYPES OF INTERVIEW AND SELECTION OF INFORMANTS DESIRED

In the previous chapter, I put forward a particular algorithm for the designing of interview work, which I called the CRQ–TQ–II pyramid (see Figure 4.3). I argued that research problems should be posed within a coherent conceptual framework embodied in a particular theory-language as theory-questions (TQs) to which empirically indicative material (EI) was sought (at least in part by semi-structured depth interview) which could provide answers to the theory-questions (ATQs). As well as emphasizing the need for precise dovetailing of theory-questions and theory-answers (based on Collingwood, Bachelard and Kuhn), I also stressed the way the theory-questions of the researcher had to be operationalized into an SSDI-design so that the designed interview questions (IQs) and other interventions (IIs) would be likely to produce the required material. As a slogan, I put forward the phrase 'a theory question is never an interview question'; I suggested that in the interview, quite often, interviewer questions (IQs) should be minimized in favour of other types of 'interviewer intervention' (IIs). I also argued that between the theoretical concepts used in theory-questions and the practice of the SSDI interview lay the 'concept–indicator gap' (see Figure 3.1) necessarily filled by an instrumentation practice (which, one hopes, is at least partially explicit as an 'instrumentation theory') which governed the pre-interview designing (and, as we shall see, also the post-interview interpreting) of the materials obtained.

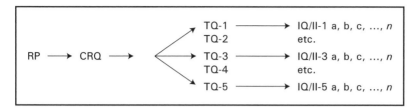

FIGURE 5.1   **CRQ–TQ–IQ Model Sideways**

How do we handle the design components? First of all, let us consider three different ways of handling the design pyramid.

Personal Points of Entry into the Design Pyramid: Top-down Deductivists, Bottom-up Inductivists, Middle-level Research Question Entrists

In general, in this book, a top-down approach is used to organize the discussion. However, empirically, when starting to design SSDI sessions, different investigators enter the logical structure at different points. You will have your own preferred starting-points. The important thing is not where you happen to prefer to start, but that you complete a well-fitting design including all parts.

The top-down pyramid model in Figure 4.3 can be laid on its side, as shown in Figure 5.1.

Some researchers are natural 'deductivists' working things out from first principles, from left to right. This text is organized in this way, starting from the *left* of Figure 5.1.

Others are natural 'inductivists', starting from imagined informant-questions on the extreme *right* of the diagram. If you are one of these, you might start by imagining an 'ideal' informant, and then writing down all the informant-questions you think you want to ask your informants, and than gradually work out what all of them signify, theoretically, what TQ those imagined IQs were for. You would find some 'logical TQ groupings' for those IQs. It might take a long time, but it is one way that some people find it best to start working, *by creative visualization of the actual interview, the end-product of the design*. You would eventually work out your CRQ, your CRO and your RP working from right to left.

Others start with a *muddle in the middle*, with a number of unsorted questions that have sprung to mind: questions that might be interviewer-questions, Central Research Questions, or theory-questions, none of them clearly distinguished from each other. That's fine to start off with. If you start with such a heap in the middle, then go on, from the centre of the diagram simultaneously sorting left and right to classify these question-candidates into the separate types of question that are needed for a logically tight and workable package of CRQ, TQs and IQs. Use either the vertical pyramid top-down model (Figure 4.3) or the horizontal left-to-right sideways model (Figure 5.1) for this sorting, whichever suits you better.

Most researchers have a bias towards a top-down (left to right), a bottom-up (right to left), or a middle-level entry point. As you find that your chosen starting-point is getting unproductive, try leaping around to another one and start from there.

In all cases, as Maxwell insists, the key imperative is that you inspect your planned initial and planned supplementary informant-questions for their 'logical necessity and sufficiency'. You want each question to be necessary; you want to ensure that the package of all your questions is sufficient. The *criteria of 'necessity and sufficiency'* of the informant-questions are those of their *linkage* to the research objectives and the central research question by way of the theory-questions.

This chapter and the two that follow are laid out in top-down mode. However, please bear in mind the remarks about starting where it feels easiest but tightening the logic between all the elements gradually: very much like tightening the bolts on a car wheel – gradually, iteratively, not too much 'finality' for any one element too early. None should be fully finalized till all are ready.

Theoretical Designing in Principle – not Including Designing of Interview Sessions or Particular Interviewing Strategies

The discussion which follows is one that takes us down from Research Purposes by way of Conceptual Frameworks to Central Research Questions and Theory-Questions, the middle of Maxwell's diagram below, down to the point where you have formulated your research questions in the light of research purposes and conceptual frameworks and resources. It then goes on to cover the theory-driven selection of interview *informants* for all types of interviewing. This is the primary content of the second section. In terms of the Rose–Wengraf diagram (Figure 3.1), it *stops short* of operationalizing the TQs into interview sessions and prepared IQs. Such operationalizing is then done twice: first, in Chapter 6 in respect of a biographic-narrative *lightly* structured interview sequence; and then, in Chapter 7, by a more pronged discussion of questions, sequencing and sessions for semi-structured depth interviewing of a *fairly-fully* structured type.

This chapter deals with preparation for *all* semi-structured depth interviewing. We deal first with the question of clarifying your purposes; and then with the development of research questions around chosen topics in terms of CRQs and TQs and the conceptual frameworks in terms of which they are formulated: this long section also deals with the practice of criticizing and improving RP–CRQ–TQ–IQ structures and with the uses (and abuses) of researching the research literature. There then follows a discussion on choosing your informants, your 'sample', and the chapter concludes with another discussion of the value of combining types of session for the same interviewee.

FORMULATING PURPOSES AND RESEARCH QUESTIONS, SELECTING INTERVIEWEES

We start in the top left-hand corner of Maxwell's diagram (Figure 5.2) and, in this section, only occasionally venture past the centre.

Purposes and Motivation

I start with purposes. This is the first element at the top left of Figure 5.2. Clarifying these can be regarded as requiring the equivalent of a depth interview with myself which, despite my own strong resistance and often anxiety to doing it properly, has to be done in a way that is not hurried and superficial.

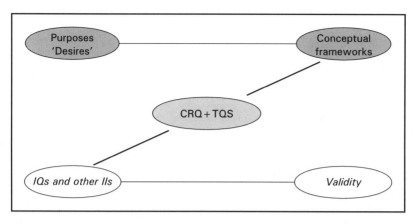

FIGURE 5.2 **Maxwell Revised with CRQ–TQ–IQ**

Let us assume that I have some desire to do some semi-structured depth-interviewing work, but that my purposes are pretty vague. The chances are that I am at the point of having one or more possible *topics*, but have not got further than that. I have not asked for what purposes I am interested in that topic, *what questions I want to ask about that topic-area*. Precise TQs can be developed only if my personal research purposes can be specified more precisely.

For most of us, it is only *after* we have done our first interview that we really feel how the lack of clear and heartfelt purposes can spoil our work.

'I had difficulty at first thinking up the questions probably I think because I was asking myself how and what my tutor would want me to say, but I realized that I needed to ask questions that would give me the answers I was looking for.' (Emma N)

'As far as developing a research intention with theory questions is concerned, I found it difficult to decide on a direction to take: the interviews themselves don't show the way. In other words, you must ask the right questions to begin with, which means spending time and lots of thought deciding *what* you want to discover from your informants.' (Christine K)

And a last quotation from an experienced researcher:

'What keeps you from asking a real question? ... it had never occurred to me that the majority of so-called questions I had asked before were merely spontaneous pleadings. *They were not really based on experience and study.* Now, after years of training, I could, as it were, feel the question, within me, but, for the life of me, *I could not get it into the right words* ... finding the exact question can be a subtle and difficult process. One word placed in one part of a sentence may produce an answer that in another part of the sentence will produce something completely different. We have to learn to be so accurate with our questions.' (R. Feild, 1976: 18, cited Moustakas, 1990: 40, italics added.)

For the most part, in what follows, I shall be trying to spell out some of the issues encapsulated in the drift of the above perceptions, and suggesting a 'technical vocabulary' for thinking about them clearly.

My research purposes, as we shall see, are to be distilled into, and then served by, a Central Research Question. This CRQ must satisfy at least two main criteria, which are interlinked:

1   The CRQ must be able to sustain my curiosity, involvement and participation with full energy and resourcefulness over a lengthy period of time. To meet this criterion about *Motivation*, I must have a degree of self-knowledge so that I know what I can stay committed to and what I can't.
2   The CRQ must be as well-formulated as possible. To meet this criterion about *Formulation*, I will have to engage in a lot of thought and study about what makes a question well formulated (a) in general, (b) for depth interviewing in particular, and (c) for sustaining my interest in even more particular. This depends crucially on the conceptual framework being used.

I shall start by considering the personal research purposes that can provide the *motivation* for sustained research.

Moustakas remarks:

> 'All heuristic inquiry begins with the internal search to discover, with an encompassing puzzlement, a passionate desire to know, a devotion and a commitment to pursue a question that is strongly connected to one's identity .... Discovering a significant problem or question that will hold the wondering gaze and the passionate commitment of the researcher is the essential opening of the heuristic process. The question as such (and the researcher's relation to it) will determine whether or not an authentic and compelling path has opened, one that will sustain the researcher's curiosity, involvement and participation, with full energy and resourcefulness over a lengthy period of time.' (Moustakas, 1990: 40)

We are all, at least partly and sometimes unfortunately so completely, socialized into accepting other people's questions that it is extremely difficult to formulate our own. I want to ask questions that will please other people. I don't even know whether I am interested in a subject or not. I am a bit interested but don't have a theory of how to get myself *more* interested so that I could become *really* interested. This has to be worked on. It means understanding and bringing to the surface different levels and types of purpose, of desires, some of which I may not be too proud and about which I may feel anxious.

Maxwell (1996: Ch. 2) usefully remarks about personal purposes as follows.

> 'Personal purposes are those that motivate *you* to do this study; they can include such things as a political passion to change some existing situation, a curiosity about a specific phenomenon or event, a design to engage in a particular type of research, or simply the need to advance your career. These personal purposes often overlap with your

continued

continued

practical or research purposes, but they may also include deeply rooted individual desires and needs that bear little relationship to the "official" reasons for doing the study .... *Attempting to purge yourself of personal goals and concerns is neither possible nor necessary. What is necessary is to be aware of these concerns and how they may be shaping your research, and to think how best to deal with their consequences.* In addition, recognizing your personal ties to the study you want to conduct can provide you with a *valuable source of insight, theory and data about the phenomenon you are studying: experiential knowledge.'* (Maxwell 1996: 16, italics added)

Generating Research Questions Around Topics

The formulation of questions is key. It is crucial, as Collingwood argued (p. 52 above), to move from topics to questions (TQs). It is then important to move from rough formulations of TQs to better formulations.

If one has no more to start with than just 'a topic', then the number of questions is infinite.

> One student wanted to study three shoplifters but was 'blocked' from having any questions, or problems with which to start. She had a topic but could not, or would not, know (or admit on paper) why she was interested in that topic. In effect, she said: 'I'm interested in anything and everything they tell me, or say to each other, but have no interest in eliciting any one type of information from them than any other'.

> This doesn't work. Until she could formulate simply, clearly, concretely and vividly what it was about shoplifting that *she* was interested in, she could not start her work. What might *you* want to study about shoplifting?

What is it that you want to study? What do you want to find out about it? As so many of the students cited a couple of pages back suggest, until you are happy with your answers to these two questions, you should not proceed any further.

- The topic may be *empirically defined*: drug-taking, families, an organization, interview communication.
- The topic may be *pragmatically defined*: how to stop drug-taking, how to solve the problems of the family, how to make the best use of a school, college or university, how to improve one's interviewing competence.
- The topic may be *abstractly defined*: deviancy, family interaction, organizational under-performance, communicative interaction.
- The topic may be *theoretically defined*: types of false consciousness among women, modes of racism among New Zealand pakeha, cultural models of emotional underdevelopment in Erewhon.

But, however it is defined – more or less abstractly, more or less pragmatically, more or less theoretically – people can always generate an indefinitely large list of questions about topics. A hedgehog diagram can suggest this, with each 'quill' representing a possible TQ (Figure 5.3).

Thinking of the variety of different research-questions that can be addressed to the same topic is always useful. However, having brain-stormed and generated a

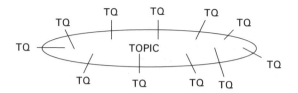

FIGURE 5.3   **Arbitrarily Large Set of TQs Around a Topic**

large number, you should then reduce them to a coherent set of 'best 5 plus or minus 3'.

Here is one student noting her failure to do this:

> 'Developing the research proposal with clear Research Purposes and Research Questions was more difficult than I expected. As I chose a very wide heading, I had a varied selection of possible angles to concentrate upon. This was my first problem. I think now it would have been more beneficial to narrow down the main subject so as to choose more inter-related questions. As my [research] questions were not related to each other very much, it was harder to draw conclusions .... the questions seemed to jump from one angle to another without exploring any particular one thoroughly. This resulted in a large collection of shallow perspectives and thoughts.' (Anna S)

EXERCISE 5.1   THEORY-QUESTIONS ABOUT SHOPLIFTING

The following is a quite unselective list of 'brainstormed' questions around a topic. You will save yourself much heartache later if you take 30 minutes to do this exercise. First of all, look at the list.

Topic: Shoplifting

Informants: Under-16 shoplifters

Question 1:   How do people come to engage in systematic shoplifting?

Question 2:   Do shoplifters feel the need to justify their shoplifting and, if they do, what justifications do they use?

Question 3:   What are the causes of shoplifting in society?

Question 4:   How do shoplifters describe and experience the activity of shoplifting?

Question 5:   What role does advertising play in increasing or decreasing the rate of shoplifting?

Question 6:   What are the effects of marrying on the practice of shoplifting?

Question 7:   To what extent are changes in the wider society responsible for the spread of shoplifting?

Question 8:   What does society think about shoplifting?

Question 9:   How do shoplifters explain why they started shoplifting, and what do they feel about the practice of shoplifting?

Question 10: Do people shoplift in order to 'escape from reality'?

Question 11: Do people shoplift because they have realized what reality is really like?

Question 12: What are the social consequences of shoplifting?

continued

continued

These are just some student questions around the topic – there could be 13 or 313 – and each question can itself be developed further and broken down into sub-questions. Some are good – well-formulated for research – and others are awful. The point that needs to be stressed here is that it is only when you move from a 'topic-title' to generating questions – each with a real question-mark – that you start thinking and evaluating clearly and moving in the area of research design. As early as possible, move from the *comfortable area* of topic-titles to the *sharper area* of questions about topics! The exercise: In respect of the 12 questions above:

1   Try to identify which of these 12 questions should NOT be best researched by interviews with three under-16 shoplifters.
2   Then identify which questions are BEST for being researched by such interviews.
3   Then identify which ones COULD be reasonably researched by such interviews but do NOT NEED to be.
4   Then go through each of the piles and make a brief note on why you put it in the pile that you did.
5   Then identify FOUR 'very appropriate' ones and say why they are better than the worst TWO in the middle demi-appropriate category.

You will find this exercise to have been helpful when you come to formulate your own research questions (TQs).

Questions	past	present	future
about behaviours/experience			
about feelings			
about knowledge			
about sensory events			
demographic questions			
about opinions or values			
about anything else (added by TW)			

FIGURE 5.4   **Patton's 6 × 3 Checklist of Possible Questions, modified (Patton, 1990: 293)**

TQs '(in)Appropriate' for (some) Depth Interviews?

Some research questions can't be answered at all by some methods; others can be, but only badly. There is an endless debate about questions which are or are not appropriate for semi-structured depth interviewing. You need to be aware of some of the issues involved.

To suggest a way of being more precise, you might want to consider Patton's attempt to categorize what topics questions might be about (Figure 5.4). They relate primarily to *interview* questions but can also help to organize *research* questions. It is perhaps more useful as a checklist of what you might be deciding to ask *no* questions about. It is a negative way of *establishing what purposes you don't have*. As an exercise, find out which of the 18 cells above you have *no* questions for, and re-evaluate to make sure that you are happy with that situation. You could then fill in the cells you *do* have questions for.

Formulating and Improving Conceptual Frameworks for your Central Research Questions

You may work more than anyone else, you may be brilliant in your discussion and painstaking in every aspect of your interviews, etc., but, if your Central Research Question is a bad one (boring and/or with an obvious answer), all your work and your eventual presentation is overwhelmingly likely to be similarly bad – whatever the quality of your intervening work and presentation.

Your product, your Answering – whatever the value of your data – can never be expected to be significantly better than your Questioning (Collingwood, 1939; de Vaus, 1996: Chs 2–3). You cannot afford not to spend time on getting your Central Research Question – and indeed all the other theory-questions – as right as you possibly can.

It is a good idea, therefore, for you *to build on a theory-and-knowledge base you have already acquired*, perhaps in previous work. It is a bad idea to think you can start on a quite new topic for which you do not already have some general concepts and some particular knowledge-base, derived from reading or at least personal experience. In 'real research life' we spend days, weeks, months or even years building up our general concepts and our research-based questions prior to the interviews.

Identify what resources you have and what further work you need to do, what further contacts you need to make, in order to have a strong basis for non-naive research. Remember Figure 1.4, and remember the key role played at each point in the research cycle of our 'knowledge, misinformation, ignorance and prejudice'.

> 'I may support my knowledge of the objective events and context of a given life-story or a given account of something by an informant from whom I wish to learn by looking at histories of the period and sociologies of the situation; I may expand my understanding of the subjectivity of the actor by looking at such documents of personal life as diaries, letters, etc.' (Plummer, 1983)

To leave background research until after you have started interviewing is to plan for a weak interview.

Conceptual Frameworks and the Improvement of CRQs and TQs

I shall now work through a number of examples of research questions and conceptual frameworks. All knowledge, and every research question (TQ), is conceptual-framework-dependent, as Maxwell's hourglass diagram indicates (Figure 3.2). We cannot avoid always using conceptual frameworks, and the more basic a conceptual framework is to our thinking, the less easy it is for us to notice it! The most powerful lever to improve your research questions is usually to improve the conceptual framework in terms of which they are formulated (see Figure 5.5).

Notice that the last question in Figure 5.5 implies that different students may be differently affected – which the previous ones did not. Might it be useful to add an 's' to make 'experiences'? Both of the last two proposed Central Research Questions feel serious for one research community or another. The first simple one is fine to start off with, but will probably produce shallow results if it is not enriched by mutation.

1 *What are the effects of university experience on the student?*
This is a first stab at a CRQ, using terms not particularly associated with a discipline, school, or social science research community. The next stage might be to find an appropriate theory-language.

2 *What are the cognitive and affective effects of university experience on the student?*
This is formulated in terms of a model of Psychology which distinguishes and defines 'effects on the person' in terms of a distinction between 'cognitive' and 'affective'. It evokes a particular theory-language which allows or requires such a distinction.

3 *What are the effects of university experience on different students in terms of their competence in transferable skills and their readiness for the labour market?*
This is a question which refers to an insertion in a different set of discourses and research languages – another conceptual framework which probably evokes (though doesn't yet specify) a list of transferable skills and a test of readiness for the labour market.

FIGURE 5.5 **Example of a Conceptual Framework: Effects of University Experience on Students**

A common-sense question may cover, or may lead to, an indefinitely large number of 'scientifically sophisticated' questions, as expressed diagramatically in Figure 5.6.

The social sciences provide a repertoire or menu of such 'theory-languages' (conceptual frameworks); you need to clarify the one you propose to use, adapt (or, less likely, construct) for generating and eventually processing your interview material.[1]

How you develop, construct, or reconstruct an adequate 'theory-language' (use an appropriate conceptual framework) for your purposes is briefly raised below.

I have argued that what is needed is a passionate curiosity. *'Uninterestingness' can sometimes lie in the failure by the researcher to find a new 'theoretical angle' on whatever the problem is, a failure that can be remedied by a shift in the question asked.*

To 'shift the question originally asked' may well require a lot of talking to other people, a lot of library skimming to see what questions other people have found interesting enough to publish about, and a lot of trying to find out what I as a person am genuinely and emotionally and personally interested in. It may require

---

1 However, at any given moment of your personal development, like *now* when you are reading this footnote, there are (A) some theory-languages that you *think with* without even noticing that you are doing so; there will be a few that (B) you can think with some degree of conscious care and deliberation; (C) there will be some that you are trying to *learn* but have not yet completed your learning of them, and you should not, *at this moment*, try to *use*; and (D) there are some that you know you cannot use and so are not tempted to pretend to yourself or others that you can.
Only use types A or B.
The danger is that you may wish to believe that a theory-language you are currently learning in social science but have not yet mastered, a type C theory-language, is at this moment for you already a type B one, or even type A. Be sure you do not try to think your research problem through with type C or type D theory-words or theory-languages: you will only be confused and confusing. If necessary, work with a type A theory-language (one you know you can use without worrying) rather than confuse a type C for a type B. If you wish to use a type B theory-language, make sure you use it with the self-consciousness and carefulness that is required for you, at the moment, not to 'mess up' by using it. *If in doubt, work instead with a (perhaps simpler but more reliable) type A theory-language.*

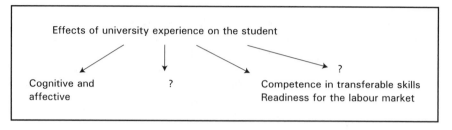

FIGURE 5.6   **Indefinite Number of 'Sophisticated' TQs**

a 'brainstorming session' in which I just pour out as many questions as possible that I can think of and, only after I have completely exhausted all the ones I can think of, going on to see which are the ones that I really feel emotionally and personally concerned to get my teeth into.

It means looking at my intentions (desires, purposes) which lie behind the asking of the different possible questions, but also looking at the formulations of questions which facilitate or inhibit interesting work. Chenitz provides a natural history of how she (re)formulated her research questions in proposal form.

In Exercise 5.1, you were asked to select and improve formulations of questions about shoplifting. Let us now look at an example of a professional researcher improving her formulation of research purposes and research questions (CRQs and TQs, though she does not use these terms).

Chenitz Improving RPs and TQs   In her excellent 'Getting Started: The research proposal for a grounded theory study' (Chenitz and Swanson, 1986) Chenitz talks about how she evolved a clear statement of her research purposes and an adequate form for the Central Research Question. Notice how she stresses the move from a first 'laundry list' of possible questions to a tighter more general formulation of 'what they were all about' and then back to a clarified larger list of questions again. Of this iterative process, she writes:

> 'The following example shows how a clinical problem [observed experience, TW] raised questions which led to the study "Nursing Interventions in a Methadone Clinic". Clarifying the problem began through a series of notes similar to the one that now follows:
>
> > I have observed the nurses in the methadone clinics now several times. With each client who approaches the dispensing window, there is a brief interaction between the nurse and client and then the methadone is given. With some clients, nurses initiate the interaction and question clients about a specific health, social, financial or legal problem. With others, nurses will initiate the interaction with a question about the patient's compliance with programme rules. I have estimated that nurse/client interaction during methadone dispensing lasts about 1 minute and 52 seconds. Yet, during that time, there are a number of nursing actions taken. What are these interventions? Under what conditions and with what clients are specific interventions used? What are the specific outcomes for specific interventions? Are there interventions to assure compliance for clients leading an addict life style? What interventions are used with clients who are getting well on the programme?'

Chenitz continues:

> 'The questions about nursing interventions continued on: a long list of questions was developed. As in this example, it is helpful for the researcher to write down the events [perceptions, TW] that stimulated the eventual research question. These ... may come from clinical or research experiences, from the literature or from a combination of both. From this, a list of questions can be generated.
>
> These questions were examined to find the real question or the research question. In our example, the central research question was "What are these interventions?" More specifically, the question was refined and again re-stated, "What are the nursing interventions during methadone dispensing in a methadone maintenance clinic?"
>
> The central research question was rewritten to form the purpose or goal for the study. In the example used, the purpose was
>
> > "to identify, describe, and provide a theoretical analysis of, nursing interventions in a methadone maintenance clinic".
>
> The purpose was written in a declarative statement. It was broad enough to satisfy all the questions in the original list.' (Chenitz and Swanson, 1986: 40)[2]

She goes on to provide what she considers to be 'a more professional formulation of problem-statement, purpose and specific research aims as interrelated in the eventual "initial proposal"'. She asks us to 'note how it locates the particular study within a context of practical urgencies and of earlier research and the lack of current research':

> 'Since its introduction in the early 1960s, methadone maintenance has become the most frequently used treatment for opiate addiction, since it is superior in drawing clients and preventing programme dropout (Rounsaville, 1983). The types of service offered with methadone maintenance range with each clinic. Most commonly, individual and group psychotherapy and counselling services are offered (Platt, Labate, 1976). In methadone maintenance programs, registered nurses are usually responsible for the management, distribution, and administration of methadone to clients. Nurses function as a central clearing house for information on clients' progress and overall health status. However since Nelson's work in 1973 and Dy et al., in 1975, there have been no published reports on the nurse's role, functions and interventions during methadone treatment. Little is known about what actually occurs between nurses and clients during this treatment time. The purpose of this study is to generate a detailed description and theoretical analysis of nursing interventions in methadone programs.' (Chenitz, 1986: 43)

Chenitz provides no explicit account of a CRQ, but as Collingwood has pointed out these can be reconstructed from statements taken as answers. Just to round off Chenitz's account in terms of the categories defined in this book, I shall formulate her Central Research Questions implicit in the last three quotations as:

---

2 Unfortunately, Chenitz does not indicate any 'intention' behind the research other than that of deficient and needed knowledge. No personal motivation is mentioned.

Research questions are called (in this text) theory-questions because

- they are written in terms of one particular vocabulary for describing and explaining (rather than any other such vocabulary)
- they are dependent, therefore, on earlier vocabularies (conceptual frameworks)
- the answers to them that you may develop may create new descriptions/explanations (theories) which may involve partially new vocabularies (conceptual frameworks).

Theory-questions are not written in the language of the informant; they are not put to the informant. Any question with a 'you' in it is NOT a theory-question.

FIGURE 5.7 **Research Questions are Called Theory-questions Because ...**

1 What happens in detail between nurses and clients during methadone treatments?
2 Given a conceptual framework relating 'roles' to 'functions', what can a theoretical analysis of such described interventions show?

Chenitz's description of how she moved from her original formulations of research purposes and research questions and her example of a crisp final formulation will, I hope, be useful as you move from relatively under-theorized and under-conceptualized initial formulations to ones which are better grounded in appropriate discourses of appropriate professionals and researchers and in relevant theory-languages.

The Five 'Theory Questions' for your Central Research Question: or, your CRQ Spelled Out   Let us now move to the differentiation of a Central Research Question and its supporting theory-questions (Figure 5.7). I shall give a number of examples in outline and then consider one or two CRQ–TQ structures in more detail.

By dint of talking to other people and doing library research, you will improve your CRQ couched in the theory-language of your academic or policy or occupational 'research community'. Gradually you will also find yourself developing TQs derived from the CRQ and dealing with different aspects of it. Set yourself the target of identifying 5 (plus or minus 3) of these TQs. They are theory-questions because they are couched in terms of the conceptual frameworks used by researchers and because the research community wants answers couched in terms of concepts that are researcher-friendly and that advance conceptual frameworks and the theory or theories of the field.[3]

When you have finally stabilized these, you should feel that you have say two to six theory-questions that, *once each one of them* has been answered *separately*, would put you in a clear position *to go on to give a satisfactory answer to the overall Central Research Question* as you finally formulated it.

Figures 5.8–5.15 are diagrams of the CRQ–TQ logical structure. Use diagrams to think with as often as possible. The most general form is shown in Figure 5.8. There follow some examples of the above structure made more concrete. Some

---

3 Bear in mind that I am using the term 'theory' in a broad sense to include descriptions, or 'models', of particular realities. See the Rose–Wengraf model, p. 55.

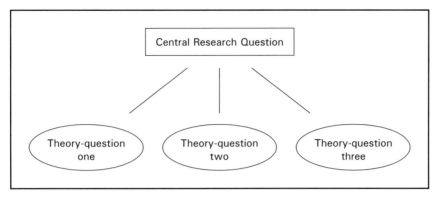

FIGURE 5.8   **CRQ–TQ General Model**

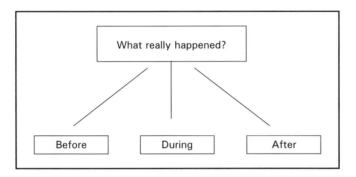

FIGURE 5.9   **CRQ–TQ: Before, During, After an Event**

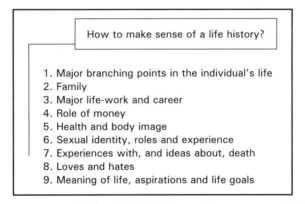

FIGURE 5.10   **CRQ–TQ: Making Sense of a Life History (Adapted from Birren, 1998)**

are examples in which *the CRQ is about happenings in a time sequence*. Others are examples where *the CRQ is about structural aspects* of a complex phenomenon. Others are mixes of 'happening' TQs and 'aspects' TQs.

For each one, it would be helpful to tentatively identify the principle by which the TQs appear to be constructed and differentiated from each other. You could

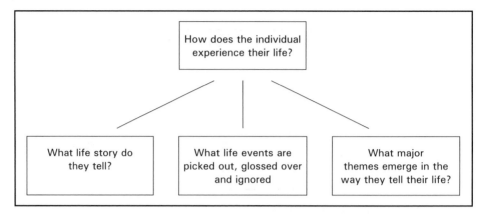

FIGURE 5.11   **CRQ–TQ: Life Events and Life Stories**

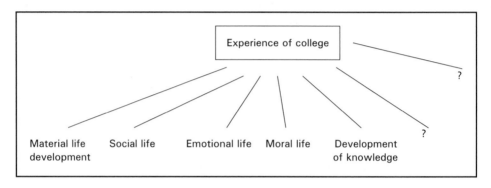

FIGURE 5.12   **CRQ–TQ: Experiences at College**

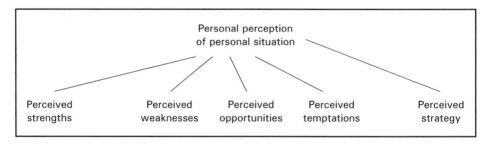

FIGURE 5.13   **CRQ–TQ: Personal Perception of Strengths, Weaknesses, Opportunities, Temptations, Strategy (SWOTS)**

also think of a different set of TQs that would serve the same CRQ equally well, or better, or worse.

Another set of questions may be motivated by interest in how the individuals tell their life stories (Figures 5.11 and 5.12). We may be interested in documenting the subjective perceptions of a given individual (Figure 5.13).

We may be interested in exploring their perceptions and deciding how correct or incorrect a view of reality the individual has (Figure 5.14). A final example

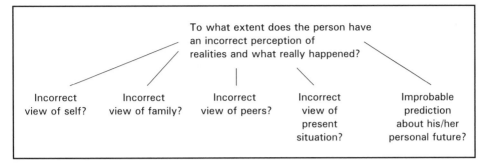

FIGURE 5.14   **CRQ–TQ: Incorrect Perceptions of Reality?**

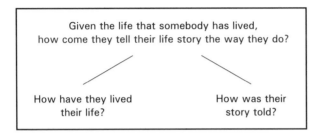

FIGURE 5.15   **CRQ–TQ for BNIM**

identifies key questions of the biographic narrative interpretive method (BNIM) (Figure 5.15).

Some of the above questions are purely subjective (and one interview with one person would be enough): for example, questions about 'their perceptions'. Some are purely objective: for example, 'what really happened'. Some are mixtures of the objective and the subjective: for example, 'what are the person's incorrect views of reality and what really happened?' All of them might be possible first-drafts of CRQ–TQ designs.

A More Complex Designs Discussed: Miles and Huberman Example   The next examples are fuller and more complex, to indicate how a bundle of CRQ–TQs + IQs can be criticized to enable it to be further improved.

Let us start with Miles and Huberman (1994) who, in their 'Study of the dissemination of educational innovations by their adoption by different schools', spelled out their questions as shown in Figure 5.16 (I have added the 'TQ's). They have, as it were, below the level of the CRQ, *two* levels of research-question, two levels of theory-question. Here, the theory-questions are starting to be spelled out in the way that they would need to be for a research project using powerful conceptual frameworks. But only starting.

Note that, in terms of our discussion earlier, some of the categories in Miles and Huberman's discourse involved are at the common-sense level. Others presuppose some existing sophisticated conceptual framework.

1b entails a sophisticated model of modes of decision-making; 3a involves a developed model of conditions for implementation of educational innovations. On the other

---

TQ1. How was the adoption decision made?
  (1a) Who was involved (for example, principal, users,
      central office people, school board outside agencies)?
  (1b) How was the decision made (top-down, persuasive,
      consultative, collegial-participative or delegated styles)?

TQ2. How much priority and centrality did the new programme have, at the time of the
     adoption decision?
  (2a) How much support and commitment was there from administrators?
  (2b) How important was it for teachers, seen in relation to their routine
      'ordinary' activities and any other innovations that were being
      contemplated or attempted?
  (2c) Realistically, how large did it loom in the scheme of things?
  (2d) Was it a one-time event or one of a series?

TQ3. What were the components of the original plan for implementation?
  (3a) These might have included front-end training; monitoring and
      debugging/trouble-shooting unexpected problems; ongoing
      support?
  (3b) How precise and elaborate was this plan?
  (3c) Were people satisfied with it at the time?
  (3d) Did it deal with all the problems anticipated?

TQ4. Were the requisite conditions for implementation assured before it began?
  (4a) These might have included commitment, understanding, materials
      and equipment, skills, time-allocation, organizational backup.
  (4b) Were any important conditions seen as missing?
  (4c) Which were most missing?

FIGURE 5.16 **CRQ–TQ: Miles and Huberman, modified (Miles and Huberman, 1994: 35)**

hand, 2a, 2b, and particularly 2c seem not very developed as categories in a theory-language, and might need replacement later on.

Note also, that there is a mix of researcher theory – categories (1b) and of ordinary-language folk-categories (2c, 4b, 4c). These could be virtually final formulations of informant-questions to be put to people or they could be initial-formulations of research-questions to be formulated within a coherent theory-language. At an early stage of formulation, the two are usually not well distinguished: it takes time to sort out and remodel research-questions into theory-language and informant-questions into informant-language. 4b is about folk-perception at the time; 4c is about the researcher's perception now.

TQs and IQs Critiqued to Promote Conceptual Development: Case Study (Marion L) So far, I have restricted myself to exposing the importance of conceptual development and frameworks in the elaboration of well-formulated research questions at CRQ and TQ level, and I hope that the general principles of the CRQ–TQ model are clearly established. As a bridge towards the later discussion of interview questions (IQs and other IIs), the next level of the CRQ–TQ–IQ model, it is now time to show how they are used in a more real-life example and provide another example – to go along with Chenitz's exposition cited earlier – of how they can be usefully critiqued for further development.

CRQ: The right to decorate, furnish, re-arrange objects within, and have more access to ... spaces within the home.

TQ1: How much of the space in a family home is shared, and how much of it is personal?
> *1a: What do you call the different rooms in your house, and why?*
> *1b: What is each room used for?*
> *1c: Who uses each room?*

TQ2: Are any rooms or spaces perceived as personal/exclusive to one member of the family?
> *2a: Do you have a room or part of a room which you consider to be yours – more yours than anybody else's?*
> *2b: If 'yes', then which room/part of room?*
> *2c: What about other members of the family?*

TQ3: Whether or not the informant has a perceived/recognized personal space, is there somewhere within the home where they can be alone?
> *3a: Where do you go if you want to be alone – or just have 5 minutes peace?*
> *3b: Is it clear to other members of the family that this is what you are doing?*
> *3c: What about other members of the family. Where do they go if they want to be alone?*

TQ4: If the informant has a personal space, how much control do they have over the decoration, items it contains and how they are situated?
> *4a: Who chose the decorations for this room?*
> *4b: (if exclusively): Did you choose the decorations for all the rooms?*
> *(if not): Is the way the rest of the house is decorated a joint decision?*
> *4c: Are the things in this room yours?*
> *4d: Did you decide where the things should go?*
> *4e: Would you mind if somebody else moved a chair from here to there? Would you move it back?*

TQ5: Is the concept of personal space important to the individual?
> *5a: Is it important for you to have this space?*
> *5b: Would you like to have some space in this house which you COULD call your own?*
> *5c: What would you do if A wants to go into B's room, and B doesn't want A in his room? Do you support B's right to be alone or do you insist on sharing?*

FIGURE 5.17   **CRQ–TQ–IQ by Marion L: Space in the Home**

Figure 5.17 gives a lengthy example of a proposed complete CRQ–TQ–IQ schema by a postgraduate student, Marion L, for a semi-structured depth interview and my response. She put forward a very good set of five theory-questions, and interview-questions for each of these TQs. Her proposed schema is shown in Figure 5.17, and my comments are given below.

Note that I have moved to considering IQs as well as the TQs and the CRQ. The response moves between various components of the design (as Maxwell identifies the components), in an attempt to promote further 'tightening up of the whole design'.

Although TQs are best first formulated and first considered without reference to their IQs but only in reference to the CRQ and the Research Purposes, in actual practice, when a design is considered as a whole, all elements need to be inspected together.

My comments on Marion L's draft schedule were as follows. I was trying to help the student develop a more coherent and powerful theory-language by work on the conceptual structure and by eventual recourse to relevant research literature:

'The question here is to try to identify the *dimensions* of the concept of "personal space" in a systematic way. The way that you write about it suggests that you have not yet found a "systematic treatment" of the concept by a researcher, and that you are having to invent it yourself.

If you can find a systematic treatment, perhaps by an anthropologist, then I would use it, it will get you to a higher level of sophistication faster than trying to do it by developing your home-grown variety. I know that the French sociologist Pierre Bourdieu has written on "space in the Kabyle house"; I vaguely remember that somebody called Ardener may have written on the subject. ET(?) Hall has written on time and space, I think in his "Silent Language". [Other] tutors should be able to suggest items.

You are interested in *'rights to space'* in a number of ways:

- *strongest:* exclusive right to space, no access for others to that space without permission, full freedom to decorate and arrange without reference to others;
- *weaker:* shared right to space, certain others have equal access, negotiation needed to determine use, decoration, re-arrangement ... and is the other negotiating on equal or unequal ground?

Units seem to be rooms and parts of rooms (toilets and bathrooms are places where one has exclusive temporary use, but for how long?), with decoration-of-rooms and the choice and distribution of objects.

You also seem to be interested in *"rights to access to people"* and in particular in the woman's right to have sole access to herself and to insist that other people do not have rights of access to her attention. This "access to persons" seems to be analytically distinct from "access to places": I can say "you are welcome to work in this room providing you don't disturb or talk to me", thus giving access to personal-space on the condition of non-access to the person who "owns" the personal-space.

I think you also need to work out the conditions under which a default-right of "exclusion" can be over-ridden by "unusual conditions". Your questions seem to stay at the level of "ordinary default" and so may risk being banal. There may be shared or not-shared ideas of "conditions under which default-rules" can or should be over-ridden, and teasing out those "special circumstances" would be very interesting.

E.g. if they think the kids are smoking drugs, making too much noise, having illegal sex, not doing their share of the chores, do they think that parents have a right to "violate kid-space"?

What kinds of household "emergency" warrant shouting requests or information through the loo door, insisting that the bath be "hurried up", etc.?

Can "space" be generated by a special "emotional display" (end-of-tether plea)?'

I then went on to make brief comments on each TQ/IQ bundle.

'Theory-questions:

TQ1

> Degrees of sharing should be focused on; and there might be room that is shared by not all the family: e.g. a kids-room for all kids; a grownup's "parlour" or shared bedroom
>
> IQ1c: who uses this room normally? who uses this room (for what) sometimes non-normally? Can you remember it ever being used by somebody else, or not being shared as it is usually?

TQ2/3/4   OK.

TQ5

> (5a) How much more space would be fair? What sort of space?
>
> (5c) When do 'fair-shares' not seem so fair? How do you think other members of your family would view the existing situation/an attempt to change? What arguments would you expect them to put? How reasonable do you think those arguments are? To avoid error, ask whether other members of the family have more choice of decorations, placing of things, re-arrangement power than she does.

Informants

> If you get two people from the same family (mother/daughter/husband), you would find out whether their perception of the other's perception of rights/powers/spaces matches or doesn't match.

A note on method

> You are using, and trying to develop, an expert-concept of "space as personal". Your organizing concept is of "rights over space". As suggested above, you may need to read research in order to improve that expert-concept.
>
> You do not focus on exploring the informant's own concept of "space" which may or may not be as oriented to the "rights of persons" as is your expert-concept. Your expert-concept of "more or less rights of persons over space" is deeply Western: look at C.B. MacPherson's *The Rise of Possessive Individualism* for an expert-discussion of the limitations of Western thought and the language of "individual rights".
>
> As long as you interview somebody as deeply imbued with "possessive individualism" as your approach is, interviewing them in terms of your expert-concept may do no harm.
>
> But it will block other understandings: one, for example, in which space does not more or less belong to individuals but (a) is only usable by categories (gender in the Kabyle house, Bourdieu); (b) is to be appropriated for time-specific functions by whoever is performing those functions.
>
> How could your questions catch the informant's own categories, even if their mode of experiencing and using space is not solely in terms of "possessive individualism" but couched also/instead in other terms?'

In the above discussion and example, I have tried to suggest how the design elements of conceptual framework and theory-language need to be considered in the procedure whereby research questions (CRQ + TQs) are 'instrumented into' (operationalized into) interviewer questions (IQs) and other interventions (IIs) and into session design.

By now, you should be convinced of the importance of the primary words of the Central Research Questions (and of all other questions) of any piece of research. You should have a sense of the 'directivity' of concepts, which, by pointing you in one direction, necessarily point you away from others.

By now, you should appreciate the way that the concepts you use in your questions need to be connected in a framework of concepts (a conceptual framework); they need to be mutually coherent and they need to be clear. You need to be very conscious of the problems of operationalizing your concepts in respect of the 'instrumention assumptions and arguments'.

> You may wish at this point to revisit the exercise on 'shoplifting' and re-examine and perhaps re-work your solutions and choices in the light of the above discussion and examples. This will ensure that you profit fully from the above discussion.

Here, I shall conclude my discussion of the work of developing coherent conceptual frameworks with which to pose our questions. Clearly, I should be able to find coherent conceptual-theoretical frameworks and models when I look at the research literature, but sadly this is not always the case.

For and Against Literature Searches for Conceptual Frameworks

It might seem natural to assume that coherent and powerful conceptual frameworks are to be found in the research literature on any given topic, and, consequently, the best thing for a researcher to do is to take somebody else's conceptual framework from a piece of published research, or a from a book of theory, and just use it. There are arguments against doing this which need to be considered. The first relates to a general avoidance of research literature; the second is that a closed conceptual framework can block creativity.

Those who argue for Grounded (Emergent) Theorizing sometimes argue the extreme case for the conscious avoidance of library research. Chenitz writes:

> 'The grounded theorist maintains a cautious and sceptical attitude about the literature throughout the study. This is particularly important during the early stages of the project, since at this point the researcher can unconsciously fall into accepting what is written. A concept or an ordering of concepts may linger in the researcher's mind. The researcher can then categorize incoming data into the learned concepts ... closing off further analysis. Also, consciously or unconsciously, the researcher may look for these variables, concepts and relationships identified in the literature. Further research in the discovery mode is fruitless, since the researcher has already closed off analysis and theory development.' (Chenitz and Swanson, 1986: 44)

Glaser and Strauss (1968), the proponents of the grounded-theory movement, originally argued more strongly for complete abstention from any reading of supposedly 'relevant literature' and particularly of any school of existing theory. This hostility to the dominant school of theorization in American sociology of the 1950s (incarnated in the writings of Talcott Parsons) can also be found in Mills (1959).

A relatively historical approach to social research data suggests that this year's juvenile delinquents may act in a different way from last year's, that, in the same year, the American Mafia may operate differently from the Russian Mafia, and by next year both may be different from what they were, thanks to the changing operations of the British government. With such a historically conscious understanding of socio-historical research data, any account (theory, model) of previous social realities may be seriously misleading if applied uncritically to a different time or place. An apparently universal 'theorization' is particularly apt to mislead one into thinking that a particular study in a particular location (e.g. Vaughan, cited on p. 325–7) in the past provides a universal statement for all times and places. Hence the danger of an uncritical acceptance of old theorizations, particularly when they purport to capture universal cross-cultural and cross-temporal truth.

I share Chenitz's concern for 'premature closure' of the theory-generation struggle, but I would also argue that one should start with a coherent and potentially productive Conceptual Framework with a Central Research Question and subsidiary Theory-Questions *that do not foreclose the further theorizing and conceptual innovation that they will, one hopes, trigger off.*

The theory-language you use and develop, and the theory-questions that you pose may well be *derived from – not be reducible to –* existing theory and research in a current research field. That is why – to avoid struggling to 'reinvent the wheel' (as did Marion L with the concept of personal space in the home) – you need to look carefully at existing relevant research fields and disciplines. Whenever they argue for a 'theorization', that theorization, as we have seen, is couched in terms of an implied or explicit conceptual framework.

Remember that one of the things you can do is to explore using concepts and findings developed in one area to look at another: transferring intellectual technology. That is what conceptual frameworks are: *transferable intellectual technology;* for example:

- using religious models to look at neo-liberal political economy
- using models of political process to look at religious transformations
- using market models to look at interpersonal relations
- using sexual attraction models to look at economic behaviour.

George Lakoff and Mark Johnson's *Metaphors we Live By* provides a stimulating account of the rich fertile way in which our experience of all social relations is profoundly metaphorical. This text that you are reading brings together bits of 'intellectual technology' from a variety of different fields: the sources on which I depend and which I have also attempted to develop come from a whole variety of intellectual and practical 'fields', and the same is likely to be true of your work.

Within a given conceptual framework, as we have seen, a variety of competing and complementary theorizations can be developed, considered, refuted or supported. A theorization is an answer to a given CRQ or TQ. A counter-theorization is *couched in the same conceptual framework* as the first theorization, but *to the same question* the counter-theorization puts forward *a different answer.*

However, whether I start from our own ordinary language or whether I start from published research, the chances are that I shall have to work at grasping and improving the conceptual frameworks (and the theorizations) that I inherited.

Grant McCracken has a very good passage on the use of doing library work:

> 'Some researchers have taken qualitative methods as license to ignore the scholarship that bears on their investigation. They contend that qualitative methods are so powerful and uniquely illuminating that they take the investigator "where no-one has gone before". This, they contend, makes the existing literature an irrelevance (and at worst a positivist distortion). This strategy may be ill-advised. A good literature review has many virtues. It enables the investigator to define problems and assess data. It *provides concepts on which percepts depend*. But the literature review has a special importance for the qualitative researcher. This consists of its ability to sharpen his or her capacity for surprise .... *The investigator who is well-versed in the literature now has a set of expectations the data can defy*. Counter-expectational data are conspicuous, readable and highly provocative. They signal the existence of unfulfilled theoretical assumptions and these are, as Kuhn ... has noted, the very origins of intellectual innovation. A thorough review of the literature is, to this extent, a way to manufacture distance. *It is a way to let the data of one's research project take issue with the theory of one's field*.' (McCracken, 1988: 31, italics added)

I would completely agree with this. I would add that it is as important to engage in a very systematic inventory of one's own prejudices, stereotypes, phantasies, hopes and fears, ideological and emotional desires and purposes and to *record these very systematically in writing*.

Such an activity brings to a manifest and a reflexive level a variety of assumptions and purposes that might otherwise lurk unseen as a quasi-unconscious theory about 'one's field'. A review of one's conscious and unconscious interest in the field is also a way of manufacturing distance, and creating a space in which the data of the research project can take issue with the quasi-unconscious assumptions and ideologies of one's research purposes.

While uncritical acceptance of past theorizations and, to a lesser extent, of past conceptual frameworks in terms of which those theorizations have been couched is to be avoided, ignorance of previous knowledge and research about the field is also to be avoided, for the reason that McCracken makes so clear. The important way of using past research is

- to have the attitude that you want to be able to *add to* knowledge and understanding, not just replicate it, and
- to have the working hypothesis that, in a historically evolving world, *the new cases you are studying will turn out to be subtly or grossly different from the previous cases* from an earlier period and perhaps a different location as expressed in already published literature.

With such an attitude and such a working hypothesis, you will let the new data of your research project take issue with the past theory of your field, your past theory of 'reality'.

Summary   I hope I have shown the importance of working on the words in the question, the conceptual framework behind the theory and knowledge, in order to improve your research design. Prior research pays off in 'clearer expectations that the data can surprise' (McCracken). A constant and careful attempt to develop the

CRQs and TQs at the centre of the revised Maxwell hour-glass (Figure 3.3, p. 59) requires a process of ensuring that they match the various research purposes they are meant to serve (especially your own) and match also the needs of the 'communities' (research communities, policy communities, natural communities) who have stakes in the outcome of good research. A full logical research design means developing appropriate interview questions and other interview interventions for each of your chosen TQs. Refer back to the CRQ–TQ–II model, Figure 4.3 (p. 63). The example of Marion L's inquiry into personal space may help you to see how conceptual frameworks are critiqued and developed as the 'slow tightening' of the elements of research design, including the IQs, continues.

After I have dealt with the identification of informants and sampling, the next step necessary to create a schedule of questions and a strategy of interventions for the interview is that of deriving and formulating IQs and other IIs. But, remember, the clarification of research purposes, of your central research question, and of your theory questions should normally be given pride of place. If you are clear about these elements, then you have clear criteria for selecting your informants and for designing interview sessions, whether lightly or fairly-fully structured.

The complexities of developing IQs and other IIs for a given piece of research can only be done by working through a number of examples. I shall work through a small number of examples in relation to BNIM in Chapter 6, and then, in Chapter 7, in relation to certain FFSDI non-narrative interview designs.

However, before dealing with the way that TQs dictate IQs, I shall be dealing with the way that TQs – by way of the instrumentation theory – dictate the selection of informants, of interviewees.

Sampling and Identifying Possible Informants

If you are interviewing one or more named persons for their own sake, then you do not have a problem of selection or sampling, and this section is not relevant for that piece of research. If, however, you have a choice of informants, then you have a question of selection and the issues raised here are relevant. In general social research, we tend to be interested in types of persons, and so the question is: how do I select samples (even a sample of one) of that type?

Your CRQ and TQs taken together will determine the character of the 'relevant material' to be gathered from the 'appropriate people'. There is an obvious interaction between the selection of the type of informant and the development of a sequence of interview questions appropriate for them.

Apart from the 'general specification of type', you will need to think about the criteria which distinguish good examples of the 'type' from ones less useful for your research purposes. The most obvious one is that you need to have access to the person; others are their probability of talking honestly and non-manipulatively to yourself or a person like yourself[4]. Other criteria might include the amount of experience they have of the subject in question, and their capacity to express that experience in words, as opposed to, say, in painting or in action.

---

4 If all in your 'pool' can be expected to be equally manipulative, then select one for whom you think you have enough contextual knowledge to detect their manipulations more easily.

You should *avoid haphazard selection of informants*. You need a deliberate or purposeful selection, or a randomized selection (see below), but *not* a haphazard or 'at random' selection.

In whatever way you find and select your informants, in your analyses and reporting you do need to make clear how you did seek out or come across them, *and specify any direct or indirect relationship you have with them or they have with each other*. In this way you and your reader can allow for how non-interview relationships might impinge on the interview data that are generated in the interview (see Figure 2.6, p. 43 and the John and Lorna vignette on pp. 16–17). A woman's discussion of 'criteria for marriage' with a complete stranger may be valid and reliable; asked the same question by her live-in lover or potential marriage-partner, the data are likely to be less so (or more?). Always specify your relation with your informants and the procedure for selection that you undertook. At least the reader of your report should know what the situation is.

More importantly, make sure that *you* take into account the matrix of real relations when planning the informant questions, when interpreting the significance of replies within the interview, and when interpreting the meaning of the interview for analysis afterwards.

Engaging in a research programme involving depth interviews, you will probably be 'interviewing' at a number of different points of time for a variety of different purposes, using a variety of designs. Your study of the research literature will have started to sensitize you to the types of informants you should try to get interviews with, and, as your study proceeds and as your 'theoretical model' is enriched by more data, you will develop your understanding both of what informants you still need to interview, what to re-interview old informants about, and what kinds of questions to ask them. Your prior design of 'desired informants' will be modified by your emergent further knowledge. In this section, I focus particularly on the selection of your 'prior' or first informants.

Named Informants or Which 'Whole Population'?

For some research purposes, usually pragmatic or clinical ones, I may be in the fortunate position of being able to interview everybody concerned – the 'whole population' as defined by my CRQ and TQs. For example, if I wish to understand why a family, or a couple, or a small team in a particular organization is not 'functioning properly', I may be in a position to interview all the members of the family, both parties to the couple, all the members of the small team. In such cases of 'whole population sampling', I have no problem of selection *within* the group defined by our theory as 'the whole population'. At least no problem of prior selection. I may have a problem about whom I re-interview, whom I interview at greater length, and so forth, as our study progresses, but I do not have a problem of prior selection. If you are in the fortunate position of being able to interview the 'whole population' in the sense described above, for immediate practical purposes, be grateful!

However, if your theoretical concerns are to develop not a particular theory of this household, or this small organization, or this tribe or village, but, say, a particular theory of a large extended family, a large organization, an urban neighbourhood, or even a general theory of families, organizations, tribes and neighbourhoods, then you *do* have a problem of selection. The rest of this discussion is concerned therefore with sampling.

Sometimes your theoretical concerns can be achieved by randomized sampling, sometimes by what is called purposive (or 'theoretical', in a narrower sense) sampling, and very often by a combination of the two. I deal with these in turn.

Randomized sampling (equal-probability sampling) is the mode of sampling discussed in all the textbooks on survey methods, (e.g. de Vaus, 1996) and, if you are in a position to undertake it, then it has very powerful advantages. I will deal with it only very generally. This does not mean that I am advising you not to undertake it: rather the opposite. For many research purposes, it is the first thing to consider doing: other methods of collecting informants restrict the scope of generalizations and inferences that can be drawn.[5] If you have a sampling frame and *can* sample in this way, then there are advantages in doing so.

You should bear in mind, however, that, given the comparatively small numbers of informants that a process of semi-structured (as opposed to fully structured) interviews can be applied to, given finite resources, you will not be able to do many interviews. Consequently, the chances are that the numbers you collect will not be enough to enable you to draw any statistical inferences from them. They will have the real advantages of randomization except that you cannot generalize on statistical grounds to the population from which the random sample was drawn.

For some researchers, the fact that semi-structured and lightly structured interviews can be applied only to a statistically insignificant number of people and that, consequently, statistical inference cannot operate, is enough to make randomization a waste of time. For others, the chances of getting 'theoretically surprising diversity' from a carefully randomized low-N sample may make it worth the effort.

Representative Randomized Sampling from a 'Frame' of a Listed Population

If you have a list of the whole population from which you will be selecting informants, you are then in a position to use randomized (or known-probability) sampling. This means that you can use a list of random numbers to select a sample (say 10) out of a whole population (say 100 or 1,000) so that each member of the 100 (or the 1,000) has a known and equal chance of being selected as a member of the 10 (the sample) that you propose to interview.

You have your list of the whole population and each name has a unique number. You find a way (by computer, or a random number table) of getting 10 names 'at random' from the list of the whole population.

- If your list of the whole population contains 100 names, then all of them will have a 10% and equal chance of being in your randomized sample of 10.
- If your list of the whole population contains 1,000 names, then all of them will have a 1% and equal chance of being in your randomized sample of 10.

Let us look briefly at the sorts of elaborations that can be made of this mode of selection.

---

5 Many researchers wish to define themselves as 'anti-quantitative' and so find reasons for not using statistics. Good research is multi-method (Brannen, 1992), and it is the purposes of the research that should dictate what methods you use. It should not be your 'favourite method' that dictates what methodology you refuse to envisage. But, for those who do define themselves as quantitative or qualitative, the selection of 'depth interview informants' can be appropriate for both.

Assume that you wanted to see whether staff and students in a school were happy or unhappy, and there were 10 staff and 100 students. You can afford to depth-interview about 10 people.

You could add the lists of names of staff and students together (110), get out the book of random numbers, and do a randomized sample of the whole (10/110 = a) little less than 10%. If your theory treats the 'whole population' as homogeneous for your purposes, then this is perfectly OK.

If you think that the 'whole population' might be divided (in this case into two groups), and that one group might be very happy and the other might be very sad (sadistic teachers brutalizing unhappy students; sadistic students intimidating unhappy teachers), then you have a problem. The first 10 names drawn out of the hat or the computer in a properly randomized way might all be from one group or all from another. Or there might be nine sadistic happy teachers and one unhappy student.

So your 'theory' of the population might make you proceed to get your 10 names in a slightly different fashion. You might go for a stratified random sample. You treat the 'population of 110' not as homogeneous but as heterogeneous, and you create two separate lists.

You would have two lists now: one for all the 10 teachers; one for all the 100 students. You want to get a randomized sample of the students, and a randomized sample of the teachers, and interview accordingly. What are your choices then?

- You could do a 10% sample of each category (or subsample). So you would get 1 from the 10 teachers and 10 from the 100 students. So you would do 11 interviews.
- You could do an equal number of interviews with staff and students. You would draw 5 names out of 10 teachers (50% sample with known and equal chance of being in the staff sample) and 5 names from the 100 students (5% sample with a known but equal chance of being in the student subsample).

If your 'theory of the population' is that 'newcomers' might feel one way and 'long-stayers' might feel another, then you would create subsample lists on a different basis.

The importance of such randomized (equal and known probability) sampling is that you then have some reasons for inferring from what you find in your (sub)samples to what is true for the whole population from which you drew them. *Were the numbers large enough, the inferences could be made statistically. Since they almost certainly won't be, the reasoning and inferring has to be logical rather than statistical.*

With other methods (with which this chapter is mostly concerned), such 'inference' is more controversial. So if you can, do use randomized probability sampling as described in nearly all social research methods textbooks dealing with surveys and other quantitative research methods. In case you are in the happy position of being able to do so, I have found Ackoff's sampling chart (1953, reproduced in Hessler, 1992: 122–3) helpful: it describes each type and their key advantages and disadvantages.

Non-random/Non-probability Sampling Statistically randomized sampling is possible only if you have a sampling frame in order to achieve randomization. You may not have a list of the whole population. Alternatively, you may have such a list but be looking to use principles of sample-selection other than those of randomization.[6] While the concepts for discussing different randomized samples are well-developed and well-agreed, this is not true of non-probability sampling. Each book you turn to will have different distinctions drawn for different purposes.

Some Discussion   Honigman (1982: 80–5) discusses both 'traditional anthropological sampling' and a variety of other methods. He remarks as follows:

> 'I am stressing the deliberateness with which subjects are chosen .... The ethnographer uses his prior knowledge of the universe to draw representatives from it who possess distinctive qualifications. He may for example select informants ... according to the class strata, occupational status, sex, age, or length of residence in the community ...'

The point worth making is that it all depends on your 'prior knowledge of the universe' (Honigman's term), your 'theory of it' (my term), as to what you are looking for and whom you select to get that information.

The concept of 'theoretical sampling' parallels my re-labelling of research questions as 'theory-questions'. Burgess discusses theoretical sampling (theory-driven sampling) as follows:

> '"Theoretical sampling is the process of data collection for generating theory whereby the analyst jointly collects, codes, and analyses his data and decides what data to collect next and where to find them in order to develop his theory as it emerges (Glaser and Strauss, 1968: 45)" .... basic questions [are]: what groups and subgroups are used in data collection? For what theoretical purposes are the groups and sub-groups used?

> Denzin (1970) [considers that] theoretical sampling does not end until new concepts and categories do not appear, while statistical sampling ends when a predetermined sample has been observed. Secondly, theoretical sampling is judged by the quality of theory, while statistical sampling is judged by the extent to which it conforms to the "rules" of sampling theory.' (Burgess, 1982: 75)

Lummis's Example   Trevor Lummis (1987) remarks of 'quota sampling' that

> 'this method requires only that the general size and distribution of the group to be investigated are already known'. (Lummis, 1987: 35)

This 'only' condition of course is not always satisfied easily, and for some features of some populations only a rough guess can be made. Library research of course, and/or being a 'native' of the population concerned, will help a lot.

Lummis then goes on to describe how he constructed a non-probability sample for the Oral History Archive at Essex University. Note how much knowledge he 'takes for granted' as he 'strategises' about all the different 'quotas' that need to be filled. His 'quotas' are produced by his prior 'theoretical model' of the composition (or 'sector' or 'location') of 'the fishing industry'. Did he get the knowledge presupposed from coming from a 'fishing community' himself? Did he get it by

---

6 Of course, you may draw two samples (both a randomized and a non-randomized one) from the same population: Honigman, in Burgess (1982: 88–9), discusses some results of this briefly.

library research? Did he get it by talking to those who 'knew' the 'fishing industry'? He had to get it somehow. Your sample construction may need (or at least benefit from) similar prior knowledge.

'My research on the fishing industry of East Anglia allowed for sixty interviews with fishermen or the women from fishing families. Had I simply gone and interviewed the first sixty 'fishermen' I found there is little doubt that, as *individual* accounts, they would have been as informative as those collected. But, given the variety of experience to be found in even one occupation in a single region, they would have been most unlikely to have included the full range of experience. Finding the informants with quota sampling in mind obliged me to seek an appropriate number of informants who worked in the steam drifting, sail trawling and the inshore sectors. I also had to find those who worked in different positions, not just skippers whose status in the community meant that they were almost invariably suggested to me as the most suitable informants. As the industry contained a number of fishermen-owners, I needed to interview the self-employed as well as the employers or employees. A balanced view of industrial relations and social conditions could emerge only through interviewing all sections. But occupation is not the only area of experience which affects attitudes and values: many of these are formed before starting work, and so it was important to include the different localities and communities the fishermen had lived in, such as rural and urban areas. Subsequent analysis of the interviews confirmed how constructive this sampling had been, because there were marked differences in social attitudes between the coastal villages where fishermen predominate and the rural villages where the fishermen were in a minority. The resulting collection of interviews is much more informative because, instead of being able to simply analyse the results as the experience of 'fishermen', it is possible to compare and contrast the values and attitudes of the various sectors within the industry and from the various locations within the region. In other words, instead of being simply a collection of individual biographical reminiscences, it is now historically and sociologically more informative.' (Lummis, 1987: 35–6)

Lummis also points out the extreme importance of *knowing what types of informant or experience are absent* from our quotas: the equivalent of non-responders in survey methods.

'If oral interviews are to be used as a systematic source from which to make general historical statements, I must be aware of what sort of experience our interviews represent – and which areas of experience they leave untapped. A piece of research from Canada illustrates this point.

Jane Synge interviewed people born between 1890 and 1908, using a quota sample of various socio-economic groups both from industry and agriculture focusing on "how families cope with such crises and potential crises as care of the aged, bereavement, orphanhood, and unemployment". This quota approach should have provided the basis for a sound analytical study, the results of which could be taken as typical of the population at large. But, as she writes:

Analysis of the experience of successive cohorts shows the extent to which the family lives described by my respondents were atypical of those of the whole adult population

continued

continued

of the early twentieth century. Our respondents are talking of homes with children. But of the cohort born in 1890 who reached adulthood, 41% either did not marry or were childless.

This emphasises the point that oral historians are interviewing only survivors and, had Synge not been alert to the limitations of her material, the experience of little more than half the population would have been accepted as the experience of all. She acknowledges that:

"... had I examined the demographic patterns of the era more closely prior to the development of the questionnaire, I would have recognised the importance of studying the high incidence of bachelorhood, spinsterhood and childlessness, and would have introduced specific questions to elicit more detailed material on the lives of unmarried and/or childless relatives and neighbours (Jane Synge 1981)"

As it stands, she did collect quite a lot of evidence about the unmarried and childless simply because her informants talked about the unmarried and childless relatives who lived with them or the nature of their family's contact with other kin. This is one of the great strengths of oral history: one is not only collecting biographical material, but the informants' observations of their wider social world: they can tell you something about how other people behaved.

And if the opportunity to use this material in a systematic, rather than anecdotal, manner has been lost in this case because this aspect of representativeness was not foreseen, it is unlikely to have even been identified had Synge not been alert to the significance of sampling.' (Lummis, 1987: 36–7)

EXERCISE 5.2   QUOTA SAMPLING

Taking a course that you have done, are doing, or might do, if you were doing an oral history of the cohort of students who were in your course at the beginning, how would the above considerations affect the 'quotas' you might construct and the 'questions' you might ask of those in your quota?

You might then wish to consider the following questions in relation to an actual or hypothetical research project of your own:

How do the considerations identified by Lummis suggest possibilities to you for constructing

1   adequate quota categories for a set of informants with whom you are concerned?
2   for those informants to whom you *are* likely to have access, appropriate questions about relevant persons to whom you *cannot* have direct access as informants?

The general point that needs to be made is that, in order to have a non-misleading or merely 'haphazard' range of informants, you must think hard and you must have preliminary knowledge about 'the [relevant] variety of [relevant] experiences' that your Research Purposes formally concern themselves with. You need insider information, you need library research, you need imagination to design theoretically well-designed questions for a theoretically stratified 'quota' sample.

Patton's Typology of Randomized and Purposive Sampling   This necessarily brief survey of sampling may usefully end by referring you to the discussion of Patton (1990) and by his highly condensed summary of the types of sampling, focusing on what he considers to be 'information-rich' samples (1990: 169–83).

Type	Purpose
A. Randomized probability sampling	*Representativeness: sample size a function of population size and desired 'confidence level'*
1. Simple random sample	Permits generalization from sample to the population it represents
2. Stratified random and cluster samples	Increases confidence in making generalizations to particular subgroups or areas
B. Purposeful sampling	*Selects information-rich cases for in-depth study. Size and specific cases depend on study purposes*
1. Extreme or deviant case sampling	Learning from highly unusual manifestations of the phenomenon in question, such as outstanding successes / notable failures, top of the class / drop-outs, exotic events, crises
2. Intensity sampling	Information-rich cases that manifest the phenomenon intensely, but not extremely, such as good students / poor students, above-average / below-average
3. Maximum variation sampling – purposefully picking a wide range of variation on dimensions of interest	Documents unique or diverse variations that have emerged in adapting to different conditions. Identifies important common patterns that cut across variations
4. Homogeneous sampling	Focuses, reduces variation, simplifies analysis, facilitates group interviewing
5. Typical case sampling	Illustrates or highlights what is typical, normal, average
6. Stratified purposeful sampling	Illustrates the characteristics of particular subgroups of interest; facilitates comparisons
7. Critical case sampling	Permits *logical* generalization and maximum application of information to other cases, because, if it's true of this one case, then it's likely to be true of all other cases
8. Snowball or chain sampling	Identifies cases of interest from people who know people who know what cases are information-rich; that is, good examples for study, good interview subjects

continued

Figure 5.18   continued

Type	Purpose
9. Criterion sampling	Picking all cases that meet some criterion, such as all children abused in a treatment facility. Quality assurance
10. Theory-based or operational construct	Finding manifestations of a theoretical construct of interest so as to elaborate and examine the construct
11. Confirming and disconfirming cases	Elaborating and deepening initial analysis, seeking exceptions, testing variations
12. Opportunistic sampling	Following new leads during fieldwork, taking advantage of the unexpected, flexibility
13. Random purposeful sampling (still small sample size)	Adds credibility to sample when potential purposeful sample is larger than one can manage. Reduces judgment *within* a purposeful category
14. Sampling politically-important cases	Attracts attention to the study [or avoids attracting undesired attention by purposefully eliminating from the study politically-sensitive cases]
15. Convenience sampling	Saves money, time, effort. Poorest rationale, lowest credibility. Yields information-poor cases
16. Combination or mixed purposeful sampling	Triangulation, flexibility, meets multiple needs and interests
C. Mixed random and purposeful sampling *Sequenced combination of elements of A and B*	Triangulation, flexibility, meets multiple needs and interests; enables some claim to statistical representativeness, and some purposeful sampling unhampered by the requirements of randomness

FIGURE 5.18   **Patton's Table of Sampling Strategies, Modified**

He is primarily concerned with purposive non-randomized samples.

'The logic and power of purposeful sampling lies in selecting information-rich cases for study in depth …. For example, if the purpose … is to increase the effectiveness of a program in reaching lower socio-economic groups, one may learn a great deal more by focusing in depth on understanding the needs, interests, and incentives of a small number of carefully selected poor families than by gathering standardised information from a large statistically representative sample of the whole program … there are several different strategies for purposefully selecting information-rich cases.' (Patton, 1990: 169)

Other Ways of Thinking about your 'Interview Sample'

Single-specimen Research   In general, semi-structured interviewing is normally part of a comparative research design. A number of people will be interviewed, and the common questions that form the 'structured' part of the 'semi-structure' will be put to all of them.

- This may be to illuminate a single case of which they are all a part or to which they are all witnesses: for example, the single case of one family may involve many interviews with members of the family and others connected to it.
- Alternatively, each of the interviews may be treated as illuminating different cases: for example, each interviewee may be illuminating the separate family or society or organization that he or she alone 'represents'.
- Or, perhaps, each interviewee or their life-story or their idiolect (personal world-discourse) or their personal culture *is* the 'case' that is being studied.

In general, cases are of interest because they promise to contribute to knowledge which is of more than just that one case. Hence science searches for relatively general or universal truths and generally has a bias towards multi-case (comparative) studies.

Obviously, the more information of different sorts I have from as many sources that I can engage with, the greater are the chances that our eventual understanding will be robust. *Five viewpoints from averagely observant witnesses on the same contradictory and controversial event are, other things being equal, more likely to produce an objective understanding than one viewpoint from one of them.*

However, *this does not mean that the study of single cases is not important for science.* Until recently, geologists and climatologists could only study the geology and climate of a single planet. Social sciences have only been able to study the phenomena of one small planet. Despite this considerable single-case restriction, *the intensive study of one single case can produce insight which the superficial study of many cases can in no way equal.* These insights derived from single-case analysis can then be used in and enriched by a multiplicity of comparative studies.[7]

So don't apologize if your research design is a single-case study involving depth interviewing of a single individual: do the study in such a way that it can be part of past and future comparative multi-case studies.

Triangulated 'Linked Lives'   Socio-historical research is quite reasonably unhappy with accounts from one source only that cannot be evaluated in the light of other material. Consequently, many researchers attempt to develop research designs which provide varying degrees of cross-referencing, or 'triangulation'. This enables cross-checking to be made. I can think of three-generation samples, of 'cousin position' sampling, of couple interviewing, and thus of the synthesis of their different viewpoints on the at least partially shared reality.

- *Three generations.* One principle is that of taking several generations of one family. Each has their own view on past, present and future, and their views and

---

7 Thomas Scheff (1997) has published a timely and very largely convincing demonstration of the value of single-case studies which move from the 'minutest particulars' to the 'most general wholes' of which they are part and in which context they are to be understood. He analyses the very fine detail of interview interactions. Kroeber's book-length study of an American Indian, *Ishi: the last of his tribe*, is an exemplary study of a single tribe whose way of life, whose history and whose culture had only one surviving witness. If a Martian culture found you as the last human survivor, as a 'single', you could illuminate more than just your own life and your own time. See my discussion in Wengraf (2000a).

experience relate to each other in complex and enlightening ways. Bertaux and Delcroix (2000) discuss these in relation to biographical resources in poor families, and Rosenthal and her collaborators (Rosenthal, 1998) do three-generation analyses of the families of victims and perpetrators of Nazi persecution in Germany 1939–45.

- *Cousin 'positions'*. Organizational research has the problem of considerable differences of power between different positions in organizational hierarchies. This tends to inhibit free expression in organizational research interviews. One partial solution which is valid for organizations with many similar-structured branches is to interview managers from one branch, foremen from another, and rank-and-file workers from a third branch. Such diagonal rather than vertical sampling reduces the fear of those involved. Obviously, to the extent that conditions in branches are genuinely different, it can lead to dangers of misleading conclusions.
- *Couple interviewing*. Interviewing husbands and wives (or other close partners) separately and guaranteeing confidentiality to both is a highly tricky business, not only because it makes publication of detail pretty impossible but also because the fact that both have given secret confidential interviews to a third party changes the dynamics of the relations between the partners. See Hertz (1995).

The same problem of the unpredictable alteration of relations by the act of interviewing occurs with the interviewing of children and of parents. Even the interviewing of friends can be a very tricky business: in order to maintain the friendship, certain realities may need to be hidden; if certain realities are communicated, then the relationship will be changed in significant ways: see the vignette of John and Lorna on pp. 16–17.

Obviously, the less intimate the discussion, the less dangers are raised for those inside and outside the interview relationship.

Multiple and Partial Viewpoints Voiced and Synthesized You need to develop a theory of 'contrasting informants' and hypotheses about the 'socially conditioned partiality' of all the viewpoints expressed by each. Our search for the most useful sample is a way of looking for a form of 'triangulation'.

This enables you to 'place' and give the correct 'weight' to the 'necessarily partial' informant. Your interpretation is not a 'mirroring short re-description' of what they say, but *an opportunity to evaluate and synthesize the partial viewpoints* expressed by each of the informants. For example, *teachers and students on a given course see an enormous amount of relevant information that the other does not*, and see from perspectives which are themselves quite different. Good research would certainly attempt to give voice (partially in the form of direct quotation) to members of each group, but it would also go beyond the partial viewpoints to evaluate and synthesize and place in historical and theoretical contexts.

Access to 'Rich and Willing' Informants At a very basic level, the informant needs to be trusted to turn up. He or she needs to be trusted to try to tell the truth, to be able to articulate their knowledge and ideas well enough. J.P. Spradley argues that they need to be good story-tellers and *not* to be too analytic. Others disagree, arguing that the 'ideal informant' needs to be thoughtful and reflective. It depends on purposes and strategy.

Some of these are very personal qualities: e.g. reliability. This can be very much a question of interpersonal chemistry.

> 'I was reluctant to ask people to be interviewed until I had a schedule of questions I wished to ask. I now feel I should have selected and made appointments with my informants as soon as I had a research proposal, working on any questions later. I say this because of the problems I had with informants, letting me down, turning up late, or generally not being found to begin with.' (Christine K)

> 'I narrowed the initial number down to the two I thought made the most interesting combination and who could be relied on to go through with the interview, turn up and participate. I also selected "reserve" informants .... This turned out to be a wise precaution as I did have to use a "reserve" ....' (Patricia E)

This does not mean that they should be friends. Many students found that interviewing 'friends' (or 'relatives') could be a mistake, for a variety of reasons. Note the difficulties reported by one student:

> 'I decided to interview Norma, a close friend of the family ... [with whom] ... I have got on well in the past. Because of our prior acquaintance, I felt that it would be easy to be straight with Norma, and therefore ask direct questions. However I am very conscious of people's feelings and was very aware of being too intrusive. I know that Norma is a proud lady, and I did not want to jeopardize our friendship by asking impertinent questions.' (Amanda B)

The most important one is that both sides care about the post-interview consequences, for themselves and their mutual circle, of having asked for and having given (or not given) 'revelations'. You are therefore both tempted to avoid asking 'dangerous-to-the-later-relationship' questions and giving 'dangerous-to-the-later-relationship' answers.

You need to think carefully about the best 'approach strategy' to adopt. The one you adopt without sufficient thought may undermine either the potential of that interview or those of other interviews.

- If you approach hourly-paid labourers in an organization within a framework of doing research for management, you may meet resistance to being interviewed or non-co-operation or slanted replies within the interview.
- If you obtain access differently (e.g. trade union official or relative of someone on the shop floor), you might get better results.
- But bear in mind: if you enter a mutually knowledgeable organization or network, such as a firm, getting good access to the shop floor by way of a trade union official may then spoil your chances of good access to middle-management, who may see you and your research as 'pro-union'.

Your 'personal reality' and social identity combine to be the 'instrument' with which you do interview research. *Nobody's personal and social identity is an appropriate research instrument for all informants.* You need to be similarly aware of the real personal and social identity of your informant to determine whether 'they' are a suitable research instrument for who you are and what you are asking of them.

Designing Sequenced Combinations of Interviewing Practices

As was said earlier, I am attempting to identify 'pure design elements' in order that sequenced combinations of such elements can be designed by you. I conclude the two

(1) Reading of the relevant published literature (if any).
This will enable me to get a sense of the area and what research questions arise but are not yet answered. On this basis, I would be able to prepare some quite precise questions and some very open questions for my first interview.

(2) My first interview will be with a professional researcher who has already done research on homeless people.
I would get a more up-to-the-minute sense of debates and material not yet in the published arena, and of how I might go about my research. He or she might also be an important source of contacts both with other professionals but also with those who could facilitate my contact with homeless people for eventual interviewing.

(3) My second interview, on the basis of the first, will be a very lightly structured interview with at least one case-worker whose task it is to deal with some numbers of homeless people and who has at least three years experience as a case-worker.
I will get a sense of issues and possibilities and priorities different from that to be gained from my previous interviewee since it comes from a field of constant practice and contact in a professional rather than a research role. Again, he or she should be a source of support who could facilitate eventual contact with homeless people themselves.

(4) Planning for eventual different types of interview with actual homeless people.

(5) The interviews and their analysis:
   (a) one intensive biographic-narrative interview run and analysed by the BNIM procedures
   (b) six biographic-narrative interviews run and analysed according to other procedures
   (c) several fairly-fully structured depth interviews not concerned with narrative, analysed appropriately
   (d) some survey research on large numbers for theory-testing.

(6) Presentation of results of my analysis in focus groups where first some homeless people and then professional researchers and professional caseworkers can group-interview me about my results.
This will enable me to be clearer about the validity and the relevance of my findings to different possible groups of research-users.

FIGURE 5.19   **SSDI in a Cycle of Research on Homelessness**

sections on concepts and approaches to the designing of sessions and the choosing of informants as well as the designing of theory-questions and informant-questions by briefly indicating some of the combinations you might wish to think about.

Sequenced Location of SSDIs in the Overall Research Cycle
I might decide that I wish to use SSDIs (semi-structured depth interviews) at a particular point in the research cycle. Assume I am interested in the experiences of homeless people. A possible sketch for one sequence of preparatory work is given in Figure 5.19. A sketch of this sort suggests the way that different types of research practice can be located over the research cycle.

Sequenced Combinations of Lightly Structured and Heavily Structured Interviews with the same Informant(s)
If our research cycle included only model-building and model-testing, I might have still two places to locate different types of SSDI with the same category of

person. For the exploratory phase I might have a very lightly structured depth interview (LSDI) in order to gather the maximum number of hypotheses about an area I am conscious of not knowing much about. Having developed some hypotheses and possibly used other methods (for example, a survey) in between, I might then do some very rigorous testing of a particular hypothesis through another depth interview at the end, but this time a fairly-fully structured depth interview (FFSDI) strongly structured by the theories I developed during the main period of the research after the exploratory phase.

In terms of Figure 5.19, I might have

(5) The interviews and their analysis:
    (5a) lightly structured exploratory interview to generate hypotheses
    (5b) survey method for testing of emergent hypotheses
    (5c) rigorous testing of crucial hypotheses through fairly-fully
        structured depth interview[8]

Obviously, this is just a simple example; the important point to remember is that the overall research cycle may locate interviews at different points in order to perform different functions.

Sequenced Combinations of Minimal, Active, Interrogational Listening, Prompting, Probing Tactics

Within a given session, there may be a planned sequence of types of interviewer practice. You may plan to start with minimal intervention so as to build up knowledge of, and rapport with, the interviewee, then shift to a more interrogational style, and then end with a much more relaxed and conversational mode. Alternatively, you may decide to start with a number of very precise small questions, then go to a more minimalist position with some very open questions, then conclude with more precise questions again, followed by an 'anything else you want to say?' concluding question. Swanson, in Chenitz and Swanson (1986: 74–5) discusses two possibilities:

'Gorden (1975) suggests the funnel/inverted funnel approach .... In the funnel approach, the interviewer starts with a general question, and follows with more specific questions. For example, the interviewer asks, "What do you think are some of the most important health problems found by women in today's world?". A more specific question follows: "Of all those you have mentioned, which one do you consider the most important to solve?". Yet a more specific question is asked: "Where have you received information about this problem?". This approach is used when: (1) the interviewer wants to discover unanticipated responses; (2) the respondent is motivated to give detailed description of an event or situation; and (3) the interviewer wants to avoid imposing his/her frame of reference on the respondent.

---

8 Alternatively, if I am very clear about the dimensions that I wish our theoretical model to focus upon, the first interview might be very strongly structured by the dimensions. The final interview might be very lightly structured in order to ensure that I was not contaminating the evidence, or it might be very strongly structured to ensure that all our hypotheses about all of the dimensions were taken into account.

The inverted funnel approach, in contrast, starts with specific questions and follows with more general questions. For example, the interviewer asks, "About how many staff members were on the unit when the power failed?". The following questions become more and more general: "How many additional staff came to the scene?", "How long did they have to wait until the emergency generator took over?", "Did anyone give emergency care on the ward?", "Did you?", "In general, how well do you think the emergency operations were carried out?". The use of the inverted funnel approach is helpful when: (1) the respondent is not motivated to speak spontaneously; (2) the respondent's experience is not important to him/her; and (3) the interviewer desires a judgment and facts are known to the respondent and not to the interviewer. Use of this approach will stimulate respondents to respond whole-heartedly and to base their judgments on the facts reviewed, in contrast to presenting facts solely as a rationale for initial judgments.'

Obviously such intended sequenced combinations are only your plans; the strength of semi-structured depth interviewing is that actual contact with the interviewee may and should lead to your revising your initial plans in order to fit the person and the situation as it actually arises.

Such a readiness to revise plans should *never* be taken as a suggestion that it is better to have made no plans at all. The process of making any plan has as its major function that of forcing you to think carefully through the issues that might arise and the strengths and weaknesses of handling them in different ways: it is that thinking that needs to occur beforehand. *Carefully developing some plan is the best way of achieving this general state of readiness.*

SUMMARY

So far, I have completed the abstract design of some of the components of interview design:

- Research purposes
- Conceptual frameworks
- Research questions – CRQ/TQs
- Selection of informants relevant in principle for some sort of SSDI.

I have not moved to the identification of what sequenced combination of lightly structured or fairly-fully structured SSDI sessions I wish to undertake. Neither have I considered the question of what prepared and unprepared interview questions (IQs) and other interviewer interventions (IIs) I wish to make – and refrain from making – in such sessions to get materials for their TQs. In terms of the Rose–Wengraf diagram (Figure 3.1, p. 55), I have not operationalized or instrumented the theory-concepts and theory-questions. In terms of the Maxwell–Wengraf diagram (Figure 3.3, p. 59), I have not yet moved to the left-hand position on the bottom line.

I now move to that bottom line of the designing of interview sessions and particularly of interview questions and other interventions. I deal first with a type of lightly structured depth interview design and then with more conventional moderately and heavily structured interview designs.

Our example of a lightly structured interview design will be that of biographical narrative interview based on an initial single-question aimed at inducing a biographical narrative. Even those who do not wish to develop lightly-structured depth interviews (LSDIs) such as single-question narrative interviews may find it useful to skim through the next chapter before going on to Chapter 7. It deals in detail with issues that are then dealt with in a more varied way in the chapter on moderately and heavily structured depth interviews. Ideally, therefore, read both in order.

However, if you are in a hurry to design your fairly-fully structured research, and as long as you are prepared to go back to the chapter you skipped, then pass over the next chapter and move directly to Chapter 7.

6

Preparing Lightly-Structured Depth Interviews: A Design for a BNIM-Type Biographic-Narrative Interview

I now proceed to the discussion in detail of developing the general CRQ–TQ specification into a design for a lightly structured depth interview (LSDI). I will do this by giving very precise details of one particular type of LSDI, namely that developed by the biographic-narrative-interpretive method (BNIM) approach. This restricts interviewer interventions initially to a single (narrative) initial question, and, until a subsequent late stage in the designed multi-session interview process, interviewer interventions remain very restricted.

After this, I proceed, in Chapter 7, to develop the general CRQ–TQ model into a design for fairly-fully structured interviewing (FFSDI). After completing the reading of both of these sections, you will have completed the book's application of the CRQ–TQ–II model to the designing of interview sessions at both the very structured and the very unstructured ends of the spectrum. You should therefore be in a position to design complex combinations anywhere within that spectrum.

'SINGLE QUESTION AIMED AT INDUCING NARRATIVE (SQUIN)' IN CONTEXT: AN INSTRUMENTATION THEORY AND A DESIGN FOR NARRATIVE INTERVIEWING

Overview

An interview design that focuses on the elicitation and provocation of story-telling, of narration, can be called a narrative interview design. After noting that there are a variety of ways of designing interviews to elicit narratives, I focus on a particular design: that which starts from a single initial narrative question, and a particular focus of such a question – part or all of the individual's life story, their biography. I conclude by outlining the purposes of such biographic narrative interviewing and the instrumentation theory that justifies such a design strategy.

> Narration is not the only type of verbal performance that a lightly structured or single-question strategy might focus on eliciting. Others are dealt with in the following section, but I might just note examples. An example of a single question designed to induce an expression of explicit values/ideology might be 'What is the most important thing

in the world for you?; to induce theorizing about the self, a self-theory, 'How do you explain the way you are?'; to induce a description of the life-world, 'How would you describe the world in which you live?', etc. Further discussion of questioning not designed to induce narrative flow but other types of verbal flow can be found on p. 162 onwards.

Similarly, not all narrative questioning need ask for biographical narrative. Roe (1994) is concerned with policy narratives, and others are concerned with particular life-events, critical incidents, the histories of organizations and so forth.

Variability of Narrative Interview Designs

In some types of narrative interview design there is quite a high level of rapid interviewer intervention as the informant unfolds his or her narrative account. McLeod (1997: 120; and p. 202) cites Sluzki's (1992) range of therapist interventions ('transformative micro-practices: invitations to narrative change') that may, in narrative *therapy*, be used by the therapist during the narrative flow. The narrator is asked to justify their narrative, explain it, deal with alternative stories, etc.

Clearly, the researcher wedded strongly to a receptive mode of interviewing will not engage in such an operation, except reluctantly. Holstein and Gubrium, active interviewers, might press such 'invitations' to narrative change quite early on in the narrative flow, and quite forcibly (Holstein and Gubrium, 1995). Clearly, therapists – concerned to *change* the mode of functioning of an individual – will definitely be active disruptors, but active narrative researchers working in a semi-structured mode may well do some rather similar things.

However, the design of narrative interviews I present in this book in detail is characterized by a more minimalist interviewer intervention. I shall deal with such a mode of narrative interviewing partly on its own merits, and partly because it *does* stand at an extreme end of the research interview intervention spectrum and illuminates the whole spectrum from that position. I also briefly present different, more structured, designs for biographic-narrative interviewing on pp. 145–49 onwards. Partly, too, because learning this extreme form is a difficult but powerful method for learning how to not-intervene and how to listen – very difficult for those 'naturally' trained to intervene in interviews because they love participating in conversations. It is therefore a good practice within which to start to become a research interviewer.

The steps and modes of interviewing and analysis of the biographic-narrative-interpretive method (in future in this text, BNIM) have been developed in the context of interactionist and phenomenological research traditions by Gabriele Rosenthal and Wolfram Fischer-Rosenthal (see references). In their academic teaching and research since the late 1970s and in specific training seminars of their Berlin-based *QUATEXT: Institute for qualitative social research*, they combined and developed the practical skills of narrative-style interviewing as introduced by linguists like Labov and Waletzky (1967), in Germany by Fritz Schütze (1977, 1992), with elements of 'grounded theory' (Glaser and Strauss), phenomenological sociology of knowledge (Alfred Schütz; Aron Gurwitsch; Peter Berger and Thomas Luckmann) and structural-hermeneutic analysis (Oevermann, 1979). The achievement of Rosenthal and Fischer-Rosenthal is their focus on biography and its methodical and sociological elaboration (see in general Fischer-Rosenthal, 1995, 2000). Biographical communication is used both as a research tool and also as a means of structuring modern society via biographical work and schemes.

On the level of interviewing and producing textual data Rosenthal and Fischer-Rosenthal refined and profiled a mode of narrative questioning, as will be shown below. On the level of analysis they produced a set of techniques and methods of triangulation in order to reconstruct case histories and their typologies with respect to lived, experienced, and narrated life (for the complete model and this distinction, see the basic texts of Rosenthal, 1993, 1995). The complete model of this biographical case reconstruction is represented explicitly in Fischer-Rosenthal and Rosenthal (1997a, 1997b, 2000) (see, as exemplary, a one-case analysis by Fischer-Rosenthal, 1996). This biographical reconstruction is not restricted to the sociological understanding of persons (as acting units in society) but is also aimed at the understanding of society in its historical and social structures (limiting and enabling interaction).

This is why the school's approach to biographical interviewing and analysis – called BNIM throughout this text – can be used as a tool for a wide variety of research questions.

As for the interviewing part, with which I am now dealing, its characteristic is that the interviewee's primary response is determined by a single question (asking for a narrative) which is not followed-up, developed, or specified in any way during that subsession. In this first subsession, after the posing of the initial narrative-seeking question, interventions by the interviewer are effectively limited to facilitative noises and non-verbal support. Any other type of intervention effectively terminates the session with extreme prejudice to the research purpose of the BNIM interview. (There are two other subsessions in this three-subsession design, which I deal with later.)

This makes it rather distinctive. One way of understanding the philosophy behind a minimalist-passive reception of interview narrative is that of the *Gestalt* principle, as discussed briefly above (p. 125), which requires the spontaneous pattern of the speaker to complete itself fully and so be fully exposed for analysis.

Single-question Interview Sessions

Single Question – Minimum Further Intervention
One of the prejudicial assumptions and mythologies of many research interview interactions is that of the 'conversation' where each partner participates equally. Indeed, together with the researcher's idea that he or she 'should run' the interview, the model of the conversation where there can be unrestricted participation by the interviewer can – despite the best intentions of both – turn into that of the strongly structured and strongly controlled pedagogic interrogation (or therapy session).

Within BNIM, on the other hand, in the interview session in which your content-full contribution is limited to a Single Question (aimed at *Inducing Narrative*), a SQUIN, and in which all your other interventions are reduced to a minimum and drained of any particular content, for as long as possible you give up control, refuse to take up offers of partial control, and maintain the maximum of power-asymmetry *against* yourself. The Briggs–Wengraf power see-saw (Figure 2.6) stays strongly tilted towards the silence of the interviewer.[1]

---

1 Silence can be a form of exercising power; at this point I am dealing with a simple model of the overt use of power.

A Variety of TQs can be Served by SQUINs

Such biographic-narrative material is relevant to a variety of theory-questions (TQs): I may be interested in the individual's biography for his or her own sake; I may be interested in that biography because the individual is being treated as a sample case of a particular type of person or their history is expected to show the working of particular social mechanisms in a given culture or milieu; I may be interested in particular ways of thinking, feeling and doing that I hope will be revealed by the individual's biographical account of their life in particular contexts in a particular historical time. I may be interested in a combination of some of the above, and quite different things, besides.

If I am interested in biographical narratives for their own sake, if our TQ is about such accounts, then obviously (single or several) questions inducing biographical narrative are what I am going to use.

If however our TQs are not about biographical narratives as such but about other theoretical entities – such as basic cultural assumptions, psychological strategies, historical contexts, sociological mechanisms, etc. – as indeed they may be, then I must be prepared to *justify by an appropriate instrumentation theory* (Rose–Wengraf diagram, Figure 3.1, p. 55) why I think that collecting biographical narratives in a particular way and processing the data according to certain procedures will help to produce answers for TQs that are *not* intrinsically biographical.

Such an 'instrumentation theory' or justification is required because information about basic cultural assumptions, about psychological strategies, about historical contexts, about sociological mechanisms, etc. can be gathered by means other than biographical narratives of particular persons, and for many purposes they should be. Some of these other methods of data-collection may involve semi-structured depth-interviewing that is non-narrative and moderately or strongly structured (as suggested in the next chapter). Others may not involve any form of semi-structured depth-interviewing at all, but rather the study of documents, participant observation, psychological tests, and other modes of social research.

There has however been, in the last two decades or so, an upsurge in the interest in biographical narration as a source of material relevant to a variety of social research purposes (see the introduction to Chamberlayne et al., 2000). There are good and bad reasons for this: I shall here just suggest some of the good reasons put forward by proponents of biographical narrative methods.

To do so, however, I need to have a clear and useful model of what meaning can be given to the concept of 'narrative'.

Narrative in Itself and as a TQ–IQ Indicator

What is 'a narrative' anyway?

The (Western) Genre of Narrative (Labov and Waletsky)

Much research has gone into the study of narratives. In this discussion, I shall deal only with the genre of narrative as it has developed in Western cultures, leaving open the question as to whether this genre is a universal for all cultures (as some Western researchers believe) or whether story-telling in other cultures may be organized differently.

In Western culture, when asked to tell the story of their life, normally socialized adults have a culturally developed sense of what is required by the genre. This largely unconscious sense operates perhaps the more strongly for being less conscious.

A classic account of the components of narrative was provided by Labov and Waletsky in 1967.[2] McLeod (1997: 47; see also 28–53) summarizes their account as follows:

'Labov and Waletsky (1967), working with spoken rather than written language, suggest that the grammatical structure of stories found in everyday dialogue consists of six key elements.

1. First of all, the teller offers an "abstract", in effect a summary of the story.
2. Woven into this may be "orientation" information in which time, place, and persons are identified.
3. Then follows the "complicating action" which comprises the core of the narrative, and takes the form of a series of clauses describing "what happened next".
4. There is then a "resolution" which conveys the result of the action.
5. An "evaluation" in which the teller conveys the point of the story.
6. A "coda" which returns the speakers to their present, here-and-now situation.'

This has been schematized (by Linell and Jonsson, 1991: 87) as shown in Figure 6.1. The description makes it clear that the classical narrative has (i) a kernel of a Central Event Sequence. Prior to this core narration, I find (ii) a description of background in order to orient the listener for the narration to follow and, after the completion of the (iii) central event sequence, (iv) a further description of the new situation that has arisen as a result of the narrated action (which might be a restoration of the status quo) and, finally, (v) then an evaluation or explicit theory of the significance of the events narrated, its 'moral'.

We can see that a 'narrative' in the narrow sense (sequence of events) is only part of a 'complete narration' (account).

Embedded Versus Articulable Norms and Knowledge

One of the key arguments used to justify narrative research is that many of the assumptions and purposes, feelings and knowledge, that have organized and organize a person's or a society's life are difficult to access directly. The less contested and controversial they are, the less an interviewee will be aware of them and able to talk about them. Conversely, to ask for a person's explicit knowledge and approach is to access only material that they themselves experience as consciously controversial and needing articulation and therefore capable of fairly quick articulation in words.

In addition, the people responding have considerable conscious control of how they present and argue such explicit knowledge and norms. Goffmann, *The Presentation of Self in Everyday Life* (1959) is the classic locus for a powerful framework for understanding the presentation of self, even in everyday research interviews.

The advantage of narrative, say the narratologists, is that, *precisely by what it assumes and therefore does not focus upon*, narrative conveys tacit and unconscious assumptions and norms of the individual or of a cultural group. At least in some respects, they are less subject to the individual's conscious control.

I find this a convincing argument and one proven in practice. Clearly, narrative in the broad sense of a 'complete account' with all the components identified by

---

2 See also the special 1997 issue of the *Journal of Narrative and Life History*, Volume 7.

Abstract 'what it is going to be about'	ABSTRACT
Orientation 'relevant background'	BACKGROUND
Complicating action 'something disturbing the normal'	
Events	CENTRAL EVENT SEQUENCE
Climax 'turning point, resulting in'	'NARRATION'
Resolution 'returning to [a new?] normality'	
Evaluation: 'the point of the story'	EVALUATION
Coda 'that was it'	CODA

FIGURE 6.1   **Labov and Waletsky on Narrative (Simplified and modified from Linell and Jonsson, 1991: 87)**

Labov and Waletsky *also* conveys the narrator's *explicit* assumptions and norms as well, for example, in the Coda or Evaluation where we find explicit evaluative theorizing, but there the evaluative theorizing is being done in a concrete relation to particular event-stories (rather than in just an abstract fashion as might happen in an 'attitude' survey), and is sometimes contradicted or 'exceeded' by them.

Narratologists, therefore, argue that biographical narratives are powerfully expressive (and so symptomatic indicators) of the natures of particular persons, cultures and milieux, and they are valuable instruments for a large range of social and psychological research theory-questions *because* they present to the researcher embedded and tacit assumptions, meanings, reasonings and patterns of action and inaction.

The Constraints of Narrative Practice on Self-representations (Schutze/Alheit et al.)

This argument should be spelled out in a little more detail. Normally, as I discussed when analysing interview interaction and the models of Foddy (p. 39) and Briggs (p. 43), the individual is likely to experience themselves as being 'at risk' within the interview interaction and will consequently have an interest in representing themselves and their life-world in one way rather than in another to the interviewer and, through the interviewer, to anybody who reads about them in any publication that might emerge. Consequently, the self-representation of the interviewee is also a self-preserving self-presentation, and a strong argument against the 'validity' of narrative-biographical evidence has been made as follows:

> 'By attempting to reconstruct the memory of the past, [a narrated life history] becomes a 'retrospective illusion' determined equally by the past, the present, and the future. It is not only the person one has become that speaks when life history is being narrated, but also the person one would like to be (in the future, too). Narrated life history thus becomes the presentation of a self-image serving to protect the identity of the subject in question, an ontology of self, a mythology.' (Osterland, 1983: 285, cited Alheit, 1994: 10)[3]

Alheit, who cites the above critique, argues against some of its implications. He argues that one of the singular aspects of biographical narrative is that the genre, once the speaker accepts to 'do narrative', has certain compelling effects of its own upon the verbal flow of the speaker. This restricts, or makes obvious, attempts to evade certain aspects. The best account I have found of this is quite difficult – the translator has not solved the problem of translation from the German at all satisfactorily – but is at least suggestive:

> 'Narration itself, as a medium of recapitulation, also contains zugzwang (interactive compulsion) elements that cannot be violated arbitrarily (Kallmeyer and Schütze, 1977; Schütze, 1982, 1984). Anyone consenting to give a biographical narrative ... is compelled to accept certain interaction norms that are relatively fixed (for the following details, see Schütze, 1982: 577ff).
>
> Every event worth recounting has specific contours; it possesses a prehistory as well as a history of successive events [future consequences?]. If the narrator wishes to present the special nature of the event, he becomes compelled to develop "a design of the event". This is the "compulsion to complete the gestalt", Gestaltschliessungszwang.
>
> At the same time, he is also pressurized to narrate only what is really indispensable to the relevance of what is recapitulated, so that the real point of the narrated story can be elaborated. This is the "compulsion to condense", Kondensierungszwang.
>
> In doing so, however, the decisive links between the "event modes" must be carefully presented so that the course of events can be understood, not only by the narrator himself, but also by the non-involved listener. This is the "compulsion to go into enough detail to make causal assumptions and connections clear", Detaillerungszwang.' (Alheit, 1994: 12, modified)

As we shall see, the attempts by the interviewee to avoid the compulsions of narrative – sometimes by a simple refusal to narrate, sometimes by inadequate detailing or peculiarities of 'drawing the moral of the story', sometimes by interrupting the story-telling by digressions into other sorts of speech-activity and in

---

3 An echo of the Briggs–Wengraf notion of past and future histories. However, some narrative accounts are attempts to *modify* the identify of the subject, and to do the opposite of *preserving* a former one.

other ways – provide the researcher with as many clues to personal and cultural reality as does the explicit narrative content itself. I shall deal with this in the chapter analysing biographic-narrative interview materials (Chapter 12). I just signal it here. The events that the individual does not talk about or make clear, the 'moral of the story' that does not seem to follow, the 'way of reacting to a particular event', the way of talking about something that seems odd and slightly or grossly inappropriate … all these appear in the flow of a biographical narration, and can be reflected upon later by the researcher.

To sum up. Narratologists argue that narrative is peculiarly difficult for the speaker to control completely, and therefore it provides less capacity for conscious and unconscious manipulation by the speaker. This is the instrumentation theory (see discussion of the 'gap' between theoretical concepts and empirical indicators discussed on pp. 60–3 above) that justifies the use of biographical narrative as valuable material for answering many theory-questions that are not formally concerned with biographical narrative as such.[4]

Stories of action and inaction enable the researcher to consider both the conscious and the unconscious *contexts and conditions* of action as well as the observed and the less observed *consequences* of action.

Having attempted to indicate in principle why the elicitation of biographical narrative material may be seen as generating particularly rich and usable empirical material for a variety of social research questions – though this does not mean accepting any given narrative account at face value, rather the opposite – I shall now turn to the pragmatics of eliciting such narratives.

THE DESIGN OF SQUINS FOR THE PURPOSE OF THE BIOGRAPHIC-NARRATIVE-INTERPRETIVE METHOD (BNIM)

The subsections that follow could not have been written without the training and the materials provided by Roswitha Breckner und Susanne Rupp. As members of the international SOSTRIS research team (Sostris, 1999), working at the University of East London and elsewhere, qualified in the methods which they have been using as researchers and training others within SOSTRIS and in the further vocational seminars for researchers at the *QUATEXT: Institute for qualitative social research, eV, Berlin*, they provided me with the complete model, its basic structure, detailed material and necessary exercises. Format, contents and didactical structures of the method and methodology have been developed in QUATEXT seminars over the last ten years and academically by the institute's seniors and directors Gabriele Rosenthal (1993, 1995, 1998) and Wolfram Fischer-Rosenthal (cf. Fischer-Rosenthal and Rosenthal, 1997a, 1997b, 2000).

Many of the formulations and exercises in this text are taken straight from such materials, and I am very grateful for permission to do so. Neither particular individuals nor the QUATEXT collective are responsible for the use I make of such materials in this text, which differs in certain respects from the original at least in terminology. I have also developed the corpus in ways that I hope are helpful.

---

4 There are other celebrations of the narrative form which identify it as the most complete mode of thinking, man as an essentially story-telling animal, etc., but such arguments are not necessary for the purpose of understanding the value of narrative material for a large range of social research questions.

Overview: Three Subsessions, and Usually at Least Two Interviews

The Biographic-Narrative-Interpretive Method (BNIM) interview is composed of three subsessions. The second subsession should occur relatively soon after the first, and can perhaps best follow on after a 15 minute break, while the third subsession requires at least a preliminary analysis of the results of the first two. The need for the third subsession is variable; it is always useful but may not always be necessary. The first two subsessions are normally scheduled on the same day, and may be experienced by the interviewee as a single session, while there would be *at least a week's interval and perhaps a month or so* between the second subsession and the third one.

The design only produces its desired effects, in terms of the types of material produced, if the interviewer's behaviour specified for each of the first two subsessions is strictly adhered to.

Subsession 1: Initial Elaboration of Story Around Topics
In the first subsession, the interviewer asks a single initial question designed to elicit the full narrative, a single carefully designed question which I have called a SQUIN,[5] and indicates that there will be no interruptions or 'helpful prompts'. The kernel of the classic form is this:

> 'I would like you to tell me your life story, all the events and experiences which were important for you.
>
> Start wherever you like. Please take the time you need.
> I'll listen first, I won't interrupt, I'll just take some notes for afterwards.'

The interviewee is encouraged to answer this question with, if necessary, reassurances and prompts for more story. On no account should you as interviewer change this question or 'spell it out' in any way, whatever pressure you feel yourself to be under.

While the story is being told in this first subsession – which might last five or ten minutes, or might last two or three hours – you note down the topics that the narration is about. You need to learn a special type of topic note-taking to be used in subsession 1. This is described on pp. 131–35.

> Both the practice of self-restraint *to avoid* 'directional supporting' and to *achieve non-directional supporting,* as well as the *practice of topic note-taking* for subsession 2, requires a fair amount of self-training in co-operation with somebody else.

The initial narration continues until the interviewee indicates clearly that they have no more to say: there should then be at least a *15-minute break* for you to review your notes and prepare questions.[6]

Subsession 2: Extracting More Story from the Topics
In subsession 2 – which is best done on the same day or, if the narration is very long, in a follow-up interview as soon as possible later – the interviewer asks for

---

5 Single Question Aimed at Inducing Narrative. Hence the notion of SQUIN–BNIM.

6 I have found such a break helpful, particularly in training. However, Fischer-Rosenthal and Rosenthal advise against such a break because they want to keep up the co-operation and spirit of trust, which has just been developed, for further joint text-production in subsession 2.

more story about the topics that were raised in that initial narration, following strictly the order in which they were raised and using the words (the language, the key words and phrases, the terms of the discourse) of the interviewee in respect of those topics. The question is strictly for more story, designed to elicit more narrating about the topics initially raised. No question can be asked which is not a story-eliciting one; no question can be raised about a topic not raised by the interviewee in the initial narration. Nor can a question about a 'raised topic' be put out of sequence. There is 'directionality' given by the interviewer in this subsession, but it is highly restricted. During the subsession, while the interviewee is responding, you continue to note the topics as they arise, for yet further follow-up questioning.

> This type of 'return to narrative' prompting and questioning required in subsession 2 requires oddly-difficult work to get right. What is most difficult is to learn to ask 'narrative-pointed' questions only. Whereas much semi-structured interviewing (and subsession 3) fosters asking 'open-ended questioning' (a practice difficult in itself to learn, see pp. 163–64 onwards), subsession 2 requires using only questions that are (in one sense) strictly closed because they attempt to *exclude* non-narrative answers.

> In subsession 1, you can only ask the one SQUIN; in subsession 2, you are restricted to the topics raised by the interviewee, and to asking only narrative-pointed questions about them (TQUINs): *T*opic *Qu*estion aimed at *In*ducing *N*arrative.

> The more you have been socialized into other modes of interviewing (open-questions, therapeutic counselling, etc.), the harder it will be for you to learn to ask only 'narrative-pointed' questions (TQUINs) in subsession 2 about the topics explicitly raised in subsession 1. How to do this is dealt with later (p. 126 onwards).

When this sequence of 'following the topics and asking for more story' has been completed, and not until, then the *first interview* (two subsessions) is over. Immediately afterwards and in private, as undisturbed as possible, you then complete your *self-debriefing* (see pp. 142–44 below).

Subsession 3 – Further Questions Arising from Preliminary Analysis of Subsessions 1 and 2

The last subsession – subsession 3 – is always a separate interview. To prepare for it, you will need to have completed a preliminary analysis at least of the materials gathered so far in subsessions 1 and 2. On the basis of that preliminary analysis and in the light of your research purposes and theory-questions, you will develop a set of questions which *may include* – but probably *won't be restricted to* – the type of narrative-pointed 'asking for story' questions to which sessions 1 and 2 are restricted. Strategically, subsession 3 is completely structured by the interviewer's concerns which gives a strong directionality to the flow of the interview. Here any questions can be asked about 'topics not mentioned'; *the questions need have nothing to do with 'narrative' at all.*

But though subsession 3 of a narrative interview using the BNIM approach may not have a single narrative question in it, the previous two subsessions have *only* narrative questions in them.

I shall now deal with each of these subsession activities of the SQUIN–BNIM method in more detail.

Subsession 1 and Interviewer Self-restraint: Note-taking, Active Listening with Non-directional Prompts but Never Probes

Full and Partial SQUINs

The Full SQUIN Request for 'Biographical Narrative' The question *addressing the life story* is the most open framework, in which the interview*ee* can decide in the course of the interview, how, when and in which contexts he or she introduces relevant aspects of his or her personal experiences.

> This field always is already to some extent focused since, during the search for interviewees, at the moment of initial contact, the research-project was presented in some fashion prior to the interview itself; consequently, this need not to be repeated in the initial question. You will need to have decided, prior to this initial presentation of the project to the prospective interviewee, how strong and clear or how weak or fuzzy you wish their awareness of project details to be. You may wish to be very vague or very precise, very transparent or rather inexplicit. This is a technical and ethical question. You must always think hard about the in-interview and post-interview implications of the choices you make about such 'pre-interview framing'. Technically, the weaker such earlier framing, the less their in-interview gestalt is affected by their pre-interview awareness of your framing.

The SQUIN for subsession 1 is as follows:

> 'I want you to tell me your life story,
> all the events and experiences which were important for you, up to now.
> Start wherever you like.
> Please take the time you need.
> *I'll listen first, I won't interrupt,*
> *I'll just take some notes for after you've finished telling me about your experiences.'*

NB: note the final italicized phrases. At the end of all initial questions (SQUINs), don't forget to add these phrases.

Requests for Partial Biographical Narratives[7] Most initial SQUINs are more restricted than the above 'completely open' 'whole life story' version, though for many purposes the above version is the best.

Some examples of thematically or temporally focused, but open, initial questions (1 and 2):

1 The question can be *conceptually focused* on a phase of life (e.g. youth), a specific biographical strand (e.g. professional career, family, etc.), biographically relevant historical phases (e.g. wartime). Any *temporal focus* should be formulated in a fuzzy pro-subjective way such that the interviewee decides, at which point in the 'objective' or 'historical time', the focused time-period begins and ends for him/her personally. For example:

---

7 QUATEXT material. The original English version by Roswitha Breckner, mainly following Rosenthal (1993, 1995) has been slightly modified.

> 'I want you to tell me about your youth / your professional career / the war ... , maybe you could start by telling me about the time that adolescence / the war / the working life began for you personally / became important for you personally ... and continue telling how things developed for you ... up to this period / came to an end in your personal experience / up to now.'

So, try *not* to pre-empt by giving indications like 'from 1939 to 1945' 'from confirmation up to marriage' / 'from the first employment up to your dismissal or retirement'. The interviewee should always be given the space/required to decide when and how to start the story, and what initial descriptive background or prologue (if any) they feel is needed, and when and how to end the story.

2   The initial question can focus on *special issues/topics:* e.g. the experience of a migration / an illness / a segment of college or professional life etc. Here also a non-specific temporal perspective should be established in order to evoke a narration. Narrations refer always to things happening *over a period of time*. They presuppose a temporal perspective. For example,

> 'Please tell me about your experience of xyz ... since it became important in your life, how things happened, up to now?'

In designing SQUINs for particular uses, the principle of deliberate vagueness which allows and requires the interviewee to impose their own system of relevancy on a fuzzy possibility is always adhered to.[8]

Given the absolute centrality of the SQUIN in the crucial first subsession, it must be carefully designed, written out in full, and delivered without modification.

Figure 6.2 provides a set of phrases and formulations with which you can compose a SQUIN appropriate for your Research Purposes and for the Central Research Question of your research project.

Severely Restricted 'Facilitative Non-directional' Support: Relaunching

In subsession 1, an interview session devoted to enabling the informant to provide a narration responding to the carefully designed SQUIN, the role of the interviewer is not to ask questions about the story, but just to enable the story to be told in the way the informant feels comfortable telling it. You are trying to get them to complete their spontaneous gestalt. *You are a story-facilitator.*

Any questions you may have about the story – and you will have many, all feeling very urgent – *should not be asked in the initial narrative session*. Such further questions *should be kept back*.

> This simple rule – just keep facilitating the story-telling, occasionally asking for more story, but never specifying what it would be about, never specifying the referent – feels unnatural and is very difficult to follow.

---

8 There is a parallel with the work of Neuro-Linguistic Programming (NLP) which starts from Chomsky's transformational grammar to stress the impact of incomplete specification and deliberate fuzziness for a subjectivity-evoking set of purposes. See Bandler and Grinder (1975).

List of Single Questions Aimed at Inducing Narratives

1. Can you please tell me about how ... happened ... and
   how it all turned out ... the/your story of ...
   your experience of ...

2. all those events and experiences which were important for you,
   how it all developed up to now/till it stopped being personally relevant

3. You could start around the time ... began for you personally
   The period in your life when ... became personally important
   when you started ... .

4. Begin wherever you like.

5. Please take the time you need ... // We've got about ...
   minutes/ ... hours

6. *I'll listen first, I won't interrupt, //*
   I'll tell you if we are running seriously out of time //
   I'll just take some notes for after you've finished telling me
   about the experiences which have been important for you

A. *Full SQUIN*   The life story

B. *Conceptual focus*

   A specific phase of life   e.g. youth; getting old; during the war
   A specific biographical strand   e.g. professional work; family
   A specific strand and phase   e.g. your family during the war

> The temporal focus for any question should be formulated
> 'pro-subjectively', not specifying time or event,
> so that it is the interviewee
> who decides where and when, for him or her,
> 'it' starts and 'it' finishes

C. *Special issues or topics*

   A migration   A personal experience of a collective
                                       historical event
   An illness or period of
     bad health   A type of situation, or relationship
   A segment of personal life
   Your overall project CRQ translated into ordinary speech

FIGURE 6.2 **SQUINs Design Sheet**

It is crucial, though, that you do *keep back all your questions*, whether you understand what is said or not, whether you see 'the point' or not. Your questions, from your system of relevancy, come later.[9]

---

9 This rule, like all others, should not be followed to the point at which you have no idea about who or what is being talked about. We recently recorded a Frenchwoman with a very complex extended family history who never mentioned any proper names of persons or places. She jumped about between generations and situations, and referred only to 'he' and 'she'. I became hopelessly lost, and playing back the tape only compounded the confusion. Had I asked before the interview for a family tree, I could then during subsession I have asked whether she was talking about Uncle X or Uncle Y when she jumped to

continued

Very briefly, in the first and second session of the BNIM narrative interview, you are helping the informant uncover the life-history that is relevant to him or her, helping the interviewee to follow their own 'systems of relevancy'. To do this, you must put your own system of relevancy (as would be expressed in your spontaneous questions) to one side until later (subsession three).

In Figure 6.2, a number of phrases are offered on the basis of which you could compose your own partial SQUIN for subsession 1. These are to be found in the box in the top half of the figure. You should note that it will typically consist of five components all of which should be delivered as a whole.

The components in the top box can be understood as follows:

1 This identifies the overall topic for an overarching narration, and alternative possibilities for this topic can be found under A, B and C on the remainder of the figure.
2 This stresses the plurality of events and experiences of which the over-arching topic-narrative is liable to be composed.
3 This is relevant for any specified partial topic – not for the whole life-history.
4 This is crucial to avoid forcing a chronological discipline onto the informant.
5 Where the time does have to be formally limited, give a rough limit in hours or minutes, but do try, in the interview, *not* to constrain the time strongly. If necessary, reduce your planned allocation of time for subsession 2. *It is more important that the interviewee takes the time they need to complete their initial narration* in subsession 1 than that you ask questions in an immediate subsession 2. If necessary, you can always reschedule subsession 2 for a later date, but the informant has only the subsession 1 chance to tell and complete the story in his or her way.
6 This is important so that the informant knows that they will not be interrupted and that they don't need to worry about time. It also restates 'experiences' in the plural to facilitate little narratives as a component of the overarching story and to stress the expected subjectivity of the account.

To begin with, stick to the formulations above, omitting the phrases which don't seem to be liable to work.

Once you have worked out your version, then write it out carefully for you to use at the beginning of the session, and stick to it. Don't be tempted by the interviewee to give any more 'directions': if, for example, they say 'Where would you like me to start?' just refuse to suggest a starting place or suggest that no one alternative is better than another; simply respond 'Wherever suits you' so as to re-emphasize that it is their choice. If they ask you to give them more precise (semi-structured interview) questions, just repeat that you want to know how it all was for them and that you don't have any special questions. This is the importance of the 'pro-subjective vagueness' identified as necessary in the second box in the figure:

'The second world war' is a better phrase than the '1939–45 war' because for people in Central Europe or Spain, German attacks and invasions started well before 1939; for

---

continued

speaking about what the un-specified uncle's response was to this or that event. But only when you start feeling *completely* at sea should you break the rule of not interrupting the system of relevancy of the interviewee, and you should do it as unobtrusively as possible.

Americans the war only started after Pearl Harbor in 1941; for many people their 'sense of the war' started sometime in the 1930s peculiar to them, and, for many, 'the war' by no means stopped on a particular day in 1945.

Even if, as a private individual, you would love to indulge your own system of relevancies and impose them on the speaker, *as a professional* doing this type of interview, *in such a session*, you mustn't do it, not before subsession 3.

To avoid misunderstanding, in nearly all actual 'single-question narrative sessions', you may well have to restate the initial question in a number of ways, all amounting to the words 'Is there any more story you can tell me?...'. You may also have to re-assure the informant that you really want them to go on telling the story in the way they are telling it, that they are 'doing OK'. But such contributions from you do not violate the 'SQUIN' principle. Your interventions must be facilitative but – apart from being oriented towards facilitating narrative by narrative-pointed questions – non-directional.

Concept of Non-directional Facilitative Support   The concept of non-directional support is, in one way, merely a rewriting of Freud's original concept of 'free association'. However, the term of 'non-directive counselling' is particularly connected to the work of Carl Rogers (e.g. 1978) who developed suggestions as to how such an attitude of mind and practice could be developed and expressed.

While Freud and Rogers are concerned to promote *therapeutic* experience, this is definitely not the concern of the BNIM researcher. We deviate from the free association rule by framing the interaction as a research interview rather than a session of psychoanalysis or of therapy or of counselling. We also deviate because we start the first session by a request not for any free association but for a very specific type of account: a biographical narrative.

Having started the first subsession in this way, however, and thus given it a very specific direction, we then – for the rest of the subsession – refuse to give any more direction to the interviewee: at most, we repeat in different words the original direction given, but refusing to add anything to it. After that initial framing as a research interview, and after the SQUIN question giving a specific directive to the interviewee, we then shift to something rather like the role prescribed by Freud and Rogers. We avoid giving any further directions or directionality to the interviewee in order that their spontaneous *gestalt* is given the space to express itself.

Some interviewees – once they are quite sure that they have really been given the permission inherent in the SQUIN question – start talking and don't require any interviewer intervention at all. In this case, all you have to do as interviewer is to listen attentively and keep careful track of the topics raised by the interviewee and make the requisite notes for subsession 2 (I deal with this below).

Most interviewees, however, may need to be *actively supported but not directed* in their narrating activity. Such need for active non-directional support is likely to be felt particularly at the start of the session – where the interviewee is making sure that you meant what you said in the SQUIN and that he or she is giving you what you want. After that, intermittently throughout the subsession, you may need to give further reassurance in this direction.

Your task is always to *remain actively listening* – interviewees will immediately sense when you have stopped listening to them, and this 'no longer listening' will end or distort the expression of their gestalt – *and always to be prepared to notice that*

Topics in the order mentioned and in the terms used by the interviewee		Plausible questions which only 'allow for' a narrative response but don't point very strongly at one, or indeed 'point elsewhere'	Questions 'pointed at narrative' (TQUINs)
Father		Can you tell me more about your father? What do you think/feel about your father?	Can you remember any event involving your father?
Mother	'angry when I was small'	What was it like?	Can you remember a situation when you were small and she was angry?
	'hit me when I wouldn't go to school'	Did you feel she was justified at the time? How did you / do you explain her behaviour? Why do you think that happened? What do you think was the result of that?	You said she hit you when you wouldn't go to school. Can you remember how that came about? Can you tell me in more detail how that happened?
Always feeling stupid		What was it like, to always feel stupid? What do you mean by 'feeling stupid'?	Can you remember any occasion on which you felt stupid?
Being in the countryside		What was good about the countryside? What sort of countryside was it like?	Can you remember anything particular that happened, any incident or occasion, while you were in the countryside?

FIGURE 6.3 **'Narrative-pointed' Questions from Topic-notes**

the interviewee is needing support, not necessarily verbal, from you to continue in this often difficult task of responding to the SQUIN.

In addition, the interviewee, to avoid dealing with difficult material, or for other cultural reasons, may put a little or an enormous amount of sometimes quite subtle pressure on you to resume the control of the interview and give fuller directions. They may say 'if you ask me precise questions, I will be able to answer them', or they may respond to your initial SQUIN question by saying 'nothing comes to mind when you ask me as vague a question as that'. You must be able to resist this unconscious or conscious pressure by the interviewee upon you, to take on an actively directional and directive questioning role beyond delivering the SQUIN. You must work hard to keep open the space for their free response to the SQUIN, a space that *they* may often attempt by a variety of tactics to get you to close. They may tend to demand 'direction', and you must succeed in giving them only support.

Since *active listening but non-directive responses and support* are not, for most people, easy to achieve and maintain, and for most people require painful *unlearning,* Quatext have provided some exercises, which I present here.

These are first with 'return to narrative only' then with 'active listening only' and then what you will actually do in a real interview, namely 'active listening *and* return to narrative'.

'Return to Narrative Only' Questions   A key distinction that seems easy in principle but is extraordinarily difficult to get right in real situations is that between 'questions pointed at narrative' and questions which 'allow' narrative. Most people can easily create open-ended interventions which allow any response (e.g. 'tell me more about X') and very difficult to create interventions which point firmly at narrative.

Let us consider one or two negative and positive examples. A narrative question is a 'closed and pointed' question which aims to induce a narrative response and to discourage a non-narrative response, such as the production of a theory, an argument, an unhistorical description, a justification, a declaration of official values, an expression of felt emotions, etc. (see Figure 6.3).

You should practise improvising 'pointing at narrative' questions and get somebody to argue why each of your improvisations might be less 'narrative-pointed' than you think, or might even be, without your realizing it, pointed at asking for feelings and evaluations, for descriptions, for theories, etc., at non-narrative.

Notes on the Exercises

You are recommended to do the following exercises on a pencil-and-paper basis with at least one other person. Do them first on your own. Do several answers if necessary for each question. Then compare results with those of your friend, and then discuss how they can be improved. At the end, you and your friend should attempt to come up with one answer per question that you both agree is clearly directed *only* at narrative. The discussion between you is more important than the results!

For each numbered exercise, assume that the interviewee has said the words and a longish silence has begun that you sense is in danger of becoming unproductive. The numbers in brackets indicate a period of silence (in seconds). The exercise might take you 2 minutes or more per item.

EXERCISE 6.1 'RETURN TO NARRATIVE' QUESTIONING

During a narrative interview you, as an interviewer, would like to give the interviewee ('I') the possibility to narrate as extensively as necessary about his/her experiences. Try to induce more particular narratives first by formulating an appropriate question aimed at inducing return to narrative.

For this exercise, *avoid* inventing responses to show empathy, understanding, sympathy or anything else. They come in later exercises.

1   '... *my mother was someone special (crying) and that she had to work like this (1) she who hadn't even had any idea about where the kitchen was, never (2)*'
2   '... *during the summer I had another short love affair, but now I'm changing the subject again (3)*'
3   '... *you're so young you didn't live through this time (1); I think that one can't understand this time looking back from today (2)*'

Active Listening Principles   In any real narrative interview, just having the skill to ask narrative-pointed questions that don't point towards any particular subject for that narrative is not enough.

Rachel Pinney (1981) argues that genuinely listening to somebody else is such a rare accomplishment that it can be seen as 'unnatural'. Certainly the genre of *conversation* implies that, while listening to what somebody says, you are also reflecting on what you think about what they are saying, and preparing a response in terms of your position and experience. My own experience is that listening is a difficult activity to sustain.

Bearing in mind that, in the context of narrative interviewing, all 'active listening actions' should be subordinated to the need to 'return to narration', active listening is needed in all interviews throughout their phases. Originally derived from the work of Carl Rogers and those researching and teaching communication skills, it has different forms.

POSITIVE FORMS OF ACTIVE LISTENING[10]   Most communication is *non-verbal* – one scholar has claimed that 93% of communication occurs around the words and only 7% is carried by the words – and so you will need to learn and practise non-verbal expression of active listening. This is shown partly by an attentive *listening posture,* a *degree of eye-contact,* and *non-verbal sounds* like 'hmm' and so forth which indicate that you are listening.

In particular, you need to *allow the interviewee the length of pauses, of silences,* that they need to think through or recall the material they are trying to access. Sometimes they may be watching images or a film in their heads which need to be fully and silently accessed before they can start telling you about it. Bad interviewers interrupt, or, during silences, stop attending. *Good interviewers don't. They give non-verbal support in a non-intrusive way and stay quietly focused and attentive* while the interviewee struggles to retrieve memories and other resources for 'answering in depth'.

If strong *emotions* arise during the interview, you should be prepared, if necessary, to 'mirror' them. This will give the interviewee the feeling that you accept them and their expressed emotions, and that they do not have to avoid feeling those emotions for fear of upsetting you.

For example, if they start to cry, you should not rush in to 'rescue' them by quickly changing the topic with a new 'objective question' or in some other way. It is more helpful and accepting to say 'That's still hard for you', 'It's still painful for you to remember that', 'That makes you sad when you think about it' in an empathetic and non-judgmental way. But always as little as possible, as minimally as possible: ideally, they should remain scarcely aware that you have done anything.

If they express feelings of anger, you might say 'You feel angry about it' to show that you understand what the emotion is that they are expressing, in such a way that they can stay with the emotion or emerge from it in their own time.

Empathetic and un-intrusive 'mirroring' is an important skill to acquire. If they attempt to communicate their feelings, and you feel that they will not proceed well without some evidence from you that they have been 'heard', if you do make a verbal intervention, it is important to use *their words-for-feelings* – and indeed

---

10 The following section involves a considerably reworked version of an original paper by Roswitha Breckner in her (March 1996) training materials for SOSTRIS. She is not responsible for the version presented below.

their words-for-anything – rather than use your own, which may mean something different to them.

You have to be very tentative about offering *any* words for their experiencing. Such words *might* fit or they might be useful by provoking the interviewee into getting a better self-expression for themselves. Try to use only their words – even if you don't understand them, or find them odd. You are not, in that initial subsession of the BNIM interview, there to understand; and you want them to have no cause from you for worrying about you and your reception of what they are saying.

> You might offer the words 'You are perhaps *worried* about it' in such a way that, barely noticing that it was you who suggested such an interpretation, they move into realizing and perhaps saying 'No, I'm not *worrying* about it; I think that I am feeling *rather sad* about it'.

> Such tentative action might (but, in BNIM, only very occasionally) go as far, if required, as paraphrasing. This is to summarize the significant aspect of the content of what has been said, *in your own words* (not repeating back their words in a mechanical way). This lets the interviewee see that you have understood what they are trying to say. If you are not certain about what they are trying to say, then offer it – as in the previous paragraph – as a self-conscious possibility to help them clarify for themselves what they are trying to say.

> You do not need to understand their reference. In one interview the interviewee said that 'Working in a London local authority in 1991–92 felt like fighting the battle of Stalingrad'. The much younger interviewer had never heard of this (1942) battle, but she did not need to. She could recycle this metaphor – which clearly meant a lot to the interviewee – without herself knowing the meaning of the reference. After the interview, she asked for the information that she needed; in the interview, she did not let her incomprehension interrupt the informant.

NEGATIVE FORMS OF ACTIVE LISTENING   Since the main purpose is to enable the speaker to go on speaking because they feel listened to, the thing to avoid is anything which cuts that flow of narrative.

- *Don't console:* e.g. 'It can't have been as bad as all that' or 'Things will get better'.
- *Don't give advice* as to how to deal with a problem, how to avoid something, how to do (or have done) something better ('I would have tried to convince the doctor …'). Do not try to 'fix it' in the past or in the present.
- *Don't 'interpret':* 'I think the problem is your father' and offer them some 'analysis' of your own.
- *Don't intrude yourself and your life-history* with comments like 'I felt that too' or 'I had a very similar experience'.
- *Above all, don't suggest what the interviewee might next well talk about!!*

Instead, when the interviewee 'dries up' or even tries to get *you* to define what they should focus upon, don't let them evoke your system of relevancy (it will be tempting!). Don't try to 'do therapy' (by giving them directions).

> *You are doing research. Try to get more story / any more stories:*
>
> - 'Any other things you remember happening?'
> - 'Do you remember/recall anything else?'
>
> *without specifying what the storying should be about.*

The temptation is to ask for more story *about a topic they have just been talking about.* However, they may have stopped precisely because a *new topic* is struggling to surface in the field of consciousness, or because a topic *raised some time earlier* is struggling to return. And you must not block such out-of-awareness processes.

When you have completed Exercises 6.1 and 6.2, only then move on to 6.3. In Exercise 6.2, you are not trying to induce a narrative – as in the previous exercise – but are trying to formulate an 'active listening response' not particularly interested in narrative.

EXERCISE 6.2   ACTIVE LISTENING ONLY – DO NOT ATTEMPT
TO INDUCE ANY NARRATIVE

5   '*... during the summer I had another short love affair, but now I'm changing the subject again (3)'*
What is the interviewee expressing?
How can you show her, that you understand her and you are interested in what she's going to tell you?
6   '*Obviously I think this is not the moment to go into details of my private life'*
What is the interviewee expressing?
How can you show him that you've understood him?
7   '*... my mother was someone special (crying) and that she had to work like this (1) she who hadn't even had any idea about where the kitchen was, never (2)'*
What is the interviewee expressing?
How can you show her that you've understood her feelings?
8   '*I don't think I had a choice (1) I didn't sort of have any choices because Caroline was born, handicapped and it sort of just went on from there, I've never sort of made a positive choice whether to keep her at home or not it just sort of (laughter) the situation just developed and that was it really, you know what I mean (2)'*
What is the interviewee expressing?
How can you tell her that you've understood her?

Since BNIM subsessions 1 and 2 require you only to ask questions which return the interviewee towards a narrative response ('narrative-pointed' questions), any response by you in these sessions must subordinate active listening to the task of helping the interviewee to return to (rigorously unspecified) narrative.

For subsession 2 prepared questions, you *do* specify the topic of narration from your topic notes. However, once they have started a subsession 2 narration, once more you do *not* specify what the topic of further sub-narrations should be. Developed by Roswitha Breckner and Bettina Voelter for the April 1995 BISP International Seminar, Exercise 6.3 goes further. Don't do them till you've done the previous sets.

EXERCISE 6.3   RETURN TO UNSPECIFIC NARRATIVE FOR SUBSESSION 1
WHILE ACTIVELY LISTENING

During a narrative interview, during subsessions 1 and 2 of a BNIM-interview, you, as an interviewer, would like to give the interviewee ('I') the possibility to narrate as extensively as necessary about his/her experiences.

continued

continued

- Assume that the informant interrupted their stream of narration in the following cases.
- Think about how you would react in such a way that the interviewee

  - realizes that you're still listening
  - feels that you understand what he/she means
  - returns to the stream of narration
  - but without you specifying what they should narrate *about*.

9   '.... *my mother was someone special (crying) and that she had to work like this (1) she who hadn't even had any idea about where the kitchen was. never (2)*'

What is 'I' expressing?

How can you show her that you've understood what she was saying and that you're ready to listen to what she's going to say, while helping her to return to the stream of narration, but without specifying what it would be about?

10   '... *during the summer I had another short love affair, but now I'm changing the subject again (3)*'

What is 'I' expressing?

How can you show her that you're interested in what she is going to tell you, while helping her to return to the stream of narration, but without specifying what it would be about?

11   '*you're so young you didn't live through this time (1) I think that one can't understand this time looking back from today (2)*'

What is 'I' expressing?

How can you show him that you've understood him and that you're ready to continue listening, while helping him to return to the stream of narration, but without specifying what it would be about?

12   '... *ah, I'm talking and talking, how did you experience this political change (2)*'

What is 'I' expressing?

How can you establish that there won't be a change of role between interviewer and interviewee but still convey that you understand what he's saying, while helping him to return to the stream of narration, but without specifying what it would be about?

13   '... *it was so horrible (1) you can't explain it to others (1) I still see the pictures in my mind (long pause)*'

What is 'I' expressing?

How can you tell her that you've understood her, while helping her to return to the stream of narration, but without specifing what it would be about?

Exercises 6.1 to 6.3 – particularly if you take enough time and you compare answers with a critical friend, but probably not otherwise – should give you the sense of some of the difficulties involved in this apparently simple practice, particularly in asking for narrative but not specifying what about.

Tape-recording, but Making Topic/Keyword Notes   So far I have focused upon the function of 'active listening while attempting to return the interviewee to unspecified narrative', the primary skill required for BNIM interviewing.

The other skill that is required is that of taking topic-keyword notes (primarily in subsession 1) so as to organize your questioning in subsession 2. It is to this skill that I now turn.

THE PRINCIPLE OF NOTING TOPICS USING THE INFORMANT'S KEYWORDS   For the sake of your later analysis, the main record of the interview experience is in the tape-recording (and in the post-interview debriefing). Consequently, you need to make very few notes in the interview. Your main focus should be on active and supportive listening.

However, you do need to make some notes, because without them you cannot run the second subsession. You need to make *notes that record the succession of topics raised by the interviewee, using their keywords*. What this will later enable you to do, in the second subsession, is to remind the interviewee of some or all of the topics that he or she raised, so that they can tell you more narratives about each of them. Without adequate notes on the topics raised in subsession 1, you won't be able to do this in subsession 2.

What do I mean by 'a topic' in this context? The term at this point merely means a topic, a referent, that which is being talked about. In this context, you need to have a list of topic-descriptions which will instantly remind the interviewee of what they were talking about. They must be in the interviewee's language and use their keywords, the key terms in their own language, their own discourse, their idiolect.

Putting the same point differently, you are *not* starting to do your own analysis in your own words of the unconscious underlying *themes* of the discourse of the interviewee; you certainly don't have to understand the 'thematic thread' that explains the distribution or treatment of topics: this is a task for later analysis. You are listing his or her topics in the sequence he or she raised them in his or her words so that they can recognize them without effort.[11] Again, at this stage, you don't even have to understand the topic-words: it is enough that *they* will recognize and do understand them. (I say 'at this stage', because, after subsession 2, you will need to explore and remedy any lack of information or understanding that you feel is important.) Your task is merely to record the sequence.

THE PRACTICE OF NOTING TOPICS   There is an art in recording the topics raised by the interviewee which is only acquired by practice. They need to be recorded as succinctly and as vividly as possible. Normally each item may take only 2–4 words: perhaps a noun plus an adjective or adverb; or a name and a verb, a phrase. Bear in mind that the only purpose of these topic / topic notes is to enable you in the second subsession to remind the interviewee of some particular thing they said, with the words and in the way that they said it, such that they can be asked to tell you more narrative about it.

For reasons I have already covered, the narrative focus of the SQUIN–BNIM methodology involves a constant gentle pressure on the informant to provide

---

11 I think it useful to distinguish between the interviewer's conscious 'topics' and the researcher's later analysis of 'themes' which may underlie the choice and treatment of topics. I have not found this distinction so clear in the German use of the term *thema* (English 'theme'). Where the *Quatext* tradition refers to thematic notes, I refer in this text to topic notes.

more narratives and narrations. The core of narrative in the broad sense of Labov and Waletsky is a narration about a succession of events (p. 116 above). Consequently, our notes on topics will be as far as possible event-focused, to make it easier to ask 'narrative-pointed' questions in subsession 2.

I can distinguish points in the subsession 1 initial narration where the interviewee refers specifically to *particular incidents, happenings, occasions*. These are particularly easy to note and use in subsession 2 narrative questions. At other points in the subsession initial narration, the interviewer may talk in *more general terms of situations, of a time or a phase*. This will be a little more difficult to turn, in subsession 2, into a narrative question.

Figure 6.4 provides a notepad structure for taking topic-notes. You might find that you only make notes in the extreme left hand column, or that it is useful to use the second and third column instead. Its use may be indicated as follows:

Let us say that, in the subsession 1 of a particular BNIM interview, the interviewee refers to his 'father' and then to his 'mother' and then tells a succession of stories about the mother.

In the first column, you could note down the term 'father' in the first line and then 'mother' in the second line. In the third and subsequent lines, you note down (perhaps in columns 2 or 3) keywords for each of the particular stories told about the mother.

In subsession 2, you can raise the topic of the 'father', because he was mentioned – if only in passing – by the interviewee in subsession 1. (If he had not been mentioned at all in subsession 1, then you could not refer to him at all in subsession 2, but only eventually in subsession 3.)

Having the topic of the father raised by the interviewee on the first line of the first column in the notepad, gives you permission in subsession 2 to formulate a narrative question about that topic because it was explicitly raised in subsession 1. Ideally, you would attempt to formulate a question using column 3 terms about incident, happening, occasion: for example, 'You mentioned your father; can you tell me about any incident or occasion with him that you remember?'[12] If, for any reason, this seems slightly difficult to pose as a question 'that arises' as Collingwood would say (see above, p. 52), then you might wish to lead towards such a column 3 question by asking a preliminary question in column 2 terms: for example, 'You mentioned your father; can you recall any particular time or situation with him?' Once he has responded, you could then use keywords from that response to formulate a further follow-up particularizing (narrative-pointed) question asking for a narrative about a particular incident, event, occasion or set of happenings (i.e. story).

I call this a SHEIOT notepad, using the initial letters of the words *Situation, Happening, Event, Incident, Occasion/Occurrence, Time*.

Even if you decide only to write into *one* of the first three columns of the SHEIOT notepad, as is likely at the start, when you are in subsession 2, the other

---

12 If he had referred to his father as 'Jack', you would need to use the term 'Jack'. If 'Daddy', then that would have been the term that you would have noted and used. His usage may vary in the course of the interview, and at each moment your note should stick to his precise usage at that moment.

			ILLUMINATION ONLY by MORE STORY
Themes in the order mentioned and in the terms used by the interviewee	Relatively *General* terms about *Situation, Time, Phase*	More *Particular* terms about *Incident, Happening Occasion Event* 'How it all came about' 'How all of that happened'	e.g. *You said* *'XXXXX'* *– can you tell me more about how all that happened?* or *– do you remember any particular incident or occasion when XXXX?*
	Their keywords for your eventual return-to-narrative questions		*Full versions* of your eventual return-to-narrative questions
father			
mother	'angry when small'		
		'hit me when wouldn't go to school'	
		'shouting at me for playing in mud'	
	'nicer to me when went to secondary school'		
		'birthday cake at 14'	
		'party at 16'	
Julia [sister]			
'always feeling stupid'			
'being in the countryside'			
An actual notepad would have 2–3 pages of blanks under the headings above			
It would just have two columns like this row and that above			

FIGURE 6.4 **SHEIOT Notepad for Noting Topics, with Sample Notes**

columns – even if nothing is written in them – may help you to formulate questions around the topics raised that are *topic-questions seeking narratives* (TQUINs) and not the many other types of question which so easily come to one's lips.

In the example below, I have filled in a way of noting topics raised in an imaginary interview like the one described above. Obviously, the notepad prior to use would be blank from the third line down, and would look like the last two rows of the figure. Given the difficulty in rapidly creating 'narrative-pointed questions', you are advised to make notepads using the first two rows of the figure at the top of *each page* of your SHEIOT notepad. This will give you general and particular narrative-provoking words (SHEIOT-words and phrases) that, in the short 15-minute break between subsessions 1 and 2, you can pull down from the top of each and every page to construct your narrative-pointed questions around the noted-down topics/keywords and phrases.

It is very important that you note down *their topic-words* and only use their words in your subsession 2 narrative questions. If they refer to 'Dad', don't say 'you spoke about your father'; if they talk of 'going to college', don't refer to 'entering higher education', or 'getting a college education'.

Note the phrases in the headers, referring to 'how it all [unspecified] happened / came about' and to, in the third-column header, the construction of two-part questions of the type 'You said [keywords/phrase used by interviewee in subsession 1]; do you remember any particular incident when …'. These are formulations which will help you construct subsession 2 questions rapidly.

Don't be afraid of using pretty similar terms and questions in subsession 2; normally speaking, provided you stick to their words and phrases, the informant's attention will be focused on their answering, not on your elegance and variety of formulated questions!

You are trying to move towards 3rd/4th-column narrative questions. You may be able to do so directly, or you may have to first get answers to 2nd-column, more general questions and then use those responses to ask for 3rd/4th-column questions.

BALANCE OF NOTE-TAKING AND ACTIVE LISTENING   There is a tension between the task of active listening and that of making topic notes for later questions. Too much concentration on active listening, and you find you have stopped making notes. Too much concentration on making notes, and you find that the informant has started to feel that you aren't listening to him or her and has got discouraged. One solution is for a two-interviewer situation in which one person takes responsibility for questioning and listening while another first takes notes in subsession 1 and then asks the questions in subsession 2, while in subsession 2 the interviewer of subsession 1 becomes the note-taker.[13] This can work well but it can lead to a change in the dynamics of the interviewer–interviewee relationship which may result in its own problems. The main point is the issue of balance and the importance of giving priority to ensuring the interviewee feels properly listened to.

A final point about note-taking is that it may be taken by the informant as an index of being 'interesting' or not: in one case, the informant told the interviewee

---

13 The SQUIN would then need modifying to indicate that the notes for possible questions may be taken by either of the interviewers in subsession 1. I shall in general assume a single interviewer in this text, however.

that she knew she was being 'boring' when her interviewee started not to take as many notes as before. Such unconscious signals need to be avoided.

Towards the Ending of the Initial Narration – Their Ending   Having discussed the first subsession and how the interviewer should attempt to ensure constant active listening and support for the interviewee throughout their initial narration, and indicated the principle of topic/keyword note-taking, obviously there will be a point – 10 minutes or 2 hours after subsession 1 starts – when the initial narration and subsession 1 will be brought to an end by the narrator. But, be careful. Not every 'silence' indicates a complete ending.

It's certainly not for you to end the session; you are restricted to accepting the ending determined by the interviewee. If it is *you* who ends the session, their gestalt is broken. The interview is spoilt and they will feel emotionally 'thrown'; then *you* will feel emotionally thrown when you discover that you interrupted their gestalt and so your research. Just as the point of the telling of a joke resides in the 'punchline' at the end which retrospectively gives a crucial (and new and unexpected) meaning to all that went before, and an interrupted joke is pretty worthless, the same is to a large extent true about the completion of the initial narrative by the narrator to his or her satisfaction. At all costs avoid destroying the 'ending' that would have given the crucial sense to all that went before.

Real and Fake Endings   If you are successful in enabling them to tell their story, they will nearly always spontaneously end their narrative by saying something like 'Well, that's it, that's my story, that's how it happened'.

An informant being silent is *not* the same as an explicit ending. A silence, or a pause, and it might be quite long, is a period in which the narrator is wondering whether to go on, in what way to proceed, or remembering something.

Your informant's silence should not be interrupted, however helpful you think your interruption might be. If they don't explicitly end the session, you can be sure they are slightly ambivalent about ending it. You might then just test this by saying, for example, after a serious pause where the NVC definitely seems to be suggesting 'stuckness', 'any other event, anything else, that occurs to you before I finish?', a deliberately weak form of attempted relaunching using something less than the SQUIN. This might then be taken by them as a relaunch, or they might just reaffirm that the narrative has ended by saying 'No, that's it', or something similar.

Just stay focused, and in active listening mode. Eventually, they will nearly always say something quite explicit that closes the session for them. Subsession 1 must only be closed by the interviewee.

Difficult Cases: Limited Relaunching   The above principles and exercises should help you cope with the difficult task of listening actively and helping the interviewee to return to narrative at moments of difficulty.

Some interviewees may not be able to undertake the task after all. You may attempt to relaunch them by repeating the original SQUIN question, perhaps fractionally modified so that you don't sound like a parrot.

If, however, they just cannot or will not cope with the SQUIN question, then they are not suitable subjects for this SQUIN–BNIM interview. You may then decide to end the interview as nicely as possible or to interview them in a more conventional narrative or other semi-structured depth-interviewing format as discussed in the next chapter. Bear in mind that they have put themselves out for you, and do not make them feel that they have let you down. Your task is to make them feel as good as they can about the experience: if you succeed, they might then be able to give you the interview you want at a later stage, reassured by your supportive and non-punitive response to the first occasion. You certainly don't want them to go away feeling bad about themselves or you.

I have dealt with the two key aspects of BNIM interviewing: namely, that of active listening and supporting and non-directional returning the interviewee to their narration; and that of taking notes of keywords and topics raised during the first subsession to prepare for the second subsession. The actual preparation of questions for the second subsession can best be done in the intersession gap.

The Intersession Gap

Setting the Gap, Provisionally for the End of Session One
It is useful to have planned subsessions 1 and 2 as a whole, giving yourself and your interviewee anything between 10 and 20 minutes for a breather, particularly if their initial narration was of reasonable or considerable length. A prolonged coffee/snack break is a useful social ritual, and 'wanting to look at your notes so as to ask questions in the next session' is a socially acceptable justification for being on your own during this break.

Using the Gap before Subsession 2
The most important thing to do in your, say, 15-minute break, is that of reviewing your SHEIOT notepad notes in order to prepare TQUINs (topic questions aimed at inducing narrative) for subsession 2.

If you are lucky, then your estimated time available for subsession 2 will be enough for *all* the topics. More frequently, and with practice, you can foresee that you will *not* have the time to gather further narratives about all the topics/topics that you have noted down. The more detailed your notes, the more time used by the informant to provide a given narrative, the less likely this is to be true. In this more usual situation, during the intersession break you must make a provisional selection of the topic/keyword notes you decide to focus upon.

Be prepared for this shortage of time in subsession 2. On your SHEIOT notepad, during the short break, highlight (perhaps with a coloured highlighter) the topics which you consider the most important and most necessary to gather further stories and narratives about and which you guess are the ones most likely to be productive of such narration. Be prepared to find out that you are quite wrong in your guesses and to instantly replan accordingly.

On the basis of subsession 1 behaviour, make a guess as to what amount of time will on average be taken by the interviewee to respond to each of your priority TQUINs, look at the time you actually have available for the whole of subsession 2, and develop a guesstimate of the number of TQUINs that can actually be addressed and responded to in the whole of the time available.[14]

Having done so, you may or may not have time – usually not – to formulate the precise wording of questions-seeking-narratives for each of the topic/topics, and

---

14 Bear in mind that you are also guessing at the number of such TQUINs that will, in their turn, produce subsession 2 narrations *with further subtopics* that could or should also be followed up by further TQUINs.

especially the ones you have highlighted. For self-training purposes, full or partial formulations could be put into column 4 of the SHEIOT notepad illustrated in Figure 6.4, p. 134, using the SHEIOT 'narrative pointed words' of the general or more particular variety.

Self-debriefing (if a Longer Period) to Tape or Paper

If, for whatever reason, the gap between subsession 1 and subsession 2 turns out to be two hours or more, then it is wise to engage in a self-debriefing session in which you 'free associate' to tape or directly to paper about the session. Based on the principle that short-term memory fades very rapidly, such self-debriefing enables the recording of experience and ideas at a level of detail which will become impossible after other events or sleep have deleted them. It is crucial that you consider this task of post-interview debriefing as being as central to understanding the interview and advancing your professional competence for interviewing in general as is the recording and the analysis of the interview itself. See pp. 142–44 for discussion.

Subsession 2: Asking for More Story About Topics Raised Spontaneously in Subsession 1

After the intersession gap described above, which should be planned for and safeguarded and used in the ways described above, it is time to move to the second subsession.

Overview

Subsession 2 is based on the SHEIOT topic/keyword notes from the first subsession. In the first subsession, only one question could be asked, a question asking for a narrative, the SQUIN. In the second subsession, the only questions that can be asked are also narrative questions, but this time TQUINs, *topic* questions aimed at inducing narrative.

The order of the questions is strictly prescribed. Just as the exposition of the original narrative took a particular sequence of raised topics – and not the same topics raised in a different sequence – so the sequence of questions raised in subsession 2 must take the same order, starting from the first topic raised in subsession 1 and proceeding to the last topic raised in subsession 1. Topics may be missed out, but an earlier topic cannot be raised once a later one has been addressed. The reason remains the same: the gestalt of the individual being interviewed must not be destroyed by the intervention of the interviewer.

Since you may not have selected all the themes that were originally raised, and since the informant may have been stimulated by their earlier responses into a train of thought they had not originally had, it is useful to have, right at the end of subsession 2, a question like 'Is there anything else you would like to add at this point?', the only non-narrative question in the first two subsessions. This allows for further narrative, but also for explanations or rectifications which the informant feels are important to make. Otherwise all subsession 2 questions must be narrative-pointed ones.

Topics in Sequence

Let us say that, in a given subsession 1, the interviewee addressed nine topics/ topics in the (non-chronological) sequence shown in Figure 6.5. This then becomes the prescribed sequence for asking narrative questions about each topic. You may miss out one or more topics, if you have to, but you must not go back to a previous one after a later one has been asked about.

In addition, topics that reappear more than once should not be condensed into a single topic for the purpose of asking a single narrative question. Topic 2 or topic 9 might conceivably be missed out by the interviewer; however, it would not be permissible to ask a consolidated question at either point, like 'You mention that your mother was sometimes angry and sometimes giving towards you, and that you admired her appearance: do you remember any particular events connected with these points?' The interviewee thought about the mother's appearance only after thinking about the primary school; she thought about the mother's negative then positive attitudes after thinking about the father and before thinking about her sister. Although I do not know why the sequence is as it is, it must be respected.

Similarly, the individual leaps from the death of her grandmother (before she herself was born) forward to her own career, then backward to university and backwards in time again to her primary school. The thought about the death of her grandmother is in some way connected to her prior topic of 'always feeling stupid'. During the interviewing process, I do not have to understand how these topics are connected and emerge in this way; however, my interviewing sequence in subsession 2 must respect the gestalt which expressed itself in the initial interview in the sequence that it did.

There are no exceptions to these rules: never go back to earlier topics, never combine topics. Always use *their* words and phrases for topics, never paraphrase or replace. And, obviously, as I have already discussed, the questions that you put in subsession 2 (with the exception of the last one which is super-open: 'anything you feel you want to say …?') must always and only be TQUINs, ones that are clearly 'pointed at narrative' in the way already discussed (p. 126 onwards).

The Curly Diagram for Sequence Management: Further Notes for Further Subtopics

It is normally the case that, when answering a narrative question about a particular topic, the interviewee develops an account which itself embodies further topics (subtopics to each initial topic). This sequence must then be respected in the same mode of non-reversible sequence.

In our imaginary example in Figure 6.5, when asked in subsession 2 for 'more things that happened' in respect of time at university, topic no. 7 of subsession 1, the interviewee might then provide an account with four topics in the following order:

- her marriage in the final year at University
- her loneliness when starting University

1	Father
2	Mother – early negative, later positive attitude to interviewee
3	Julia [sister]
4	Always feeling stupid
5	Grandmother's death before subject was born
6	Career
7	University
8	Primary school
9	Mother – appearance

FIGURE 6.5   **Nine Topics in Order**

1 Father	
2 Mother – early negative, later positive attitude to interviewee	
3 Sister	
4 Always feeling stupid	
5 Grandmother's death before subject was born	
6 Career	
7 University ─────────────────┐	
8 Primary school	7a marriage in final year
9 Mother – appearence	7b loneliness starting University
	7c desire for grandfather's support
	7d reasonable University results

FIGURE 6.6   **Sequence of Nine Topics Plus Four Subtopics**

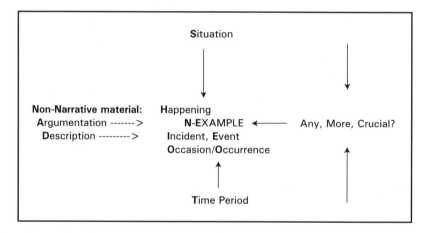

FIGURE 6.7   **SHEIOT Cross – Trying to get to Narrative**

- imagining how she would have liked to have her grandfather's support
- her reasonable results in her University examinations.

At this point, after that further account with the above four topics, the interviewer may ask narrative questions relating to all or none of them (providing the order is respected) but, once the interviewer has posed a question around topic no. 8 or 9, *none* of the extra four topics can be addressed:[15] this would make them out of sequence.

A diagram may be helpful (Figure 6.6). Clearly, any response to one or more of responses 7a–d must be dealt with in the same strict fashion. No topics must be addressed out of sequence!

Even if the time is long, and the number of topics initially raised is few, you will be at some point deciding not to follow-up subtopics or sub-subtopics raised. So

---

15 Except in subsession 3, where anything can be raised.

selection – in the sense of not following up all the responses to all the topics initially and subsequently raised – is inevitable.

> It is a matter of judgment whether or not you raise in subsession 2 one or more of the initial topics raised in subsession 1. The chances are that the judgment will be affected by your overall project CRQ and your sense of what narrative development of which topics will be most productive.

Despite the above, obviously it is best if you can ask TQUINs about all the topics in the *initial* narrative, even if only a few of the further accounts may be able to be followed up in their turn.

SHEIOT askable Questions in Subsession 2

On the SHEIOT notepad, when identifying key terms that could be used in formulating narrative questions for topics raised in subsession 1, I used the mnemonic SHEIOT. In Figure 6.7, I make the same point but in a different way. The interviewer's intervention (question) tries to move the account given by the interviewee towards the centre of the cross-shaped diagram. (I'm sorry that the arrows on the right-hand side of the diagram spoil its logic!)

You always ask for more narrative/story. Your questions always go for more narrative/story, a narrative example, (N-Example) with the terms 'happening, incident, occasion (or event)'. The diagram refers to non-narrative material (Argumentation and Description); the meaning of these terms for types of non-narrative material will be made clear later (pp. 174–80; 243–45).

You are always trying to get to narratives about particular happenings, incidents, occasions, and examples. The point of the right-hand-side of the diagram is as follows. If you are given an argumentation or a description (non-narrative material), to get narratives/story, you ask the following kinds of questions.

> 1   Can you give me ANY example of an occasion when?
> 2   Can you give me any MORE examples of similar events, incidents at that time / of that type?
> 3   Was there some particular CRUCIAL incident or situation or time that you can recall?

All these are examples of narrative questions that can be used in subsession 2 to get the speaker to return to narrative.

Bear in mind, always, that although it is your responsibility to put gentle pressure for the use of narrative by asking narrative-seeking questions, if the interviewee responds sometimes or even always – this happens rarely but it can happen – by not providing a narrative, this does not have to be a negative result. The instrumentation theory of BNIM specifies that, if asked properly for a narrative by way of a narrative-pointed question, a speaker decision to provide non-narrative is as illuminating for subsequent analysis as is a decision to respond to the narrative-pointed question by in fact providing narrative. Ask for narrative, in subsession 2 as in subsession 1, but, as long as you did ask properly for a narrative, be perfectly happy if, at certain points, you don't get it. From one point of view of interviewer behaviour, a technically perfect practice in subsession 2 can be seen not as one in which you only received perfect narrations (this never happens); it is one in which you managed to ask only N-pointed questions. This will become clearer after I have discussed (in Chapter 12) the way we analyse BNIM interview material.

Checking Contact for Subsession 3

Once you have completed going through the original and the emergent list of topics in the correct sequence, then effectively subsession 2 is completed.

As both you and the interviewee should know, there will be a sizable time-gap between the end of subsession 2 and the next interview, because you will have to do a preliminary analysis of the materials in order to prepare subsession 3, that next interview. It is therefore probably best to leave the time and place of subsession 3 vague, and to be fixed later by phone once you have completed your preliminary analysis and know what questions you wish to ask.

However, if there are points of information which you know you lack and you know your informant could provide easily and quickly, you could ask for such points of information there and then. You might also, or alternatively, ask for permission to make contact by phone or by letter in order to clear up any such points of information, dates for example of key life-events. This can be regarded as an early form of subsession 3 activity.

In addition, you might invite him or her to write or phone you if they need any points of clarification, or, upon reflection, want to add to or qualify anything they have said. A depth interview, if it is successful, results in the interviewee exploring areas, depths and connections that are not perfectly familiar: they may say things they don't quite expect to say, or miss out things they do want to say. Obviously, any further information or correction that they wish to make will need to be itself evaluated, rather than simply taken at face value. Nonetheless, it is important that they feel that it is easy for them to add to, or correct, the information or responses that they gave you.

Self-debriefing on Subsession 2 to Paper or Tape

Principles

Post-interview debriefing is central to your understanding the interview and to advancing your professional competence. The principle is easy to grasp. Just as you wanted your interviewee to free-associate around the broad topic of their life-history experience, now they have finished you want yourself to free-associate around the much narrower topic of your particular-interview experience.

Making notes immediately after the session – 'field-notes' or 'session-notes' or 'debriefing-notes' – is a key operation often neglected or mistakenly left till later or treated as being of minor importance. You need to think of your 'product' from the interview field as being composed of two sorts of materials, both of which are necessary to understanding the other and to being the fullest possible record of what happened: interview-tapes and debriefing-notes.

Why give so much attention to this instant debriefing? This record of interview experience and what memories, ideas, *anythings*, it stimulated in you is vital for your subsequent analysis of this particular interview (as well as being of great importance for your professional development as a social researcher). Discussions of such free-flow writing can be found in Field (1981), Progoff (1975), Rainer (1978) and Ericcson and Simon (1980). The notes are material from your short-term memory that will be lost as you talk to people, leave the building, take public transport and do other things. You have only one opportunity to get the maximum benefit and the data from your brain: immediately after the interview before you do, or think about, anything else.

Procedure

Preferably stay in the same room. Although *their* structuring initial question asks for a narrative, the initial question for *you* in the debriefing should not be narrative-focused at all. Make the assumption that your tapes are wiped and that the only recollection of the interview is now in your head. You therefore need to write down everything that you can remember about it: content, feelings, process, anything and everything. Write in a free associative flow, *not trying to order, organize, or censor anything*. For the 30–60 minutes period, *just write*. It can be sorted later.

You may find that you start by the last few things that were said and then your mind jumps in apparently senseless ways in and out of the interview, from the beginning to the end, from the expression on the informant's face to a detail of what he or she said. Just write it all down till you have nothing left to write ... and then write some more.

The *gestalt* principle central to the biographic-interpretive method is clearly central to the practice of instant subjective debriefing.[16] If you find out *eventually* that what you remembered in your debriefing notes and what happened as recorded on the tape is significantly or subtly different, this is a very important discovery that will help you in your study.

Aneeta Minocha's comment (cited Sanjek, 1990: 97) summarizes the activity:

> 'During my talks, I scribbled key words in a small notebook. Later I wrote extensive reports of my conversations, and also recorded my explanations and interpretations as they occurred to me at that time. I also recorded the contexts in which particular conversations took place, as well as the general physical and emotional condition of the informants, their appearance and behaviour and the gestures they used. Usually it took me three to four hours to put on paper five to six hours of fieldwork. It is because of such immediate recording of my field experiences that I was able to recreate the atmosphere in which each conversation or event took place. Even now, as I write, I can vividly feel the presence of the participants.' [1979: 213]

A Sample Fragment

Ariane Schorn (2000) has a similar procedure and a sample fragment. Immediately after her 'theme-centred interview', she writes (I have corrected the English translation):

> 'A postscript is made which contains the first impressions. This includes ideas and feelings referring to the interview partner and the interviewer. Of special interest is

---

16 You may also wish to generate formally structured fieldnotes of a non-subjective type, with a 'schedule' of areas to be attended to and have notes written about. Sanjek (1990) is very helpful in discussing the whole issue, as well as being fun and fascinating to read.

everything that – so to speak – took place "between" the protagonists (their interaction, atmosphere of conversation, dynamics of conversation, specific "scenes", etc.).

> Example: Mr P welcomes me with a firm handshake. While sitting down, I try to talk about the frame of the interview when Mr P suggests using first names .... I agree, a little dumbfounded, with the feeling of being taken a bit by surprise.' (Schorn, 2000, section 2)[17]

Summary

To sum up: what are the different functions served by such free-associative notes made instantly after the closure of the interview?

- First, you will be making a record of some non-linguistic data that the tape-recorder will not catch.
- Second, your tape-recorder may not function or, after recording, you might lose the tape. The 'nightmare assumption' might become true.
- Third, and most important, in making such notes, your brain is already re-ordering the material in a free-associative flow. It is already making connections within and outside the interview itself; it is already providing material about emotions and feelings; it is already complementing the dry chronology of the tape-recording with the data-provision of your own brain. It is therefore your 'closest-to-experience' start of your eventual theorizing of that experience.

Subsession 3: Questions Arising, and the Theoretical Relevances of the Interviewer → SSDI

This session has no BNIM-prescribed structure, and in it you may or may not ask for narratives. Designing it involves you in reflecting upon two principal components:

- questions arising from preliminary analysis of the material from the first two subsessions
- further questions arising from the theoretical and practical concerns of the specific research project which the SQUIN–BNIM narrative interviews are designed to serve, the overall Project CRQ and its Project TQs (see p. 150).

In Part IV, I will describe in detail the process of analysing the material from the first two subsessions and how questions for subsession 3 may arise from them. This will therefore not be repeated here. See p. 207 onwards.

Exceptionally, you may be interested in pure BNIM research into people's biographies and have no further theoretical or practical concerns. In this case, you will have no prior research questions that would lead to any special 'pre-designed content' for your subsession 3. This is very exceptional. Most researchers have some project-defined theoretical and/or practical concerns, and consequently such concerns will govern the design of their subsession 3 prior to any 'matters arising' from subsessions 1 and 2. For example, Hollway and Jefferson (2000) had

---

17 Schorn also suggests using the model of a clinical supervision for discussing the interview afterwards. Arguing that even research interviews involve 'transference and counter-transference', she says that such research-related supervision sessions make that flow accessible for reflection, and gives a good example.

both certain theoretical and practical concerns relating to the fear of crime, and these governed the production of 'default questions' for their equivalent of subsession 3. Chamberlayne and Curran (unpublished, as yet, 2001) are designing research into the needs and experiences of homeless people sleeping rough in London. It may very well be that, say, a half or three-quarters of such default questions designed for subsession 3 do not in the end need to be asked because they turn out to have been answered in subsessions 1 and 2. Nonetheless, the possibility of *none* of them being answered in the first two subsessions must be envisaged, and consequently a subsession 3 needs to be designed as if no particular information could be *guaranteed* to be provided by the eventual subsessions 1 and 2. The designing of such subsession 3s is dealt with in the next chapter, after the interlude.

In the 'interlude' that now follows, I consider, very briefly, alternative models of obtaining biographic narratives which you may find useful to include in your particular research design and which contrast in significant ways with – and can also complement – the model just put forward. After the interlude, a short conclusion places BNIM within your broader research context.

INTERLUDE: COMPLEMENTARY (OR ALTERNATIVE) RESEARCH DESIGNS

The narrative-focused design of SQUIN-BNIM interviews is very expensive in time, and research based upon it with the three subsessions under normal conditions of close-to-zero funding can only cope with a small number of cases, perhaps only one, perhaps only two or three, rarely more than five or six. We therefore consider briefly three alternative methods of collecting biographical narrative.

Lieblich, Tuval-Mashiach and Zilber's Narrative-Interview Design

One project using life-story materials is that of Lieblich, Tuval-Mashiach and Zilber (1998).

'Given the large number of participants included in the study, our chosen method for procuring a life story presents a compromise between the wish to obtain free and rich self-narratives, on the one hand, and the need to limit allocated time and the amount of material per person, on the other .... [T]his kind of interview facilitated some kinds of analysis while limiting others .... In opening the interview, the interviewer introduced the task of "stage outline" as follows:

Every person's life can be written as a book. I would like you to think about your life now as if you were writing a book. First, think about the chapters of the book. I have here a page to help you in this task. Write down the years on the first column – from zero, from the day you were born. When did the first stage end? Write it here. Then go on to the next chapters, and put down the age at which each one begins and ends for you. Go on till you reach your present age. You can use any number of chapters or stages that you find suitable to your own life.

... The directions for the second task were given when the chapters were all recorded, as follows: "Now, please, think about the title you would give each one of these chapters, and write it in the next column".

continued

continued

When the interviewee had completed the stage outline, the interviewer placed it where it would be visible to both of them and said, "I will be asking you several questions about each one of the stages you proposed". Our instructions led the narrators to focus on four questions / directions for each stage:

1   "Tell me about a significant episode or a memory that you remember from this stage."
2   "What kind of a person were you during this stage?"
3   "Who were significant people for you during this stage, and why?"
4   "What is your reason for choosing to terminate this stage when you did?"'

(Lieblich, Tuval-Mashiach and Zilber, 1998: 25–6)

According to this compromise designed to 'limit allocated time and amount of material per person', the 74 interviews carried out produced 4,500 pages: some 61 pages per person!

From the theoretical position of BNIM with its three sessions and its insistence on only asking for narrative, of the above four standard questions, only question 1 is fully satisfactory: the other three standard questions elicit self-theory, description and argumentation. Indeed, the whole approach of insisting on sequential chapters with prepared titles in chronological order would be antithetical to the BNIM approach which is designed not to elicit the *conscious* self-theorizing and life-periodizing of the interviewee but rather to make inferences from the free-associative gestalt. BNIM-theory would argue that the interview strategy above would lead to a more controlled and less expressive performance.

On the other hand, Lieblich, Tuval-Mashiach and Zilber would argue that, given their purposes, using their theory of interviewing practice, their compromise was adequate for those purposes. You might wish to consider what theory of 'good-enough interviewing' they must have for them to feel happy about their compromise. You might also wish to consider what theory of 'sufficient numbers' BNIM practitioners must have to be satisfied with their more intensive methodology. It is certain that Lieblich et al. managed to interviewed a very much larger number of interviewees than they would have achieved with the more-intensive BNIM procedure: an advantage not to be underestimated. Figure 6.8 suggest this trade-off reality.

Dolbeare–Schuman–Seidman's Narrative-Interview Design

Seidman (1998) provides an account of a three-interview mode of in-depth phenomenological interviewing designed by Dolbeare and Schuman (Schuman, 1982). The first interview is described by Seidman, on whom I rely for this account, as being a focused life history; the second asks for a 'reconstruction of the details of experience'; the third asks the informant to reflect on the meaning of their experience. Each interview lasts some 90 minutes and they take place about 3–7 days apart.

Interview 1: Focused Life History:

'In the first interview, the interviewer's task is to put the participant's experience in context by asking him or her to tell as much as possible about him or herself in the light of the topic up to the present time .... We ask them to reconstruct their early experiences in their families, in school, with friends, in their neighbourhood and at work .... In asking them to put their student teaching or mentoring (*the topic*) in the context of their life history, we avoid asking "Why did you become a student teacher (or mentor)?" Instead, we ask them how they came to be participating in the program. By asking "how?" we hope to have them reconstruct a range of constitutive events in their past family, school, and work experience that place their participation in the professional development (*sic*, their?) school program in the context of their lives.' (Seidman, 1998: 11)

Interview 2: The Details of Experience

'The purpose of the second interview is to concentrate upon the concrete details of the participants' present experience in the topic area of study. We ask them to reconstruct these details. In our study of student teachers and mentors in a clinical site, for example, we ask them what they actually do on the job. We do not ask for opinions but rather the details of their experience, upon which their opinions may be based.[18] In order to put their experience within the context of the social setting, we ask the student teachers, for example, to talk about their relationships with their students, their mentors, the other faculty in the school, the administrators, the parents and the wider community. In this second interview we might ask them to reconstruct a day in their student teaching from the moment they woke up to the time they fell asleep. We ask for stories about their experience in school as a way of eliciting details .... Ask: "What is your job? What is it like for you to do what you do?"' (Seidman, 1998: 12/20)

Interview 3: Reflection on the Meaning

'In the third interview, participants are asked to reflect on the meaning of their experience .... The question might be phrased, "Given what you have said about your life before you became a student mentor and given what you have said about your work now, how do you understand mentoring in your life? What sense does it make to you?" This question may take a future orientation; for example, "Given what you have reconstructed in these interviews, where do you see yourself going in the future?" .... The combination of exploring the past to clarify the events that led participants to where they are now, and describing the concrete details of their present experience, establishes conditions for reflecting upon what they are now doing in their lives. The third interview can only be productive if the foundation for it has been established in the first two.' (Seidman, 1998: 12)

---

18 Compare Spradley (1979) – TW's note.

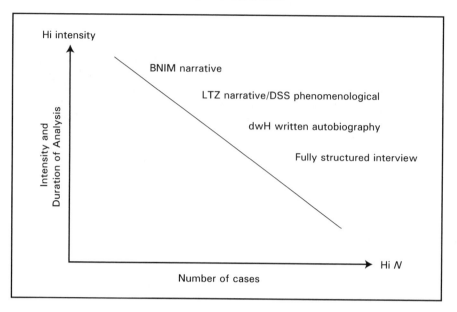

FIGURE 6.8 **Trade-off Between Number of Cases (N) and Intensity of Interviewing Method**

Again, there are clear similarities with BNIM as detailed earlier, and significant differences. There seems to be more of a specification of particular standard phases and situations, and also a gap between 'past origins' (the life-history) and 'present experiences' (interview 2), and those appear to be seen in terms of 'what they actually/ typically do', again with a prepared specification of relationships – 'with their students, their mentors … the wider community'. The final session asks for a quite specific self-theorizing of the past and present previously described, what BNIM would define as 'argumentation' about the meaning of the life, Labov and Waletsky's 'moral of the story'. The 'details of experiences' are not necessarily asked for in terms of narrative, certainly not exclusively, though there are references to story, and clearly narrative would be a welcomed mode of response. However, 'what is your job? what is it like to do what you do?' clearly does not require narrative, though it may definitely get at description and argumentation in a valuable and powerful way.

de Waele and Harré's Written Autobiographical Method

This is very similar to the structure proposed by J.P. de Waele and R. Harré in their 'Autobiography as a psychological method' (1979). This is reported by W.M. Runyan (1984: 183–4) as follows:

'Another idiographic method … is that of the "assisted autobiography". In this method, an individual "is assisted by a well-trained team in the production of a document, which is a representation of how he views his own life-course, his own knowledge, beliefs, interpretive schemata and principles of action and judgement".

continued

continued

The first step in the method is for the person to produce an autobiography written in his or her own terms.

A team of skilled interpreters then raises a series of questions about the document, drawing upon an intensive nine-part Biographical Inventory. Questions may be raised about topics not covered in the initial autobiography, about apparent contradictions and inconsistencies in the autobiography, about the experience of producing it, about the meaning and interpretation of particular events, and so on.

Accounts offered by the participant can be compared with data collected from other sources .... Questions can then be raised about the relationship between this new information and the initial autobiography. Finally, through a dialogical process, a revised and negotiated autobiographical document is produced.

This final autobiography "is not a record of happenings and responses to them, but is a record of interpretations of happenings, the planning of responses to them, the understandings of successes and failures in these matters. In short, it provides a cognitive map both of how the individual now represents his life to himself and how he represents his resources by which he sees himself to have coped or failed to cope with the problems and crises of that life as it unfolded".' (De Waele and Harré, 1979: 206, cited Runyan)

The above suggests a primarily non-oral development of a personal biography, which can also be built into the development of a research programme, as well as biographical-narrative interviews of one sort or another.

To conclude. All design strategy is a compromise, and any implementation is a further compromise. Your theory of interviewing subjects and process, and your overall research design, dictates what is an acceptable compromise and what, in given conditions, is unacceptable or counter-productive for your particular research purposes.

CONCLUSION: SQUIN–BNIM AND THE GENERAL CRQ–TQ–II MODEL

Having concluded our detailed discussion of the BNIM model of biographic-interpretive interviewing based on a single initial question aimed at inducing narrative, an example of what might be seen as a lightly structured depth-interviewing strategy, and its brief comparison with other models, I should now show how it fits into the general CRQ–TQ–II model used in this manual.

Figure 4.3 (p. 63) provided the general framework in the pyramid shape from CRQ at the top through TQs to the IIs serving each TQ. I can apply this to the SQUIN-BNIM research programme in Figure 6.9.

A fuller diagram is given in Figure 6.10, in which I have indicated the way that biographic-narrative interviews of the BNIM variety and the CRQ that governs them can fit into any overall CRQ of a complex multi-method project (Brannen, 1992). This is indicated by the 'nesting' of the CRQs in the middle of the figure within the structure governed by the Project CRQ at the top of the figure.

The above discussion has demonstrated the way in which the research design may quite specifically require interview sessions or subsessions that operate in

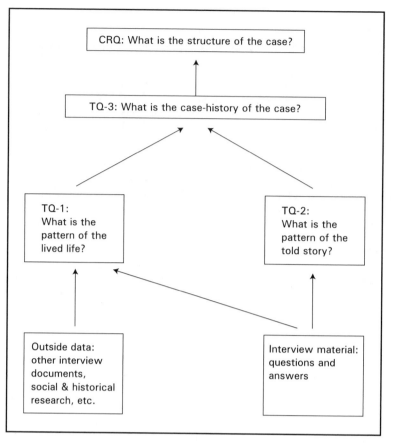

FIGURE 6.9 **BNIM in the CRQ–IQ Structure (1)**

quite different ways. They obviously do not exhaust the field of possible multi-subsession design, but only suggest possibilities.

I have already discussed the instrumentation theory which identifies the importance of always asking for narrative in the first two subsessions. In Figure 6.10, it is important to notice that

1 the CRQ and the TQs determine the choice of informant, the initial narrative IQ (the SQUIN), and the final subsession 3 pre-prepared IQs;
2 the goal of the initial IQ, the SQUIN, in subsession 1 is in large measure to allow the 'system of relevancy' of the informant to express itself in the first and the second subsession;
3 subsession 3, the final subsession, is more organized under the control of the 'system of relevancy' of the researcher.

Although the interviewee's self-expression in the first subsession is initiated by a SQUIN determined by the system of relevancy of the researcher, and therefore it cannot be called in the strict sense completely free association, it is pretty close to being unstructured by the researcher. It is at the 'free associative' end of the interview spectrum.

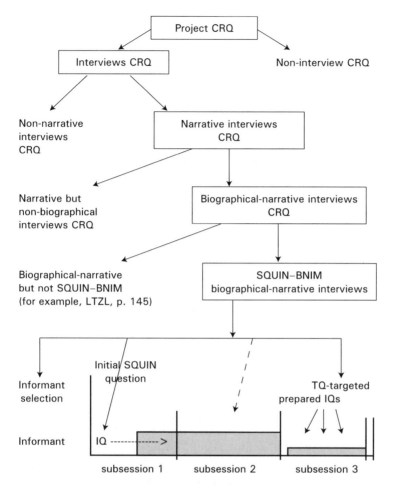

FIGURE 6.10 **Project CRQ and the Use of BNIM**

The final subsession 3, with its TQ-derived pre-prepared questions, is at the more structured end of the spectrum. Some or all of the questions may be fully structured.

Figure 6.10 may be easier to understand once you have read Chapter 12 on the analysis of BNIM interview material. You may wish to come back to it then.

7

Preparing Moderately- or Heavily-Structured Interviews

I have already argued that the design of all interview sessions is determined by the CRQ–TQ model, by the chosen conceptual framework, the chosen theoretical focus and by the knowledge/prejudice-base of the researcher as these produce theory-questions. See Part I and the earlier discussion in Part II.

In the previous chapter, I outlined in detail how this worked out in respect of the first two subsessions of interviews for the Biographic-Narrative-Interpretive Method of interviewing for narratives, using primarily a single question to induce such narratives. Such SQUIN–BNIM interviewing can be seen as an example of lightly structured depth interviewing (LSDI).

In this chapter, I go on to consider more broadly the general issues of designing more-structured depth-interviewing sessions: fairly-fully structured ones (FFSDI). These are characterized by the need for a wide repertoire of prepared informant questions and other interviewer interventions (IQs and other IIs).

> It should be remembered that, in the case of FFSDI sessions arising from earlier BNIM subsessions, the theory-questions (TQs) that are the core of such designs arise also from the knowledge-base enriched by working on subsessions 1 and 2 to produce them.

Our pyramid model of SSDI design has already been presented (p. 63 onwards) and I shall not repeat it here. Instead, I shall take the discussion further. Since we are talking of the designing of interview sessions which are fairly-fully structured by the interviewer, where the interviewer expects to have quite a high rate of pre-prepared and follow-up questions and other interventions, I shall start by considering variations of interviewer style and interview genre: from passive to active listening, and across a range of genres of active interviewer style.

I shall continue with a general discussion of formulating interviewer questions and other interviewer interventions, and conclude with a more specific discussion of such interventions and questions, firstly stressing the importance of the different psychological self-setting of yourself as interviewer, and then going on to elaborate precise and targeted IQ formulations.

I already argued that the precise formulation of TQs and the CRQ was essential for clear research design. I stressed the care that had to be taken with the formulation of an initial IQ for BNIM narrative interviewing so that it precisely did *not* provide specific directions for the interviewee beyond its brief. As we shall see, in dealing with moderately and strongly structured SSDI, where the goal is different and sometimes the instrumentation theory is different, we often have to improvise IQs that are very precisely targeted to leave the interviewee relatively *little* room for manoeuvre.

VARIABLE STANCE: PASSIVE LISTENING TO 'ACTIVE' INTERVIEWING

I start with the listening strategies of the moderately or heavily structured inter-view session and what they mean in terms of the 'psychological set' they suggest. It is useful here to draw a broad contrast between two opposite poles of a spec-trum. These can be seen either as the spontaneous style of an interviewer or, given sufficient interviewer flexibility, as a consciously chosen strategy for a particular interview.

Listening and Genres of Interviewing Experience

I have already discussed the practice of 'active listening' above, with special but not exclusive relevance to BNIM. It is important for us to be conscious of our personal spontaneous style, its strengths and its weaknesses. It is important to develop our capacity for a range of styles appropriate to the interview task and situation and to be conscious about the strategy and tactics of mixing assertive and receptive practice.

How have such styles been described? I shall look at two attempts: by Massarik and Dillon, respectively. A style can be seen as either a posture that the interviewer takes up, or as an experience that the interviewee undergoes. Experience and phantasy both enter into the experiencing of the InterView (to borrow Kvale's, 1996 typography) between two people.

Massarik (1981: 205) summarizes a typology of experienced interview relations from the point of view of the interviewee as follows:

- 'In the *Hostile interview*, the interviewer is the *Enemy*, and the relationship is of combat with specific information and its consequence the prize of war.
- In the *Limited Survey interview*, the interviewer appears as *Automaton*, punching certain buttons, seeking to elicit mechanical response.
- In the *Rapport interview*, the interviewer emerges as *Human-Being-in-a-role*, not denying his/her humanity and acknowledging the humanity of the interviewee, while still focusing essentially on subject-matter and on specific replies.
- In the *Asymmetrical-Trust interview*, the interviewer is defined as *Sage*, as source of counsel and wisdom, and the interviewee as petitioner, holding the weak side of a power-balance. [Or vice-versa? TW]
- In the *Depth-interview*, interviewer and interviewee, in substantial balance meet as *Peers*, their humanities expressed in circumscribed terms but with continuing emphasis on the specific goals of response content.
- In the *Phenomenal-interview*, interviewer and interviewee become *Caring Companions*, mutually committed to the enhancement of understanding, their respective humani-ties richly and actively revealed.'

As regards the last two 'types', readers of this manual will recognize that the direc-tion is welcome but that the account is perhaps a little thin.

A different way of thinking about questioning style or strategy is suggested by Dillon (1990). He identifies a number of domains of questioning practice in society, each one of which is characterized by a particular style of relationship between questioner and questionee. His work is too long to develop here, but his feel for the differences of atmosphere and questioning practices makes his list of domains suggestive. I can ask myself whether my interview might feel to the interviewee at some point or other like one or other of the following:

- classroom questioning
- courtroom questioning
- clinic questioning: psychotherapy
- clinic questioning: medicine
- personnel interviewing
- criminal interrogation
- journalistic interviewing
- survey questioning.

Reading Dillon's detailed account of the pattern of questioning in each of these areas, it seems to me that most, if not all, of these modes of questioning and relating can be seen as deviations from the style of questioning and interaction that is normally most suitable for semi-structured depth interviewing for social research. Some are a considerable distance away from the normative model which I would suggest is normally most productive; some are much closer. However, research interviewing is not identical with any of the above.

If my interview feels too much like one of Dillon's categories – either during the interview or afterwards when reading the transcript or listening to my voice on the tape – then I urgently need to consider the impact of that style on the intersubjective experience of my interviewee and consequently on their response in the interview.

Receptive and Assertive Practices

Broadly speaking, we can perhaps distinguish between a relatively passive receptive style or strategy, on the one hand, and a relatively active assertive style or strategy, on the other.

Receptive strategy is close to Carl Rogers's model of psychotherapy. It empowers the informant, enabling them to have a large measure of control in the way in which they answer the relatively few and relatively open questions they are asked. This was exemplified in the section on BNIM interviewing, first subsession. The flavour of this 'active listening' approach can perhaps be conveyed in Rosenthal's description of the first part of her BNIM interviewing strategy:

'At the beginning of every individual interview, we made the following request to the biographer:

"please tell us your family story and your personal life history. Anything that occurs to you. You have as much time as you like to tell it. I won't ask any questions for now. I will just make some notes on the things I would like to ask you about later, if I haven't got enough time today, perhaps in a second interview."

continued

continued

By posing this initial narrative question, we are not specifying any particular theme in the first part of the biographical-narrative interview. Generally, this request to hear the interviewee's family history and life story is followed by a long biographical narration (i.e. biographical self-presentation) often lasting for hours, not interrupted by questions from the interviewers at any time. The interviewers use non-verbal and paralinguistic expressions of interest and attention to encourage this narrative .... This leaves it up to the biographer to determine which themes are addressed, and in how much detail, as well as how they present them, and in what sequence.' (Rosenthal, 1998: 3)

At the other end of the spectrum is one with a very interviewer-assertive strategy, like Massarik's 'hostile' or Dillon's 'courtroom' strategy. Assertive strategy close to legal interrogation enables the interviewer to control the responses, provoke and illuminate self-contradiction, absences, provoke self-reflexivity and development (Potter and Weatherell, Holstein and Gubrium). Its flavour is perhaps suggested in Holstein and Gubrium's' *Active Interview:* they give an example of an interview in which the interviewer encourages the interviewee to explore the same situation from a variety of 'stand/view/points' (my terms).

'Neither elaborate narratives nor one-word replies emerge without provocation. The active interviewer's role is to incite the respondent's answers, virtually *activating narrative production* [italics in the original]. Where standardized approaches to interviewing attempt to strip the interview of all but the most neutral, impersonal, stimuli (but see Holstein and Gubrium, 1995, for a discussion of the inevitable failure of these attempts), the consciously active interviewer intentionally provokes responses by indicating – *even suggesting* – *narrative positions, resources, orientations and precedents* [italics added]. In the broadest sense, the interviewer attempts to activate the respondent's stock of knowledge[1] and bring it to bear on the discussion at hand in ways that are appropriate to the research agenda ....' (Holstein and Gubrium, 1995: 123–5)

My personal preference is for a receptive strategy rather than an assertive one as the dominant characteristic of semi-structured depth-interviewing. However, I recognize that assertive questioning may play a key role in some interviews, and, in others, even play a dominant part. Even where the interview as a whole is characterized by a relatively receptive style or strategy, at a particular point it may be very important to deploy a very assertive style or tactic. And vice-versa.

Nevertheless, I would argue that assertive strategy should be a rather subordinate, late or even absent part of most semi-structured research interviews. It depends on a very considerable rapport or, more usually, very considerable power-over. It will feel potentially threatening and controlling. It is unlikely to leave the interviewee feeling good.

---

1 To 'activate a stock' might be best understood as to 'explore the stock' by a variety of provocations. What about the 'complex stack of evaluations' and the 'stack of emotions' which might also be activated and explored as means or as ends or both? See Scheff (1997) for a further discussion of the complexities of 'message stacks'.

The success or failure of parts of the interview will depend on the subjective experience of the interviewee, and this is the more dependent upon your attitude and structuring as your interview design and practice moves away from the lightly structured towards the strongly structured end of the spectrum.

FORMULATING IQS AND OTHER IIS FOR TQS
AND CRQ – GENERAL LOGIC

I am now at the bottom line of the CRQ–IQ pyramid shown in Figure 4.3, as revised in Figure 7.1. In the revised version, the shaded levels of the informant questions are co-determined largely by the TQs which they serve but also partially by the characteristics of the particular informant to whom those questions will be put. This model applies to all varieties of semi-structured depth interviews.

The chapter is divided into two principal parts. In the second part, from p. 162 onwards, a number of different surveys of interview questions / informant questions are introduced. They are not there to replace or to constrain your research imagination and freedom to design appropriate IQs for each of your TQs; they are there to stimulate that imagination and to maximize that freedom.

Before that, in this first part, a more general orientation to the development of interviewer questions, prompts, probes and activity within the interview is suggested.

General Orientation for the Development of Interviewer
Questions and other Interventions

A few points from earlier discussions to bear in mind:

- Interview interventions are in the folk-language and the emergent idiolect of the interviewee.
- The theory-language of our particular social-science discipline is not the language that you use in the interview. A TQ is not an IQ, is a useful slogan. You should always 'translate' a TQ (in your theory language) to one or more instrumented-IQs (in the interviewee's natural language).
- We shall see how this works later, but a general rule is that you will have contaminated your interview if you find that you have told your interviewee what your CRQ and your TQs are. This is my general rule; others, more concerned for a 'democratic' or 'equal' relation between the two parties (Okeley) or with a different instrumentation theory (Pawson), may have different general rules.

Preparation for Reading this Chapter – Reading Transcripts
Find examples of detailed interview transcriptions in Dillon (1990), Lieblich et al. (1998) and Mishler (1986) and anywhere else you can. This will help you to get a sense of (a) the flow of an interview, (b) the questions, prompts and probes of the interviewer as they operate productively or counter-productively within that flow to get the material required.

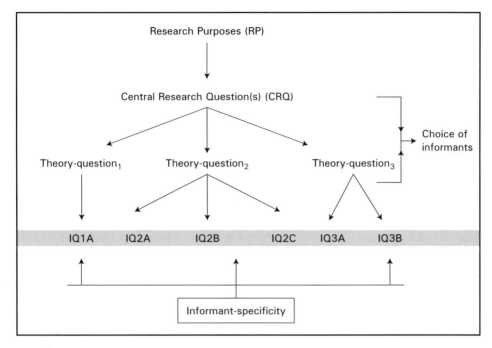

FIGURE 7.1   **CRQ → TQ → IQ and the Informants: Pyramid Model of the Co-determination of Initial Informant Questions by the TQs and by the Specificity of the Informants**

The TQs Largely Determine the Design of the Initial Informant Questions and Accompanying Stimulus Material

As an exercise, you may wish to look at one or more of the incomplete CRQ–IQ diagrams (p. 85 onwards) to sketch in some draft IQs (interviewer questions) for each of the TQs specified there. You will benefit more from the discussion below if you then imagine two completely different and contrasting informants, and, for the same set of TQs, construct appropriately different IQs for the two informants.

The theory of informant subjectivity-in-context also determines (in conjunction with the TQs) the designed structure of interview questioning. Considerable research in the area of survey questionnaire design particularly has been done on the way that the formulation of questions affects the answers given. The discussion of the models of interview communication of Foddy and Briggs in Part I suggests how this happens.

In addition, you need to consider what stimulus material can accompany your questions, prompts and probes.

1   In old people's homes, researchers have brought photographs of places, music and films of a previous period, household products of a certain time, newspapers. In such cases, the interviewer provides material which they hope will stimulate memory.

2 In research into the design of the home, researchers interview people in their home and ask about how they came to live in that particular place, and decide on interior decoration, and acquire particular artefacts: the interviewees in context provide the stimuli material that the interviewer uses.

3 Other stimulus material might include constructed vignettes, press cuttings, tape-recorded excerpts, or anything else you think might be appropriate. You might want to present the individual with something he has said or done or written or produced in the past: personal documents and artefacts.

Clearly, your sense of 'what is appropriate' for eliciting the interview material you want depends on your theory of subjectivities in general and your developing theory of (understanding of) the particular subject you are going to interview.

Informant Subjectivity: Hollway and Jefferson on the Defended Anxious Subject

Your 'model of subjectivity' (what could be called 'a model of human nature in interview') will be operating as a background assumption in your questioning-design work.

In Part I , I presented a model based on Briggs and others of the interview situation in general (p. 43 above). I now put forward the model of Hollway and Jefferson. Even if you disagree with their model put forward by them of human subjectivity in the interview situation, they are an example of an explicit 'instrumentation theory' for the designing (and interpreting) of interviews. Let us look at their argument.

Criticizing the British Crime Survey, they argue (Hollway and Jefferson, 2000, ch. 1) that much qualitative and quantitative inquiry shares a theory of the 'research subject' (the subjectivity of the person being researched):

'As we have already suggested, [the assumption] that an interviewee can "tell it like it is" still remains the starting point for most qualitative, interview-based, research .... The subject assumed by the BCS question and by all survey-type questions assumes that a person is one who

- shares meanings with the researcher
- is knowledgeable about his/her experience
- can access this through an imaginary scenario (which he or she may or may not have experienced)
- can capture it satisfactorily in a single concept
- can make distinctions in amount, such as the difference between "fairly safe" and "a bit unsafe".

Taking a research subject's account as a faithful reflection of "reality" similarly assumes a person is one who:

- shares meanings with the researcher
- is knowledgeable about him or herself [his or her actions, feelings, and relations]
- can access the relevant knowledge accurately and comprehensively (that is, has accurate memory)
- can convey that knowledge to a stranger listener
- is motivated to tell the truth to a stranger listener.'
  (Hollway and Jefferson, 2000: 10–12; last line modified, TW)

Hollway and Jefferson argue that the evidence shows that a *different model* of human nature, a different theory of subjectivity, is needed both to conduct depth interviews properly and to interpret their results satisfactorily. They indicate the nature of their own psycho-social model as follows:

> 'Threats to the self create anxiety ... this is a fundamental proposition in psychoanalytic theory where anxiety is viewed as inherent in the human condition. For psychoanalysis, anxiety precipitates defences against the threats it poses to the self, and these operate at a largely unconscious level. The shared starting point of all the different schools of psycho-analytic thought is this idea of a dynamic unconscious which defends against anxiety and significantly influences people's actions, lives and relations .... Anxiety and the defences which it precipitates are complex responses to events and people in the social world, both present and past. Defences against anxiety affect the discourses that people "choose" through which to perceive/fear crime, and this affects people's actions. The conception of an anxious, defended, subject is one which is simultaneously psychic and social. It is psychic, because it is the product of a unique series of anxiety-provoking life events and the manner in which they have been unconsciously defended against. It is social in three ways: first, because such defensive activities affect and are affected by discourses [systems of meaning which are a product of the social world]; secondly because the unconscious defences that we describe are intersubjective processes; and, thirdly, because of the real events in the external, social world which are defensively and discursively appropriated. It is this psycho-social conception of the subject that we believe is most compatible with a serious engagement in researching ....' (2000: 19–24)

Some sense of intersubjective anxiety within an interview can be found in the analysis of the two ways in which Isobel's interview with W could be understood (p. 34; see also Bar-On's harrowing 1999). Clearly, the concept of anxiety being used in that discussion was not much more than common-sense: even at that level, however, the notion of the self defending against anxieties is a powerful tool for understanding interaction. *Designing a semi-structured interview interaction* in this perspective means that you must not ignore, or hallucinate away, the problem of anxiety but explicitly cater for, and monitor, it.

I would argue that an 'instrumentation theory' combining the Briggs–Wengraf general model but integrating into it the above Hollway–Jefferson model of anxious defended subjectivity is a good starting point for depth-interview research. Obviously, the key problem is applying it in the design of interview sessions and of interview questions and other interventions, prepared and improvised.

Basic Unit of the Semi-structured Interview: The Open Question with Prompt-supported Answering and Interviewer Listening

As I have already said, in the typical design of a semi-structured-interview, what is designed are the initial questions. With an 'active follow-up strategy', questions, prompts, probes, statements and other interventions by you will be pretty constantly improvised and invented by you during the interview. Not knowing how they are going to answer to your prepared initial questions, you nevertheless must prepare to respond to their answering!

```
Theory-question A:
        Informant-question A.1  _____
        Informant-question A.2  _____

Theory-question B:
        Informant-question B.1  _____
        Informant-question B.2  _____
        Informant-question B.3  _____

Theory-question C:
        etc.
```

FIGURE 7.2   **Logical List of IQs for TQs**

One student prepared 43 initial questions for a supposedly semi-structured interview of 30 minutes. Four or three, not 43, open-ended questions might have been more appropriate.

The most frequent and typical unit of a semi-structured interview takes the form of an *open question* and then a *comparatively lengthy response* which the interviewer holds back from interrupting.

The Structure of a TQ–IQ Question Schedule

In general, generating or studying typologies of questions is a way of sensitizing myself to old and new ways of formulating questions by *systematically considering dimensions* on which interview questions might vary. Good typologies can also serve as a *map of options* to inspect at any given moment to stimulate and discipline my creative imagination.

Clearly, the number of questions that could be asked is infinite, as is the number of typologies that could be usefully generated or studied. I can only suggest some that have been fruitful.

Always remember that interview questions should serve their purpose within a design, and above all, they should serve to help answer the theory-questions that serve the central research question. If you wish them to serve their intended function, consider the *timing* of your interview-questions: the *right question* posed at the *wrong time* is the wrong intervention.

The Format of the Logical Schedule of Informant Questions

For each theory-question, I generate 3–7 informant-questions for specified informants on the basis of which I hope to get adequate theory-answers. I list them as shown in Figure 7.2. This, as is done for example in Figure 7.3, lays them out visually for quick inspection of their 'logic'. Once I have laid them out, *I get friends* to help me check them. Are the informant questions necessary for answering the TQ under which they are slotted? Together, are they sufficient? It is *absurdly easy for me* not to see how there are obvious informant-questions which I have wrongly left out, or informant-questions which I should have left out, or modified, or moved to the slot of another theory-question. *It is much easier to see the flaws in other people's draft lists.* Do it for them; above all, get others to do it for you!

Figure 7.3 gives extracts from such a list by an undergraduate student, Ferhat A, doing research into a university module-course entitled IT 100. This is an example of a good logical TQ–IQ design.

'... *Theory-question 1:   How well-organized as a course do the students feel IT 100 is?*

1.1.   How do you feel about how the course was planned?
1.2.   How do you feel about the time given for assignment deadlines?
1.3.   How much did you feel you had to study at home in order to prepare for or understand the next day's lecture?
1.4.   Did you find the lecturer and/or seminar group leader lagging behind or ahead of schedule?
1.5.   Did you feel there was enough equipment for everyone to use?
1.6.   Did you feel you were getting enough help from the staff during the workshop session?

Theory-question 2:   Did the informants find the context of the course relevant to their particular interest in computers?

2.1.   To what extent did the material of the course deal with contemporary issues?
2.2.   To what extent did you feel the students could relate to the examples given by the lecturer to illustrate how computers work?
2.3.   To what extent did the course satisfy your particular interest in computing?
2.4.   How much did the course justify your decision to take it in the first place?
2.5.   To what extent do you think IT100 was relevant to the other set of modules that you took?

Theory-question 3: Did the students find there was sufficient variety of content within the course? ...

Theory-question 4: What degree of satisfaction did the students experience from the way the material was presented and taught? ...

Theory-question 5: How did the informants feel about the fairness of the assessment?

5.1.   Were the questions of the assignments written in a way that was clear enough to be understood?
5.2.   Were explanations of the subject matter clear enough to enable you to grasp what had to be answered?
5.3.   Did the tutors make the answer format they preferred clear to you? ...

FIGURE 7.3   **Extracts from a TQ–IQ Structure (Ferhat A)**

Although many of the answers to the above might be *yes/no*, clearly the interviewer who is prepared to ask follow-up questions to such *yes/no* answers can enable the interviewee to expand their initial response in a semi-structured and more open way. Sometimes the initial-question schedules for a semi-structured depth-interviewing session may appear identical to those for a short fully structured interview: the difference lies in the intention of the interviewer to use each initial question to develop a series of follow-up questions on the basis of the initial responses. The example above is typical of such a strategy. For training purposes, however, you are recommended to develop initial IQs of a more 'open' sort, as discussed below.

The Structure of the Planned Sequence for the Session

Please note at this point that the *logical schedule* may or may not be identical to the *sequence schedule*. When I come to plan the sequence of IQs for the session, I don't necessarily bunch all the IQs that serve a particular TQ together; there may be very good reasons for separating them.

The logical schedule is designed to enable us to ensure that there is a tight fit between the CRQ–TQ–IQ levels. Once this has been achieved, then there is a question of the order or sequence in which the required IQs are to be posed to the interviewee. A 'sequence schedule' is then created. The sequence of the questions to be put in the interview may, therefore, be very different from the structure of the logical schedule.

> For certain purposes, particularly if it is not wished that the interviewee should rapidly understand the theoretical point of the interview questions, the IQs relating to a particular TQ should be carefully separated.

> This would be one inference from an instrumentation theory where, once an interviewee grasps the theoretical point of the questioning, then he or she may consciously or unconsciously change the way in which they respond, thereby – according to this instrumentation theory – reducing the validity of those responses. That instrumentation theory then provides a basis for a structuring of the interview 'sequence schedule' in which *questions that logically relate together must be carefully not posed together* – must be carefully placed well away from each other – to avoid triggering the self-defensiveness of the subject.

> For example, interview research designed to explore 'unconscious racism' (a) might use indirect rather than direct questions and (b) might separate the relevant indirect questions and intersperse them with others relating to other apparent topics.

Having discussed the difference between the logical schedule of TQs and IQs and the actual interview schedule of IQs, we now need to focus upon the designing of the informant questions and other interventions.

FORMULATING IQS AND OTHER IIS FOR TQS AND CRQ – IN DETAIL

The number of types and typologies that exist or could be generated is infinite. I distinguish here between (i) typologies of interview questions that are concerned with functions in the interview process and (ii) typologies of interview questions that focus on substantive areas of research interest.

I shall look at open and closed questions, the avoidance of biased and leading questions, and at IQs designed to constrain (a) the generality or the specificity of answers and (b) the amount of detail and the length of the answer wanted. I then go on to present Kvale's process typology and then argue for the necessity for constantly adapting the informant-questions to the language-patterns of the informant.

Open and Closed Questions

Semi-structured interviewing is characterized by an emphasis on relatively open questions. However, you may wish also to put certain closed questions. Consequently, what is crucial is the capacity first to recognize the difference between open and closed questions and, secondly, to be able to generate the one or the other rapidly in an interview situation. It is always surprising to discover how difficult this is, not so much in theory but rather in practice under pressure. Here, as elsewhere, getting training and practice beforehand is invaluable.

Open, not Closed; and Design the IQ-sequence so as to Free and to Widen the Range of Legitimated Answers

We have already considered the BNIM of the Berlin *Quatext* School which has a first session that 'takes as long as it takes' in which a first completely open-question is put and no follow-up or further questions are put, in order to elicit the maximum amount of free response in the informant's own words to complete the informant's gestalt.

The opposite can also apply. Clearly, if you want precise information, it is stupid and misleading not to ask directly for what you want. Do not ask general questions like 'What is your background?' when you just to want to find answers to precise points, such as

1 whether their mother ever had a full-time job, or
2 whether they were discouraged by their teachers from staying on at school.

As always, the important thing is to know that some TQs require precise information that may entail closed-ended questions, and that other TQs will require open-ended questions. Hence the crucial role of developing clear TQs, so that the IQs serve their theoretical function clearly.

Learning to Distinguish Open from Closed Questions, and Overcoming the Tendency to Closure!

Patton (1990: 298–99) has a very good transcription from a training workshop which indicates the difficulty of asking genuinely-open questions, rather than closed ones (Figure 7.4). The transcript is in the left column; the right-hand column records truly open-ended alternatives to the dichotomous questions actually asked.

Leading and Biased Questions Contaminating the Response

Most informants feel somewhat vulnerable in 'opening up' to an informant: if you let them know in any way that you have a preferred response to one of your questions, they are more likely to 'tailor' their response to what you seem to be hoping for. A few will go the other way, and be determined to give you what you seem to be hoping not to hear. Either way, you contaminate the responses.

Much of this is 'read' by them from your tone of voice and general body behaviour (non-verbal communication) and will be dealt with later. But it takes a lot of work to eliminate loading and bias from the prepared questions, let alone from the spontaneous follow-up ones. Here is an example of 'leading' questions.

> TQ. 'How do students feel about the idea of lectures in terms of the amount of knowledge gained?'
>
>> IQ1. 'Do you find lectures too long and impersonal?'
>> IQ2. 'Do you feel that in hindsight you were misinformed about the contents of the course?'

It is much better to indicate how wide the range of possible and legitimate answers is and to indicate why all of them might be reasonable and so welcomed by you. For example, the IQs above might be reformulated as:

1 'Some people find lectures too long; others find them too short. What would you say your perception was?'
2 'Would you say that, in hindsight, before the start of the course, you were well-informed or rather misinformed about the contents of the course?'

The most frequent mistake is to unconsciously urge the listener to give the response that you are expecting or desiring. An example might be:

> 'Would you agree that Mrs Thatcher was / Mr Blair is / an uncaring Prime Minister?'

Instruction: Okay, now we're going to play an interviewing game. I want you to take turns asking me questions about an evaluation I just completed. The program being evaluated was a staff development demonstration project that involved taking professionals into a wilderness setting for a week. That's all I'm going to tell you at this point. I'll answer your questions as precisely as I can, but I'll only answer what you ask. I won't volunteer any information that isn't directly asked for by your question.

Actual interview	*What the interviewer really wanted to know: open-ended question*
Question: were you the evaluator of this program? Answer: yes	What was your role in this program?
Question: were you doing a formative evaluation? Answer: mostly	What was the purpose of the evaluation?
Question: were you trying to find out if the people changed from being in the wilderness? Answer: that was part of it	What were you trying to find out in the evaluation?
Question: did they change? Answer: some of them did	How did participation in the program affect the participants?
Question: did you interview people both before and after the program? Answer: yes	What kinds of information did you collect for the evaluation?
Question: did you also go along as a participant in the program? Answer: yes	How were you personally involved in the program?
Question: did you find that being in the program affected what happened? Answer: yes	How do you think your participation in the program affected what happened?
Question: did you have a good time? Answer: yes	What was the wilderness experience like for you?
Question: are you reluctant to tell us about the program?	I'd like to find out more about the program. What would be the best way for me to learn more from you about it?

FIGURE 7.4 **Closed versus Open Questions – Patton's Demonstration (Patton, 1990: 299–300)**

Alternatively, much more usefully, one could ask a number of more indirect questions, and see whether the concept of 'caring' is an informant-dimension or not. If it is not, then the design shown in Figure 7.5 allows the informant's own keywords and discourse to operate. This more complicated indirect preparation is more likely to produce eventual theory-answers of value[2] than is the apparently more direct and straightforward original blunt informant-question. *Practising going two steps back and re-approaching more indirectly* will give you the necessary practice.

---

2 Including insight into the *variety* of folk-concepts behind the term 'caring'.

(a)   'What are important aspects of policy and style for Prime Ministers to have?'

(b)   'What are their relative importance, which ones are more important, which ones are less?'

and only then:

(c)   'How does/did Prime Minister X rank on the (*informant-defined-dimension*)?' and, if nothing like the concept of 'caring' has come up, only then asking

(d)   'Does the word "caring" mean anything to you? If so, what?' and, if there is a positive answer to the first part of (d), only then asking the rather leading question:

(e)   'Would you agree that Mrs Thatcher was / Mr Blair is / an uncaring Prime Minister?'

FIGURE 7.5   **Prime Ministers as Caring? Informant Terms and Definitions**

EXERCISE 7.1   IMPROVING INTERVIEW QUESTIONS

(a) 'Some students are irresponsible, others do well.
Which would you say is true of most students?'

Improve this question!

(b) The example of a TQ–IQ structure given by Ferhat A was that of a good logical structure. However, it is a flawed example of a semi-structured depth interview, since the IQs are often too closed and non-neutral. As an exercise, review the IQs on p. 161; identify which ones are not genuinely open and improve each one of them to make them conform to the criteria of openness and non-leading neutrality.

Let us consider some further examples. One student had a 'leading question':

TQ2 ... to ascertain how the informants respond to society's stereotypes and enforced guilt? ...

IQ 2.6 'Do you feel guilty about going out to work? Do you feel that society tries to make you feel guilty?'

I remarked:

'You lead very strongly by (i) implying that she has a tendency to "feel guilty" (which may not be true) – she may feel a mixture of positive and negative emotions and positive and negative evaluations; and (ii) that something called "society" might be "trying to make her feel this". Far too much a "leading" question ....'

Similarly another IQ under the same TQ ('Society has characterized you as a housewife: do you resent this?') is also leading in a very similar way.

On another student's design for a study of homeless people, I commented

'Some of the IQs are leading. 2.4, "When you were homeless was there a consensus that the homelessness crisis was the government's fault?", is an obvious example. So is 3.3 which asks for a single-cause explanation ("Who or what is responsible for homelessness") rather than asking "Is there a problem about explaining homelessness?", which might get at more complex arguments.'

The prejudice in the TQ may be also supported by 'loading' in the IQs. If you don't notice the bias in one of the design elements, you are less likely to notice it in another, as in the following example:

'TQ3. To gain a personal view about the informants' views towards nannies and whether they feel nannies have an adverse effect on children ...

> 3.1. Have your children had nannies? What are your views on nannies? Do your views differ about child-minders?
> 3.2. Do you think nannying has an adverse effect on children at an early age, getting attached to someone who is not permanent in their life?
> 3.3. In your opinion, are children spoilt by parents who go out to work and therefore may over-compensate?'

I should stress the problem is with the IQs, especially the last two, not with the TQ. Theory-questions may well be legitimately prejudiced – as when they are testing a particular hypothesis – but then particular care needs to be taken not to contaminate the IQs designed to get unbiased material to test the 'prejudiced TQ'. Karl Popper (see Lakatos, 1970) would even argue that the IQs should be slanted in the direction opposite to that of the TQ so as to enhance the chances of the TQ hypothesis being falsified.

In hypothesis-testing, the hypothesis should be a controversial statement about reality. "Informants feel nannies have an adverse effect on children" is an excellently arguable hypothesis. However, to avoid the least suspicion about the validity of the evidence, the IQs must be manifestly unbiased. TQs may be open or unidirectional (i.e. biased), but IQs must aim for maximally valid evidence. Biased IQs normally invalidate inferences you would like to draw from answers. The more the TQ has a favoured hypothetical answer, the more care must be taken to ensure that the IQ is not *slanted towards* producing material favourable to the favoured TQ hypothesis.

The extract from a CRQ–TQ–IQ design, given in Figure 7.6, shows a structure strong in logic but also strong in (removable) bias. The CRQ was fine. The TQs were a bit odd. The IQs were badly in need of improvement. My comments were:

- 'IQ1A, 1B all assume that there is some effect. They inhibit anybody who wishes to declare that there is no effect. 1B focuses on thoughts, should there not be a 1C on behaviour?
- Is 2A really about distinguishing fact from fiction, rather than distinguishing the two but deciding that TV is an "adequate" (accurate) representation? Or are two distinct questions forced into one sentence?
- IQ3C is begging for the answer "more likely".
- IQ4A assumes that TV must play "a part" and makes "no part at all" difficult to say.

The researcher's CRQ was *In what ways, if at all, does the depiction of violence on TV influence teenagers' behaviour and state of mind?*

Her TQ–IQ structure was as follows:

TQ1: How does the informant believe the depiction of violence influences teenagers?

1A: Some people believe the *amount* of TV violence watched affects teenagers; others believe it is how *graphically* the violence is portrayed that affects them. Do you think that either or both of these views has any merit?

1B: In what ways if at all do you see the violence shown on television as influencing teenagers' thoughts?

TQ2: To what extent does the informant believe that exposure to TV violence cultivates teenagers' attitudes and sensitizes or desensitizes them to actual violence?

2A: Would you say that fictional TV life is accepted by teenagers as adequately representing reality, or do you think that they can distinguish between the two?

2B: It is claimed that violence on TV either teaches teenagers to accept actual violence or makes them more fearful of it. Do you have any thoughts on this?

TQ3: Does TV promote actual violence to [?] teenagers from childhood either directly or indirectly?

3A: To what extent do you think that watching TV teaches teenagers how to behave?

3B: It has been said that violent characters on TV are portrayed as heroes to teenagers; others argue that the harmful consequences of resorting to violence are always shown. What do you think?

3C: If violence is shown on TV as a socially acceptable way to solve problems, is this more or less likely to result in teenagers committing acts of violence?

TQ4: Is TV violence alone enough to turn a teenager to actual violence, or must its influence work in conjunction with other factors?

4A: Do you think watching violent scenes on TV can directly lead a teenager to commit actual violence, or do you think that other factors must play a part alongside TV?

4B: In recent years, lawyers have sometimes used the violent scenes in particular programmes or films shown on TV as defence for violent crimes committed by teenagers; others argue that TV cannot be held responsible. What thoughts do you have about this?

4C: Some argue that a teenager's upbringing strongly affects how they interpret and act upon the violence they see on TV; others argue that the connection is not strong. What are your thoughts on this?

FIGURE 7.6   **CRQ–TQ–IQ Bias: Violent TV and Teenage Violence**

'In general, there is a strong bias in your questions taken as a whole. The logical connection of the IQs to the TQs is strong, but the bias of the IQs makes them less valid.'

The above examples should have shown the distinction of open and closed questioning, and the difficulty of avoiding leading and biased questions. The more practice you can get in groups of at least two in brainstorming possible IQs for your TQ, and then having them critiqued, the better.

Generality/Specificity of Answer

This is a tricky point, but an important one. Often, in social-science research – this is less true of the historian of unique events – I am struggling to get evidence for generalizations. I am trying to infer from particular cases to more general truths. If I want to know about football hooligans, I may be asking one or two people

Level One: Universal statements about all societies
'I just talk the same way to everyone. I always refuse to take notice of how high-up they think they are.'
'Human nature being what it is, ... You can't change human nature.'
'. . . That's just the way things are, I guess. It's always the way it goes.'

Level Two: Sub-universal cross-cultural descriptive statements
'I talk differently to some men, but then it depends on whether I fancy them or not, doesn't it?'

Level Three: General statements about a particular society or culture group
'I can't see the point of having a phone. You have to pay for it, even if you don't use it. Besides, people can always pop round if they want to talk to you. I suppose it's different in large cities, though.'

'Everybody lives so far away from each other nowadays, that, if it weren't for the phone and the plane, we'd never make contact with anybody.'

Level Four: General statements about one or more specific cultural scenes
'I love weekends. I always have a special meal with all the family there . . . and nobody has to do any work.'

Level Five: Specific statements about a cultural domain
'I don't give a stuff about the decor of a pub: it's the people I go for.'

Level Six: Specific incident statements
'At this point in the conversation, she seemed to get quite agitated, screwing up her face and twisting her hands several times for about a minute.'

'On Wednesday, I decided that, for our new house, I would not have a dish-washer installed. I don't think he likes the idea, though, since he's the one who does the washing up.'

FIGURE 7.7 **Six Levels of Abstraction Specificity (after Spradley, 1979: 210)**

about them, but I want to get at their approach to football hooligans in general, and I would like to generalize from our two informants (or 422 informants) to the population of informants from which I have only taken a sample. I am therefore driven by an itch to generalize and to ask our informants for generalities: 'How do you feel about lectures in general?' To get at *my* theoretical generalizations, I wrongly think that I have to ask my interviewee for *their* generalizations.

J.P. Spradley expounded a 6-level grid (1979: 210) of the types of statements that can be made: from the most general to the most particular (Figure 7.7). Think of it as illustrating a principle rather than as a definitive statement. The examples are mine.

The important thing is that you need to formulate questions which make it more probable that the informant will *talk at the level of generality–specificity you want*. And you need to find follow-up questions to 'fight back with' in the potential power-struggle if the informant is uncomfortable speaking at that level, but you decide that you still want to press him or her to do so. They may want to be at Spradley Level Six when you want them to talk at Spradley Level One, or vice-versa. Remember that it is your TQ and your instrumentation-theory that determines the level of generality and specificity that you need.

Your prepared informant-questions may need to move backwards and forwards between Spradley levels from the very general to the very specific, but, as has been

'How do you feel about lectures in general? *general question*

'Could you give me the names of one good lecturer, one bad lecturer, and one other lecturer that you've heard in the last two weeks?'
Going through each name in turn:

'Could you describe what happened in their lecture?'
'What was good about that lecture?'
'What was bad about that lecture?'

Searching for sub-generalities:
'Are there any other things about lectures that make them good?'
'Are there any other things about lectures that make them bad?'
'Have you ever in the past wanted different things from lectures than you now want?'

'Summing up, how would you say you feel about lectures in general?' – *general question*

FIGURE 7.8 **Generality-IQs through Particular IQs**

said, 'depth' involves a fair amount of focus on 'detailed specifics' and on contradictions and non-contradictions between general and specific statements.

If generalizations from your informants are important to get, it may be rather better to have a sequence of informant-questions which only asks the 'generality question' within a context of much more particular ones. See Figure 7.8, for example.

The chances are that you would find a much richer answer to the 'general question' *once you had gone in depth into particular cases* … and that, even if his or her answer to the concluding general question was pretty banal, *you would understand what was meant by the banality much better* than you did before you *first* asked the 'general question'.

Length of Answer (Amount of Detail) Wanted

You may find it necessary to indicate the length of answer that you want. This can to some extent be given by the prepared informant-question.

* You can preface the clear and distinct question by a short statement saying something like 'I am now coming to a really important question. I would like you to take your time in answering it, and any detail you can give me will be really appreciated. The question is the following. *Have you …?'*
* Alternatively you might ask for less detail. 'I have been going into quite a lot of detail, and will again. This is very helpful to me. But, just before I do so, *can you just tell me briefly whether you have …?'*

As interviewer the informant will normally be co-operating with what he or she takes to be your purposes and your timing. It is up to you to give them leads so that they can co-operate as well as possible. Remember they cannot know what you have in mind until you tell or show them.

This concludes our discussion of some generalities about interviewer questioning. They may be of help in planning your prepared interview questions. However, they will probably be of most value when you listen to a tape of yourself interviewing or read a transcript of an interview you have done and are trying to understand and improve your practice. Gradually by preparing questions and getting a friend to critique them, by doing interviews and going over your interventions carefully (as we did in the case of the interview with W, p. 20), you will raise the quality of your questioning.

What I have done in the preceding discussion is to think about interviewer questioning in general. To conclude this discussion, I present a sequence for an interview in terms of types of questions at different stages of the interview.

Kvale's Process Typology

In his *InterViews* (1996: 133–5), Kvale offers the following typology of interviewing questions which broadly follow the possible phases of an interview as a whole, or a segment of an interview on a given topic.

'Introducing Q

"Can you tell me about …?", "Do you remember an occasion when …?", "What happened in the episode you mentioned …?", and "Could you describe in as much detail as possible a situation in which learning occurred for you?" Such opening questions may yield spontaneous rich descriptions where the subjects themselves provide what they experience as the main dimensions of the phenomena being investigated. The remainder of the interview can then proceed as following up dimensions introduced in the story told in response to the initial question.

Follow-up Q

The subjects' answers may be extended through a curious, persistent and critical attitude of the interviewer. This can be done through direct questioning of what is said. Also a mere nod or "um" or just a pause can indicate to the subject to go on with the description. Repeating significant words of an answer can lead to further elaborations. Interviewers can train themselves to notice "red lights" in the answers – such as unusual terms, strong intonations, and the like – which may signal a whole complex of topics important to the subject. The key issue here is the interviewer's ability to listen to what is important to the subjects and at the same time to keep in mind the research questions of the investigation.

Probing Q

"Can you say something more about that?", "Can you give a more detailed description of what happened?" "Do you have further examples of this?" The interviewer here pursues the answers, probing their content but without stating what dimensions are to be taken into account.

Specifying Q

The interviewer may also follow up with more operationalizing questions, for instance: "What did you think then?", "What did you actually do when you felt a mounting anxiety?", "How did your body react?" In an interview with many general statements, the interviewer can also attempt to get more precise descriptions by asking "Have you also experienced this yourself?"

continued

continued

Direct Q

The interviewer here directly introduces topics and dimensions, for example: "Have you ever received money for good grades?", "When you mention competition, do you then think of a sportsmanlike or a destructive competition?" Such direct questions may preferably be postponed until later parts of the interview, after the subjects have given their own spontaneous descriptions and thereby indicated what aspects of the phenomenon are central to them.

Indirect Q

Here the interviewer may apply projective questions such as "How do you believe other pupils regard the competition for grades?" The answer may refer directly to the attitudes of others; it may also be an indirect statement of the pupil's own attitude, which he or she does not state directly. Careful further questioning will be necessary here to interpret the answer.

Structuring Q

The interviewer is responsible for the course of the interview and should indicate when a theme has been exhausted. The interviewer may directly and politely break off long answers that are irrelevant to the topic of the investigation by saying, for example, "I might be able to get back to this later, but, given the time, I would now like to introduce another topic".

Silence

Rather than making the interview a cross-examination by continually firing questions, the research interviewer can take a lead from therapists in employing silence to further the interview. By allowing pauses in the conversation, the subjects have ample time to associate and reflect and then break the silence themselves with significant information. Practise lengthening the milliseconds that you leave before you break into a pause or silence. During a period of silence, both you and your interviewee have a chance to reflect more deeply on what has been said and what could be said.

Interpretive Q

The degree of interpretation may merely involve rephrasing an answer, for instance: "You then mean that ...?", or attempts at clarification: "Is it correct that you feel that ...?", "Does the expression ... cover what you have just expressed?" There may also be more direct interpretations of what the subject has said: "Is it correct that your main anxiety about the grades concerns the reaction from your parents?" More speculative questions can take the form: "Do you see any connections between the two situations of competing with the other students for grades and your relation to your siblings at home?"' (Kvale, 1996: 133–5, modified)

Kvale's very useful account above does not – apart from the discussion of 'silence' – consider the necessarily improvised 'alternatives to questions' suggested by Dillon (pp. 199–200). Otherwise you should find it usefully summarizes points already made and adds further reflection. In particular, you may wish to consider whether it provides a model of a useful approach to sequencing types of questions in any interview that you might design. You might wish to compare it with the model of ethnographic interviewing that Spradley (1979: 58–68) presents both abstractly and in his enjoyable transcript of an imagined interview with a waitress.

INDIRECTION AND STRATEGIES OF INTERVIEWEE TEXT-PRODUCTION

The core of the approach in this text has been distinguishing the language of the researcher embodied in research questions (TQs) couched in a theory-language, and the formulation of interviewer questions couched in the idiolect of the interviewee (IQs) in designed interview sessions and sequences that, according to the instrumentation-theory interpreting the relationship between the TQ-level and the IQ-level, have the best likelihood of producing the desired material for analysis.

I explore below

1   the use of indirect IQs for answering TQs
2   the types of text that you wish to elicit from your interviewee.

IQs 'Echoing' or not 'Echoing' TQs

Some IQs 'echo' the TQs they serve, others are indirect.

We have already cited, on p. 79, Patton (1990) as providing us with a 6×3 checklist of possible questions with past, present, and future options. In Figure 7.9, I have used this six-fold system twice:

• once to classify research/theory questions (TQs), and
• once to classify interview questions (IQs).

This gives us a minimum of a 6×6 table. In Figure 7.9 *'ppf'* stands as a reminder that each of the tables could be further subdivided by past-present-and-future – creating 18×18 cells. The 'echo' or 'direct' interviewer question, the interview question that is a simple echo or re-write of a corresponding theory-question, is marked as a shaded entry.

Why bother? For some theory-questions, *the best interview question is not one that simply echoes the theory-question*, but one that gets at the material *indirectly*. Kvale made 'indirect questioning' a particular category. Earlier, I noted a general rule about working to satisfy controversial TQs by asking indirect interview questions, as in the example around discovering people's views of Mrs Thatcher as a caring or not Prime Minister. See some of the examples on p. 165 onwards, above.

So, in our diagram above, to answer a TQ 'What are his values?', it would be *possible* to ask an IQ 'What are your values?', the direct 'echo' interview question. Possible, but not very useful, our instrumentation-theory suggests.

Alternatively, it might be *better instrumentation policy* to follow the rule of indirection and ask a different interview question, such as 'What have been the three most important decision-making experiences in your life?' and be ready to follow up any answer that suggests an experience of value-dilemmas and eventual value-choice that could be explored. To get at TQ6 information, ask a variety of IQA.

Obviously, for certain research questions, there may be no point in indirectly beating about the bush. If you wish to know somebody's age or nationality or occupation (demographic questions), other things being equal, ask them directly. To get at TQ5 material, ask IQE.

	Interviewer questions (IQs) about					
Research/ theory questions (TQs) about *ppf*	A behaviours/ experience *ppf*	B feelings *ppf*	C knowledge *ppf*	D sensory events *ppf*	E demo- graphic questions *ppf*	F opinions or values *ppf*
1 behaviours/ experience						
2 feelings						
3 knowledge						
4 sensory events						
5 demo- graphic questions						
6 opinions or values						

FIGURE 7.9   **Patton–Wengraf 6 × 6 TQ by IQ Table**

Indirect interview questions, non-echo IQs, are more difficult to imagine and require more preparation time. The point of the 6×6 diagram above is just to encourage you to explore alternatives to the direct 'echo' interview question. See the previous discussion of the two examples of bad echo questions, pp. 64–5.

Please note two implications:

- *for each theory-question* that you might wish to ask (a given row), there might be six interview questions that could be used: the 'echo' interview question, shaded, *and five others*;
- *given an interview question*, the design might be such that you can obtain material relevant for any of the six theory-questions: the 'echo' theory-question – *and five others*.

Since the six categories of Patton by no means exhaust the range of functions of interview questions, the degree of real flexibility and imagination involved is much greater than 6×6 or even 18×18. You need to think flexibly about typologies of research questions and typologies of interview questions.

Students of interviewing who have not tried to learn about the different forms of questions, or have learned vaguely about them but have not practised them, have put in a lot of work *and* have ended up with disappointing banalities. Imaginative practice at indirection pays off in imaginative responsiveness in actual interviews.

What Kind of Verbal Response (Text) is Wanted?

One important way to think about your draft IQs is to ask yourself the question 'What kind of response do I want to elicit by this question?' But I mean this in a very precise sense. Literary criticism has developed typologies of textual production in which distinct types of text can be identified in any textual product. Since the sense of 'text' covers the vocalization that occurs in interview discourse, I can apply their distinction directly to informant responses to interview questions.

The typology of textual product I have in mind is that which distinguishes:

- Narration
- Description
- Argumentation

Narration (Specific Stories)

A narration is fairly clear: it is a story. Whenever you find a text in which there is a sequence of events – 'first this happened, then that' – which may or may not be causally linked – 'that happened afterwards because this happened before' – then you can define that text segment as being a narrative. These sequences of events may be factual or fictitious. The effect is one of an 'unfolding story'. This has been discussed at length in the section on Narrative Interviewing; see above, pp. 114–18 onwards.

In terms of the Patton–Wengraf 6 × 6 diagram (p. 173),

- You might ask for a story (IQA) simply because you want an account of a historical experience: your IQA echoing your TQ1.
- Or you might ask for a story (IQA) because you wanted to get at opinions and values (TQ6).
- Or you might ask for a story (IQA) because your TQ was about knowledge (TQ3).

And so on .… You might practise exploring each of the non-echo uses of asking for story (IQA).

Description

'The decisive feature distinguishing descriptions from narratives is that descriptions present static structures' (Kallmeyer and Schütze, 1997: 201). What you find in these texts or text segments is a description of the qualities or the features of situations, including the representations of actions and events, but these actions or events are explained as an expression of fixed qualities of situations or essences. The account of the situation is ahistorical, not in the form of a narrative sequence. The effect is one of a 'still photograph'. Change over time is bracketed out. In terms of our diagram, IQD might be most often of use.

Many – though not all – ethnographic questions produce ahistorical text of a de-historicized descriptive sort. See Spradley (1979) for the concern to get descriptive material of particular situations, or societies, etc. In terms of our 6 × 6 diagram above, IQD might be most often used.

Argumentation

The distinctive feature of such texts and text segments is that they involve lines of reasoning, arguments and general and particular evaluations. Argumentations show the speaker's general orientation and what he or she thinks of themselves and of the world. They imply that some other position is possible, but are not confined to what is called 'argument' in ordinary English. There may be no other explicit position nor, even if there is, need there be 'overt disagreement' with it. In terms of our 6×6 diagram above, IQs B, C and F might be most often used.

Getting at Argumentation and Evaluation: Some Examples

Since narrations have already been dealt with in respect of biographical narration, and description has been dealt with well in other literature, especially Spradley (1979), we shall therefore look briefly at strategies by which researchers have tried to get at argumentation and evaluation.

Argumentation (Kuhn)

Sometimes, your research purposes may require getting the informants to engage in argument. This was the case with an interview schedule developed by Deanna Kuhn (1991: 299) and reproduced in part below:

1. What causes prisoners to return to crime after they're released?

1A *(Probe, when subject completes initial response)* Anything else?

2. *(If multiple causes mentioned)* Which of these would you say is the major cause of prisoner's return to crime?

3. How do you know this is the cause?

3A. *(Probe if necessary)* Just to be sure I understand, can you explain exactly how this is the cause?

4. If you were trying to convince someone else that your view [that this is the cause] is right, what *evidence* [verbal emphasis] would you give to try to show this?

4A. *(Probe, if necessary)* Can you be very specific, and tell me some particular facts you could mention to try to convince the person?

5. Is there anything further you could say to help show that what you've said is correct?

6. Is there anything someone could say or do to *prove* [verbal emphasis] that this is what causes prisoners to return to crime?

7. Can you remember when you began to hold this view?

7A. *(If no)* Have you believed it for as long as you can remember?

7B. *(If yes)* Can you remember what it was that led you to believe that this is the cause?

8. Suppose now that someone disagreed with your view that this is the cause. What might *they* say to show that you were wrong?

etc.

Despite appearances, Kuhn was not interested in crime at all.

She was interested, as her book title suggests, in the extent to which people of different classes and different levels of education and types of occupation had or had not mastered different skills of argument. These included handling causal theories (multiple vs. single), being able to marshal supporting evidence, being able to generate and/or entertain alternative theories, counter-arguments and rebuttals of counter-arguments. She had three schedules: one about prisoners' return to crime, one about unemployment, and one about failure at school. These were just alternative topic-areas around which individual capacities for argument could be demonstrated.

From the point of view of the interviewee, there was a hard-hitting set of IQs about a topic; from the point of view of the TQ, the topic was only a means of exploring the 'capacities for argument' of the interviewee.

In our next example – of a set of IQs eliciting evaluation, there is also a very clear structure – but the research purposes are different.

Evaluation (Rowe)

Getting at 'values' is always difficult. We all have an 'official set of values' which we are quite ready to trot out at a high level of abstraction (e.g. politicians on the 'basic values of our society') but which have a peculiar relation to the values actually implicit in our behaviour (consider those same politicians when there's trouble on their patch).

It is best, therefore, to be concrete and incident-specific when you want to get material with which to explore the informant's values. Start with particular evaluations and infer very carefully up to 'values' in the abstract. Avoid, the word 'values' in your informant-questions, especially the first one. We look at a couple of examples.

Rowe describes a process, which she calls 'laddering', in which she tries to get at what the informant thinks is 'important'. The sequence of inquiry is similar to that developed in Psychology as 'personal construct theory'.

'When I teach a psychology class about the structure of meaning, I often, as a demonstration, call for a number of volunteers to go through a process of questioning which demonstrates how the most trivial decision which we make is based upon a series of judgements, each more abstract than the one preceding it, and all ultimately dependent upon a judgement about the nature of the individual's sense of existence.

I begin by asking the person to name three kinds of some particular class of object. The object could be food, or flowers, or musicians, or anything about which the person has some experience. One object frequently chosen is motor-cars. So I begin by asking "Would you give me the name of three kinds of motor cars?"

The person can reply in many different ways but, for the sake of this example, I shall say that the person says "Chevrolet Corvette, Ford Escort, and Cadillac".

I then ask, "Can you tell me one way in which two of these are the same and the other one is different?"

Here the person can reply in many different ways but, whatever is said, the person is using a construct which he or she uses to evaluate these objects.

Suppose the person replies with "One of the cars is cheap and the other two are expensive".

I then ask, "Which do you prefer, an expensive car or a cheap car?"

continued

continued

The person can choose either "expensive" or "cheap" [their folk-categories, TW], and, for whichever is chosen, I ask the same question. I ask "Why is an expensive car important?"

To answer this question, the person has to give a construct which is connected to his or her construct of "expensive" and which is important to him or her.

Suppose the person says, "I prefer an expensive car because expensive cars are more reliable than cheap cars".

I ask "Why is reliability [folk-category] important to you?"

The person may give an elaborate answer to this, but one which says, in effect, "Because people depend on me?"

I ask "Why is it important that people depend [another term in their idiolect or conceptual framework] on you?"

The person may answer in many ways, but [let us assume that] the essence of what this person says is that the whole point or purpose of his or her existence is to be needed by others, to relate to others, to be part of a group.

I then ask, "Supposing that things changed in your life so that no-one in the entire world needed you, or depended on you, or wanted to relate to you in any way. What would happen to you?"

This is an extremely cruel question, for I am asking the person to contemplate and put into words the very conditions which would bring about the annihilation of that person's self as he or she experienced it ....

Supposing that another person says, "An expensive car is always an individual car. It's different".

I ask, "Why is being different and individual important to you?"

Here the person can answer in terms of being an individual, being distinct from all other people; or the person may talk in terms of individual achievement, not simply in the sense of having expensive and individual possessions, but in the sense of developing, becoming an individual. Such answers contain at their core a sense of the ongoing development of individual clarity, authenticity and achievement ....' (Rowe, 1988: 63–4)

I have cited the above example at length, because it illustrates the value of starting with plain and simple questions and then of asking 'Why is X important?' questions using the folk-terms supplied by the informant, and then, to be used with great caution, an emotional-provocative question at the end.[3]

---

3 Rowe remarks, it is worth noting, 'I would not ask these questions in such a direct and persistent way of someone who was greatly troubled. These questions can often seem threatening and disturbing' (1988: 65).

Both Kuhn and Rowe are concerned to research quite deep structures: of skills at argument, in one case, and of basic values, in the other. They both designed their IQs to get the informants to start from quite concrete material and to move in such a way as to reveal the more abstract and deeper structures gradually.

Rowe's approach is relatively direct. One of the reasons for an indirect approach is given by the gap between tacit 'knowing-how' and verbally articulated 'knowing-that'. Many things that I know – like riding a bicycle – I cannot describe in words.

As Spradley writes (1979: 9):

> '... a large part of any culture consists of *tacit knowledge*. We all know things that we cannot talk about or express in direct ways. The ethnographer must then make inferences about what people know by listening carefully to what they say, by observing their behaviour, and by studying artefacts and their use. With reference to discovering this tacit cultural knowledge, Malinowski wrote:
>
> "... I cannot expect to obtain a definite precise and abstract statement from a philosopher belonging to the community itself. The native takes his fundamental assumptions for granted, and if he reasons or inquires into matters of belief, it would always be in regard to details and concrete applications. Any attempts on the part of the ethnographer to induce his informant to formulate such a general statement would have to be in the form of leading questions of the worst type because, in these leading questions, he would have to introduce words and concepts essentially foreign to the native. Once the informant grasped their meaning, his outlook would be warped by our own ideas having been poured into it. Thus, the ethnographer must draw the generalizations for himself, must formulate the abstract statement without the direct help of a native informant."' (Malinowski, 1950: 396)

Like Rowe, BNIM narrative questioning (e.g. Rosenthal, 1998) is also concerned to explore deep structures of basic values and assumptions about self, others and context. However, the methodology it uses is that of 'asking for story/ies' (narratives) working on the assumption that story-telling is more expressive of 'deep structures' than is the Socratic questioning of Rowe. People's explicit theories in response to questioning may tell you one thing; the assumptions and asides in their story-telling may tell you something else. Such 'triangulated' multiple sources of evidence need careful 'interpretation'.

Evaluation Via Vignette (Kohlberg, Gilligan, Shweder)

Another way of getting at values is that of the prepared vignette. I used the vignette method in relation to the cases of John and Lorna. Research into the development of personal and social moralities owes much to the research of Kohlberg, who used vignettes of moral dilemmas to identify what he alleged to be 'the stages of moral development' of children and adolescents. His work was re-evaluated by Carol Gilligan who used the same vignettes but interpreted the data in a way contrary to that of Kohlberg to argue that girls developed a higher complex grasp of moral issues than did the boys.

The vignette turns on whether a husband should steal a drug to save his sick wife or not. Gilligan contrasts the responses of Jake and Amy:

'Jake at eleven is clear from the outset that Heinz should steal the drug. Constructing the dilemma ... as a conflict between the values of property and life, he discerns the logical priority of life and uses that logic to justify his choice:

> For one thing, a human life is worth more than money, and if the druggist only makes $1,000, he is still going to live, but if Heinz doesn't steal the drug his wife is going to die. (*Why is a life worth more than money?*) Because the druggist can get a thousand dollars later from rich people with cancer, but Heinz can't get his wife again.

Asked if Heinz should steal the drug, [Amy] replies in a way that seems evasive and unsure:

> Well, I don't think so. I think there might be other ways without stealing it, like if he could borrow the money or make a loan or something, but he shouldn't really steal the drug – but his wife shouldn't die either.

Asked why he should not steal the drug, she considers neither property nor law but rather the effect that theft could have on the relationship between Heinz and his wife:

> If he stole the drug, he might save his wife then, but if he did then he might have to go to jail, and then his wife might get sicker again, and he couldn't get more of the drug, and it might not be good. So, they should just talk it out and find some other way to make the money ...

Seeing a world comprised of relationships rather than of people standing alone, a world that coheres through human connection rather than through systems of rules, she finds the puzzle in the dilemma to lie in the failure of the druggist to respond to the wife. Saying that "it is not right for someone to die if their life could be saved", she assumes that, if the druggist were to see the consequences of his refusal to lower his price, he would realise that "he should just give it to the wife and then have the husband pay the money back later". Thus she considers the solution to the dilemma to lie in making the wife's condition more salient to the druggist or, failing that, in appealing to others who are in a position to help.' (Gilligan, 1982: 26–9)

The same vignette used in India (with 'Ashok' replacing 'Jake') produces a quite different response than those of the Western young people studied by Kohlberg and Gilligan. It illuminates a whole different 'cosmology and moral universe'.

'*Interviewer:* Should Ashok steal the drug?

Babaji: No. He is feeling desperate because his wife is going to die, and that's why he is stealing the drug. But people don't live forever, and providing her with the drug does not necessarily mean she will live long. How long you live lies not in our hands but in God's hands. And there are other ways to get money, like selling his landed property, or he can even sell himself to someone and can save his wife's life.

First-order expansion:

Ashok is feeling desperate because his wife is going to die. It is his desperation that impels him to steal the drug. Because he is desperate, he overlooks the fact that stealing

continued

continued

is wrong, insufficient and unnecessary. If he were not desperate, he would recognize that there is a natural limit to a (given) human life; that providing his wife with the drug will not necessarily prolong her life; that it may be this woman's destiny to die at this particular time; and that if that is the case the drug will not prolong her life. It is God's intention and not human intervention that ultimately determines matters of human life and death. It follows that providing the drug is neither a sufficient nor a necessary condition for saving the woman's life. From the human point of view, the result of providing the drug is unpredictable.

Moreover, other means are available to raise needed money. Ashok could sell his property or, if necessary, sell himself into indentured servitude in order to raise the money. Since those alternative means exist and have not been exhausted, stealing is not a necessary condition for obtaining the drug.

Since the drug itself cannnot be assumed to be effective in determining the course of events, and since one can assume the existence of alternative means to obtain the drug, there is no justification for stealing.

Second-order expansion

The argument attributes the intention to steal to confusion deriving from desperation, in contrast to a well-considered and informed motive. The argument locates the ultimate efficient cause (including necessary and sufficient conditions) for human life with divine agency, rather than with human intervention in events. The understanding is that human destiny is an expression of divine intention, and that human destiny is an actual plan given to an individual by God. The implication that follows from that proposition is that any specific human intervention is neither a necessary nor a sufficient condition in the determination of life and death.

Having set forth that implication in the first part of this piece of reasoning, the Babaji then changes the focus of logical evaluation to a different locus in the causal structure of events. Having first dealt with the question of necessary and sufficient conditions and the ultimate causal course determining matters of life and death, in the latter part of his response he considers causality from the viewpoint of possible human interventions.

The argument takes administering the drug as the proposed intervention, which presupposes that the drug must be obtained. That goal then becomes the focus of evaluative reasoning. The argument asserts, in essence, that even if one were to admit that administering the drug is the best intervention, stealing the drug is not a justifiable means of obtaining it; there are other ways to raise the money to buy it at the asked price. Assuming, for the sake of argument, that the goal is to obtain the drug, the argument contrasts stealing to obtain the drug with an alternative causal or instrumental sequence (sell one's property or oneself) with the additional meaning that the alternatives are to be preferred.' (Shweder, 1991: 204–6)

Given a research purpose to identify different 'cultural universes', we have seen how this can be achieved by a variety of different 'instruments', including the structured schedules of Kuhn and Rowe and the device of a vignette + open question. The only one which is pretty sure to produce meagre results is the direct echo-like interviewer question: 'What sort of cultural/moral universe do you live in and what assumptions do you make?' The chances of such a direct 'echo' IQ, deriving too directly from its TQ, producing very useful results is – as Spradley and Malinowski would predict – rather close to zero.

Let me conclude this discussion of the type of textual production liable to be elicited by differently phrased IQ strategies. Strategies differ. The same TQ might lead to three different sets of IQs: one set would be designed to elicit narrations (e.g. Rosenthal), another descriptions (see Spradley's (1979) structural and similarity/contrast questions), a third, argumentations (e.g. Rowe or Kuhn). All three might be aiming at 'reconstructing the native's view of his or her world', but with different theories of informant subjectivity and therefore different instrumentation-theories, and therefore perhaps different degrees of success.

Do not feel that any one strategy of text production is the best for all purposes. Frequently, you may find that your IQ-schedule needs to elicit different text-types by combining different questioning strategies. For some research purposes, certain types of text may be more useful than for others. But certainly think clearly about the type of text a given question is likely to evoke and think clearly about whether that is the type of text you need.

CONCLUSION

The principles developed in Part I have been applied in Part II to the designing of theory-questions, interview sessions, selection of informants, and of interview questions to elicit different types of textual response. I distinguished broadly between lightly structured interview sessions (of which the single question inducing biographic narrative was the exemplary case) and the fairly-fully structured interview sessions where the interviewer prepared and improvised a far greater number of interviewer questions and other interventions, including the use of vignettes, etc. However, irrespective of the degree of interviewer structuring, all such interview questions (IQs) either directly echoed or more often indirectly served the theoretical questions (TQs) that were generated by the central research question (CRQ), which itself was governed by the complex of different semi-conscious desires and formalized purposes behind the enquiry. Similarly, it is typically theoretical questions and assumptions that guide the choice of informants – sometimes the whole population; otherwise through a randomized (quota) or a purposeful sample or possibly both.

I attempted to show that the gap between the TQ-level and the IQ-level was the domain of an operationalization or an instrumentation practice, to be made as explicit as possible, and that often implicit different models of human subjectivity suggested different direct and indirect ways in which TQs could be translated most effectively into IQs. Questions of avoiding 'bias and loading' in IQs were addressed, and clarification of what was meant by 'open questions' and 'questions pointed at narrative, argumentation or description'. I also discussed questions of guiding the degree of abstractness/specificity that was wanted and the length or degree of detail of an answer.

I stressed the key importance of learning and using the idiolect of the informant, and the strategy and tactics of asking and listening some more; as well as the desirability of intervening as little as possible and then, often, not by questioning but by some other mode of interviewer intervention (see pp. 199–200). The translation of the logical schedule of interview questions into a process schedule of a planned sequence of questions in sessions, based on your general model of human subjectivity and your working model of the subjectivity of yourself and your selected informant, was emphasized as being a distinct task.

Having worked through the text this far, you should be in a good position for generating a relatively integrated $CRQ \rightarrow TQ \rightarrow II/IQ$ research design for one or more sessions with appropriate interviewer questions, stimulus material, and a readiness to improvise follow-up responses that are likely to occur.

In the next, shorter, Part III, I deal with the period around the interview.

III

AROUND THE INTERVIEW: CONTACT MANAGEMENT – THEORY AND PRACTICE

Up to this point, I have been talking about 'design issues' in a way somewhat divorced from leaving your research desk and divorced from the real time of fieldwork practice.

If you have not completed the TQ–IQ design, and if you have not selected in *principle* who you would like your interviewees to be, then I recommend that you postpone doing more than, at most, skimming quickly through the following pages. Once your CRQ–TQ–IQ design in principle is finished, once you have identified your sample (of one or more) in whichever way you have, you are about to plan real contact. This is the best point at which to read this part, which is a primarily practical one.

8

Before Making Contact and Starting
the Fieldwork Phase of the Research Process

ETHICS, LEGALITIES AND PRACTICES

Questions of Informant Access to Tape, Transcripts, Interpretations

In general, you will need to develop your own preferred solution to the question of interviewee control over the use you make of interview material. The legalities and the ethics are complex and controversial, and the legal situation varies from country to country.

At one end of the spectrum is a not-very-ethical strategy which is to focus on ensuring and assuring anonymity and confidentiality, and to minimize any other guarantees to the interviewee. You attempt to keep ownership of tape and transcripts and complete control of any interpretation. A legal document specifying researcher ownership and his or her right to use the material in whatever way he or she thinks fit that does not compromise the interests of the interviewee can be helpful, particularly if you are expecting to publish some of the material in some way.

An alternative strategy is one in which you attempt to involve the interviewee as a co-researcher and even as a co-producer of any interpretive text that uses their material. This involves them in an ongoing process of negotiating real and publishable meanings and uses of their material[1] and even in a final right of authorship over produced texts. This model safeguards the position of the interviewees, but can be frustrating for the researcher/interviewer, who may never be allowed to come to, and to publish, their own interpretation of the material.

Legalities and Ethics

One professional US researcher's summary of some questions of US legalities and more general ethics runs as follows:

---

1 For example, in this text, I have extensively used the case of 'Harold'. His name and certain other characteristics have been changed. In addition, I sent him the manuscript and asked him if there was anything that he was unhappy about in respect of his data and the interpretation. He said he had no objections to the use of the material as presented in the text. I am grateful to him for his support.

'Like a cat about to go into a yard full of dogs, step with full attention into this matter of legalities and ethics. The amateur just turns on the tape recorder and lets the tape roll. The professional reads as much as possible about the law, uses a release form, and saves hours of worry – and maybe a lawsuit. The main areas of legal concern to researchers recording people's words are copyright, libel and privacy .... But often a legal issue is also an ethical issue, as well .... responsibilities of interviewer to narrator, consideration of harm to others, and truthful presentation of research ....

Narrator and interviewer have joint copyright .... A release form signed by the narrator is required before the interviewer can use the information in a publication. When the interviewer deposits the tape in the archives, a release form from both narrator and interviewer is necessary so that the public can have access to the tape. If a tape is to be sealed for a time, or the narrator requests anonymity, make sure the archivist is willing and able to ensure that these provisions are carried out.

Do not promise anonymity unless you are certain you can enforce this provision. Beware of publishing confidential information in a way specific enough for the information source to be identified. Discuss with the narrator the ways identity will be disguised and the information presented.

Warn the narrator about making assertions about others on tape that could result in a lawsuit ... and in publishing or repeating information from a taped interview, be aware of the possibility of defamation, a false statement that harms someone's reputation. Respect the right of privacy by not publishing personal, intimate details of a person's life unless this is absolutely necessary to the meaning of the study.

Be sure to get on tape permission to record when you begin an interview. Tell the narrator what the project is about, how the taped information will be used, where the tape will be placed, and who will have access to it. Inform the narrator of rights – such as withdrawal from participation and refusal to answer every question or discuss a topic. Be sensitive to the possible harm that can come from encouraging a narrator to "tell all".

In researching and writing *commissioned* histories and institutional or community studies, the researcher must insist on a contract specifying access to information and narrators .... Ownership of data and eventual access must be made clear. In a situation towards where the commissioner wants to delete or change passages, the researcher must resist if such a change would seriously alter the truthful presentation of the research evidence. But in many cases educating the commissioner at the beginning of and all along the project can help avoid an impasse. The researcher must be aware, too, of the inclination to like the individuals involved which may affect the kinds of information sought or colour its presentation.

Power in the interviewing situation is most often on the side of the interviewer. Accept that there is inequality in the interviewing situation, but know also that the narrator's immediate and long-range good may not be sacrificed for the researcher's gain. Give the narrator a chance to review the transcript or relevant manuscript paragraph ....' (Yow, 1994: 111, italics added)

The above passage indicates some of the issues involved. Not all of these may be relevant to your work, but many may be.

The situation in the UK has been summarized by Alan Ward for the Oral History Society <http://www.essex.ac.uk/sociology/ohs/copyright.html> as follows. I am indebted to Rob Perks for this information. The UK Economic and Social Research Council is apparently drawing up its own version.

Currently, the ownership of the copyright in the words spoken is vested in the speaker, but can be assigned in writing to anybody else (for example, the interviewer) with any conditions imposed on subsequent use. The purpose of the assignment is to enable routine consultation of interviewees to take place as agreed with the interviewees subject to any conditions they impose on all or parts of their spoken material either in general or up to a particular date. If the recording (owned by the person who made the recording or their employer) or the words spoken by the interviewee (owned originally by the speaker) are to be placed in taped or transcribed form in an archive, then the possible uses to which the material may be put should be specified; the British Library's standard clearance form states:

> 'All material will be preserved as a permanent public reference resource for use in research, publication, education, lectures and broadcasting. If you wish to limit public access to your contribution for a period of years (up to a maximum of 30 years) please state these conditions .... I hereby assign the copyright in my contribution to the British Library National Sound Archive ... signed etc.'

The Oral History Society ethical guidelines should also be consulted. They can be found on the internet at <http://www.essex.ac.uk/sociology/ohs/ethics.html>. They involve ensuring that information on copyright ownership and restrictions on use are recorded in writing, preserved, and transmitted to those who may be concerned, and that access is restricted where 'the interests or social and professional standing of the interviewee or of others involved with the interviewee or mentioned in the interview could be harmed by providing access' even where this has not been explicitly foreseen or mentioned by the interviewee.

Sometimes, the heavy formality of the operation suggested above may intimidate the interviewee, who suddenly feels that a heavy legal apparatus has arrived, one more appropriate to a police interrogation than to the interview they thought they were having. Seidman (1998) ch. 5, 'Affirming Informed Consent', is a helpful discussion.

Particularly if the tape is *not going to be deposited* in a public archive, and if any use of the material will be in an *anonymized form* – this is most likely to be the case where you are using 'representative' informants from a randomized or purposive sample – then some of the measures recommended may be less necessary. But, where you are going *to interview a named individual* and hope to publish in such a way that the *individual's identity will not be anonymized but clear* – classically, a celebrity or named-individual – then the full apparatus recommended by Valerie Yow is clearly appropriate.[2]

---

2 Since this book was prepared, Hollway and Jefferson (2000) have published an excellent chapter on 'The Ethics of Researching Psychosocial Subjects', critically evaluating certain guidelines of the British Psychological Society and the British Sociological Association. You should also be aware of current Data Protection Legislation.

Questions of Confidentiality and of Anonymity in any Publication or Use

There is an important distinction between anonymity and confidentiality.

Anonymity is a question of degree. It can be satisfied in a weak form, at least sometimes, by changing certain identifying details (name, place, age, occupation, etc.) sufficiently so that, were people who are not friends and relatives of the individual to read the account, they would not recognize their friend or relative as the one who had given the interview. A stronger version is one in which friends and family would not recognize the person. The strongest is one in which the informant would not recognize himself or herself in the published account.

Confidentiality is a stronger requirement, since it indicates that certain confidential material may not be used in any form, however anonymized. This is more typical of what journalists consider to be 'confidential background briefing', by which can be meant that the details of what is revealed may not be published, that the fact of any background briefing or contact may not be revealed either. The event, apart from the traces in the head of the reporter, 'never happened'.

Clearly, confidentiality of a whole interview means that nothing of what was said can be used in a published document. The chances are that you are unlikely to meet, or want to interview, someone who insists on such a degree of confidentiality overall. However, you may need to assure the interviewee that you will keep certain information confidential, and that in general you will ensure sufficient anonymization for the level they require.

Anonymity and anonymization is a matter of degree of skill in changing details sufficiently so that the reader cannot identify the individual concerned but in such a way as not to destroy the social-science research value of the final report. Too much loss of detail will degrade the value of the report, but not as much as the 'changing of detail'. From the point of view of the research purpose, certain changes of detail will be trivial while others will be disastrous.

> For example, in research into labour markets, it may be trivial to change a miner's location from one mine to another; it would be a disaster to describe a miner as a white-collar worker of some sort. However, for research into a particular mining disaster, it might be a non-trivial change to alter the location of the miner, but it could be conceivably less important what particular type of work the person was doing in the mining industry in that stricken location.

PILOT THE DESIGN: REHEARSE THE SESSION WITH A VOLUNTEER

Pilot your 'design purpose' and the 'fitness of your design for those purposes' on somebody or a couple of somebodies before you 'go for real' on the 1, the 10 or the 100 people you have as your sample. Almost certainly, your design and your practice will be improved in unexpected ways.

Bear in mind that the process of depth-interviewing is expensive in time and money and energy. If you only have two or even one 'depth interview slots' (the number will always be low), then you need to have alternative interviewees as well as your 'first choice'.

GETTING A LIST OF POSSIBLE INTERVIEWEES AND MAKING A SHORTLIST

You need to get a long list of possibles, then a shortlist, and only finally decide after reviewing all the possibilities. A phone discussion's manifest function may be to ask 'if X would be prepared in principle to take part'. At least as important a latent function is that of your finding out the 'degree of being worth interviewing' of that person compared with other people you haven't yet talked to. You need to draw up a person specification, as if for a job!

> One student identified an informant as a 'nurse in a gynaecological ward where abortion patients stay'. However, she did not indicate how long the nurse's experience was to be of such a ward, nor whether the nurse was to have any knowledge of post-hospital re-evaluation by the patients.

> Another student wanted to study the causes and consequences of homelessness in London. Of his informant, who combined a number of different interview potentials, I remarked

>> 'You need to be clear what different contributions the person might make: as experienced in having been homeless, as currently being a housing advice officer, or as currently studying a degree in Housing Policy and Theory.'

The issues involved in sampling (pp. 95–106 onwards) should have been carefully considered before any attempt at contact is made.

MAKING INITIAL CONTACT AND THE CALCULATION OF 'FRAMING'

Bertaux's remarks (1997) are useful:

> 'Let us place ourselves in the most tricky situation: you have not yet met the person in question, she has never seen you. However someone whose confidence you have gained and in whom she herself has confidence has told her that you will ring her up to ask for an interview. You must persuade her to give you an interview.

> You must be clear, precise, natural and to the point. Practice your phrases before making the call. Put yourself in the position of the other person: she has no *a priori* desire to tell her life story to an unknown person, and, besides, this is not what you want. You are interested in her experience only as a member of a social category. The point is fundamental. So, to begin with, you will start by saying who you are ("I am working on a dissertation, a thesis, a book on ..."); you will mention the social object in everyday terms, leaving aside the entire sociological vocabulary; and you will make certain that you introduce the verb "to tell" or an equivalent (for example, "so and so has told me that you have interesting stories you could tell me"). If the person hesitates, if she says for example that she has nothing interesting to relate, say that it is just people who think like that in whom you are interested. Add that it would take about an hour. Press a little but not too much: respect for the other person must be a priority. In any case, you cannot force anybody to see you who does not wish to see you. If your efforts are unsuccessful, remain courteous, express your regret, and act as if your paths could be expected to meet again in the future.

continued

continued

If the person accepts the interview proposal, don't let her start to tell her story on the telephone but propose a rendez-vous. People are constrained, have work schedules and daily rhythms that you will learn to understand. As long as you don't know what they are, let your subject choose time and place. However, bear in mind that the success of the operation depends in part on the context: the ideal context is a time and a place where you will be alone in a one-to-one situation, without interferences, without a telephone, and with a good stretch of time in front of you. Fix the earliest possible time; if you can, leave a telephone number where she can ring you or leave a message. If the person changes her mind and cancels the appointment, show that you are disappointed and try to arrange another rendez-vous.

Everything will be much easier if you have already been able to meet the person, exchange a few phrases and arrange the appointment on such an occasion, because she will already know whom she will have to deal with.

Remember that we live in a society structured into classes, fractions of classes, and professional sectors: relations between social groups pre-exist research contacts and 'structure' them in advance. We cannot change them, nor change our social belonging: we can only come to terms with them. However, ever since sociologists have done fieldwork, they have always found one method or another for overcoming these barriers (Mauger, 1991; Picon and Picon-Charlot, 1997).

One of the norms of our society is that one should not refuse to communicate without good reason. This will help you, particularly if you present yourself as somebody who is attempting to understand a situation which your interlocutor, by virtue of their experience, knows much better than you do.' (Bertaux, 1997, my translation)

Care needs to be taken about the approach to interviewees in the field. Foddy's model Figure 2.4 (p. 39) suggests that the potential interviewee is going to encode *whatever you say and do* into a 'frame' in terms of which they will understand the forthcoming interview event. This will happen whether they realize it or not. So you must realize it, and work to avoid 'the wrong framing' by the informant.

Your interview design may involve, and usually does, not giving too much information about yourself or your research purposes to the interviewee. The more information that you give, the more they will inevitably 'slant' what they say in the light of their interpretation of 'who' they think you are and what they think the effect of the research will be.

However, you may be tempted, in order to obtain the consent of a valued potential informant to become an interviewee, to give them much more information than you should or to give them slanted information. This then becomes their unconscious or conscious frame for the future interview that they are agreeing to. Having thus created a more powerful prior frame for the interview than you had intended, your attempt within the interview when it occurs to act in such a way as to 'not give too much information away' may only serve to help you forget that you gave that information away long before the interview occurred; this will maximize the chances of underestimating such prior framing when you or somebody else comes to interpret the interview transcript. A similar problem can arise when you reveal your concerns to an intermediary who then finds an interviewee for you: unknown to you, your intermediary may have 'framed the event' in a way that you may find it difficult to uncover.

If you are aware of these and similar possibilities, you can find ways of perhaps forestalling some of them and of allowing for the effects of others.

QUESTIONS OF ARRANGING INITIAL AND POSSIBLY LATER SESSIONS

Many, though not all research designs, involved a plan for one or at most two sessions. You need to allow for needing a further follow-up-session, perhaps only on the phone, to clear up questions that arise during the period of analysis.

9

The Session

TECHNICAL MANAGEMENT UP TO THE SESSION

Long-term Forward Planning

You have to arrange with your informant time and place and context for your interview. This may be highly constrained by the timetables of the parties involved, or there may be a degree of choice.

You want a *setting* as free from interruption and as comfortable and non-distracting as possible. You want to avoid interruptions by phones, by noise from outside, by other people. Ideally, this usually would mean an 'interview room' in the home or workplace of neither party. Not very feasible.

You want a *clear stretch of time* so that you know what amount of time you can plan for. You need to know if there is any leeway so that the interview could continue if necessary. You need to count for yourself on a minimum of 30 minutes setting-up time before the informant arrives. You need to count on having an *hour* or so after the close of the interview and the departure of the informant on your own to make undisturbed session notes (debriefing, field-notes). So, make sure you add 90 minutes to whatever time you allow for the interaction with the informant. (see Figure 9.1).

So the 45-minute interview – even assuming the informant arrives on time and the interview starts on time – might require almost three hours.

You must allow enough time to feel unhurried about all the operations involved and try to ensure that your informant is also unhurried, and that you are free from interruption and outside 'noise' for the full three-hour period.

You will also need to make sure you have all your materials, and that they work! Any interview will require the following:

- A tape-recorder (preferably one that gives an audible signal at the end of the tape; preferably two tape-recorders in case one fails), twice as many blank tapes as you think you will need; back-up batteries and cables to the electricity supply (make sure your extension lead is long enough and has two sockets for whatever is already in the wall-socket of the room you are using!).
- You will also require a note-pad (with spare pens, the one you start with always runs dry) and maybe two small bottles of mineral water in case either of you gets thirsty in mid-flow.

On your own		With the informant		
Setting up time	30"			
		Pre-interview arrangements		10"
		Warm-up period		5"
		Interview itself	*for example*,	**45"**
		Saying goodbye		10"
De-briefing session	60"			
TOTAL	90"	TOTAL		70"
	Time before + time after + interview time = 160"			

FIGURE 9.1   **The Time Interviews take – add 90 Minutes**

- You will need to have your question-schedule in some unobtrusive form that you can nonetheless read without difficulty and any other stimulus-materials (like old photographs, etc.) that you may wish to use.

You will also need to ensure that your informant has the opportunity of co-arranging whatever he or she wishes with you. Well-handled, this will increase their commitment and the chances of their turning-up and being in a good frame of mind.

To help your informant, you therefore should consider providing him or her with something like one side of A4 which outlines the material arrangements, explains the point of the exercise and the time and place, and reassures them about the confidentiality and the anonymity of the material. It could advise them how to contact you both before and after the interview with any questions or comments or requests they may have. McCracken (1988: 69–70) has a short 'ethics protocol' which you could use as part of an 'interview memo' which acts also as an informal contract/release form.

Three Weeks Before the Interview: Pre-interview Material

PRE-INTERVIEW QUESTIONNAIRE FOR THEM?   It may be part of your research design to ask them to fill in a pre-interview questionnaire so that you do not have to take up interview time with demographics or similar. If so, you need to let them have it in good time so that they return it to you a couple of weeks before the interview.

PRE-INTERVIEW MATERIAL FROM THEM TO YOU?   You will need time to reflect and digest any such material that they send (it may also be relevant to ask them for any documents – personal or official – which might make your interview questions more directed and informed than they otherwise would be). The more material they send, *the earlier* you must ensure you receive it. If you don't, they will come expecting you to have read it and you will be obliged to ask them questions based on not having read what they sent.

7–10 Days Before the Interview

You need to contact the informant, confirm their and your availability, give/get any information about the interview room, and pick up any anxieties that they may have. Their and your anxiety is likely to rise as the interview approaches, and both of you will need 'coaxing along' in order to arrive on time in good heart, ready to use the adrenalin for a good lively interview!

By this time, you should be reading any material that the informant has sent, and revising your question-schedule in the light of any new information that has emerged or any new concerns that you have.

The Day Before the Interview

You need to make quite sure that you have all the material required by your long-term plan; that you have made your last revision to your question-schedule and produced a version that is instantly and easily legible. You should also review the place of this particular interview within the evolving designed research and the information you have so far. This will mean that you have a clear grip on the purposes that the interview is meant to serve, the theory-questions you are now trying to get answered, as well as on the detailed question-schedule itself.[1] It is also wise to re-confirm the appointment again with your informant and deal with any last-minute problems the night before.

You should make sure that your equipment is working, your spare batteries are present, that your tapes are provisionally labelled, that all material supplies and resources are in order.

The things that need to be borne in mind are:

- time of and around the session
- location
- preparing and testing the apparatus and tapes
- 'leaving'
- arrangement for instant de-briefing after the session.

MANAGING THE SESSION

Overview and Introduction

The main purpose of this chapter is that of helping you to sensitize yourself for the interview interaction. It therefore recapitualates some points previously mentioned that are perhaps especially relevant to recall the day before the actual interview, without requiring you to read the whole volume again up to this point.

Getting Ready for Your First Interview: The Briggs–Saville-Troike
Model of the Interview Process as Communicative Interaction
You will only fully appreciate the complexities of communicative interaction when you transcribe and comment upon your first interview transcript. An approach and a model of the interview as a communicative process was sketched in Chapter 2,

---

1 I stress the need for such re-review of the purposes of, and the information for, the coming interview, because so many of the informant-questions will have to be invented on the spot during the interview flow. Particularly for beginners, without a solidly re-confirmed sense of what the interview has to be about, any difficulties in the interview will lead to a failure to listen to the responses and a failure to improvise the right follow-up questions and responses. That is why the context and the preparation the day before are so important.

and you should re-read that to help prepare yourself for understanding what goes on. I shall merely review some of the points made there.

Key Points in General

The key points are: the need to maintain double attention throughout the interview; the need to monitor especially what is happening to the balance and expression of power and emotion during that process; the need to model and induce the mode of answering that you want. You need to ensure that you listen to the answers rather than rushing through the questions; under some conditions, you may have to improvise prompts, probes, silences and support as well as just questions; you need to be able to deploy a tactic of challenge within a context of support, and you need (which sums it up) to be alert to obstacles to your own listening – I provide a list of 13!

Double Attention

By 'double attention', I mean that you must be both listening to the informant's responses to understand what he or she is trying to get at and, at the same time, you must be bearing in mind your needs to ensure that all your questions are liable to get answered within the fixed time at the level of depth and detail that you need.

Listening attentively to what is being said while simultaneously managing the time to ensure it doesn't run out and that the direction and level of talk are appropriate to get the interview material that you want … this is a skill you will develop gradually.

Bear in mind the earlier discussions of interview style and strategy in Fred Massarik's model (p. 153) of the types of interview and the discussion of the assertive and receptive approaches to interviewing.

Power and Emotion within the Interview Process

The above discussion has suggested I hope that the interview is an interaction between real people and that there are issues of both power and emotion involved, issues not normally a prime focus of discussion. See the Briggs–Wengraf model (Figure 2.6, p. 43). In the following extract, a student is reporting on the interview process. She is studying obsessive fans. She identifies on-going emotion and denial in the informant, while not noticing rather similar mechanisms in herself:

One student noted earlier that in her first interview, 'Andrew' was unhappy about admitting that he was a fairly obsessive fan. When challenged as to whether he felt embarrassed by his admission, he replied 'It's a bit of a weakness really, 'cos people can use it against you'. In his second interview, he expands 'Well, they can manipulate you I think, can't they, take the piss out of you …. My brother takes the mickey quite a lot'. In her report, the researching student notes that 'all three informants were reluctant to answer direct questions as to how obsessive they really were'.

Later on, the interviewer's report suggests unintentionally that the interviewer herself may well have been one of the persons that an obsessive fan might be wary of answering directly and honestly. She, too, might be experienced as taking advantage of a revealed vulnerability.

continued

continued

The strength of her report enables us to see how such a mechanism might have worked. In her Interpretation section, she writes:

'Simple Minds performed concerts in aid of Anti-Apartheid and Amnesty International. Andrew later became a member of both these organizations due, he said, to the band's involvement. Before Simple Minds took up defending these groups, Andrew had never heard of, or knew little about, them.

When I tactfully challenged this by saying that Simple Minds' motives may not have been as pure as were presented to the fans, he was quick to defend the Simple Minds against this charge. He reaffirmed the band's commitment by explaining that Simple Minds were beating the drum for these causes long before any other pop group joined the bandwagon. He believed that Simple Minds motives were totally genuine.

He found *questions which may be considered as a form of attack* on the band less than straightforward to answer. This is not to say I was hostile in my questioning of Simple Minds; (?). it was when he went off on a tangent about the greatness of Simple Minds that I *had gently to remind him that no one is perfect*. The way he defended the band was very personal indeed, as if he were defending a member of his family.'

It was clear that the use of *questions which may be considered as a form of attack* did usefully make clear the strength of the informant's readiness to defend the band from questioning. On the other hand, the student may have been less 'tactful' than she likes to think. *Why did she 'have to' tell him that 'no one is perfect'? Almost certainly, she shouldn't have done.* Her honesty in the last paragraph in describing the situation suggests that she is half-conscious of having perhaps 'not got it quite right' in the interview and still half unconscious. Unless one is being consciously provocative – like Kuhn – none of one's questions should normally be capable of being seen (either in their words or in their delivery) as a form of attack.

It is very important to be constantly alert to the 'emotional micro-process' in the interview interaction, and to see when you, as emotional co-manager of that process, are going wrong. At the beginning of this text, I explored the 'interview with W' in terms of alternative experiencing of that slightly dodgy start. The *Simple Minds* example shows a half-awareness; what follows is an interpretation of another student's interview which shows better sensitivity to such micro-emotional processes and their significance in terms of the expression and repression of feeling.

Cassie B is discussing the long-term effects of the physical abuse of children. She writes:

'Anne is a strong and confident person when talking about herself in the present:

"Umm, I don't really think it has ... I mean, I've never had a relationship with my father, he's just always been a supplier ...".

continued

continued

Though when she's talking about the past, she becomes overflowing with emotion. In the extract below, she talks of feelings in the past, and is very close to tears: to

"... I think, (long pause) that when I was younger, what it was, what it basically was, I tried so hard, I really did, I mean, he'd do such horrible things and I'd, I'd still try to love him, to have him love me ...".

This is a pattern that Anne follows quite regularly throughout the interview, of being quite brash and sarcastic at the beginning of an answer, and then losing herself in her emotions as the middle approaches. This shows just how unsure about her own person she really is.'

My comment on this sensitive account was:

'I would guess that Anne's "brittle confidence" is based insecurely on a denial of the emotions she suppresses and still feels, and that only when she can acknowledge and work through those emotions safely, will she be able to be less flooded out by repressed emotions ... and be able to be less brash and sarcastic in order to keep them at bay.'

Elsewhere, Cassie B's account of Anne continues:

'... difficult to express emotions. Anne exhibits this by being rude or sarcastic any time an emotion is about to be expressed. When the list of abuse she suffered is given, she could have been reading a shopping list with the amount of emotion she put into it. Before she gives me any details about physical abuse, Anne seems to gather herself and her feelings together:

"... I don't feel that you should be, abuse is like out of order. I'd, I don't know ... OK, um, here I go, relating to my own experience ..."

The first part of this extract is very stuttered and confusing. The gathering herself together allows Anne to stop any emotional outflow [that might] give away her "weakness". At other times, when mentioning abuse, she will make sarcastic jokes, but very bitter:

"... He used to use belts, and I used to have strap marks (and I tell you they weren't the kind you get from sunbathing)."

Anne's responses are all carefully planned in order not to show anything of herself. However she does at times drop her pretence and show emotion.'

This text involves a description of a structure of feelings based on observation of emotional practices throughout the interview. To the extent that the interviewer was aware of the emotion-handling pattern as 'Anne' expressed it in the interview, she would have been better able to assess the significance of what was going on and manage the interview better.

The dimension of power in interviews is most important. As already argued, neither party leaves behind any asymmetries of power in the wider society when they anxiously enter a room for an 'interview'.

Briggs (1986) has given us an excellent description of his struggle to impose himself as the 'authoritative interviewer' on his Mexican informants, and the way he gradually learnt that he had to earn the right to ask certain questions by developing a competence and approach more like that of an 'attentive pupil'. Other references are Ann Oakley's 'Interviewing women: a contradiction in terms' (1981) and Shulamit Reinharz's (1992) chapter 'Feminist interviewing research'.

Power-sources outside the interview situation inevitably have to be taken into account in understanding successes and failures. In addition, even in the ideal case of the two parties having some notional total equality of external power resources, there could still be *asymmetries of communicative power* developing within the interview itself.

The typologies of 'experienced interviews' of Massarik and Dillon previously cited (pp. 153–54) suggest power asymmetries and, indeed, the likelihood of usually covert and often only semi-conscious struggles over the co-steering of the interview process itself.

You may wish to review the 'interview with W' transcript (p. 20) as one in which the interviewer is struggling to establish or maintain a 'frame for communication' which the interviewee perhaps seems to find rather uncomfortable to accept to begin with.

Prepare for your own interview by staying relaxed even if the start of it seems difficult.

Modelling the Mode of Answering that you want

In preparing your question schedule try to ensure that the informant has an accurate perception of what you are currently wanting. As you will recall, Foddy's symbolic interactionist model (p. 39) stresses the importance of the informant's perception (and misperception) of what it is that the researcher wants. You need to think of the type of text (e.g. the level of generality and specificity as in Spradley's six levels; the proportions of narrative, argumentation and description), the amount of detail, the particular content (Patton–Wengraf 6 × 6, p. 173) and so forth that you wish to get as interview material for your different TQs.

McCracken (1988: 35) suggests starting by a (Spradley, 1979) 'grand-tour' question which enables the informant to reply at some length (detail, depth) thus starting to set their frame of expectation that this is the sort of degree of depth and detail and length of answer that is the norm. He then suggests the use of what he calls 'floating prompts':

'Once "grand-tour" testimony is forthcoming, it is relatively easy to sustain it in an unobtrusive way. The simplest way of doing so is through the use of "floating prompts" through the careful exploitation of several features of everyday speech (Churchill, 1973; Dohrenwend and Richardson, 1956). Simply raising one's eyebrow (the "eyebrow flash" as it is called in the paralinguistics literature) at the end of a respondent's utterance nearly always prompts him or her to return to the utterance and expand it. A slightly more conspicuous device is to repeat the key term of the respondent's last remark with an interrogative tone. (Respondent: "so me and my girl friends decided to go out and get wrecked". Interviewer: "Wrecked?" Respondent: "yeh, you know, really, really blasted"). If these techniques are not effective, the interviewer can be more

continued

continued

forthcoming ("What do you mean 'blasted', exactly?") but not more obtrusive ("Do you mean 'intoxicated'?"). The object here is to watch for key terms (such as "wrecked" and "blasted") as they emerge from the testimony and to prompt the respondent to say more about them.' (McCracken, 1988: 35)

Patton (1990: 321–4) discusses a variety of 'prefatory statements' that can be prepared in advance or invented during the interview in order to alert the informant that a new type of area is about to be covered, that there is now a shift from a broader to a narrower question, or that the next question needs to be answered in a new type of way.

Non-verbal communication is of great importance. The tone of voice and the speed with which you say anything – how you ask your questions, make your statements, etc. – will send powerful messages to your informant which may quite over-ride your words. *Saying 'take your time' in a rush* will lead to the informant responding – not to the words of your statement, but to the pace of your delivery.

Even if your para-linguistics are congruent with your words, your body-stance may send a different message. Consequently, very necessary to good interviewing is a high level of sophistication about listening to the paralinguistics of yourself and of your informant, as well as staying aware of the non-verbal communication coming through body-posture and body-movement.

Rushing through the Questions rather than Working with the Answers?

Rushing or listening? Earlier, I insisted on the need for a generous provision of planned time. Only if you are using completely-structured question-schedules can you evade the need to spend most of your energy in the interview in listening to the answers. Why? Because only listening to the answers in an alert but unhurried state will enable you to maintain 'double attention' and stay focused on developing your responses (follow-up questions, silences, etc.) to their answers to your initial questions. The slightest suggestion of hurry will destroy your capacity for what might be called 'deep listening to yourself' and destroy their capacity for 'deep listening to themselves'.

Not listening to the answers – perhaps because you are in a hurry to complete too many questions in too short a time – leads to silliness:

'I suppose my leisure activities are reading, gardening, and cooking.

So which one of these leisure activities do you do at home? All of those, then?

Yes, obviously gardening I do in the garden . . . .

Do you do them at a special time or just when you can find a break?

Just when I can find a break. Mostly the gardening I do at weekends because it's dark when I get home from work. The cooking I do in the evenings because I have to do it. The reading I do in the bath and because I have to do it.

So you don't have a special place that is set aside in your house that is just sort of your leisure space . . .?'

I commented:

'*Could* there be a "leisure space" for all three activities? Think about it. A kitchen with a garden she can work on at eye level, while she reads a book to the side of the stove. You are not thinking hard enough in relation to her specific responses.

And also, you are giving her your "forced choices" [at a specific time *or* when you can find a break]. Had you asked for each of them, "when do you do them?" you would have found out whether she talks spontaneously of "breaks" at all, and, if she does, whether she thinks of herself as "finding a break" or "making a break". You could have found out her categories of "time and activities"…'.

In relation to her other informant, there is a similar mad rush which starts to sound like a film script:

'*Do you have any leisure activities that you do at home?*

No, I do all my leisure activities, no, not all, yes I do them at home, but not all.

When do you do them, what part of the day, specific time?'

I commented:

'She hasn't said what they are, these "leisure activities", you don't ask the natural question "What are they?", but ask "When do you do them, what part of day, specific time?" in a rather Prisoner-of-War-interrogation style. Are you interested in the answers? Would she have thought at the time that you were interested'

Your informants will notice if you are 'in a hurry to get through the interview' and they will probably co-operate by giving shorter and shorter and diminishingly interesting answers. Remember you are learning to go 'in depth' rather than speed through the shallows!

Facilitation and Challenge, Questions and Alternatives to Questions

Semi-structured depth-interviewing has a characteristic pattern of a small number of prepared interviewer-questions followed by further questions improvised to follow-up the interviewee's response to the original question. We have already discussed the value of indirect questions, and it is important to realize that there are alternatives to questions as such.

Dillon (1990: 176 onwards) provides a technical and systematic account of alternatives to questioning which repays careful study. He reviews the research on a variety of alternatives to questions and provides an argument for not using an interview question (IQ) when some other mode of interviewer intervention (II) is more appropriate, as it very often is. I cannot here give his full typology of alternatives to questions together with examples of each type, though it – Table 12.1 in his book – repays careful study. He summarizes his argument as follows:

'At any given juncture of talk the practitioner can choose either to ask a question or to use an alternative. The most common juncture for choice is where the partner has just finished making a contribution, as in response to a [initial, TW] question:

continued

continued

> *Practitioner:* Question
> *Partner:*   Response
> *Practitioner:* Question or alternative

What else can the practitioner do at that point other than ask a question?

The practitioner may use four different kinds of alternatives, encompassing a dozen specific ones – declarative statements, speaker questions, signals and silences. There are also various other alternatives of mixed types …. At the juncture where the partner has just finished a response, the practitioner can, instead of asking a question, choose to:

> 1 make a *statement* of his selected thought in relation to what the speaker has just said; or
> 2 provide for a *speaker's* [further] *question*[2] related to the speaker's contribution; or
> 3 give some *signal* of receiving what the speaker is saying, without himself taking and holding the floor; or yet
> 4 say nothing at all but maintain a deliberate, appreciative *silence*.'

(Dillon, 1990: 176–7)

He argues that, 'used together with well-chosen questions, a mix of alternatives gives the greatest promise of enriching the cognitive, affective and expressive processes' in 'certain types of interview'. By implication, in certain types of interview, his argument suggests that *reliance solely upon unrelenting questioning* can be counter-productive.

In our earlier discussion of 'active listening' (pp. 127–30), we stressed the importance of facilitating the further self-expression of the informant by attentive silences and other devices (verbal and non-verbal), implementing Dillon's third and fourth alternative to questions.

Patton (1990: 329) stresses the importance of providing reinforcement and feedback to the informant about how the interview is going. Patton gives a useful example and suggests that the interviewer:

> 'provide reinforcement and feedback [such as]
>
> *"I am about half way through the interview now, and I think a lot of really useful things are coming out of what you're saying"*
>
> or

continued

---

2 Dillon (1990: 180) defines this as an attempt to provide for the interviewee (the speaker) an opportunity to 'formulate a question about what he is struggling to think and say'. A generic formulation that Dillon provides is when the interviewee says 'Something is the case, I don't know' and the interviewer says 'Relax for a minute and think up the question that is still bothering you about that', permitting and enabling the interviewer to grapple explicitly with the problem involved in finding the right question to ask him or herself.

continued

> *"I really appreciate your willingness to express your feelings about that. You're very much helping me to understand."*

The interviewer can get clues about what sort of reinforcement is appropriate by watching the interviewee.

When verbal and non-verbal behaviours indicate someone is really struggling with a question, going mentally deep within to form an answer, after the response it is entirely appropriate to say:

> *"I know that was a difficult question and I really appreciate your working with it because what you said was very meaningful and came out very clearly".*

At other times, the interviewer may perceive that only a surface or a shallow answer has been provided. It may then be appropriate to say:

> *"I don't want to let that question go by without asking you to think about it just a little bit more, because I think you've given some really important detail and insights on the other questions and I'd like to get more of your reflections on this one".'*

(Patton, 1990: 330)

This final example of Patton's shows a move towards what might be defined as a more challenging response rather than a simply assenting and receptive one. There are certainly times when a relatively challenging or even an extremely challenging response may be appropriate.

I previously cited Patton on six types of interview question, differentiated by content (see p. 79 above). Schatzman and Strauss (1973) have four types of follow-up question differentiated by function, the first two relating to events and the second two to coherence:

- *chronology* ('and then? when was that?')
- *detail* ('tell me more about that, that's very interesting')
- *clarification* ('I don't quite understand; but you said earlier …')
- *explanation* ('Why?' 'How come?')

(Schatzman and Strauss, 1973: 74, typography revised)

If we turn our attention to relatively challenging interventions in a narrative flow by the informant,[3] Sluzki (1992) – cited by McLeod (1997: 120) – suggests ways in which a *therapist* might intervene in or after a narrative account by a therapy-client (Figure 9.2). McLeod talks of subverting taken-for-granted realities and practices by such micro-interventions. He sees them as trying to 'change the story' and produce a better one.

Whatever its legitimacy in therapy, is this highly assertive–aggressive response an appropriate research operation? Holstein and Gubrium's *The Active Interview*

---

3 Within the biographic-interpretive method of BNIM, such challenges to the narrative would only be permissible in the third subsession. With other narrative methods, they might be legitimate at any point.

Example of a client narrative:
'This has been bothering me for the last ten years. It all started when I lost my place in college after failing some exams. It just made me so anxious in any situation where I felt I was being assessed, like in a job interview. And every time I failed to get a job, my mother used to get really angry with me. She keeps saying how stupid I am, but I know she only gets so upset because she cares so much about me.'

Narrative dimension	Examples of questions that invite a narrative shift
Time	'Why do you consult me *now*?'*
Space	'In what circumstances/situations is the problem more or less noticeable?'
Causality	'What was going on *before* this problem emerged?'
Interaction	'Throughout these confrontations with your mother, who was the grown-up and who the child? Who was supposed to look after whom?'
Values	'How do *you* act towards someone you care about?'
Mode of telling	'Would you describe for me what actually happens when you are in a job interview, as if I were witnessing it?'

*Obviously, this question is not relevant for a research interview!

FIGURE 9.2 **Transformative Interventions: Invitations to Narrative Change (Sluzki, 1992)**

suggests a fairly frequent use of a degree of such active provocation and challenge. What you decide to do depends on your general model of human subjectivity in interview and, in addition, on your derived model of *this* person's particular subjectivity as it emerges and evolves in *this* interview. It also depends on your purposes and your ethics.

Thirteen Obstacles to Listening
The main function of the interviewer in semi-structured – largely improvisatory – interviewing is to listen carefully to the responses of the informant so that the improvisations will be appropriate to both the TQs and the CRQ of the research design but also to the unfolding development of the interview itself. It is therefore perhaps useful to end this chapter by focusing on the difficulty of listening.

In their *Messages: the communication skills book* (1983), Matthew McKay et al., identify some 12 blocks to listening. They are things that happen inside us as we try to listen, things we do to stop ourselves from listening. Although their list is concerned with listening in ordinary conversation, much of it can be applied to research interviewing. I've added the first item which makes 13!

- Paper-focused on schedule-watching and note-taking
  You are too busy making notes and looking at your question schedule

- Comparing
  Constant comparing what the speaker reveals or says with yourself, your own experience, your own history

continued

continued

- Mind reading
  Constant attempt to figure out what the other person is really thinking and feeling

- Rehearsing
  You're rehearsing what your follow-up question will be or thinking about the next planned question or topic

- Filtering
  You listen to some things that you are looking for, and filter out what you consider 'irrelevant'

- Judging
  You make rapid factual or evaluative judgments about somebody and then react in terms of that hasty premature labelling which you don't then re-evaluate

- Dreaming
  You're half-listening because something said triggers off in you a whole host of private associations which then completely drive out what the person goes on to say

- Identifying
  You refer every experience back to a similar one of your own

- Advising
  A concern to help somebody 'fix it' rather than just stay with the account

- Sparring
  Arguing and debating, the put-down of others and the discounting of yourself. A desire to disagree and correct

- Being right
  This could be worst of all!

- Derailing
  Suddenly changing the topic (interaction-cutter) or 'joking it off' or 'comforting it off'

- Placating
  Wanting the other person to like you, you just semi-automatically agree rather than giving full attention

(Summarized and revised from McKay et al., 1983: 16–19.)

Only as you practise reviewing your interviewing, by listening to the tapes and looking at the transcript and at your post-session notes, will you become fully aware of how frequent these obstacles are, even to those with the best intentions! With more practice, you start to recognize them as they start to happen and are so enabled to stop them quicker.

I shall end with a counter-quotation from Lofland (cited by Patton, 1990: 349) which sums up some of the complexity of the 'double attention' and flexible responsiveness to verbal and non-verbal communication that is required of the interviewer:

'One's full attention must be on the interviewee. One must be thinking about probing for further explication or clarification of what he is now saying; formulating probes linking up what is currently saying with what he's already said; thinking ahead to putting in a new question that has now arisen but was not taken account of in the [prepared interview schedule] plus making a note at that point so one will not forget the question; and attending to the interviewee in a manner that communicates to him that you are indeed listening. All of this is hard enough simply in itself. Add to that the problem of writing it down – even if one takes short-hand in an expert fashion ....'
(Lofland, 1971: 89)

You may wish to consider how Lofland's advice can be reconciled with the 13 points derived from McKay. Both seem useful to me.

Key Points for BNIM Interviewing

Emergent Answers and Prepared 'Default' Questions
I suggested earlier that, if your BNIM three-subsession interview is undertaken within a project with its own theoretical and/or practical concerns, you should have designed your subsession 3 as if *none of these* project concerns was answered at all by the actual subsessions 1 and 2.

Normally, however, this 'catastrophic hypothesis' never occurs, and consequently a significant proportion of your default questions designed for subsession 3 will have been answered by material produced in subsessions 1 and 2, and therefore you should not ask them again.

Nothing irritates an interviewee more than to be asked twice for the same material, since the second request gives unmistakeable evidence that you as interviewer have not been listening to the answers you were getting. So before subsession 3 you need to strike out all questions to which the informant has in fact already provided sufficient answers in earlier subsessions.

Three Analytical Subsessions but not Necessarily
Three Separate Interviews
Although the three subsessions are analytically distinct from the point of view of the researcher-interviewer, they do not necessarily mean that the interviewee will experience all or only three apparently different interviews. Typically, subsessions 1 and 2 blend together into a 'first interview'and subsession 3 is a 'second interview'.

However, it may be that, with a very productive and detailed initial narration, subsession 1 might have – for reasons of practicality – to be taken as two 'interviews' because there is just too much material that the informant wishes to express. Alternatively, with a very unforthcoming informant who provided only a three-minute initial narration and cannot be persuauaded into more than five-minutes worth of subsession 2 production, you might go straight into your subsession 3 and complete all three subsessions in 'one interview'.

You need to be prepared for a variety of eventualities.

Leaping Subsession 2 into a (Narrative) Subsession 3
Under certain conditions, it is possible that the specific requirements of your overall research project push you to 'leap over' subsession 2. A discussion with Andrew C and Isobel F involved the following scenario.

Assume you are concerned with pregnant women who are substance abusers. Assume that you have asked for their life story in the classic SQUIN, and that, in their initial narration, they have completely ignored the period of pregnancy and the topics of babies and substance abuse, but have given you voluminous narratives on everything else, and that your remaining time is short.

According to BNIM rules, you cannot ask, in subsession 2, for narratives about any topic not raised by the informant in subsession 1. The narrative material you have on all the topics that were raised in subsession 2 is ample.

In such a case, you decide to move to subsession 3 where you ask perhaps narrative-pointed questions and then perhaps your other default questions about the topic-areas that are of key concern to your research project but were not raised at all by the informant in subsession 1.

ENDING THE FORMAL INTERVIEW WELL: THE LAST FIVE MINUTES AND THE REMINDER OF 'POST-INTERVIEW' ARRANGEMENTS

The interview can be a tiring experience for both parties. You need to ensure that the interview 'ends well'. You should always invite the informant to say anything else that he or she thinks might be relevant to the topic or the interview process that has not yet been mentioned: if you give enough time to this, you may find a whole new area of information emerging quite at the end.

You should always confirm that you can be contacted afterwards as per your 'contact sheet' and just confirm that the informant might be asked if they would consider giving a short (phone or face-to-face) follow-up interview in case material comes up in the transcript which isn't quite clear. Invite the informant to send you any written comments or make contact by phone if they think later of any points they would like to make.

Make sure that the informant is aware of your appreciation of the time and energy they have already committed to your research by agreeing to and undertaking the interview.

Make sure, however, that you do not take time from the full 'hour on your own' for instant debriefing, as discussed next.

AFTER THE SESSION: INSTANT DEBRIEFING TO SATURATION

This very important function has already been discussed; please refer to pp. 142–44 above.

IV

AFTER THE INTERVIEW: STRATEGIES FOR WORKING THE MATERIALS

OVERVIEW

We start, in Chapter 10, by a discussion of the importance of *indexing and copying* material and then consider the question of levels and types of *transcribing* appropriate and inappropriate for different research purposes; choosing between (and combining) different transcription practices always involves choosing between different costs and different benefits. I then address the key role of using the time of transcribing simultaneously as a time of *constant memo-izing* and journal-keeping. After that there are two basic chapters.

In Chapter 11, the principles for designing data-collection procedures through interviews developed in Part II and which I summarized as *CRQ–TQ–IQ* (Central Research Question → Theory-Questions → Interview Questions) are applied as principles for designing data-analysis procedures. I put forward a general model of moving from Interview Material to Answers to Theory-Questions to an Answer to the Central Research Question, *IM–ATQ–ACRQ*.

In Chapter 12, I look in great detail at one complex method of doing such interview analysis, namely the Biographic-Narrative-Interpretive Method (BNIM) of analysing life-story interview materials generated according to the three-subsession design presented in Chapter 6.

The general ATQ–ACRQ model in Chapter 11 and its detailed application to biographic-narrative material in Chapter 12 should suggest to you how such depth analyses of depth-interview material can usefully be provided for a broad spectrum of uses.

10

Copying, Indexing and Transcribing

INDEXING – CLEAR STRUCTURE FOR RETRIEVING DATED MATERIAL

You need to develop a system of 'indexing' your material (transcripts, fieldnotes, reading notes) so that you can find it again. You need to label your tapes with time, date, place, informant. You need to have a separate file for each interview with each informant, with enough data to enable you to re-contact them for follow-up interviews.

Otherwise, as anybody who has worked in an office will tell you, you will have mounds of stuff that you cannot get at because it is 'all in there, somewhere' but 'you cannot immediately lay your hands on it'. You will suffer from information overload and the analysis will take ten times as long.

As you analyse the materials, you will produce new annotated versions of earlier material; you will produce a whole variety of memos to yourself on a very large variety of topics; you will produce secondary data presentations (I will talk about these later); and you will produce drafts of interpretations and analyses of segments of text and of the text as a whole.

If you have your own computer, indexing and retrieving and 'pasting' of material – and, above all, its eventual analysis – is greatly aided by software programs devoted to qualitative data analysis: Atlas-TI; Ethnograph; NVivo; Nudist; etc. If you are planning to do a number of interviews, one of them will be invaluable. CAQDAS at the University of Surrey is a very good starting point for understanding the implications of different software packages. The web address is <http://caqdas.soc.surrey.ac.uk>.

COPYING – WORK ONLY ON COPIES OF TAPES

Your first technical task is to make a copy of the tape. Better still, two. Without a copy of the taped interview, you run the serious risk of losing all your data, should you mislay the original, or should a tape-recorder mangle it, or for a number of other reasons. So make a copy and keep the original master-tape in a very safe place. If your copy needs to be replaced, make another copy *and still keep the original unused.*

TRANSCRIBING TO SPARK OFF MEMO-IZING
AND (ALSO) TO PRODUCE A TRANSCRIPT

Some people think that you first transcribe your interview tape into written form, and then you start to think about it. This is a terrible mistake.

Thus far in this text, I have frequently stressed the importance of an 'instant post-interview debriefing' in order to lose as little as possible of your experience of the interview. *During an interview*, stopping to make notes on what is going on is not possible without breaking contact and rapport with your informant. The informant cannot wait, and shouldn't.

However, *while you are transcribing*, the audio-tape can wait indefinitely while you make notes on your experience and ideas stimulated by that re-hearing of the audio-tape. You should take full advantage of this. Since you don't *have* to wait till later, don't wait. The audio-tape can wait, and should.

When you listen to the tape for the first time, but only for that first time, a flood of memories and thoughts will be provoked. These memories and thoughts are – like your post-session thoughts and impressions discussed in the previous chapter – available only once. You could argue – almost – that the only point of doing the slow work of transcription is to force the delivery to your conscious mind of as many thoughts and memories as you can, forced as you are to *work slowly through a technical task* (writing down the words onto a piece of paper) while *your mind has time to think fast and widely about the material and the event* in which the material was gathered.

You only hear your taped interview in this way for the first time once. In subsequent listening, the flow of stimulated memories and ideas is much less. If, at the end of the process of transcription, all you have is a perfect transcript, and no theoretical memos, you have wasted 60% or more of this window of opportunity.[1] Better to have *no* transcript and all the theoretical memos, than the other way round!

Another way of saying this is that you are, in attempting to get an answer to your CRQ, struggling to be constantly moving towards a 'sense of what it's all about', you are struggling towards a 'holistic sense of the whole' which is only slowly distilled from a 'holistic sense' of what the little bits you are looking at are all about. This 'holistic sense' calls on much more than the conscious intellection part of your brain; it requires a constant *practice of pausing* to let what might be called your 'whole mind–body response' get access to your conscious mind, giving your conscious mind time and opportunity to generate and sense new understandings of 'what it's all about'. A very useful little book that can help you develop effective practices of letting your holistic senses of parts and wholes express themselves is Gendlin's *Focusing* (1981). See also Claxton's *Hare Brain, Tortoise Mind* (1997). It's when this response starts to flow onto the pages of your notebook or computer that you are starting to do the mental work that eventually will move you on towards a higher-quality answer to your CRQ.

Strauss (1987) underlines the need to consider the work of transcribing as running along the ground in order to jump into the air, or pushing a car along the ground to

---

1 If somebody else does the first draft of the transcribing, you will nonetheless, when *you* listen to the tape for the first time and checking the draft transcription, have a similar once-off opportunity to hear the tape freshly.

get the engine started. The point is to spark off many theoretical memos for yourself in this crucial interaction of active struggle with the transcript and active struggle of your mind as it remembers the original interview experience and also reflects on possible interpretations of that original interview process, and the data generated.

What were you feeling and conjecturing at different points in the flow of interaction? What do you think the informant was feeling about what they were saying at a particular point? From how serious a level were they making the point they were making? Was the informant trying to convince you that they were not a certain sort of person?, etc. These subjective perceptions are themselves hard data: hard data about your subjective perceptions. And when evaluating the interview you need all the hard data about your own previous subjective perceptions that you can get.[2]

The tape will always wait patiently to be transcribed; the ideas that spring from you as you write will vanish quickly. This way, the inevitable 'drudgery' of transcribing will be subsumed into the highly creative one-shot activity of what is the equivalent of a depth interview of yourself as you experience the transcribing of the tape.

When you find you are not getting any 'ideas about the transcript' as you transcribe, then you are not doing 'transcribing creatively' (creatively, that is of notes and memos). If so, stop until you can find a way of making that physical effort do more than just produce a good transcript.

The above may be experienced as rather a counsel of perfection. If you are working with quite large samples, you may find that you cannot give each work of transcription the amount of memoizing attention that you would like to. You then – as always – have a situation where you must balance a higher degree of time and attention to a small number of interviews against a larger range of interviews to each of which you can only give less attention. For training purposes in the craft of doing semi-structured interviewing, you should do one or two. This will heighten your selectivity and sensitivity when you get on to doing larger numbers of cases in less detail. In a research project, very often the very first interviews are analysed in great depth, later ones less so.

Transcribing to Produce Memos

Short notes-in-the-margin and free-associative unstructured writing are not the only 'products' that you should produce while you are transcribing.

Barney Glaser in his *Theoretical Sensitivity* (1978) devotes a whole chapter to what he calls the 'writing of theoretical memos'. Although he links this with coding and I link it with interviewing and transcribing, his points are very valuable:

> 'The *core stage* in the process of generating theory, the bedrock of theory generation, its true product is the writing of theoretical memos. If the analyst skips this stage by going directly from coding to sorting or to writing – he is *not* doing grounded theory. *Memos are the theorizing write-up [of ideas about codes and their relationship] as they strike the analyst while coding.* Memos lead, naturally, to abstraction or ideation. Memoing is a constant process

---

2 You might eventually decide that some or all of these subjective perceptions were quite mistaken. That would be another very interesting finding and would tell you more about the interaction. But you could not come to that discovery without having previously recorded the hard data about those earlier subjective perceptions. That is why it is so important to record them at the time. They become objective data about a past state of your subjectivity.

that begins when first coding data, and continues through reading memos or literature, sorting and writing papers or monograph to the end. Memo-writing constantly captures the "frontier of the analyst's thinking" as he goes through his data, codes, sorts, or writes.

As he is "sparked" by his work …, the *prime rule* is to *stop and memo* – no matter what he interrupts. If he does not, the analyst may lose the thought as his mind goes on to new thoughts and the mechanics of more coding, sorting, writing. While the idea may be tacit or infused in the next set of ideas, it will usually be lost through forgetting, confusing, or supplanting it, because grounded theory constantly generates a proliferation of ideas. Thus the only way to store ideas is in memo writing. The analyst generates a memo fund so they can be forgotten for the moment and referred back to later as codified, and somewhat formulated, theoretical ideas.' (Glaser, 1978: 83)

Glaser's insistence that one should constantly 'stop and memo' – when you are transcribing, when you are coding, when you are sorting, when you are writing up, when you are reading contextual literature – is very important.[3] They may be 'a sentence, a paragraph, a few pages' but they can be seen as the building blocks of your 'interpretation section'.

They are 'building blocks' in a double sense. Some of them may end up almost unaltered as paragraphs or pages of your final report. More likely, they help to 'build the evolving process of your own reflection'. By making explicit your 'momentary ideation about the material' at one moment (i.e. by writing a memo to yourself about it), you lay the basis for moving your thought about it on still further. You subsequently have the 'first memo' on which to reflect and re-theorize at a second, a third, or whatever stage. The constant writing of memos to yourself provides material for final writing; it also provides a basis for improved reflection at a later stage by having full access to critically reviewing and improving your spelled-out thoughts at the earlier date. *To make going along worthwhile*, as you go, *stop and memo*!

Kiegelmann (2000), studying brother-sister incest, talks of a 'first reading' to identify content and what she calls 'researcher's response'. She gives an example of interview text, part of which we cite, and then makes a memo-like note about it:

'Back then he was my big brother and I would do anything to, to protect him and make sure nothing happened to him, and whatever else, you know, and do whatever he told me to do. And [1] now, that, [1] I know better [laughs] you know, like I take care of myself first, and you know, like he comes later and [inhale] I care about him as a person 'cause … (interview with Elena, p. 16; Numbers in [brackets] are indicating pauses in seconds)

When I first read this paragraph, my attention shifted immediately to her statement 'I take care of myself first'. I recognized in myself a desire to encourage this strategy and noticed that I did not want her to excuse her brother. Thus, I realized that I needed to be careful not to let this reaction interfere with the analysis of Elena's interview. In addition, I became aware of the possibility that already during the interview my questions might have discouraged her from expressing her full range of experiences with her brother.' (Kiegelmann, 2000, Section 5)

---

3 There is a whole chapter in Strauss (1987) – ch. 5, 'Memos and memo-writing' – which takes Glaser's analysis further and makes excellent reading. See also Sanjek (1990) for a discussion of field-notes in anthropology, especially 'scratch notes'.

Figure 10.1 is a good example of a reflection on reading the transcript that might (in shortened version) be inserted in a side-column of the transcript, or (in expanded version) treated as a separate memo, or both.

Line no. or box no.	Notes	Transcript	Other type of notes
001 page 1			
002			
003 etc.			

FIGURE 10.1   **Transcript Matrix Blank**

Transcribing to Produce a Transcript

Though transcribing to produce notes and memos, thoughts and reactions, is perhaps the crucial function of creative transcription, you are also transcribing to produce a transcript. This is a long process. Use a word-processing program, right from the start.

Earlier chapters contain examples of transcripts. On my computer I keep a blank matrix with numbering to use for future transcripts, and then, for each interview, I fill in the three columns. An example of the start of such a matrix is given in Figure 10.1; I find it useful to have references to pages as well as line/box numbers, in order to move rapidly through a long transcript. Some word processors and qualitative data analysis software programs have a system of automatic line numbering, and it makes the process much easier. Notice that the matrix has side columns – in order to enable you to insert a variety of materials and comments – and continuous numbering. A transcript is the written version of the interview with as many annotations and commentaries as you see fit. It is like a stage script for a play except that there was only one performance and you are, as unique historian, trying to convey the exact quality and detail of that improvised performance. Recall the use of the columns in the 'Interview with W – ONE and TWO' (Figure 2.3, pp. 34–8).

The three-column structure for transcription is designed to enable relevant comments and material to be placed in one or other of the side columns, so that the data loss involved in just producing all the words spoken by both parties – and nothing more – in the central column can be to some extent overcome. Session notes material can be inserted or referred to, in these side-columns.

Also, of course, such side-columns can be left blank, used for comments and coding that are developed during the analytical and interpretive process later (I shall discuss this).

The Verbatim Principle for Transcript Version Zero
One student, Fraser C, analysed carefully how his attempt to economize by 'selective transcribing' – always horrifyingly tempting – didn't work.[4]

---

4 If you are learning how to interview, you must have full transcripts in order for you, and anybody who is helping you learn, to have access to the data of what happened. Once self-training is less important, then you may be more selective about omitting passages of content which seem to your now-trained perception not to be relevant.

'I found it necessary to transcribe in full the interviews. I at first attempted to *note down only key words and phrases* whilst listening through my tapes, and to use these along with notes taken during and after interviews. This proved impossible, because the keywords seemed to lose their meanings out of the context of the interview, and comparison between different keywords from different informants did not point to the real similarities and differences relating to a question, without first referring back to each tape. I found that, *in order to move quickly between interviews, and to allow me to properly quote passages of interview*, I had to transcribe in full my interviews before I could analyse them. This proved a very labour-intensive policy, [though] having produced 96 narrow-ruled sides of transcripts, with keywords highlighted and quotations numbered for easier reference, it was much easier to find relevant passages, to analyse interviews, to quote verbatim, and to compare and contrast answers.'

People do not speak in grammatical written sentence form: an example from Dell Hymes is given below (pp. 218–19). Your questions are not always delivered as you intended them, too. People speak over each other. They do not answer your questions efficiently and briefly. For reasons that will become apparent, you need to keep this first transcript verbatim. Without such a verbatim (version zero, in Poirier et al.'s, 1983, useful phrase) transcript, you will not be able to analyse the interview as a communicative interaction adequately, because you will miss out on hesitations, gaps, difficulties of formulation, inconsequentialities, changes of 'tack' in mid-sentence when you or your informant slightly changes their mind about what to say and how to say it … all of which may be valuable clues to the state of mind and the state of feelings of your informant.

Later on, you may produce 'cleaned up' versions (post zero), but you should always start with a clean verbatim one.

Put Words in a Central Column; *have a Wide Column on each Side for Other Material* There are many systems for transcribing into the central column of the transcript. You need to indicate who is speaking by the initial of their pseudonym, and the questions should be in a different colour ink or in italics so that you can quickly look for questions on their own and answers on their own.

You will be looking at the transcript frequently as you attempt to understand it; you should therefore make it very legible. Leave spaces between the verbal equivalent of paragraphs, double spaces between utterances.

All the Words of both Parties For the reasons described above, and the need to avoid going back constantly to check, the first transcript should be as complete and unedited as possible. Verbatim means 'complete' with nothing left out. The essence of a transcript is (a) all the words spoken, (b) page and reference numbers, to enable you to find particular passages rapidly.

Ways of Numbering, Turns of Speakers, Units of Meaning You will need to decide whether numbering is by physical line numbers or by speakers' turns plus units of meaning, and when and where you will use broadbrush and when fine-brush units of meaning.

The least problematic method is numbering by physical lines as produced by your word processor e.g. as in Figure 10.2. In that example, text is poured onto the paper and the only additional rule is that a new speaker starts on a new line. The lines are numbered.

> 1. *Isobel: OK. Now I've switched on the tape I can start talking. Thanks for the tea and*
> 2. *biscuits, they are wonderful*
> 3. W: You're welcome
> 4. *I: Thank you for giving up this time for me*
> 5. W: Well, I don't see it as giving up the time, more as contributing ...
> 6. *I: Well, for giving me the time, contributing the time, thank you very much*
> 7. W: If it furthers someone's psychological understanding even a tiny little snippet, it
> 8. can be of value to me and maybe someone else
> 9. *I: Lovely, thank you*

FIGURE 10.2   **Numbering by Physical Line Units**

An alternative is to number boxes by speaker's turns (Figure 10.3). In that example, the box numbers actually refer to the 'turns' of particular speakers. In an interview with a constant back-and-forth between the speakers, this is fine. However, where one speaker holds forth for one, two or 22 or 122 pages, then, to facilitate both rapid reference and more thoughtful reading, you may wish to put distinctly different 'units of meaning' (the equivalent of a sentence or a paragraph) into their own boxes in such a transcript. The 'numbering' would then refer to distinct units of meaning (Figure 10.4).

In that extract from the same interview, something more like a 'unit of meaning' principle is at work, with a relatively fine distinguishing brush. A broader-brush approach might bunch 39–46 in one 'box', 47–50 as another, and 51 as a third, as shown in Figure 10.5. (You might do a different broadbrush differentiation.) Twelve units of adjacent meaning with a fine brush; three units of adjacent meaning with a broader brush.

Any system of numbering other than that of simple physical line numbering is going to be arguable; consequently, straight from the start of transcription, it does make you think about distinct and complex meanings, and this is certainly useful.

1		*Isobel: OK. Now I've switched on the tape I can start talking. Thanks for the tea and biscuits, they are wonderful*	
2		W: You're welcome.	
3		*Thank you for giving up this time for me*	
4		W: Well, I don't see it as giving up the time, more as contributing ...	
5		*I: Well, for giving me the time, contributing the time, thank you very much*	
6		W: If it furthers someone's psychological understanding even a tiny little snippet, it can be of value to me and maybe someone else	
7		*I: Lovely, thank you*	

FIGURE 10.3   **Numbering by Speaker 'Turn' Units**

039		W: Well, I was six when he left.	
040		I don't remember much about him from those days,	
041		I know him now as a man,	
042		but my relationship with him when I was younger seems to be	
043		that I was afraid of him,	
044		didn't really know him,	
046		yes I was kind of glad when he went	
047		I think I was probably	
048		really jealous and possessive of my mother.	
049		She was always the one I felt emotionally close to	
050		very very much so.	
051		And one senses that he was in the way of that.	

FIGURE 10.4 **Numbering by Adjacent Units of Meaning – Finebrush**

1		W: Well, I was six when he left. I don't remember much about him from those days, I know him now as a man, but my relationship with him when I was younger seems to be that I was afraid of him, didn't really know him, yes I was kind of glad when he went.	
2		I think I was probably really jealous and possessive of my mother. She was always the one I felt emotionally close to very very much so.	
3		And one senses that he was in the way of that.	

FIGURE 10.5 **Numbering by Units of Meaning – Broadbrush**

For many purposes, all the words plus 'unit reference numbers' (to physical lines or to units of meaning and to speakers' turns) may be sufficient. For some purposes, and normally only for relatively short chunks of transcript, you may find it important to give some sense of the way the words were said: the paralinguistics, usually informally but sometimes formally as well.

Transcripts with Paralinguistics

Your purposes, your theory-questions and your 'instrumentation theory' determine the level and type of detail to be included or excluded.

Paralinguistics: The Cost of Going Formal!   Learning to use an efficient system for going beyond the spoken words to the way in which those words were delivered involves a considerable investment of learning time. Once you have started to learn them, using such a system of conventions may double or triple or more the amount of time taken to transcribe any given tape.

Given that it will take you some 4–8 hours to complete a transcript of 1 hour of tape just focusing on the verbatim words, and 8–16 hours perhaps to transcribe the same hour of tape and take theoretical memos and record free-associations, then you should be very wary of moving to any of the formal systems, since this could double or triple the time again to 30 hours or so more.

Scheff (1997) argues convincingly that the task of interpretation *intrinsically* requires the attribution of meanings and connotations and strategies to the speakers in a transcript, and that the only function of *formal* notation systems is to enrich and discipline that interpretive practice of observing observables and ascribing inner states to conversational partners.

Such a contribution is very useful. Formal systems have been developed within the school of ethnomethodology known as 'Conversational Analysis' (CA), and the most frequently found system of conventions is that deriving from Gail Jefferson. In sociology, a version of this is provided by David Silverman. However, don't try to enrich *all* of the verbatim text with the *full* apparatus of any of the versions of paralinguistics conventions; the apparatuses were developed for use in analysing much smaller segments of text than the lengthy interviews with which you will mostly be working.

I shall now look at different ways of taking the paralinguistics into account: first informal (which is usable on large chunks of text, like a whole interview) and then formal (which, unless you are absurdly well-funded and have very large quantities of time, you will only use on small selected segments which require especially close and accurate description and interpretation).

Informal Paralinguistics as in the Notation for the 'Interview with W – ONE and TWO'   Consider our puzzlement about how to interpret the 'interview with W', with its lack of systematic paralinguistics in the side-columns. We put in 'alternatives' (see Figure 2.3, pp. 34–8) which gave completely different meanings to the interaction. When you transcribe your own interviews, you will want to provide the notations that will enable you and anybody else reading them to avoid that degree of puzzlement and having to speculate. Slightly modifying our citation from Tannen (p. 33 above), we could say that 'Everything that was said had to be said in some way – in some tone of voice, at some rate of speed, with some intonation and loudness …. These are the signals by which you interpreted then, and can now interpret again and perhaps differently, the meanings of your own interventions and that of your interviewee.'

If you consider the accounts given of the 'interview with W – ONE and TWO' about the role of the father, you will see that the three-column transcription allows for quite complex suggestions of 'the way the words are said'. This is achieved by treating the text as a stage-script, using words like 'said hesitantly', 'in a rush', 'rather pompously', etc.

Symbol	Example	Explanation
[	C2: quite a [while Mo: [yeah	Left brackets indicate a point at which a current speaker's talk is overlapped by another speaker
=	W: that I'm aware of = C: = Yes. Would you confirm that?	Equal signs, one at the end of a line and one at the beginning, indicate no gap between the two lines
(.4)	Yes.(0.4) yeah	Numbers in parentheses indicate elapsed time in tenths of a second
(.)	to get(.) treatment	A dot inside parentheses indicates a tiny gap, probably no more than one tenth of a second
_____	What's up?	Underscoring indicates some form of stress via pitch and/or amplitude
:	O:kay?	Colons indicate prolongation of the immediately prior sound, roughly proportional to the length of the prolongation
WORD	I've got ENOUGH TO WORRY ABOUT	Capitals, except at the beginnings of lines, indicate especially loud sounds relative to the surrounding talk
.hhh	I feel that (.2) .hhh	A row of h's prefixed by a dot indicates an inbreath. A row of h's without a dot, an outbreath. The length of the row of h's indicates the length of the in- or out-breath
( )	future risks and ( ) and life	Empty parentheses indicate the transcriber's inability to hear what was said
(word)	Would you see (there) anything positive?	Parenthesized words are possible hearings
(( ))	confirm that ((continues))	Double parentheses contain the author's descriptions, rather than transcriptions
.,?	What do you think.,?	Indicate speaker's intonation . = falling intonation , = flat or rising intonation
–	becau-	Hyphen indicates an abrupt cut-off of the sound in progress
^	drînk	A 'hat' or circumflex indicates a marked pitch rise
→	1 →	Arrows in the margin point to the lines of transcript relevant to a point made in the text

FIGURE 10.6 **Silverman's Simplified Transcription Symbols**

At one level, this is clearly not a precise objective description of the way the words were said. They indicate attributions by the listener to the speaker of 'inner states' along a variety of implicit and explicit dimensions. They could well be wrong: I thought I was being 'firm'; you heard me as 'pompous' or perhaps 'bullying'. However, they may well be adequate for many purposes. They can be seen as an informal way of going beyond the spoken words without collecting the full battery of formal conversational analysis conventions.

Formal Paralinguistics   There may be cases, however, where – probably just for a short segment of your interview text, as in the micro-analysis work which is a part of the biographic-narrative-interpretive method (BNIM) of analysing narrative life-history interviews – you may feel the need for something more formal.

I provide, below, some formal systems proposed by Silverman, by Dell Hymes, and finally by Labov and Fanshell. See also Poland (1995) and Potter and Weatherell (1987), and for a review discussion of questions of transcription, see, for example, Psathas and Anderson (1990) and Edwards and Lampert (1993). You will find it a useful experience just to consider these conventions and their uses.

SILVERMAN   Silverman's 'simplified' transcription symbols (1993: 118) are shown in Figure 10.6 (p. 217).

DELL HYMES: INTONATION UNITS SIMPLY IDENTIFIED   The complexity of the world of speech-as-spoken can only be suggested in a work of this order. One guide to meaning can be that of the intonational units, as discussed by, for example, Dell Hymes (1996).

Merely putting *pauses* and *notes on voice* into the transcript can be helpful, as can be seen in the following example:

> '[Lucy]: No [the Armed Forces] wasn't me (quiet tone) – I don't think my father would have approved either of that sort of thing (laugh). Because you know – it's a strange thing – the ones who joined the forces seemed to get a bad name – I'm not just saying they were bad – I mean I had cousins in it – and – but you know they had a name for girls – who were – and I suppose – after all who knows when it could happen – they could have died the next day, you know [strong tone].' (Pamphilion, 1999: 403–4)

A concern for thinking about *how intonation structures the delivery of meaning* is also evoked in a slightly different way in the following excerpt from a text by an allegedly schizophrenic woman. This was originally collected and presented by Gee (1991) and then reworked by Hymes (1996: 145). I have slightly modified the presentation.

In this mode of transcribing, indentation is used to convey the relation of intonation units to each other.

Well, when I was LITTLE,
    the MOST EXCITING thing that I used to do is
    there used to be THUNDERSTORMS on the beach that I lived on
And I walked down to MEET the thunderstorms
And we'd turn around and RUN HOME
    running AWAY from the
        running away from the THUNDERSTORMS.

continued

continued

That was the MOST EXCITING
    one of the MOST EXCITING times I ever had was doing things like that
  besides having like when there was HURRICANES OR STORMS out on the ocean.
The WAVES
    they would get really BIG
And we'd go down and PLAY in the waves when they got big.
And one summer the waves were ENORMOUS
    they were just about
      they went STRAIGHT UP AND DOWN
So the SURFERS WOULDN'T ENJOY them or anything like that
They'd just go STRAIGHT up and down
    the HUGEST HUGEST things in all the world.
Then they would
    they would
    they went ALL THE WAY OVER the top of the edge of the road
and went down the road TO OUR STREET
So that's HOW BIG the waves were
    they were HUGE.

Quite clearly, this presentation by Hymes is an attempt to represent on the page a complex structure given by intonation and meaning or, rather, an attempt to suggest the hierarchies of meaning which are to some extent suggested by intonation contours.

The most 'scientific' attempt to present interview material on paper with a visual display of intonation contours was that of Labov and Fanshell (1977). They used two devices: a variable persistence oscilloscope and a real-time spectrum analyser to show the amplitude of the speech pattern over fairly long utterances and to show the rise and fall of the voice (1977: 43–6) (Figure 10.7).

They use acoustic displays from these devices as part of their analysis of a particular therapeutic session to great effect. They admit, however, that 'the problem of the interpretation of paralinguistic cues is a very severe one' and that no context-free interpretation of the meaning of paralinguistic cues can be expected. Ideally, with a very large grant, I would use their recording and displaying devices at least for micro-analysing selective segments, but, even with such acoustic displays, the task of making judgment inferences about 'inner states of thought and feeling' would still be the responsibility of the researcher.

The above discussion should have given you some sense of the significance of being aware of the intonation and the way the words are said, and some sense of the range of possibilities in respect of noting them.

The Practice of Transcribing – An Example

So far, we have assumed that transcribing the words spoken from the tape is in principle straightforward. Even this is less straightforward than it might appear. In principle, transcribing means 'putting down all the words'. In practice, this is complicated and 'any translation is also a betrayal' (*traduttore traditore*), any 'decoding is also an encoding' (David Lodge). In Kay Standing's 'Voices of the less powerful', she discusses and exemplifies the implications of 'tidying-up' transcripts.

FIGURE 10.7   **Labov and Fanshell (1977) Intonation Contours**

'I had made a conscious decision to "tidy up" the transcribed words of both the women and myself, for example, to edit out some of the "ums, ahs, errs, you knows", the swearing, and my own constant "yeahs", and make "gonna" and "innit" into "going to" and "isn't it". The "before and after example" below from Maria, a white working-class lone mother with three daughters, illustrates the dilemmas I faced in transcribing the taped interviews as I heard them, and then translating them into a form more suitable and acceptable for an academic piece of research. Maria's style of speech is distinctive. She speaks quickly and passionately, at "90 miles per hour", barely pausing for breath (and certainly with no respect for grammatical conventions!). During the course of the interview she became upset and emotional, angry and heated. In the passage below she talks of her anger at her ex-husband not paying Child Support:

> I got that letter and I think ... it just don't ... oh I was fuming this morning you know how if one person had just said one thing to me I'd have jumped down their throats you know but that's it ... I think oh sod the lot of them you know I mean they've done no investigation at all I told 'em when they phoned me it's a lie he's living with someone I even spoke to me mother-in-law, I said why is he telling me this "oh well erm she's not working" and I said "so fucking what?" that's not my problem and what is the big deal [shouted] 'cos he's expected to pay something for his kids [yeah] it's pathetic you know [yeah] so erm, I can't say to the kids oh this is what you're gonna get [oh no] this is what you're worth, you ain't even worth a pound each to him you know [yeah] yeah yeah, and it's hurtful you know ...

The lack of punctuation marks makes the passage difficult to read, and sits uneasily in conventionally written text. Yet at the same time, unedited, it captures Maria's style of speech, it captures her passion and anger, the emotions which become lost in the tidied up, neutralized, 'safe' version of the same passage. The words remain the same, but much of the meaning is lost:

> I got the letter and I think ... It just don't ... Oh I was fuming this morning. You know how if one person had said just one thing to me, I'd've jumped down their throats. But that's it. I think, oh sod the lot of them you know. I mean they've done no investigation at all. I told them when they phoned me, it's a lie, he's living with someone. I even spoke to my mother-in-law. I said "Why is he telling me this?". [She said] "Oh well, erm, she's not working". And I said, "So fucking what?" That's not my problem, and what is the big deal 'cos he's expected to pay something for his kids? It's pathetic you know. So I can't say to the kids, "Oh this is what you're going to get". It's an insult. It's

continued

continued

like, oh yeah, this is what you're worth, you're not even worth a pound each to him. And it's hurtful you know.

The editing out of many of my interventions, the "yeahs", also negates the experience of the interview, when often both of us would be talking at once, and has implications for where I place myself in the research text.

By tidying up the transcripts in this way, I homogenized the women's voices, making them all sound (or read) the same. I took away their own (and my own) distinctive way of speaking, which reflects their background and culture, and made standard English the "normal" means of communication. This raises a further dilemma: by doing this, am I further negating the worthiness of the women's language, and indeed of my own? Am I just playing into the hands of the "establishment" by saying black and white working-class women's ways of speaking are wrong, are inadequate, are not as valid as the academic discourse? However, the women themselves often did not feel that their words were valid as academic discourse, and wanted to tidy up their speech to sound "more English". This compromises the character both of their speech and the data and has implications for the production and validation of knowledges.'

(Standing, 1998: 190–1)

As the above extract suggests, transcription is not a technical and transparent process. It involves complex decisions as mediation occurs between the speakers and the eventual readers of transcribed words in any published report.[5]

The Politics and Theory of Transcribing

Transcribing is an instrumentation practice, examining sound-data from an audio-tape to create visual-data for printing out on paper. This poses a considerable number of questions which can only be suggested briefly here. Mishler summarizes one of the issues clearly: the form of transcription is guided by 'theoretical and by practical considerations':

'There are many ways to prepare a transcript and each is only a partial representation of speech ....

Each representation is also a transformation. That is, each transcript includes some and excludes other features of speech and rearranges the flow of speech into lines of text within the limits of a page. Some features of speech, such as rapid changes in pitch, stress, volume, and rate, seem almost impossible to represent adequately while at the same time retaining the legibility of the text. Adding another complexity are the non-linguistic features of any speech situation, such as gestures, facial expressions, body movements, that are not captured on audiotape recordings and are difficult to describe

continued

---

5 Note how the five last lines of Maria's speech could be punctuated differently. 'So fucking what' might not be the end of the quoted speech. Where might it come instead?

continued

and record from observations or videotapes. Lastly, it must be borne in mind that the initial record – audio- or videotape or running observation – is itself only a partial representation of what "actually" occurred.

These cautionary remarks are not intended to discourage investigators but to alert them to problems that must be explicitly faced and resolved in each particular study .... That transcription problems are inherently insoluble in any sense of completeness suggests certain guidelines for preparing and using transcripts.

First, investigators must keep in mind that speech is the intended object of study.[6] At each stage of analysis and interpretation they must be wary of taking their own transcripts too seriously as *the* reality. Transcripts tend to take on a life of their own, especially given the effort, attention, and time involved in their preparation and analysis. Their form – how lines are arranged and how overlaps in speech and interruptions are marked, whether pauses are simply noted or measured in tenths of seconds – both expresses prior assumptions about the nature of talk and generates new hypotheses. *For these reasons it is important to keep returning to the original recordings to assess the adequacy of an interpretation.*

Second, because there is no universal form of transcription that is adequate for all research questions and settings, the criteria to be used in choosing or devising a system choice are theoretical concerns and practical constraints. The mode of transcription adopted should reflect and be sensitive to an investigator's general theoretical model of relations between meaning and speech [instrumentation theory], selectively focus on aspects of speech that bear directly on the specific aims of the study, and take into consideration the limitations of the basic data and of resources available for analysis.

The experience of transcribing is also likely to convince investigators of the need for repeated listenings to ensure the most accurate transcript possible for their own analytic purposes, irrespective of the notation system chosen ....'
(Mishler, 1986: 48–9, italics added)

Any representation of a complex event such as an interview interaction will be less complex and more selective/simplified than the event itself. Consequently, just as a video-tape of the interview would leave out the subjective experience of each party in the interview encounter, so an audio-tape is even less of a complete record. In turn, when you make a transcription from an audio-tape onto a piece of paper, yet further data are lost.

To remedy these losses, I have stressed the importance of instant session de-briefing notes after each interview, of journal-keeping and instantly memoizing notes while doing the transcription. If you see the importance of this apparently marginal activity, and if they are all done sufficiently and with the sufficient skill that comes with practice and the readiness to experiment, then these may go some way towards a partial remedying of such data loss.

---

6 Mishler is not necessarily correct in asserting that 'speech is the intended object of study', since I am interested in 'meanings' and 'truth' to which speech on its own may be an insufficient or misleading clue, as in the case of 'untruthful and self-defensive speech'. Accompanying NVC may be more 'communicative' of important or parallel truths.

In the end, however, for much of your work of analysis and interpretation you will be dependent upon the transcript that you generate. It is for this reason that the issues around transcribing have been dealt with at some length.

Despite the contribution, or on the basis of the contribution, of sociolinguistics and other sciences of oral and written language, the task of interpreting the contribution of the paralinguistics to meaning always requires us – after the most exhaustive formal notation – to *engage in arguable, relatively informal interpretation*, in the way that I suggested with 'the interview with W', arguing from observable data to inferred inner states.

Consequently, in a transcript, when I get beyond the difficulties of deciphering the particular words used – and conveying in writing sounds used in speech that are not words, such as 'uh' – I am starting to make arguable interpretations on paper of flows of sound in interaction. I create 'sentences' by putting in capital letters, and full stops, and produce semi-colons, commas, dashes, etc. to make reading easier. The requirements of page, and the suggestions of meaning, induce us to produce the equivalents of 'paragraphs'. This cannot be avoided but it can be made conscious and explicit. Consider the elaborate transcript in Appendix C

Where nothing hangs on a particular level or type of detail, do not attempt to provide such detail. To give the economic wealth of Britain to the nearest £M would be a great achievement; to try to give it to the nearest 1p would be totally absurd.

> Look again at the implied paralinguistics of the 'two ways of reading' the 'interview with W' – Figure 2.3.

Figure 10.8 is designed to suggest that we move from the text to the attribution of 'inner states' of the interaction flow as registered in the text and in any other registration or commentary on the way the words were 'delivered'. This may involve formal paralinguistics and NVC notation and commentary – to heighten the degree of precision, and to reduce the speed of such 'attributions of inner states' – over (usually) short stretches of text. Whatever the level of paralinguistic notation (and we nearly always use commas, full stops, to indicate simultaneously intonation patterns and switches in speech flow, and these intonation conventions carry implications about 'units of meaning') in columns 4 and 5 of Figure 10.8, whatever I do in columns 3, 4 and 5, *I do it in order to get to column 6.*

1	2	3	4	5	6
page and line/box no.	speaker	text (including chosen level of paralinguistic notation)	formal paralinguistic and NVC commentary on 'delivery observables'	ordinary language description of 'delivery' observables	ordinary language hypotheses about meaning of observables in terms of attributed 'inner states'

FIGURE 10.8   **Paralinguistics → 'Inner States'**

11

Analysing/Interpreting any Interview
Materials: Answers to TQs

OVERVIEW

Once you have both completed a version of the transcript together with side-column notes derived from *post-interview debriefing* and from notes and theoretical memos developed *while doing the transcribing*, you are in a position to begin the task of analysis and interpretation of all these interview materials.

I start by dealing with this task very formally at a high level of abstraction, using the CRQ–TQ–IQ model to indicate how the same model guides both the designing of the interview before it happens and the analysing that you do afterwards on the interview material obtained.

After that, I provide an example of how the general model of interview material interpretation presented in this section actually works out in a given interpretive practice. The interview material is that of biographic narratives; the mode of interpreting them is that of the biographic-interpretive method (BNIM).

GENERAL CRQ–TQ–IQ MODEL: IM → ATQ → ACRQ

Our approach to interview interpretation is a logical extension of the approach to interviews presented in Part I and on its implementation to interview design described in Part II. Consequently, the treatment here can be relatively brief.

The general model put forward in Part II was that of a top-down progression from your Research Purposes (RP) to the formulation of a Central Research Question (CRQ) to a number of derived Theory-Questions (TQs) that spelled out the CRQ, and then from each TQ to a number of Interview-Questions (IQs) and other Interventions (IIs) that you hope will produce the appropriate material for analysis.

RP → CRQ → TQs → IQs/IIs

It is not surprising, therefore, that the corresponding method of analysing the materials eventually produced moves back upwards. You collect the interview material (IM) produced that you see as relevant to particular TQs, you analyse them to produce an answer to each TQ, and then finally you consider simultaneously all the answers to each TQ in order to produce a unified answer to the original CRQ.

Hence the following formula, where the interview material is called 'IM', the answer to a theory question is called 'ATQ', and the answer to the Central Research Question is called 'ACRQ'.

$$IM \rightarrow ATQs \rightarrow ACRQ$$

Figure 11.1 spells out the above formula for the purposes of working up your analysis and interpretation around the interview material. In the diagram, I have assumed that, in addition to the TQs with which you started off, as a result of the work of analysis a new theory question (TQZ) has emerged which will contribute towards your eventual response to the original CRQ. The diagram also assumes that knowledge and material from relevant research literature will also be contributing towards the answering of the TQs.

In addition, there is always a TQ0 which is about the interview processes as they occurred, because these govern the use of the material for answering all other TQs. Although some find this artificial, and argue correctly that much of the interview process becomes highlighted as you struggle with interpreting the interview material for your substantive TQ questions, I have already argued that interview processes (TQ0) must always be studied in themselves quite explicitly, first, before you move to the actual substantive TQs of your study (see p. 12).

Illuminated by the discussions of process of how interview questioning and interviewer intervening can 'go wrong' and by anthropological-historical models such as the Briggs–Wengraf model put forward earlier in Part II, you will consider, for each interview, how the interview-interaction processes worked and what are the implications of your TQ0 findings for answering the substantive TQs (TQs 1–Z) with which you are concerned. Obviously you may revise these ideas later, but it is important to start by considering them explicitly and writing down some provisional conclusions.

The work of interpreting the interview material (IM) and its relevance to any individual TQ and to the TQs as a whole depends, of course, upon the review of the interview processes and the application of your particular instrumentation-theory. Just as the instrumentation-theory was crucial in the designing of appropriate IQs for specified TQs, at the design stage, the same instrumentation/interpretation theory (whatever it is) is crucial for interpreting the significance of the interview material actually gathered (IM) as would-be evidence for answers to TQs.

As you can see, the CRQ at the top left of Figure 11.1 is answered by the A-CRQ at the bottom right. This goes by way of considering each TQ in the light of interview and any other material gathered, including a review of the interview processes relevant to that TQ and a review of relevant research material, and then the producing of an A-TQ for that TQ.

	Interview processes for the two interviews	Interview A	Interview B	Research literature	Answers to each theory-question
Research questions CRQ					
TQ0	Interview processes				A-TQ0
TQ1					A-TQ1
TQ2					A-TQ2
TQ3*					A-TQ3
TQZ† ←	· - · - · - · - · - ·	- · - · - · - ·	- · - · - · →		A-TQZ
REVIEW AND SUMMATION OF QUESTIONS AND MATERIAL					
					A-CRQ

* TQs 1–3 stand for those (any number) TQs initially developed in the research design stage and exist prior to doing the actual research. In principle, they remain unchanged from beginning to end of the research.

† 'TQ-Z' can stand in for any emergent 'theory-questions' to which the interview happens to have supplied material – perhaps against the interviewer's will or 'better judgment' – but which (unlike prior TQs 1–3) was not anticipated prior to the interview. Sometimes the whole interview may run out of the control of the interviewer for good or bad reasons but provide material that can be used for exploring or developing quite different theory-questions. Rather than get 'nothing from an interview, you should always see what you can get from an interview, even if the original CRQ turns out to be un-answerable on the basis gathered. One student, Jane B, prepared an interview on the assumption that certain reforms had been instituted: her CRQ was about the 'effects' of these supposedly instituted reforms. Only in the interview – a difficult one to get – did she find out that the reforms had not been implemented: none of her questions in their original format 'arose'. The question was then: what could be usefully gathered in the interview about the topic-area more generally? A 'TQ-Z' had to be rapidly envisaged and material gathered in the interview relevant to this new TQ. Even if your TQs are all answered and your CRQ too, see what else is in the interview that could be used be used for a further TQ-Z ....

FIGURE 11.1　**CRQ–ACRQ: Developing and then 'Adding up' Answers to each Theory-question**

This is done methodically for each of the TQs, including new emergent TQs and sometimes dropping or modifying old ones for reasons that you explain and justify in the text. Having completed the ATQs, the answers to all the Theory-Questions, you then review and sum the argument as a whole, producing an answer to the CRQ (A-CRQ) as a whole.

It is important to bear in mind that the interview material relevant for the answering of a particular TQ will very often be found in a variety of places. Unlike a fully structured interview, a semi-structured depth-interview format will mean that much of the material for answering a particular TQ *should* be found around the IQs designed for that TQ but *also that much may be found elsewhere*.

Consequently, you will need to examine *all parts of the interview material* in order to ensure that interview material relevant for answering a particular TQ has not been overlooked. I recommend that you work through the transcript, identifying segments of relevant material for your first TQ and coding them in one of the side-columns for rapid retrieval (preferably by a qualitative data analysis software program on a computer). Then work through the whole transcript, coding for the second TQ; and so on. Do not try to code for more than one TQ at a time: you will just do the job badly.

I cannot here discuss the general questions of coding and interpretation of qualitative data in general and of interview material in particular. Among many discussions of coding, a good introduction has recently been provided by Coffey and Atkinson (1997) and there is little point in duplicating their excellent work or those of others who have contributed to the discussion.

However, bear in mind that a code-label is simply a little retrieval-tag attached to one or more segments of text to enable you to think of them as related in some useful way, and that a 'code-label' is a very condensed form of a more expanded 'theoretical memo' or 'gloss'. The sets of coding labels (which together make up at any time your 'codebook classifications') are your own constructions, designed for your different TQ and CRQ purposes. If a segment of text is a piece of luggage, a code-label is just a retrieval-tag attached to it. The same text segment can have a variety of different retrieval tags attached to it, and most qualitative researchers find themselves modifying and revising their 'coding system' as they work through their material; though they need to be used with caution, qualitative-data-processing packages make this process of creative revision feasible.

Be aware of the broadbrush/finebrush approach to coding: codes can be applied to make very fine discriminations (but then it may be impossible to see the wood for the trees) or to make very broad discriminations (in which case they may not enable you to distinguish anything but one or two clumps of trees in the wood). Fine codes – such as postcodes – nestle within broader codes – such as names of towns. The notion of nested structures is also important in semiotic analysis – see the Appendix and Martin (1997: 40–1) on narrative episodes 'nested' within a global narrative structure. Choose your brushes appropriately for the task in hand at the moment.

This principle of 'summativity' – of collecting all evidence from everywhere in answering each TQ – is perhaps suggested by Figure 11.2. The grandmother and the granddaughter have been asked different IQs so that, by puting their answers together, the researcher might get the material relevant for his or her A-TQs.

And a further point: *as you work through the transcript in relation to a particular TQ, always take time off to write theoretical memos or free-association notes for yourself.*

THE 'JUDICIAL MODEL'

What mode of writing should you adopt? There are different models. One you should seriously consider is described as the 'quasi-judicial method' (Bromley, 1986) as summarized in Robson (1993: 375–6). It is not dissimilar to the recommendations of Agar (1986, 1996). These relate to each ATQ separately and to the elaboration of the ACRQ afterwards. Robson cites Bromley as suggesting 10 procedural steps while keeping in mind four questions. The simplest formulation for using and examining the evidence is:

1 provide good arguments against the best possible counter-interpretations, and,
2 recognizing the problems of your own best answer to the TQs and CRQ,
3 put forward your own best answers to the TQs and CRQ.

Theory-questions Central Research Question	Informant A e.g. 'grandmother'	Informant B e.g. 'grand-daughter'	Answers to each theory-question
Theory-question 0 interview processes	all contact with her answers to IQs	all contact with her answers to IQs	ATQ0
Theory-question 1	IQ1.A.1	IQ1.B.1	]
	IQ1.A.2	IQ1.B.2	] ATQ1
	IQ1.A.3	IQ1.B.3	]
	plus relevant material from elsewhere		]
Theory-question 2	IQ2.A.1	IQ2.B.1	]
	IQ2.A.2	IQ2.B.2	] ATQ2
	plus relevant material from elsewhere		]
Theory-question 3	etc.	etc.	ATQ3
			Answer to Central Research Question

FIGURE 11.2 **Two Sets of Informant-questions but One Set of Theory-question Answers when the Informants need Different Informant-questions**

The procedure is in general terms – though not in every particular – well-suited for your discussion of interview and other data. Each answer to each TQ should be expected to be a condensed mini-judicial review, as could the later summative overall answer to the CRQ.

My revised version derived from Bromley (1986: 26) by way of Robson (1993: 376) is as follows.

The four questions:

1 What is the problem and question at issue?
2 What relevant evidence might there be?
3 How else might one make sense of the data?
4 How were the data obtained?

The ten procedural steps in the quasi-judicial method:[1]

continued

---

1 In the text below, where Robson has 'explanations', I have replaced this by the term 'interpretations'.

continued

1   State the initial questions, problems and issues as clearly as possible.
2   Collect background information to provide a context in terms of which the problems and issues are to be understood.
3   Put forward prima facie interpretations and solutions to the questions, problems and issues in the light of your instrumentation theory.
4   Use these interpretations to guide the search for additional evidence. If they do not fit the available evidence, work out alternative interpretations.
5   Continue the search for sufficient evidence to eliminate as many of the suggested interpretations as possible, in the hope that one will account for all the available evidence and be contradicted by none of it. Evidence may be direct or indirect, but must be admissible, relevant and obtained from competent and credible sources.
6   Closely examine the sources of the evidence, as well as the evidence itself. All items should be checked for consistency and accuracy. This is analogous to cross-examination in the case of personal testimony.
7   Enquire critically into the internal coherence, logic and external validity of the network of argument claiming to settle the issues and solve the problems.
8   Select the most likely interpretation compatible with the evidence.
9   Formulating an acceptable interpretation may have an implication for action, which has to be worked out.
10 Prepare an account in the form of a report. It should contribute to instrumentation-theory 'case law' by virtue of the general principles employed in interpreting the particular case. It should explicitly answer the Question, or say why it cannot do so.

Individual or group sessions struggling with the task of 'interpreting the evidence' in the light of 'the questions' can be apparently chaotic and emotional processes. The ease of such work should not be over-estimated. Normally, a considerable original disorder – in which chaos seems to be spreading – is followed later by a surprisingly swift development of a large measure of agreement. See Gelcer et al. (1990: 109–11).

If you are part of a research team, see if you can arrange panel discussions and interpretation. You may decide to start with preparation of draft answers (with evidence, dealing with counter-interpretations explicitly) to particular TQs by each individual, and then move to a group discussion of the draft answers. Alternatively, you might start with collective brainstorming and then move to separate preparation of theoretical memos on each TQ. You will soon find what suits your team best.

If you are working individually, see if you can at least find one other person to join you in a two-person team for at least one session. They do not have to be otherwise engaged in your or any research, though if they are trained in a different social research tradition, this helps; they just have to have had different experiences and a different life from your own.

CONCLUSION

In order to be applicable to any materials from semi-structured depth interviews, this account of the process of analysing and interpreting any and all possible materials has had to be very brief and extremely abstract. I have argued that, having attempted to understand the interview processes involved (TQ0), you should then identify and where appropriate code-tag with a TQ-number label all material relevant to each of the Theory-Questions (TQs) derived from your Central Research Question (CRQ) and then, using something like the quasi-judicial method of Bromley, produce appropriate answers to each of those theory-questions. On the basis of those ATQs, you can then develop your answer to the Central Research Question (ACRQ).

I hope that you find that its design principles are useful when you apply it to your own research. In the next section I apply the general model to a particular set of interpretive procedures. The general (IM–ATQ–ACRQ) model is shown in operation with biographic-narrative interview material and with a specific genre of analysing such material known as the biographic-narrative-interpretive method (BNIM). Even if you are not interested in biographic-narrative interviews in themselves – because your own research is very different – you may find it useful to read the section in order to grasp what is involved in any actual application or case-practice of analysing interview materials to produce an answer to your TQs and CRQ.

12

Analysing/Interpreting SQUIN–BNIM
Interview Materials: Answers to TQs

OVERVIEW

Preliminary Note

The account of the biographic-interpretive method of analysing narrative life-stories (BNIM) that I put forward in this chapter is derived from the work of Gabriele Rosenthal and Wolfram Fischer-Rosenthal (see pp. 112–13 above for a fuller discussion). I have modified some of their terminology, but basically this account presents their method. Although I have not studied with them, I learned their method through working with Roswitha Breckner, Prue Chamberlayne and Susanna Rupp (in England) and with others in the Sostris project, a six-country research project over three years devoted almost entirely to primary research into social exclusion using the BNIM method (Chamberlayne and Rustin, *Sostris Final Report*, 1999). Research teams from six countries engaged in 250 interviews across Europe, probably the largest co-ordinated use of biographic-interpretive interview methodology to date (I would welcome news of others!). In order to provide an introductory account in English, I have plundered handouts and notes and other material used in the training by Roswitha and Suzanna and attempted to convey my understanding and my formalization of the practices involved. My thanks to all those involved in the Sostris project, and particularly those named above. If they recognize their words and examples in some of what follows, they will be correct! They are not responsible for my use of them.

The General ATQ → ACRQ Model Applied to this Model

The structure of the design of a biographic-interpretive methodical research founded upon a single question inducing narrative (SQUIN–BNIM) can be formally and most simply defined as shown in Figure 12.1. However, what counts as a good description of 'the structure of the case / lived life / told story' cannot be made clear except through examples and practice. The specific meanings of those BNIM terms in the BNIM theory-language will be clarified throughout the remainder of this text.

The difference of life and text has been an extensive debate in the German speaking biographical research in the early 1980s. In the context of this debate and

The Central Research Question = CRQ	'What is the structure of the case?',
Two Theory-Questions = TQ1	'What is the structure of the lived life?'
= TQ2	'What is the structure of the told story?'

FIGURE 12.1   **SQUIN–BNIM's CRQ–TQ**

drawing on Gestalt-theory, Rosenthal 1995 has developed a methodological and operative tool to distinguish these two levels in an autobiographical text analytically. This operative distinction which leads to a reconstruction of a two-layered biographical structure of life history and life story as produced in communication, is not trivial. The everyday speaker (and the communication) excludes his own perspective and observing operation as production factor while communicatively observing his life, because this would lead to the question, if he might have had another life, whether he would look at it differently, and why he/she constructs it like this. In the language of Spencer Brown, the *speaker* only looks at the marked state of the distinction 'my life', namely the 'life' as objective, and neglects the unmarked state of the observation/communication as active operation of it and within it. However, *the researcher as observer can look at the presentation and process of telling the story and thus discover the structure of its construction.* Fischer-Rosenthal and Rosenthal call this technically the Thematic Field Analysis (TFA), see below.

Once the interview material has been worked over to produce answers to these two theory questions – what is the pattern of the lived life? what is the pattern of the told story and the self-presentation? – in the way that I shall try to show, this is not the end of the matter. We are also interested in *the relationship between* that structure of the lived life and that structure of the told story (compare Bollas, 1987: 46–8, 64–81). This is formulated as a further theory question to which an answer can only be given after the two initial theory questions above have been answered.

As we shall see, these answers are themselves subject to further analysis to produce answers to further theory questions which, eventually, produce an answer to the Central Research Question. The Interview Materials are worked on to produce successive waves of Answers to Theory Questions which in turn, it is hoped, produce an Answer to the Central Research Question.

IM → ATQs → ACRQ

Intermediate Processing: From Raw Material to Processed Data

The reorganization and questioning of data in stages, as suggested above for the SQUIN–BNIM procedure, is common to most sophisticated schools of data-analysis, whether quantitative or qualitative. As Coffey and Atkinson (1997) have stressed, dealing with qualitative data analysis, some approaches involve a moderately eclectic menu of alternative and loosely complementary methods; others, like the one under consideration here, are relatively rigorously defined and sequenced. However, both complex quantitative analysis (e.g. multivariate

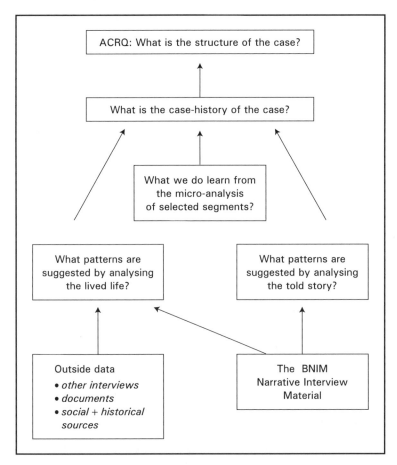

FIGURE 12.2   **BNIM in the CRQ–IQ Structure 1**

analysis) and complex qualitative analysis (e.g. BNIM) require (and requite) time, and training, and practice.

From Relatively Mechanical Craft to a Craft-based Artistry

One final point needs to be made. I have said that, like many others, this particular method of analysing data moves from a relatively mechanical activity – where the procedure is logically tight and following the procedure is likely to lead all those who do follow the procedure to similar results – to a craft-based artistry. After the relatively mechanical craftwork has been done, and the answers to the first two theory-questions obtained, then the answers developed for the subsequent theory-questions become less determined by technique and more determined by the individuality of the researcher and the sociality of the analysing team. Such a statement may anger positivists because it suggests a limit to the impersonal power of technical procedures; it may anger some enthusiasts for qualitative methods because it declares the need for relatively mechanical and routine activity before the 'individuality of the researcher' makes itself legitimately felt.

I have discussed this at some length in Wengraf (1999; and see also Wolcott, 1994) and will explore this further below. However, my firm conviction is that the inevitable artistry of interpretation can realize its full value only when placed squarely in relation to a solid and reliable craft base.

PHILOSOPHY OF BNIM INTERPRETATION

Five Stages of BNIM

Roswitha Breckner, in *Sostris Working Paper no. 2* (1998), identifies the 'Principles and Procedures of the Biographic-Interpretive Method'. She writes:

'Biographies are texts ... which refer

- to past experiences
- in a present horizon, and
- in a horizon of future expectations.

The process of analysis addresses these relations in different steps, aiming at the reconstruction of the inter-relation between the lived-through past and the present story in the horizon of future expectations. It is organized in five steps:

1 the analysis of biographical data (BDA), addressing the chronology of experiences in the lived life, the lived-through past
2 the analysis of the interview text in a thematic field analysis (TFA), aiming to reconstruct the structuring principles of the story-as-told; its gestalt
3 the construction of a "case history" on the basis of (1) and (2) addressing how events have been experienced in the past, and how the patterns of orientation and interpretation and self-presentation developed genetically out of these past experiences
4 micro-analysis of small selected pieces of text aiming to analyse in depth the inter-relation between past experiences and their presentation and to check hypotheses developed before and in stage 3 above
5 finally, based on the results of the previous four steps, a discussion of the inter-relations between the life history and the told story, contrasting the two, aims at formulating a structural hypothesis about the principle of connection between the life history [specific sequence of lived-through experiences in the past] and the told story [the present-time presentation of specific experiences from that life-history]. This is known as "identifying the case structure".'
(1998: 92, modified)

In this volume, I cannot give a full account of all these steps. What I can do is to show in reasonably full detail the working of the earlier relatively routine steps, and indicate the principles of the final more interpretive steps. However, I hope that the presentation here will provide sufficient materials and examples for you to achieve an advanced understanding of the principles and practice of the method.

TQ Zero – Analysing the Communicative Interaction

As in any interview-based study, you will first need to consider and analyse the interview interaction in which you participated. This can be considered as answering the TQ0:

How did the interview process go, and what implications has this for the different subsequent TQs relating to my CRQ?

For this, your debriefing notes after the interview and any theoretical memos developed while transcribing will be invaluable resources.

You also have the theoretical models and sensitizing examples of Part I, which can now be particularly applied to the raw materials of your own interview practice. Since these models (Foddy and Briggs) have already been presented pp. 38–9, 42ff, and since the communicative interaction in 'the case of W' transcript has been analysed at length (p. 18ff), this will not be re-presented. You should refresh your memory of this material before starting to analyse your own interaction materials.

You will need to develop an understanding of the development of the relationship between the two of you as the interview process went on. You need to develop some sense of how you and/or your interviewee moved at different points towards and away from different topics and different possible levels of truthfulness and self-defence, partly perhaps as response to what you did or did not do. The task is not to blame or judge, but to see the interview as a unique interaction between two anxious subjectivities, an interaction that has to be understood if you wish to make correct inferences to any extra-interview realities from interview material arising from that 'anxious incomplete interaction'.[1]

Although you do not have access to the 'inner experiencing by the interviewee of the interview', you do have some access to your own 'inner experiencing' of that interview process. Through and with the debriefing notes, the transcription, and the theoretical memos written during the process of transcription, you should be able to construct a plausible account of how it was for you and how it might have been for the other person at different moments in the interview when dealing with different matters.

You cannot know that your account of them is correct, but you must try to develop the most 'grounded' set of hypotheses about their experience and response that you can. This discussion and analysis will be crucial in providing a context for analysing all the data you have been careful to generate and provide. In order to avoid such a process being self-serving and fanciful, others should be asked to read the transcript and respond to your own Bromley-style (pp. 227–9) semi-judicial assessment of the interview processes. Whatever provisional conclusions to TQ0 about interview processsses you come to at this point will luckily be likely to be rectified during your further analysis of the material regarding the other theory-questions.

As you do this interview-interaction analysis, reviewing your response to the interview, the interviewee, as a whole and to particular moments in the interview process as well, you will also need to continue to *keep writing theoretical memos*. Otherwise your record of the work done at the previous stage will *not move you on* to the thinking and creative distillation required by the next stage. 'Don't move on, without at least one memo done' is a good slogan, if you want to move on *creatively* as opposed to mechanically.

---

1 References to 'anxiety' are based on the model of human subjectivity that I and others prefer to adopt for this work. It does not necessarily imply that those involved in the interview are conscious of that anxiety. Anxiety in social interaction is a postulate of the model – see Hollway and Jefferson, pp. 158–9 and the more powerful discussion in Bar-On (1999).

Lived Life – Told Story

What are the steps in the BNIM analysis? The *first stage of analysis comprises sequentializations of lived life and told text*. On the basis of the tape, the transcript is produced. On the basis of the transcript, two other documents are produced. The first document derived from the transcript describes the chronology of the interviewee's life; the second describes his or her delivery – within the interview – of the biographical account and responses to the interviewer interventions as a result of which it is told. These are then subject to further analysis.

1 The sequence of events and actions in a life is usually called a 'chronology' and I shall talk of constructing a Biographical Data Chronology (BDC) from the interview material and any other sources.[2]
2 The description of the sequence of a text has no common-sense name, so I shall talk of constructing a Text Structure Sequentialization (TSS) – for short, a sequentialization – showing the changing structure of the text, particularly that of the story told in the initial narration.

What happens then?

- On the basis of the BDC of the sequence of the life, we go on to do a Biographical Data Analysis (BDA).
- On the basis of the TSS of the sequence of the text, we go on to do what will be called a Thematic Field Analysis (TFA).

This gives us the scheme shown in Figure 12.3. I start with the theory-questions at the basis of the two early distinct sequences: what is the BDC of the person's life, and what is the TSS of his or her text? These proceed in a similar way: though one deals with life-events and actions, the other with text-events or speech-actions, the principles of construction are similar. I deal, though, with each in turn.

GENERATING THE BDC AND THE TSS

Biographical Data Chronology Constructed from Interview and Other Sources

The *lived life* is composed of the uncontroversial hard biographical data[3] that can be abstracted from the interview material and any other helpful source: it is organized chronologically in the BDC and expresses the 'objective' data about the person's life, the life-events as they happened. Since the lived life occurs over time, *sequentializing the lived life* by constructing a chronology (BDC) is an obvious thing to do. The interviewee may give these events in their chronological order to some varying extent, but you will have to collect them from all over the two or three sessions and put them in order yourself.

---

2 It could have been called a 'Biographical Structure Sequentialization' (BSS) to match the next term (TSS) but 'Chronology' is an ordinary language term and therefore BDC is easier to remember.

3 If there is or could be a controversy, then the postulated 'datum' is not 'hard enough', and is left out!

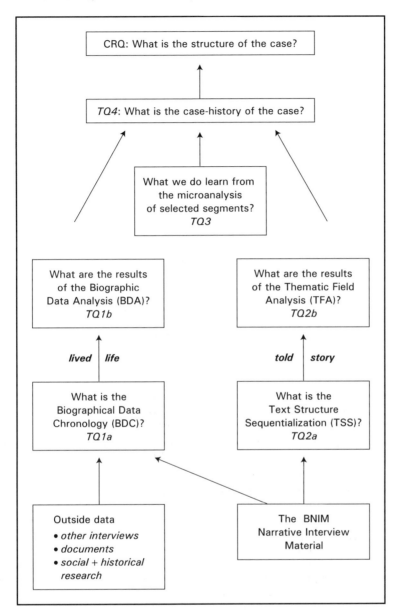

FIGURE 12.3 **BNIM in the CRQ-IQ Structure 2**

Figure 12.4 is an extract from chronology of a lived life – a biographical data chronology, BDC[4] derived from the transcript and from any other available social and historical sources.

The biographical data can be extracted from any of the subsessions of the interview and from any other source: you can probably do it within 3–6 hours, or less.

---

4 Another longer example of a BDC can be found in Breckner (1998: 93–4).

Biographical Data of
Harold Halford*

> 1944 Mother married first husband, Faulkner. They have three children (Jane b.1944, John b.1948, Fred b.1954) and then the husband dies around 1956. She remarries, Richard Halford, in 1957. A fourth child is born (Michael, b.1958)

1960	HAROLD Halford born
1963	Derek Halford born
1970	Family moves house, Harold goes to new junior school, then goes to new secondary mod
1971	Mother dies Jan 71
1971–2	Father, with long-term sickness, retires from mines
1976	HAROLD leaves school and goes into the mines
1975/76	Father marries Annie Peters with a daughter of Harold's age and six other (grown-up, left-home) adult children

etc.

*A number of these were checked by phone call, and my earlier drafts were 2–3 years out.

FIGURE 12.4   **Biographical Data Chronology – Harold Extract**

Where you have no other source of data than that presented in the interview, you may sometimes have relatively few data points, and very often hardly any clear dates. If you cannot re-contact the interviewee to ask them to fill out the dates and detail, then you just have to work with what you have got. Even if you cannot date certain episodes, you may be able to arrange them in the right sequence: 'I don't know when his children were born, but I know it was first a girl and then a boy' provides an undated sequence.[5]

If there are not enough hard biographical data arising from subsessions 1 and 2, you might eventually wish to do a quick phone interview with the interviewee to clarify, and hopefully get at least rough dating for, the sequence of 'hard facts' that make up the Biographical Data Chronology.

Obviously, a sensible design for subsession 3 would include TQs aiming to get further clarification of these 'uncontroversial objective events' that go to make up the BDC.

Biographical data can not only be drawn from the interview – though this may be sufficient for some purposes, and you may well be limited to this – but from potentially all other sources providing such data. Such sources are different types of historical research, personal documents like letters, diaries, written autobiographical texts (unpublished and published), official files, etc. Also applicable are other oral sources in the social networks of the interviewee, which is especially the

---

5 If you know that something happened, but you can't place it anywhere, and a phone call to the informant doesn't help, then you can't place it in the chronology.

case in family studies, where representatives of more than one generation are interviewed (see the three-generation approach in Rosenthal (1998)). Along these lines of obtaining materials for a BDC, and for much else, see Miller (2000).

When there is reason to believe that crucial events, actions or are being concealed (e.g. those of Nazi perpetrators, political party affiliations or incidents of victimization which might be found in objective or 'official' documents (see Rosenthal, 1998; Rosenthal and Bar-On, 1992), the researcher should consult the archives and any other accessible sources to obtain biographical data omitted or denied by the interviewee.

Generating the Told Story (Text Structure) Sequentialization from the Transcript of the Initial Narrative and Eventually from Subsession 2

The principle of developing a BDC corresponds with our normal way of thinking and provides no conceptual difficulties. The same is not true about the task of developing – from the same transcript – a Text Structure Sequentialization (TSS). This requires considerable practice to get right for most people. Unlike the concept of a biographical chronology, a TSS is a new concept, specific to the BNIM, and requires quite a lot of work to be understood and more to be operationalized and used in practice. Don't expect to grasp all of it straight away!

The Concept of a TSS and its Importance

A TSS is a description of the sequence of structural changes in a biographical account, especially of the initial narration in subsession 1.

Very briefly, when we come to analyse a person's *told story*, we address not so much the events and actions, the happenings, that occurred in a person's life (the BDC), but rather the way in which those events and actions were experienced and *are now understood from the perspective of the person giving the interview*. To achieve such an understanding, to have a description of the told story to analyse, a technical description of the structure of the text is first required, the TSS. The verbatim text of the interview is not adequate and must be 'processed' into a TSS.

As I said previously, the significance of the single question aimed at inducing biographic narrative is precisely to create a space which the speaker is obliged to fill with a textual structure of his or her own creation, a unique gestalt.

Consequently, a *full description* – full, that is, from the point of view of the instrumentation theory – of the *textual structure* created freely by the interviewee is a precondition of interpreting its significance. Depending on the length of the transcript and upon other factors, the amount of time taken by the work of generating a TSS can be very considerable. It could easily take two or three working days. A long TSS might take double or triple that time, or more.

What does a TSS look like?

TSS: Noting Three Types of Change in the Transcript

Going through the transcript, you will need to produce a document looking like that shown in Figure 12.6. This is part of a TSS of an initial narrative (subsession 1). I will explain how it was derived. Topics are indicated in the right hand column, characterizations of the way topics are talked about are in the central column.

In this mode of description, the structure of the text is held to have changed, and a new structure is said to have started, if *either the topic* has changed, *or the way a*

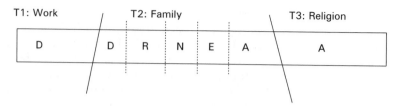

FIGURE 12.5   **Simple Model of Topic and DARNE Textsort Change**

TOPIC: GOING INTO THE MINES, LIFE IN THE MINES 8/9–13/3		
page/line no. in transcript	Summary of structure	Brief indication of content, the gist
8/9–9/2	Description/argumentation	Fascinating working in the industry 'never never a dull moment'. Physically very very demanding – never worked weekends and rarely overtime

9/3–7	Narrative episode	Waiting for the bus at 5 a.m. 'no point in coming in the pit boys it will be closed in 8 months time'
9/7–8	(still a narrative)	'3 or 5 years later it was still going, still saying the same old thing'
9/9	Evaluation	'At the time you know, I thought you couldn't come across better characters'
9/10–15	Argumentation	'As I grew more mature, and after the miner's strike, I realized how naive I was, how people can be manipulated, my attitude to my colleagues changed'

9/20	Evaluation	I couldn't have believed that I would have such dislike for colleagues

9/27–10/3	Argumentation	I would do strike again, but would approach it now with bit more open eyes

FIGURE 12.6   **TSS of Harold – Fragment**

topic is spoken about has changed, or both. If the *Speaker* had changed – which in the example doesn't happen – this would be another change of structure, a new segment would be said to have started.

In Figure 12.5, I have assumed no change of Speaker, as might be the case of a confident initial narration in subsession 1. I have identified three topics (T1, T2, T3) and four changes of textsort, the way a topic is talked about. I have given the initials of the five textsorts I will identify below:

Turning to an actual example, in Figure 12.6 the researcher has noted a change from 'Description/argumentation' (which is how topics were being talked about on page 8, line 9 to page 9, line 2) to a 'Narrative episode' account (on page 9, lines 3–8), which is then followed by an 'Evaluation' (page 9, line 9), and so forth. The meaning of these terms will be clarified later.

Because the topic, in a broad sense, is deemed to have remained the same, a definition of that topic is provided at the top of the entry. The left hand column indicates the page and the line-numbers of the segment of text whose gist is summarized – partly by quotation, partly by paraphrase – in the right hand column. Something like three pages of verbatim transcript have been 'condensed' in this way into, are being 'represented by', something more like half a page of the TSS. The summary of the gist in the right hand column is not obscure; it can be regarded as a summary of the 'aspects' of the 'overall topic'. The central column contains certain technical code-labels which now need to be explained. They refer to the type of textsort being used to deal with the main topic and its aspects.

Figure 12.7 provides a cleaned-up later version of a page of a TSS, this time relating to an interviewee known as 'Janette' (see Rupp and Chamberlayne, 1998 for a full discussion of this case). Here, something like three pages of verbatim transcript are condensed into one page of TSS.

In this version, there is a summary of the topic and its aspects together on the right-hand-side, while in the centre the highlighted materials are the *evaluations* made by the interviewee. Less detail is given about the various aspects in Figure 12.7 below than in the previous one. It is a matter for you to choose which one of these two versions of a TSS is easier to produce and easier to work from.

The principle behind the sequencing of the transcript is one in which a new 'segment' is said to start whenever there is a change of at least one of the following three features of the transcript text. The first two identifications of difference are comparatively common-sensical; the last is highly technical.

1   *Speaker change*: a change from one speaker to another (interviewer/viewee swap or overlap)

2   *Topic change*: a change in the topic being talked about

3   *Textsort change*: a change in the way a given topic or topic is being treated by the speaker. This is known as a textsort change. The terms used in the central column of the TSS segments in Figures 12.6 and 12.7 include the five different types of text currently distinguished in the BNIM typology of textsorts:[6]

- Description
- Argumentation
- Report
- Narrative
- Evaluation

continued

---

6   These have evolved and vary: I am using one version. New categorizations will no doubt develop. Procedure and definitions according to seminar-material of *Quatext*, defined by Berlin 1992ff.; Rosenthal 1995, pp 240f.; see also Kallmeyer and Schütze 1977.

continued

Using the initials of the above five textsorts, I can refer to a textsort analysis as being a DARNE analysis.[7]

page/ line	Speaker/textsort	Summary topic/quotation
1/7	I: initial question	interested in the biographies of people in Europe tell me your life story begin wherever you want
1/10	Ja: question	(giggles) my life story?
1/11	I: cont initial question	interested in everything that has been important for you take the time you need I'll not interrupt you, take some notes
1/14	Ja: interactive remark	okay
1/15	I: cont init question	ask later
1/16	**Ja: global evaluation (3)**	**'I think I'll start off saying that I am (probably) a third generation single parent'**
1/18	I: interactive remark	yeah
1/19	Ja: report	grandmother was a single parent immigrated with her daughter in the 1950s father stayed back
1/27	(end)**evaluation**	**'so she was actually a single parent while she was here'**
1/28	I: interactive remark	aha aha
1/29	Ja: report	Mum brought up in England no marriage, four children father left; J aged 18 months Mum brought them up Mum back to college, accountant married another man
2/1	argumentation	felt never the need for 'the norm' of a family strong women in the family 'shrews', against 'suppression' conflicts with stepfather older children parented younger brothers, not the stepfather

FIGURE 12.7   **Cleaned up TSS of Janette – Fragment**

7 Strictly this should be called a DARNE/topic/speaker Text Structure Sequentialization. Were we to use Spradley's concept of six levels, our textsorts would be different. Other classifications of textsort difference would produce different TSS for the same verbatim transcript.

Let us look at each of these in turn.

There is no difficulty about identifying a *change of speaker* in a transcript. In the first example above, there is only one speaker. In the second TSS segment, there were a number of changes of speaker, each one of which is a 'structural change', producing a new segment.

The concept of *topic/keywords and phrases* was raised in terms of the making of notes during subsession 1, the initial narration, of the three-session interview characteristic of the SQUIN–BNIM method (pp. 131–35). On the basis of the transcript of the whole interview, the sequence of topics can be re-identified more precisely or more broadly (or both), and calmly and completely. A summary sufficient to remind you about the thematic content is on the right-hand-side: the gist. A broadbrush identification of topic would define the whole segment as being about one topic; a finer (or 'aspects') brush provides the column 3 discriminations of what might be seen as subtopics of a main topic.

The DARNE Typology

It is the *textsort change* which is most difficult to grasp. Derived from literary theory – see Breckner (1998) for a summary and references – the five basic or pure types of textsort (D-A-R-N-E) are there because the instrumentation theory underlying the BNIM–DARNE school of interpretation holds that a change in the way that somebody talks about an old or a new topic is held to be significant. (I used to express my frustration at my slowness at learning all this by referring to 'that darn BNIM analysis'. Now that it's become easier, I talk about 'DARNEing the TSS'). The instrumentation theory considers that how the interviewee holds to or changes a topic, and how they hold to or change the way they talk about the topic at the time, is significant:

> 'The method used here to analyse narrated family and life stories is one of hermeneutical case reconstruction developed by the author [Rosenthal] over many years in combination with various other methods .... On the one hand I tried to reconstruct what the biographer actually experienced during this sequence of their life, and, on the other hand, to analyse how they present their life in a present-day interview. *In analysing their biographical self-presentations, or life-stories, what I am aiming to achieve is an analysis of the biographer's present perspective.* I interpret in what form, i.e. at what point of the text, they speak about certain parts of their lives, and I reconstruct the mechanisms behind the topics they choose to talk about and the experiences they choose to tell.
>
> I assume that it is by no means coincidental and insignificant when biographers *argue* about one phase of their lives, but *narrate* another at great length, and then give only a brief *report* of yet another part of their lives or *describe* the circumstances of their lives in detail.' (Gabriele Rosenthal, 1998: 4–5, modified)

Textsorts in a DARNE analysis can be identified as falling into one of five prototypical classifications (there are mixed cases, and subtypes), as follows.

> **D = Description,** namely the assertion that certain entities have certain properties, but in a timeless and non-historical way. No attempt is made at story-telling/narration. There is
>
> *continued*

continued

a sort of timeless 'anthropological present' about the described person, a situation, whatever.

In the Harold example (Figure 12.6, p. 240) the speaker describes 'how it always was' in the mines: 'never a dull moment', never worked weekends; always ....
(lines 8/9–9/12)

A = Argumentation, namely the development of argument and theorizing and position-taking, usually from a present-time perspective, often from a past-perspective, often a blend of the two. It is generally in a stand-alone form (not explicitly connected to the content of a particular narrative). Only sometimes is it in the form of an explicit 'disagreement' with an explicit counter-position, though one is usually implicit.

In the Harold example, the speaker (lines 9/10–15) provides an explicit theory from his present-time perspective about his evolution from naiveté to maturity. Between lines 9/27 and 10/3 the speaker again from his present-time perspective puts forward a theory about what he would do if he 'had his time over again' in relation to the strike.

R = Report. This is a form in which a sequence of events, experiences and actions is recounted, but in a relatively experience-thin fashion, such that it appears to be recounted from some distance. Very often, it provides an overview of a range of events some of which are then singled out for detailed narrative treatment. Very often, it covers a relatively long period of time. The difference between this and the next category is one of degree.

In the Harold example, lines 7/9–12 give a brief report of the speaker's 15 years in the mining industry. It is quite close to a bare chronology.

N = Narrative, namely the telling of a story by which event Y followed event X, and event Z followed event Y, either for causal reasons or just 'because they did'. The story is not told in a very 'thin' way, like a bare (police) report, but rather in 'rich detail', and sometimes even in the present tense by the narrator virtually 'reliving from close up' the sequence of events recounted. Often there are words in 'direct speech' as said by the actors in the story episode being narrated.[8]

In the Harold example, the speaker in lines 9/3–7 tells the story of his first day at work, about standing at the bus stop and then the older men telling the new boys that 'there's no point in coming into the pit, it'll be closed in 8 months time'.

This is a detail-rich story of a particular sequence of events on that particular day, and therefore is classified as a narrative rather than as a report.

E = Evaluation. The easiest way to think of this is as the 'moral of the story' – of a thin report or a rich narrative – stated explicitly as such, usually before or after the story-sequence in question.

In the Harold example, line 9/9 gives Harold's evaluation at the time after going into the pit and before the 84–85 strike of the characters in his mini-narrative; in line 9/20 he gives a post-85 evaluation of the mining characters to be presented in a narrative of the 84–85 strike that he is going to tell later.

---

8 See discussion of the concept of narrative as developed by Labov and Waletsky (1967) and on p. 116.

When I first encountered the use of these textsorts in a DARNE sequentialization, I was sure that any given text segment must fall unambiguously into one and only one of these categories, and that all segments could be described in one of these ways. I searched vainly for the unambiguous definition of the five textsorts such that I could achieve text-segmentation *by textsort* as mechanically as I could achieve text-segmentation by *speaker*.

This led to great misery. The five categories are empirical judgment categories; they exist on a spectrum where there are many mixed cases and cases which, to my mind, are not very usefully described by any one of the five categories.

In addition, very considerable changes occur in your segmentation of text depending on whether you are segmenting with a broad brush some 20–30 pages of transcript hoping to produce a TSS of some 2–3 pages, or whether you are taking 6 pages of transcript and subjecting it to a very detailed close-up analysis (I shall discuss this later) in which the 6 pages might also be used to generate some 2–3 pages of TSS.

Consequently, the correct question to ask about a draft Text Structure Sequentialization is not 'is this the true text structure sequentialization?' but rather 'is this a useful and productive TSS for advancing to the next stage, or should it be done more finely or more broadly overall or in particular places?'

A particular aspect is the question of the level of detail. If the draft TSS is too long, then it will not be helpful. If it is too short, it will not be helpful. Only practice enables us to judge how broad or narrow a brush is needed for a particular interview text at a particular stage of the inquiry. The process of doing such a text sequentialization takes a considerable period of time, and is always subject to revision, partly because you can always decide to do a broader analysis or a much finer one, closer to a microanalysis. Some accounts lend themselves well to a broad analysis; others are so intricate that a broad analysis is not very helpful, because different textsorts seem to be embedded in every sentence! For the purposes of practising, and for long initial interviews, try a broadbrush approach (with mixed categories, if necessary, as in the example above) to start with, and be prepared to refine it later if necessary. For training purposes, a target of a 2-page TSS with some 20–25 'structural segments' for the initial interview might be worth bearing in mind; obviously the nature of the actual interview structure might make this impossible.

Tips on Identifying the Structural Segments of a Transcript so as to Produce a TSS of Manageable Length for Self-training Purposes

It may be useful to indicate one possible procedure for producing a TSS for training purposes of approximately a certain number of items – I have suggested 20–25 – on approximately 2–3 pages of A4. Professionally, you would not wish to limit yourself in this way. First, identify the total number of pages used in the initial account (subsession 1). Let us say, subsession 1 occupies some 20 pages. Second, calculate that, if you aim for some 20–25 structural segments, how frequently per page you would *love* to find a structural segment. In this case, 20 pages to generate 20–25 structural segments comes out at a little under one segment change per page *on average*.

Conclusion: you will probably need a pretty broad definition of 'topic' so as not to have too many changes due to topic. You will also need to have a pretty broad definition of 'dominant textsort' to avoid having too many textsort changes.

Obviously any actual text is highly unlikely to oblige you by producing on any one of its 20 pages or even on average throughout the 20 pages the 'just under one page per text segment' that you would prefer to see; nonetheless, such a 'mission impossible' will help you to move forward in your analysis. As, by page 3 of 20, you discover that your tacit notion of topic and your tacit notion of textsort are, unless you change them, set to produce either a ridiculously high number of 'structural segments' (say 60 over 8 pages) or a ridiculously low one (say 6 over 8 pages), you will be in a position to consciously modify your tacit notions of both in order to get closer to the target region of 20–25 over 2–3 pages.

So, with your notion of an approximate number of desired 'structural segments per page of transcript', you set out to do the first 2 pages of 20. Let us look at an example to get the sense of how you work to produce your TSS over a number of revisions.

1   First you identify any change of *speaker* on your first 3 pages of transcript. In the transcript of subsession 1, you will probably find some switches on the first page or so, but not too many. In the example below, there is one change of speaker. In the 'Interview with W' (not a narrative interview), you will remember constant changes of *speaker* throughout the 3-page extract.
2   Second, you identify changes of *topic*. Again, in the example below, with a target of 20–25 structural segments, you will want to be very broadbrush about topic. In the first 3 pages out of 20, one-seventh or so of the whole, you would like to have two topics at most (keeping other changes to the notion of topic-aspects or sub-topics). That would give you a horrid total of 14 structural segmentings due to change of topic. Out of your target 20–25 changes, this would leave only some 10–11 additional changes of segment within topic before you hit your maximum of 25. With this worry in mind, you go through the 3 pages of transcript, identifying the minimum number of 'broad topics' that you can get away with.
3   Finally, identify changes of *textsort* which do not correlate with a change of topic. Over the 20 pages, you have said that you want to identify not more than 10–11 such changes; then in 3 pages – one-seventh of the whole – you don't want to identify more than one-seventh of 10–11: namely, less than two for the 3 pages.

As we shall see, such a desire to find, in the first 3 pages of the 20-page transcript, no more than two changes of topic (with perhaps correlated change of textsort), plus no more than another two changes of textsort within the segmentation of topics, is going to be very difficult to satisfy.

Let us look at an example, from Rupinder B (Figure 12.8). The change from *interviewer* to *interviewee* after line 1 requires no comment.

Topic Changes   How do we reduce the number of very broad topics to two?
1   lines 2–25: Coming to London, family and early work to end of school
2   lines 25–36: Leaving school, improving work
3   lines 37–43: Getting married and the new family.

Topic Changes and Characterizing the Textsorts   Let us look at four different solutions to the problem of getting towards our (arbitrary) target of some 25 structural segments more or less over the 20 pages (we have only a segment here).

Line/ box no's	Notes	Words	Notes
001		*Interviewer: I would like you to tell me your life story, all the events and experiences which were important for you, start wherever you like, we have about half an hour or perhaps a little longer. I won't be saying anything, I'll just take some notes for afterwards.*	interviewer: initial question
002		Interviewee: Hi, I was born in India, fifth of October 1952.	
003		I never saw my father, coz he came when I was about a year old, I don't remember him.	
004		My sister named me before I was born, couple of years before I was born.	
005		So when my father came here, I was about I was told a year old, perhaps a little bit over.	
006		Then the only thing I know about my father was through the letters what I hear and photographs seen of him.	
007		Then I stayed in India till about 10, 11 years, and after 10, 11 years I came to England.	
008		In 1963 to be precise, the day after president Kennedy was shot .... shot didn't know anything about English, came from a village to a town.	
009		It was a very [pause] changing and moving not understanding experience.	
010		Then I saw my father after about 10 years and so keep looking at him for a while trying to work out [pause] what father looks like.	
011		When I came in '63, the times were really hard, so we had to really [long pause] take precautions how to survive in England, coz my mother couldn't speak much, any, English.	
012		I couldn't speak any English, so the only breadwinner was my father and he wasn't turning a lot of money.	
013		So we stayed, we had to lodge, we were staying as lodgers somewhere.	
014		Then after about a year or so, my sister joined us, coz she stayed behind, my father and myself came over to England.	
015		Then she came, a year or 14 months later.	
016		Then we gradually saved little bit to buy a house so we bought a house by borrowing bits and pieces.	

continued

Figure 12.8 continued

017		It was hard times and when I was about 13 I was doing paper work, working in shops.	
018		Um ... when I was 15 then I started working in the bakeries coz they used to take casual workers for day or night whatever came along.	
019		So we keep doing, going to school, didn't catch up much because there wasn't many people in England who speaks much Indian only English.	
020		Parents were uneducated, they couldn't help me much, whatever I learn at school.	
021		If I forget I had to wait till the next day, to go to school to ask the teacher to explain what it meant, so that slows me down a bit.	
022		Where other people had their parents, or elder brothers who could speak English or could [pause] teach them [pause] help them catch up whatever they didn't know.	
023		So I was very good at school, gymnastics games stuff like that, maths, but English was my very weak point.	
024		And there wasn't many people well my mother and father couldn't help me much coz they were completely uneducated.	
025		So when I was about 15, I left school, then I start work, I work anywhere I could lay any type of work I could lay my hands on.	
026		I couldn't work very late because that at the time, people under the age could only work up to 10 o'clock at night.	
027		Most places where they work, where work was they finish 11 so they wouldn't take me on, wouldn't take me on coz I couldn't do the full shift.	
028		Then I [long pause] find a job where I could work early, early shifts only, but they let me work overtime too about 9.30, quarter to 10 o'clock.	
029		That's when you could say gradually the good times started.	
030		Well they were good in the way of coming in money but if you really analyse it they were pretty hard for me coz I had to work most of the time when I should have played about, enjoying myself.	

continued

Figure 12.8   continued

031		So then I worked in Granada, when I started working in Granada Motorway Services, well I started from the bottom bit.	
032		Went up to being an assistant manager, it was pretty good life I would describe it as.	
033		[long pause] I never went back home, my mother went a few times.	
034		Then my brother was born over there. He after 3, 4, 5 years more or less we put in school in India.	
035		A boarding very very expensive school.	
036		And to pay his fee and airfare it was another problem moneywise so I had to work hard, harder.	
037		[very long pause] Then after working for about 5 years, I decided to get married.	
038		I got married in 1973.	
039		Then I had my first child he was born on 19 of June 1974.	
040		Then I had my second child, she was born on 21st of April 1976.	
041		Few years down the line, I had my third child born on 5th of November, no 5th March [laughing] 1980.	
042		From 1973 to 1980 was happy times I would put it down as very happy times.	
043		Didn't have much but whatever I had was satisfying.	

FIGURE 12.8   **Rupinder B's Transcript Segment**

- *Solution A.* Using the model shown in Figure 12.9, we would have new structural segments beginning on lines 1, 2, 9, 25, 28, 31, 37, 42, ... some eight structural segments in the first 3 pages. At this rate, 20 pages would generate 8×7 segments, i.e. 56 instead of the planned 25.
- *Solution B.* Alternatively, we might just identify the three topics, and classify each of the first two as 'REPORT/eval/argumentation'. This drastic solution might have to be adopted. It gives us only three 'structural segments' on the first 3 pages, much closer to our original aim of ending up with under 25 segments from some 20 pages.
- *Solution C.* If we wish to move less drastically towards target, we might redraft our TSS as shown in Figure 12.10. Using this model, we have reduced the

1. **lines 2–25: Coming to London, family and early work to end of school**
   REPORT/Argumentation/evaluation

   2–8: REPORT: India: absent father, coming to England
   9: EVALUATION: 'a very changing and moving not understanding experience'
   10–25: REPORT/argumentation: unknown father, school, casual work, uneducated parents, left school at 15

2. **lines 25–36: Leaving school, improving work**
   REPORT/evaluation/argumentation

   25–28: REPORT: Finding a more regular job
   29–30: EVALUATION: times of good money but very hard work, not enjoying myself
   31–36: REPORT/eval: climbing Granada, cost of brother's boarding school and airfare, harder work

3. **lines 37–43: Getting married and the new family**
   REPORT/evaluation

   37–41: REPORT: decided to marry, birth of children
   42–43: EVALUATION: very happy times, didn't have much but whatever I had was satisfying

FIGURE 12.9   **Rupinder B's TSS – Solution A**

lines		
1:	Initial question by interviewer	
2–8:	**REPORT:**	India: absent father, coming to England
9:	**EVALUATION:**	'a very changing and moving not understanding experience'
10–28:	**REPORT**/argue:	unknown father, school, casual work, uneducated parents, leaving school
29–30:	**EVALUATION:**	good? times for money but harder work
31–41:	**REPORT:**	finding more regular job, climbing Granada, cost of brother's schooling and airfare, harder work, getting married, having three children
42–43:	**EVALUATION:**	happy times, though didn't have much

FIGURE 12.10   **Rupinder B's TSS – Solution C**

number of structural segments to those starting on lines 1, 2, 9, 10, 29, 31, 42, bringing it down to seven structural segments.

- *Solution D.* To bring it down further, we must get quite drastic and make very much rougher approximations. This solution is a three-segment solution (Figure 12.11), similar to that of the main headings of Solution A above.

The above examples may indicate both by what they have in common and by how they differ the complexity and difficulty of developing a TSS for training or for professional purposes. While the identification of biographical data as defined

lines		
2–28:	**REPORT**/argue/eval:	India, emigration of father, self then sister emigration, uneducated parents, casual work at school, leaving school, casual work after school
29–30:	**EVALUATION**:	good times but hard work, then harder
31–43:	**REPORT**/evaluation:	full-time job, assistant manager, supporting brother in India, getting married, three children

FIGURE 12.11   **Rupinder B's TSS – Solution D**

previously can be done fairly easily, the distinctions between one topic and another topic, and the distinctions between one textsort and another, are much less 'obvious'.

Coffey and Atkinson (1997: 32–45) show very clearly how coding of topic content can be at a variety of levels of finebrush and broadbrush detail in respect of a single interview extract, and their demonstration should be consulted.

> With respect to the above example, clearly, in neither column will you find sufficient recognition of some key bits of material, which a finer micro-analysis would bring out.

> For example, the first ten lines would be best analysed in detail to indicate the constant 'eruption of the father' into the narrative text (lines 5, 6, 10) and the 'evaluation' in line 9 which seems to refer primarily to the transition from village India to English town but also may be linked to the seeing of his father after 10 years.

I hope the above discussion and examples give you some sense of the decisions involved in choosing how fine or broad a 'segment structuring' (TSS) by DARNE textsorts you decide to do at different points in the text.

I have not indicated how to do the final element, namely compressing the verbatim text into its topic 'gists' but, once the Speaker, Topic and DARNE textsort changes have been identified, then summarizing the topic gist (as in the example of Janette, see p. 242) is fairly straightforward.

Some Additional Discussion Points About the TSS

Once you have grasped the principles of constructing the TSS on the lines indicated above, you might wish to consider the following points. They are not central to the argument so, if they start to confuse you, stop reading them straight away, and move on to the next section!

Subtypes of the DARNE Typology   Some subtypes have been developed, a few of which are identified in the previous example of the Janette sequentialization. Develop your own, but only once you are clear about the five main types.

- *Evaluations* are always connected to a narration: they may be 'start', 'middle' or 'end' evaluations, depending where they are placed in respect of that narration. In addition, most of them are by implication local to particular narrations in the text, local-evaluations; some may be 'global narrations' covering whole phases of the life or the life as a whole, for example Janette's 'I have never ever met a man who was …'.

In addition, they may be concerned with what might be called 'Rationality Values' (RV evaluations) concerned with logic, truth and rationality, or 'Ultimate Values' (UV evaluations) concerned with the good, the moral, the beautiful, etc. Though not philosophically very tenable – since for a scientist Truth may be an ultimate value – I think the RV/UV distinction may be helpful.

- *Narratives* can be long and extended with many characters and a number of episodes: these can be called 'epic narratives'. A narrative about the 1984–85 miners' strike in a single pit would be likely to be such an 'epic'. Other narratives can be of a single incident or occurrence, and these can be termed '*occurrence/episode* narratives'. Harold's 'first day waiting for the bus to go to the mines' (p. 240) would be an example of this. A *condensed situation* is one in which a small incident is constantly repeated, a type of chronic occurrence.
- *Argumentation*. With this category, it is often important to determine whether this is occurring from the narrator's present perspective or whether what is being re-constructed or re-expressed is the argumentation of an actor 'at the time' about which he or she is talking. You could distinguish, therefore, a 'now-argumentation' from a 'then-argumentation'. Quite often, in the course of a single argumentation, the speaker will slip between the two categories and at certain points it will be a blended and perhaps confused 'then/now argumentation' mixed category.
- *Descriptions*. In relation to narratives, which always have a kernel of action at the centre, they can be thought of as sometimes being subtyped as pre-action descriptions and post-action descriptions.

Finally, for *mixed category categorizations*, you may wish to distinguish predominant from subordinate components of the mixture, by the use of upper and lower case, respectively: 'ARGUE/description' would be different from 'DESCRIPT/argue' in terms of the relative dominance of the components in the 'flavour' of the text structure sequence identified. Similarly, you could have 'THEN/now' argumentation as an unequally mixed category.

Figure 12.12 sums up the five categories and the discussion of some subtypes so far.

If you are practising the method as an apprentice, a working TSS of 2–3 sides of A4 is perhaps what you should normally start with, along with a working BDC also of 2 sides or so. You should aim for some 20–25 chronological items (for the BDC) or 'structural segments' (for the TSS): if you have more than this, you should put them into 'chunks' or 'bundles' so as to keep them down to a number manageable in training.

A short example of a TSS has been given above. A longer example of such a text sequentialization using a slightly different set of textsorts is given in *Sostris Working Paper No 2* (1998): 98–9.

Supra-sorts of the DARNE Typology: A-N-D   The difficulty of DARNEing a transcript into these categories is because some of the categories are more closely related to each other, and/or differently related, than might appear from the difference in their 'tag-names'.

Pre-action[*] Post-action	DESCRIPTION	
Present- perspective A past- perspective	ARGUMENTATION	
	REPORT	
	NARRATIVE	Epic – many sequences Episodic – single sequence Condensed – repetitive sequences
Start Middle End	Rationality-Values EVALUATION Ultimate-Values	Local Regional Global
	MIXED/cases mixed/CASES	

* The 'action' in question is that of the Central Event Sequence, starting with 'One day something happened'.

FIGURE 12.12   **DARNE Subtypes**

- A REPort is a thin NARRative; a NARRative is a rich REPort.
- An ARGument is an expanded EVALuation; an EVALuation is a condensed ARGument.
- A DESCRiption is a de-historicized moment of a possible NARRative.
- A NARRative is a re-historicized combination of DESCRiptive and describable moments.

So, two of these categories can be thought of as being on spectrums of 'expanded/condensed' varieties of each other, and one of them (DESCR) on a spectrum of 'historicized/de-historicized' in respect to narrative (see Figure 12.13).

Clearly, it is important to place textsorts into the A category (could be more or less ARG or EVAL), into the N category (could be more or less NARR or REP), or into the D category (should not be confused with N). The distinction *within* the superordinate categories A, N, and D is less important than the distinction *between* them.

Textsorts in the Theory of Narratives   A final point may be made – which may help further to reduce the apparent arbitrariness of these 'practical judgment categories' that the DARNE textsorts provide.

There is good reason, I recently realized, for thinking that something like these DARNE categories would be needed in *any* narrative analysis of narrations. The reason is that they correspond rather closely to components of the Labov and

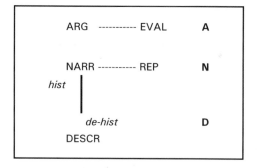

FIGURE 12.13   **DARNE Categories' Internal Relations (A-N-D)**

Abstract 'what it is going to be about'	*report*	ABSTRACT
Orientation 'relevant background'	*description₁*	BACKGROUND
Complicating action 'something disturbing the normal'		
Events and actions	*argumentation* *narrative*	CENTRAL EVENT SEQUENCE
Climax 'turning point, resulting in'		'NARRATION'
Resolution 'returning to [a new?] normality'	*description₂*	
Evaluation:	*evaluation*	EVALUATION
Coda 'that was it'		

FIGURE 12.14   **Labov and Waletsky on Narrative and DARNE**

Waletsky conceptual framework of what is liable to be found in *any*, they say, (Western) narrative.

In Figure 12.14, I have taken the Labov and Waletsky model cited earlier (p. 116) and inserted, in italics, what I think are corresponding 'places' where DARNE textsorts are likely to be found. I have distinguished between *description₁* and *description*$_2$ in the figure, since the implied or explicit situation after the action may be the earlier normality restored or it may be a new one.

The above attempt to relate Labov and Waletsky's 'components of all narratives' and the Fisher-Rosenthal and Rosenthal 'textsorts to be found in all narratives' may help you relate the two together.

> There is a problem with 'argumentation', however. This can be seen as a type of discourse which, although the narrator may not engage in very much during a classic narrative, the 'agents' in the narrative very often do – wondering which way to go in the enchanted forest, arguing who should carry off the grail or the king's daughter, whether to accept the gift from the stranger, etc.

> Also, of course, 'argumentation' can be seen as a mode of (polemical) evaluation. And the 'end-evaluation', the 'moral of the story', is a 'compressed argumentation'.

> There is an implicit evaluation-argumentation dilemma in any 'narrative action'. Similarly, anybody advancing an argumentation might (be coaxed to) find a real or imagined narrative to 'prove' or illustrate the point. Finally, every description may imply a narration of what happened before, or after, or in, the described scene.

> Narrative typically implies choices between courses of action at key 'moments of choice'. There is either an internal debate (argumentation) within each character; or an overt argument between two characters; or a suggestion by the narrator of how the character might have decided otherwise. Argumentation is therefore intrinsic to any narration of agents and action.

If Labov and Waletsky have correctly identified the components of any narrative, then there will be something like DARNE textsorts in any attempt to describe the types of text (speech-act sorts) to be found in any narrative. And the relation between the textsorts may well be fluid and complex.

DOING THE BDA AND THE TFA: CENTRAL PRINCIPLES OF DATUM-BY-DATUM ANALYSIS

As we have just seen, the raw data of the interview verbatim transcript and other materials are worked up into *a life-sequentialization* (chronology) of the evolution of objective life-events (Biographical Data Chronology) and a *text-sequentialization* of the evolution of the speech-act events, the text-events, the changing segmental structure of the interview (Text Structure Sequentialization).[9]

These new intermediate documents are then, in the next stages of analysis, 'interpreted' by interpretive panels of co-researchers (see below) quite separately but according to a single principle derived from the Glaser and Strauss (1968) school of Grounded Theorizing (GT). There are two principles:

1 datum-by-datum analysis by which predictive hypotheses are multiplied before being refuted or supported by a later datum or by later data
2 the multiplication of counter-hypotheses and tangential hypotheses in relation to the first hypotheses you think of.

---

9 Together with the emergent free-associative notes, theoretical memos, third-column transcriptions of attributions of inner states based on paralinguistics and non-verbal modes of communication (NVC).

Datum-by-Datum Predictive Analysis and Retrospective Checking

The strategy is that developed by Glaser and Strauss (1968) which they refer to as grounded theory, but which can perhaps be better described as *emergent theorizing*. A process of emergent theorizing is intended to produce by the end an emerged product called grounded theory. We will describe below how this process of emergent theorizing happens: it happens by predicting data that ought to follow and then checking back from such future data to earlier predictions.

The *process* by which the biographical life-data and the text-sequentialization are analysed in the second stage have common features described by Breckner (1998: 93) as follows:

> 'In the procedure based on abduction – which is best exemplified in the detective work of Sherlock Holmes – the starting point is an empirical phenomenon [in our case an event or a segment of text] which is to be explained by a general rule formulated as an hypothesis. *The core of the abductive program is to construct alternative hypotheses to explain a given empirical datum. The analyst is invited to think about all possible hypotheses, each of which could be regarded as sufficient to explain the empirical phenomenon*. By this, we follow not just one path – running the risk of neglecting or even overlooking relevant data – but remain open to alternative hypotheses with increasing complexity.
>
> The empirical datum to be explained is seen as part of an empirical process constituted by a *sequence* of data which has to be explained. From each of the alternative explanatory hypotheses of the datum D, *a prediction is made about what later data are likely to follow if the general rule embodied in that hypothesis about datum D were true*. Every explanatory hypothesis about datum D is then tested by looking at the data that follows subsequently as evidence for and against the [explanatory] hypothesis about datum D.' (Breckner, 1998: 93, modified, italics added)

As each new datum in the series is examined, *the next event in the biographical data chronology* or the *next topic or text-sort change in the sequentialization*, then there is a search back to see which previous hypotheses can be seen as weakened or *falsified* by this new datum. This having been done, there is then a search back to see which surviving hypotheses have been strengthened or *confirmed* by this new datum.

This having been done, then further new hypotheses are developed around the significance of the new datum, together with predictions about what will occur later in the series were the hypothesis in question to turn out to be correct.[10]

The question of formalizing the development of such 'later occurrences' might be represented by a diagram. The task of multiplying hypothetical possibilities for the individual biographical or text datum is precisely that of inventing any and all possibilities that the social and cultural knowledge of the panel can come up with. They are creatively proliferated; not systematically organized. They might look as

---

10 In *Sostris Working Paper 2*, there are longer examples of such hypothesis generation and hypothesis falsification/validation in respect of the biographical data of Tony (on pp. 94–6), and in respect of the analysis of the sequentialization as the expression of a thematic field on pp. 99–102.

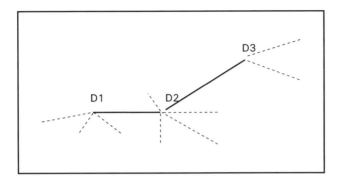

FIGURE 12.15   **Later-occurrences Diagram at Point D3**

shown in Figure 12.15. At each datum-point, a number of (dotted line) hypotheses are developed. The subsequent datum (only to be revealed to the panel after all the hypotheses for the previous datum have been speculatively multiplied) either suggests that one of these was correct or that a new one needs to be retrospectively constructed, and that the hypotheses which remain unsupported or even refuted by later occurrences *remain*, but only as *unrealized possibilities* of life-events or text-events in the particular case being studied. Realized (confirmed) hypotheses are represented by a solid line; unrealized (unconfirmed or refuted) ones remain as dotted lines.[11]

The point is parallel to that made by semiology that the meaning of any particular choice of sign depends on all the other signs that could have been selected at that point, but were not. The fuller the sense of the foregone possible alternatives, the more precise a meaning can be given to the alternative that actually occurred. This is particularly true when I am dealing with actions done or not done by the agent in situations where certain other courses of action were not ruled out of possibility by external determinations. We are looking at the track record of a response-making and often decision-making, life-living and, at the moment, lifestory-telling 'agent'.

It will be easier to grasp this rather abstract point – about refuting/confirming hypotheses after the second and each subsequent datum-point and then multiplying new ones for the next – after looking at a concrete example. This will be done below.

A final point needs to be made. In many respects, the grounded theory method of Glaser and Strauss is followed in terms of hypothesis generation and falsification. It is also followed as we shall see in the attempt to move from early close-to-data coding to later higher-order, more abstract 'coding'[12] which attempts to integrate, and find the organizing principle of, the earlier multiplicity of codes – though the term 'codes' is not used. There are two key differences.

---

11 This model is clearly a simplification. In actual practice, towards the start of the process a large number of hypotheses are generated and relatively few are refuted; towards the end of the process, there are a large number of refutations and confirmations and a smaller number of new hypotheses.

12 Strauss and Corbin (1990) distinguish between first 'open' and later 'axial' coding.

- The first is that Glaser and Strauss are concerned primarily to establish typical action of typical actors: theirs is usually a generalizing focus right from the start, not – as in this sort of biographical work – an individualizing one.
- The second difference is that the phenomenological tradition attempts to generate hypotheses through asking you to imagine the experience of a particular actor at a particular moment, to emotionally and cognitively (and temporarily) identify with whom you take the experiencing, living actor to be, and then 'generate hypotheses' on the basis of that attempt at 'imagined experiencing'. As many of your earlier 'possible hypotheses' get corrected by subsequent data, your always mostly implicit model of the 'experiencing actor' and their experience-provoking world can be assumed to be *likely* to become increasingly close to target (i.e. explain all the data satisfactorily). Rather than 'grounded theorizing with the constant comparative method' *to identify generalities right from the start*, the phenomenological insistence on attempting to 'enter the world of the agent' in their unique life-history and life-story produces a qualitatively different experiencing of analysing and a different sort of result.

Panel Work, Predictive Hypothesizing and Counter-hypothesizing

You need to find somebody else to work with on the analysis of each of these documents. The principle is that there should be a panel of at least two for this task: if you can find five or six people, so much the better! The more different from each other they are, the more 'objective' your results are likely to be. This is because such work is best done by a collective of people unlike yourself and both like and unlike your informant. If you only work on the basis of the mental models (Senge, 1990: 174–204) derived from and generated in your own personal history and your own 'case-limitations', your one-person-panel sociological imagination will be weak and partial.

If you are obliged to work on your own, then you need to pay particular attention to the task of furiously multiplying 'counter-hypotheses' which feel deeply counter-intuitive to that spontaneously developed by your intuition limited and constrained as it necessarily is by your personal gender, class, generation, epoch, locality, age, circumstances and milieux. The more the diversity of those involved, the better and more interesting the work of analysis becomes.

If you cannot ensure a panel to do all the work with you, then at least find one other person to start the work described below. A half-day panel to start the work of biographical data analysis and another half-day panel (and they do not need to be the same people) to start the work of thematic field analysis may be enough to enable you to work productively on your own.

The principle of counter-hypothesizing is crucial to all work but particularly to moments when you are obliged to work on your own. In order to expand and use your sociological imagination, you will need to move beyond the hypotheses which your intuition and common-sense will normally provide and restrict you to. For every hypothesis you find yourself spontaneously putting forward, develop a counter-hypothesis which asserts precisely or roughly the opposite of what you have just hypothesized. When you have done this, then develop a tangential hypothesis, one which is at a complete tangent to the two hypotheses you have just developed.

```
Datum X
            original hypothesis      1
            counter hypothesis       2
            tangential hypothesis    3
```

FIGURE 12.16   **Counter/Tangential Hypothesizing – Simple Model**

For each datum therefore, a mechanical rule would be that you should attempt to develop a minimum of three hypotheses: an original one, spontaneously produced; a counter-hypothesis to the first, declaring the opposite; and a tangential hypothesis which is concerned with some completely different dimension than that in which the first two hypotheses operate. There is, of course, no maximum, and particularly at the start you should aim at proliferation, as you will see.

Biographical Data Analysis of the BD Chronology

Let us now apply this general model of hypothesis multiplication and refutation to the case of the flow of biographical data in the life-sequentialization, the chronology. I am now thinking about the *lived life*, the flow of 'objective' events and actions. For this purpose I *ignore* and put to one side any knowledge of the *told story*.[13]

Analysing the Biographical Data by Multiplying
and then Retrospectively Verifying BD Hypotheses
Breckner argues as follows (1998: 93, I have changed the typography)

'The results of this first step of analysis are

- hypotheses about *patterns of orientation*, patterns which show up in interrelated sequences of action, independently of the interviewee's interpretation of them
- hypotheses about *turning-points* and about *possible meanings of single events*, again independently of the interviewee's interpretation of them.

continued

---

13 It could be argued that, ideally, to ensure non-contamination, the work would be done by separate panels (one on the lived-life analysis, one on the told-story analysis) in neither of which was the interviewer or researcher present, and the two separate panels (producing the BDA and the TSS separately) would not meet or exchange results. This counsel of perfection is unlikely to happen in most real-life cases, but try to keep *other* members of your panel in genuine, not fake, ignorance, if you wish to maximize their usefulness. As for yourself, cultivate in the early sessions of analysis a deliberate non-recall. The psychoanalyst Bion spoke of starting each psychoanalytic session by discarding 'both what you know and what you want, to leave space for a new idea' (Bion, 1980: 11, cited Casement, 1985: 222). Once you have got into the panel-process, as we describe later, you will find this not difficult to achieve as the spirit of playful exploration develops.

(A) The analysis of biographical data aims to reconstruct the societal, generational, age-, family-, and milieu-related *contexts* that an individual has lived through.

(B) Furthermore, I get an insight into the *possibilities* that were inherent in the social contexts and *those chosen, ignored, or rejected by the actor.*' (Breckner, 1998: 93)

Breckner then outlines the questions that the panel need to ask themselves about each datum in turn:

It is important that the analytical panel is presented with one block of data (one datum) at a time, and that information about future data is not provided. This ensures the free multiplication of hypotheses about possible future data.

Going through all the biographical data in their chronological order for each datum, I should attempt to *generate as many hypotheses and counter-hypotheses as possible* that answer the following questions:

1 How could *this* event be experienced, in relation to the context of age, personal development, family, generation, and milieu?
2 How could the *sequence of events so far shape* the future lived life?
3 For each suggested hypothesis under (1) or (2), *what event or phenomenon would I expect to come next or to follow* either in the sequence of biographical data or in later life-phases [following-hypotheses]?

Given the data that does come next or later in the chronology, *which previous hypotheses should I consider falsified or perhaps only discouraged*, and which are those rendered *more plausible or even confirmed? Which new hypotheses* are suggested?

• Following hypotheses – following pretty immediately or at some point
• Structural hypotheses for the whole life OR for this phase of the whole life
(Breckner, 1998: 93, modified)

Note that any and every hypothesis about the 'meaning of the experience' must be developed into a 'following hypothesis' about what might happen 'later in the life' were the hypothesis about meaning to be true. In a way that Karl Popper would approve, the speculative hypothesis about meaning is 'put at risk' by being operationalized into a prediction (operationalized into a hypothesis about what would follow in the life) about subsequent events. If the events don't happen, then the original hypothesis about meaning must be reconsidered, and may be considered to be weakened by the failure of one or more of its predictive 'following hypotheses'.

Segments of Harold's BDA
Let us now apply this procedure to a block of data, a datum, in the case of Harold. In an actual session, each biographical datum would be prepared by the presenter in a very large typeface that could be seen by all the panel on a separate sheet of paper. Let us imagine that the following 'datum block' is presented (datum 1):

1944   Mother married first husband, Faulkner. They have three children (Jane b.1944, John b.1948, Fred b.1954) and then the husband dies around 1956. She remarries, Richard Halford, in 1957. A fourth child is born (Michael, b.1958).

1960   HAROLD Halford born.

The questions are – how could the event be experienced by those involved? How could it contribute to the 'shaping' of the life? What events and actions might be expected to follow next or later in the life if those experiential and/or shaping hypotheses were correct? Figure 12.17 shows one set of hypotheses and following-hypotheses.

> Both experiential and shaping questions are asked about each BDC datum, and any hypothesis in answer to those questions which is generated must then have a 'following hypothesis' (FH) (and counter-hypothesis, and tangential hypothesis) predicated for it.

> Similarly, no predictive following hypothesis must be entered without an attempt to identify the *hypothesized experiencing and subsequent shaping* that gives meaning to it.

Note the way in which original hypotheses are typically followed by an invention of a counter-hypothesis, and sometimes both are followed by a tangential hypothesis (see p. 259 above).

After these and other hypotheses are presented – notice that many take the form of hypothesis and then the thinking-up of a counter-hypothesis – and written-up by a 'scribe'[14] then the next datum is presented, datum 2:

1963   *Derek Halford born*

What then? The *first task* of the panel is to see whether the new datum tends to confirm or tends to deny any of the *previous hypotheses*, particularly the 'FHs', the 'following occurrence' hypotheses.

- Some doubt is thrown on H5 since another child *has* been born, though of course it may be unwanted.
- FH1.2 that predicted parental separation as a result of Harold's birth is disconfirmed (so far).

None of the others is strengthened or weakened by the new datum, the panel concludes.

---

14 For such analysis sessions, you need a supply of continuous paper (butcher's paper is best, flipchart paper will do) and a number of differently coloured felt tip pens and large blank surfaces (walls?) on which sheets can be fixed in some way or other (Blu-tack or similar?). The scribe has to put up all the different hypotheses and following hypotheses in very summary form in a way that any member of the panel can instantly look at the sequence of sheets to see which previous hypotheses have been put forward, which have been rather weakened or falsified by subsequent data, and which have been supported or even confirmed by subsequent data. See Figure 12.21.

How could the event be experienced – in relation to the context of age, personal development, family, generation, and milieu?	How could the sequence of events so far shape the lived life? – Orientations – Turning-points – Meanings	What would I expect to occur next or later in the sequence of the lived life? Predictions of later (following) 'biographical data' – not necessarily immediately following
Experiential hypotheses	**Shaping hypotheses**	**Following hypotheses**
H1. Unwanted child by at least one parent	H2. Rejection by at least one parent	FH1.1. Harold is the scapegoat of at least one parent and perhaps his older sibs or half-sibs FH1.2. Parents separate as a result of too many children
H3. Child wanted by both parents – but mother wanted another girl, since Jane is already 16 and will soon leave home	H4. Mother disappointed by Harold being a boy, but treats him 'as if' he were a girl	FH4.1. Harold will develop a 'girlish' disposition FH4.2. Harold will develop a very anti-girlish disposition
H4. Two-year-older brother Michael is jealous of new baby		FH4.1. Harold will be persecuted by Michael FH4.2. Parents wil rescue Harold and persecute Michael
H5. 'Favoured last child'		FH5.1. No more (wanted) children FH5.2. Special status leading to great self confidence FH5.3. Special status leading to refusal to grow up
H6. 'Just another child'		FH6.1. Fights for attention from older siblings and parents FH6.2. Is protected by 16-year-old sister Jane against other siblings

FIGURE 12.17   **Harold – BDA Datum 1 Hypotheses**

The second task of the new panel is to ask the same questions about *the new datum*: how might it be experienced, how might it shape the rest of the life-story, what might be expected to follow in the life-sequence? This will in turn generate a batch of new hypotheses. It might produce a butcher's paper analysis like that shown in Figure 12.18.

After further hypotheses have been multiplied on the basis of the second datum, then the third datum is presented:

How could the event be experienced – in relation to the context of age, personal development, family, generation, and milieu?	How could the sequence of events so far shape the lived life? – Orientations – Turning-points – Meanings	What would I expect to occur next or later in the sequence of the lived life?
Experiential hypotheses	**Shaping hypotheses**	**Following hypotheses**
H7. Three-year-old Harold is pleased by the birth of a child who is younger than him		FH7.1. He will look after the younger brother FH7.2. He will bully his younger brother FH7.3. Eventually he forms an alliance with his younger brother against all his older sibs and half-sibs
H8. Harold ignores his younger brother as 'too little' and continues to focus on older family members		FH8.1. A cool relation will develop between Harold and younger brother FH8.2. Harold will build an alliance with one or two older siblings and 'act above his age'
H9. Father feels financially overloaded and emotionally set aside by yet a further child		FH9.1. Father will leave home FH9.2. Father will look for and find a better job
H10. Mother feels emotionally over-burdened by yet another child		FH10.1. Mother will leave home FH10.2. Mother will find a relative or neighbour to act as a surrogate parent for one or more of her children

FIGURE 12.18   **Harold – BDA Datum 2 Hypotheses**

1970   Family moves house, Harold goes to new junior school, then goes to new secondary modern school

```
Datum X

  Experiential/shaping hypothesis 1
    following hypothesis FH1.A
    counter-hypothesis FH1.B
    other at-a-tangent FH1.C

  Counterhypothesized experiential/shaping hypothesis 2
    following hypothesis FH2.A
    counter-hypothesis FH2.B
    other at-a-tangent FH2.C

  At-a-tangent experiential/shaping hypothesis 3
    following hypothesis FH3.A
    counter-hypothesis FH3.B
    other at-a-tangent FH3.C
```

FIGURE 12.19   **Counter- and Tangential Hypothesizing – Refined Normative Model**

As with datum 2, the effect of datum 3 on the confirming or disconfirming of previous hypotheses is checked, and then further hypotheses are multiplied with appropriate hypotheses about 'what would follow in the life if …'.

> You may wish, at this point, to practise (preferably with a friend or two to help make up a panel) the procedure of BDA by continuing the above datum-by-datum prediction exercise with datum 3 and subsequent data and data blocks (how you block or disaggregate them is up to you) on Harold's Biographical Data Chronology (p. 238), at each stage attempting to see which previous hypotheses are weakened and which strengthened by the new datum, before developing new hypotheses to be written up on the butcher's paper prior to the presentation of the further datum.

It is particularly important to always consider counter-hypotheses, and brainstorm to produce a reasonable number of these. The following normative model might be considered, particularly if you are not able to find anybody to join with you, and bring their different assumptions and mental models to complement your own.

This second model (Figure 12.19) involves counter-hypothesizing and tangential hypothesizing both at the first level of experiential/shaping hypotheses, and, for each of those hypotheses, a similar structure for each 'following/later occurrence' hypothesis. Again, I would stress that this provides a normative model of the minimum you would normally expect: you would hope that for most data you would be able to generate far more.

The procedure continues until all the biographical data have been analysed in this way.

Some Notes on Recording the Progression of the BDA

Hypotheses may be confirmed, or merely supported; falsified, or merely rendered less likely, by subsequent datum-points. This could be represented on the record sheets by a double-tick, a single tick, a single 'x' or a double 'x'. In addition, it is important to give a clear notation on the sheets which record the progress of the discussion what subsequent data were used to confirm or deny, weaken or strengthen support for, which 'following hypothesis' and which 'hypothesis';

(I) 1994 Mother married first husband, Faulkner. They have three
children (Jane b. 1944, John b. 1948, Fred b. 1954) and then
the husband dies around 1956. She remarries, Richard Halford,
in 1957. A fourth child is born (Michael, b. 1958)
1960 HAROLD Halford born

H1. NOT WANTED	FH1.1. Badly treated by all
	FH1.2. Parents separate (2 falsifies)
	FH1.3. Sterilization (2 falsifies)
H2. GIRL WANTED	FH2.1. 'as if girl' $\longrightarrow$ 'girlishness'
	cFH2.2. 'as if girl' $\longrightarrow$ 'macho-ness'
H3. MICHAEL JEALOUS	FH3.1. M will attack H
H4. INTENDED 'LAST CHILD'	FH4.1. Sterilization (2 falsifies)
	FH4.2. Self-confidence
	cFH4.3. 'Baby of family'
	etc.

FIGURE 12.20   **Fragment of Working Record of BDA Session**

hence in Figure 12.21 the occasional note against a hypothesis that it was 'falsified by datum X' or indeed 'confirmed by datum Y'.

A record might be as shown in Figure 12.20. Normally it would be helpful to have three colours: one for hypotheses (experiential or shaping); another for 'following hypotheses'; a third, to identify the number of the later datum that affected the 'confirmation/falsification status' of any particular such hypotheses.

A post-session record of the process might be written up as shown in Figure 12.21 – based on a development by Margaret Volante, Surrey University. Data numbers are given in roman numerals. Data are given in bold face:

- 'H' numbers refer to experiential or shaping hypotheses.
- 'FH' numbers refer to corresponding 'hypotheses about what would follow in the life-event sequence of the BDC if' the H in question were correct.
- '*counterhypothesis* →' means that the next H, or the next FH, was developed by imagining a complete or partial counter-hypothesis to that formulated previously. Always seriously entertain a counter-hypothesis to any particular H; and, with respect to any given H, a counter-hypothesis to the FH you first formulate about the H.

Notice that the falsification of an FH does not always entail the falsification of an H; however, it will typically lead to its weakening, unless alternative FHs are developed for it.

Note that, by this point in the analysis, on the basis of refutations and confirmations so far, the panel has managed to put forward a 'structural hypothesis'. It may itself be confirmed or refuted or enriched by subsequent data. The goal of the process of refuting and confirming particular predictive datum-hypotheses is to

(1)   **1944   Mother married first husband, Faulkner. They have three children (Jane b. 1944, John b. 1948, Fred b. 1954) and then the husband dies around 1956. She remarries, Richard Halford, in 1957. A fourth child is born (Michael, b. 1958)**

           1960   HAROLD Halford born

H1.

Born into a working-class family where no more children were wanted, the birth of this fifth baby is experienced by the mother, her second husband, and the other children as a misfortune

FH1.1. Harold will be treated badly by all or most of his family

FH1.2. Parents will separate straight away as a result of having too many children

later falsified by datum 2

FH1.3. One or other parents will get sterilized to avoid any further children

later falsified by datum 2

Contextual Note: Studies show (?) that, in mining communities in this area at this time, families of five or more were not unusual, and that sterilization was uncommon. If FH1.3 were confirmed by a later occurrence, this would be a more significant than it would be now or in less traditional milieux.*

counterhypothesis →
H2.

Child is wanted by both parents, but mother is disappointed that new baby is not a girl, since Jane is now 16 and leaving home

FH2.1. Harold will be treated 'as if' he were a girl, and will develop a very 'girlish' disposition

counterhypothesis →

FH2.2. Harold will be treated 'as if' he were a girl, and will develop a very 'anti-girlish' disposition

H3.

Two-year-old elder brother Michael is jealous of the new baby

FH3.1. Harold will be persecuted by Michael

H4.

Harold is the intended 'last child'

FH4.1. One or other parents will get sterilized to avoid any further children

later falsified by datum 2

FH4.2. As a result of this special status, Harold will develop great self-confidence

counterhypothesis →

FH4.3. As a result of this special status, Harold will refuse to 'grow up' in order to remain 'the baby of the family'

H5.

Harold is just another child and is neither specially favoured nor disfavoured by his parents

FH5.1. Harold will learn he has to fight as the smallest in a large family to get attention from his parents and his siblings

FH5.2. Harold will be protected by his sister Jane from the younger siblings and will learn to seek out and manufacture 'female protection' for himself

continued

Figure 12.21   continued

| (2) | **1962   Derek Halford born** |

H1 is weakened because FH1.2 and FH1.3 appear to have been falsified
H4 is weakened because FH4.1 is falsified
No previous hypotheses are definitively confirmed or falsified

H6.   Three-year-old Harold is pleased by the birth of this younger brother
FH6.1. Harold will look after his younger brother and develop a strong
            attachment to him
FH6.2. Harold will form an alliance with his younger brother against
            his older siblings

(3)   **1970–72   The family moves house to a new village. Harold**
goes to a new junior school and then to a new secondary
modern school
No previous hypotheses are confirmed or falsified by this datum

H7.   Harold is upset by this rapid succession of changes

Structural Hypothesis 1: Harold's life orientation is
changed by this cumulation of sudden changes of
place and of school[†]. He gets discouraged

---

* Please note the use of such 'contextual notes' that may be supplied by the local or global knowledge of any of the members of the panel, or on the basis of library research. The '?' indicates that the author of the contextual note was, at the time of writing it, uncertain of his or her facts and made a note to do library work to check the note out.
† In practice, you would probably not advance a 'structural hypothesis' about an orientation or a turningpoint so early in the analysis. You might wait for more data. I have put this in, however, to indicate how you would make a record of such a hypothesis about a structuring principle for the life as a whole or for a phase of the life.

FIGURE 12.21   **Post-session Record of a BDA**

move to a higher level of abstraction in which structural-hypotheses can be put forward, which may eventually allow us to move to a *structural understanding of the whole of the lived life*.

The above recording format makes it easy to view the results and the history of the work of the team doing the analysing.

After you have completed analysing the biographical data, a large number of datum-specific and also structural hypotheses will remain neither supported nor weakened by the evidence, a fair number will be refuted or rendered rather suspect and a fair number will be strengthened or supported. Those who feel worried about advancing 'wild hypotheses' (such as too psychologistic or determinist ones) should feel reassured by a procedural decision to the effect that hypotheses not supported by at least three biographical data by the end of the BDA should be considered as unproven. The free and wild brainstorming and multiplication of hypotheses after each new datum is presented is balanced by the careful and systematic elimination of hypotheses unsupported or refuted by the evidence after each new biographical datum is presented.

To sum up. I have indicated, necessarily briefly, both how a biographical data *chronology* is presented, and how it is used – in chunks – in the process of doing a 'future-blind' biographical data *analysis*. I also provided a 'later occurrence'

Harold was the fifth child of his mother, whose first three children were from a previous marriage where the father had died. His own father was a miner who had gone into the pit at 14.

Shortly after the family moved to a new village, and Harold changed schools, his mother died when Harold was 11. Harold left school without a qualification and went into the mining industry at 15.

After joining the mines, Harold's life was disrupted when his father remarried. Harold and his two biological brothers moved into the house of an older unmarried work colleague (Len) where Harold lived until he met, seven years later, the woman who was to become his partner.

Occupationally, Harold's lived life was that of a stable pattern of a male miner until this was disrupted by the eventually successful running-down of the coal industry during which the National Union of Miners was defeated by the government of the day, committed to the weakening of the trade union movement at all costs. After training, he worked briefly at the coal face until an industrial accident forced him to take a surface job as a crane-operator. He engaged in a life of pubs and clubs around rugby with his peers until at the age of 23 he was involved in the miners' strike of 1984–85.

While training in 1976 to be a face-worker, he had met and been taken up by Len, an older union militant – an older militant himself influenced by his uncle, a militant and victim of the miners' strike of 1926. Len took Harold and his brothers into his house, and socialized Harold into the left of the labour movement. Harold became involved in the 1984–85 strike as a left-wing radical activist.

After the defeat of the strike, he stayed on in the mining industry until the pit to which he he had moved after the strike was itself soon to close. He obtained a job as a mobile crane-operator in the private sector and took redundancy from the mining industry at the age of 29.

After a year of being an 'industrial gypsy' at the beck and call of his three successive employers in that year, he had an accident while playing rugby, had sickness benefit for the statutory six weeks, and was then made redundant.

Within two weeks, he had taken a job working with people with learning disabilities, and this was to prove the start of a new career in which Harold was proactive in getting or resuming the education that had stopped when he left school at 15 and only started again at the age of 30 with what has so far proved to be a career in the caring / social work sphere.

Between 1991, when he was 30, and 1997 when at the age of 36, after taking GCSEs and a BTEC with distinction, and later courses, he became a fully fledged Community Care Officer, he took the courses he needed to climb the ladder of professional qualification. He is currently thinking of going to University.

FIGURE 12.22 **Harold – BDC Narrative Summary**

diagram to show, slightly more abstractly, the logic of the process of analysis which operates by your multiplying and then verifying or falsifying hypotheses about the experience of events and their possibility of shaping the future life in one way or another.[15]

---

15 A fuller example of a biographical data analysis is given by Breckner in *Sostris Working Paper no. 2*: 94–6.

Having concluded the BDA, you should summarize the themes or issues that you see as having arisen in the lived life of the subject as analysed through the Biographic Data Analysis process. Bear in mind when you produce your own that this is an intermediate document that can be used by the researcher later in a variety of ways. It obviously goes beyond the chronology on which it is based, but should attempt not to go too far. It was written after all the BDC 'objective event data' had been subject to the datum-by-datum analysis procedure of producing a BDA. As we shall see, producing such a narrative summary of the lived life does not exhaust the use of the BDA.

Example of a Narrative Summary of the Lived Life

Producing a summary of the lived life, as shown in Figure 12.22, is an *expansion* of the BDC, useful for later analysis to refer to and useful for presentation purposes to other researchers and to an eventual audience, such as you.

Turning-points and Phases of the Lived Life

It is now useful to attempt to provisionally produce one or more models of the turning-points and the phases of the lived life. Make the assumption (which is of course subject to later revision) that there are between two and seven phases in the life you have just examined, and that each phase is terminated by a turning-point that introduces the next phase. Produce one or more phase models of the lived life, and record what you consider to be the strengths and the weaknesses of each model that you retain for later consideration.

The best way to start constructing such a phase model for your informant is to *assume* that the lived life falls into at least two phases, and to then ask yourself how these two phases can best be described in terms of the *turning-point* between them. You can fix any number – usually seven plus or minus two is a good target – and then see how fruitful is the model that you have found. If it is true that it is hard to grasp more than seven items in your head, then perhaps five plus or minus two is a better target. Alternatively, ask yourself which are the *turning-points*, and then, for each one, identify the previous and subsequent phase!

After this was done by the Sostris panel, Figure 12.23 summarized our understanding and our phantasies about the phases of that lived-life.

Bear in mind that your phase model – such as the above – represents only a little of all the work you did in the course of the *analysis* of the BDC, namely the biographical data analysis, the BDA.

The panel's activity of multiplying and refuting hypotheses about later-in-the-life occurrences is partially valorized in the *next stage* of the analysis, the panel's attempt to multiply *the ways in which the individual might conceivably tell the life* that the panel have just been considering at some length. As Breckner says, this generation of 'logically possible told stories'

> '... helps us open a horizon of possible and alternative "stories" matching the biographical data, in order not to stick to the view that [we will find] presented by [the informant] in the interview'.

Different 'Possible (Harold)-told Stories'   Having explored the actual and the possible life events of the individual whose lived-life you are examining, you now need to prepare yourself for the next stage, that of examining the actual 'told story'.

Biographical Data Analysis

Eight phases:

- Until 9   Security in large family.
- 9–11   Change of school, of village, school again and then loss of mother.
- 11–16   Housework at home for depressed out-of-work father, bullying at school for status. Left school with no qualifications.
- 16–24   Left-wing union militant in NUM and in his colliery. Secure work-community with activist mentor. Rugby and pubs and NUM travel. Starts relation with future wife.
- 24–25   Showdown between NUM and Tory government; scabs divide the NUM nationally and locally. Miners defeated.
- 25–29   After defeat of miners, moves to non-scab other pit, continues militancy till it is shortly to close.
- 30   'Industrial gypsy' as mobile crane operator in private sector. Starts to do 'O levels', has rugby accident, is ill and then made redundant. Short crisis.
- 31–37   Career shift. Voluntary work with kids with learning disabilities, and then move into Social Work and climbing qualifications and status ladder. Thinking of going to university.

Cycle of disrupted security: first the family crisis then re-security in the mines; then divided mining community and re-security in the second pit; then insecurity in private sector and re-securization in social work career.

FIGURE 12.23   **A Model of the Phases of Harold's Lived Life**

Multiplying *possible ways the subject you have analysed might tell their life story* adopts the datum-by-datum prediction procedure you have already been engaging in, but applies it to 'predicting the whole of told story [TSS]' as the next mega-datum on the basis of the whole of the earlier mega-datum: the now completed lived-life analysis (BDA).

Spend 30–60 minutes (in your panel of two or more) multiplying different ways that the story of the BDC turned into a lived-life story (such as in the BDC Narrative summary or Figure 12.23) *might* turn out to get told by the person who lived that life. What are the very different ways in which somebody who had lived their life like that might tell the story of that life?

Use counter-hypothesizing and tangential hypothesizing as much as possible to get the largest possible range. Find a way of noting these different possible told-stories on a wall-chart, so that none is lost. Have a competition to get as many as possible!

Try to summarize your 'possible told-stories' in one-liners. For example, a story of survival; a Bildungsroman; a story of heroism; a story of handled pain. You might imagine that the one-liners should also predict what sort of textsorts might be deployed in Harold-told stories if the one-liner were correct:

- so a *story of handled pain* might involve little single-incident narratives and much more distanced reports
- a story of *heroic struggles* would involve many single incident narratives

- a *Bildungsroman*, as it is called in German, a story of moral, intellectual and emotional maturation, might involve much argumentation and contrasting of naive-evaluations then and mature-evaluations now.

Let us consider the case of Harold. How might the Harold of the lived-life (Figure 12.23) *tell* his story? Figure 12.24 gives three hypotheses, each with one counter-hypothesis. Note that a draft hypothesis about textsorts is associated with each of these alternatives. For each of these hypotheses of how the story might be told, you could usefully write down what textsort structures (DARNE-styles) you would expect to find or not find in the story as told.

An intermediate document like the 'Possible told-stories' version of Harold should always be produced, *after* completing the narrative version of the BDC and *before* looking at the story actually told. It may well be that none of these specu-lative hypotheses about the possible told-story are born out. Even if our under-standing of the case has therefore to be powerfully corrected in the light of the data of the TSS, the told story, the exercise has multiplied our sense of possibilities and sharpened our expectations. We can therefore revise our diagram a little further, as shown in Figure 12.25.

The previous discussion and examples summarize where you might expect to be after completing a biographical data analysis, after recording it, and after preparing hypotheses about possible 'told-life' stories. Another example, about Tony K, is given by Breckner (1998).

The analysis then moves from the 'possible told stories' to an analysis of the 'actual told story' starting with the TSS low down in the right-hand column of Figure 12.25. It is to this actual told story (or rather its TSS) that we now turn.

Thematic Field Analysis of the Text Structure Sequentialization

I now move from life-history analysis, and speculative hypotheses about possible ways the story of the lived life *might* be told, to text-analysis of the way the story *was* actually told.

Analysing the TSS by Multiplying and then Retrospectively Verifying Thematic Field Hypotheses: Looking for Themes

We have just seen how, to develop the analysis of the lived life, the BDA, you start with the biographical data chronology (the BDC) and then do the analysis by tak-ing each datum in turn and multiplying later occurrence hypotheses and verify-ing them.

In exactly the same way, in order to develop your analysis of the sequential flow of the actually told story, you take the DARNE text sequentialization (TSS) as a basis for developing and verifying hypotheses about *later occurrences within the flow of segments of the told story, of the TSS*. A similar datum-by-datum predictive procedure is followed.

Fischer-Rosenthal and Rosenthal who developed it call this a Thematic Field Analysis,[16] and the concept needs to be laid out in some detail. The aim of

---

16 This is shorter than saying it is a Text Structure Sequentialization governed by the instrumenta-tion concepts of 'thematic field'. It might better be called: a TFA-type of TSS based on a DARNE analy-sis of textsorts with topics and speaker changes.

1. Harold could tell the story as **an interrupted-education story**, in which he might well have taken school and post school qualifications at the right time and moved straight into a professional track, had it not been for his mother's death and, or possibly or, his father's temporary depression and alcoholism in his crucial early years at secondary school. This might involve a fair amount of justificatory Argumentation.

c2.   *He could also tell a **necessary informal learning and delay** story that, as son of a miner, there is no way that an aspiration for qualifications and professional standing would have developed in him during his school days. It was only by way of the self-confidence and social skills developed through his participation in the labour movement and its struggle with the National Coal Board and the government of the day that the capacity to take advantage of educational opportunity would develop. But that capacity would only lead to actual relevant action after the closure of the mining industry which forced Harold to find a new way of earning money, and eventually made a professional career an obvious option. This might involve a fair amount of justificatory Argumentation.*

3. He could represent the **period of militancy as a period of his being duped** by his leaders and elders, and his current professional concern as being a period of mature post-ideological wisdom in which **conventional marriage and a middle-class career represent sensible mainstream values.** This might involve many shifts between then-and-now Evaluations.

c4.   *He could represent the **1990s as a terrible forced compromise with a bourgeois victory** at the collective level which forces his subordination at the individual level. His refusal to accept bourgeois socialization in the capitalist schooling system was the only correct preliminary to the life of a dedicated activist in the left-wing movement within the trade unions. His professional career could be seen cynically as an **individual cop-out** on his part, involving legitimating the capitalist state for his clients, and he could see the smashed left-wing mining communities as, in Peter Laslett's phrase, 'the world we have lost'. This, too, might involve many shifts between then-and-now Evaluations.*

5.   He could identify a **continuity for managerial responsibility for individuals and collectives,** manifesting itself first by taking financial responsibility for his family as a young adolescent, then by taking responsibility for a partner with a small child locked in a bad marriage. He then actively attempts to help lead a pit community of miners fighting to block the closure of the mining industry, and then, finally, after helping to care for children with learning disabilities, is currently equipping himself to help the individual members of the ex-mining communities to be as conscientiously supported as a grudging government will allow. This might involve Description and illustrative Narratives.

c6.   *He could represent himself as a **weak figure following the line of least resistance** as he goes into the mines without much thought, stays in the mines with no preparation for coping with the post-mines future, takes bad jobs as a mobile crane operator, and then is pushed into getting on the social-work-qualifications escalator. This might involve Description and illustrative Narratives, and negative self-Evaluations.*

FIGURE 12.24   **Some Possible Harold-told Stories Around his Expanded BDA**

Thematic Field Analysis (TFA) is to understand the told story of the life narration as constructed by, and consequently expressing, a gestalt or pattern or structure that has to be detected. The told-story is the surface under which is detected a flow in and/or of thematic fields, under which a deeper structure is then postulated to explain the two upper levels.

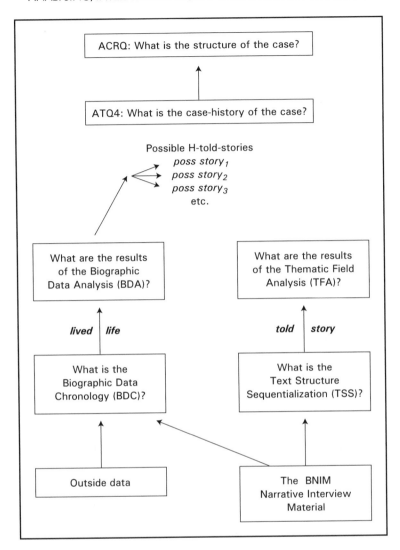

FIGURE 12.25   **Possible told Stories on the Basis of the BDA**

There are, as has been shown above, many ways in which a given set of life events and actions could be presented in a life story: As we saw, some possibilities are put forward as hypotheses by the research panel after completing the BDA (p. 272). However, the gestalt that structures the actual way in which the story is told in the interview is almost certain to be quite different from any one of those hypothesized. The gestalt of the told story that you *do* find might well have some elements of all the gestalts you predicted, as well as others you didn't, in a configuration you couldn't guess at!

Detecting the topics and their interrelation is the task of the TFA on the basis of the DARNE-TSS. The notion of a 'thematic field' was developed by Gurwitsch (1964), where he stressed the way in which any particular theme or topic derives

Transcript	Verbatim transcript
TSS	Structure of the sequence of the text (TSS)
Structural principle	Underlying principle of text production: the gestalt generating the TSS

FIGURE 12.26   **Thematic Field Analysis – Three Levels**

its significance from the 'thematic field' from which it emerges and from which it takes its colouring. The concept of 'field' is not analogous with the enclosed field of the English countryside but with the 'visual field' of visual perception, which has no hard boundaries. The theme itself is a relatively autonomous unit of meaning that can be found in a number of different thematic fields.

> 'We call *thematic field* the totality of items to which a theme points and refers … and which forms the context within which the theme presents itself, … thematic fields may so differ from one another as hardly to have in common any material element, except the theme. To illustrate: we may think of Goethe one time as a poet and creative genius of the German language, another time, as a minister in the service of the Duke of Weimar …. The proposition, 'Columbus discovered America in 1492' may be encountered in different contexts. According to differences of context, the proposition is experienced as organized along different lines of relevancy. Despite these differences which, far from being extrinsic, concern the proposition itself, it still is, and is experienced as, identically the same, whatever the context in which it is encountered. Whether we read it in a history of America, in a history of the great geographical discoveries, or take it as a mere example (as in the present discussion), in each case we are confronted with the same meaning unit.' (Gurwitsch, 1964: 322–3, 325, modified)

Not withstanding the fact of that identity of the meaning unit at one level, its significance is changed by the thematic field in which it (e.g. Columbus's voyage) is at any particular time inserted and recalled:

> 'The *appearance of a theme* must be described *as emergence from a field* in which the theme is located as occupying the centre so that the field forms a background with respect to the theme. The theme carries a field along with it so as not to appear or be present to consciousness except as being in, and pointing to, the field …. By analysing any example, we find the tinge derived by the theme from the thematic field to be the *perspective* under which, the *light and orientation in which*, the *point of view* from which, it appears to consciousness.' (319, 359)

The final point that needs to be made is that

> '… the relation between the theme and items of the thematic field may be more or less indiscriminate and somehow nebulous and obscure …. [it can be] an undifferentiated mass, somehow dark and obscure, yet specific.' (336–7)

For Gurwitsch, part of the thematic field around the central topic/theme is always relatively definite and distinct, while eventually there are always parts of the thematic field which are eventually indeterminate. Any of the items that constitute the field can be 'attended to' and so become clear, but at any given moment, just as whatever our eyes are focused upon requires a selective inattention to the material at the periphery of a field of vision, the thematic field(s) in which the topics/themes are centred leave many items off-centre. It is the task of thematic field analysis to move towards understanding the thematic fields or sequence of thematic fields in which the topics emerge and in terms of which they have their specific (and often changing) meanings. We first suggested this when thinking of how the topic of 'mother' arose twice in the example on p. 139.

Breckner's (1998: 98) rather difficult summary is as follows:

> 'Thematic field analysis [of the TSS] involves reconstructing the subject's system of knowledge, their interpretations of their lives, and their classification of experiences into thematic fields. Our aim is to reconstruct the interactional significance of the subject's actions, the underlying structure of the subject's interpretations of his or her own life, which may go beyond the subject's own intentions (Rosenthal, 1993: 61).
>
> The "hidden agenda" is supposed to structure the narrated life story, which "represents a sequence of mutually interrelated themes that, between them, form a dense network of interconnected cross-references" (Fischer, 1982: 168).
>
> "The *thematic field* is defined as the sum of events and situations presented in connection with the topic that form a background or horizon against which the topic stands out as the central focus"' (Rosenthal, 1993: 64, based on Fischer, 1982 and Gurwitsch, 1964).

This is difficult to understand: the concepts of 'themes' and 'topics' are both central and slippery in social research. Though there is no mechanical way of identifying themes and topics, the effort needs to be made. The concept of 'topic' we have already discussed: whatever the difficulties of the slippery concept of 'theme', we cannot avoid using it, and for many purposes the difficulties may not be relevant. My experience is that, for the BNIM work of using the TSS for a thematic field analysis, no particular *philosophical* problem is normally raised.

A recent writer on the subject, Boyzatis (1998), distinguishes between the moment in which you *sense* that there is, in the data, a theme or pattern of signification – which he calls 'the codable moment' and I might call 'a thematic field' – and the later moment in which you *find a name*, or code-tag, for that which you have just sensed. This distinction is very like that made by Gendlin (1981) where he distinguishes 'getting a felt sense' of what is going on, getting a clear sense of 'what *all that* feels like', from the next step in which you try to find a very few (two or three) words which may convey the 'core' of that 'all that about' meaning. Finding such an image or verbal formulation he calls 'finding a handle' for the 'felt sense' (Gendlin, 1981: 53–6).

At each stage of the TFA the process of generating hypotheses about a datum block, and refuting or corroborating earlier ones is the same as for the BDA. Similarly, on the basis of datum-hypotheses we then look for the emergence of structural hypotheses about the TSS story-telling as a whole. However, the questions to be asked about the sequentialization are different, since we are analysing the short history of a textual production in an interview rather than the long history of a lived life.

The 'later occurrences' are later TSS segments, later occurrences of speaker action, later topic content and thematic movement, and later occurrences of this or

1	Is the biographer generating a narrative or being carried along by a narrative flow in the story-telling?
2	How far is the biographer oriented to the relevance system of the interviewer, and how far to to his or her own relevance system?
3	In which thematic field is the single sequence embedded; what is the hidden agenda?
4	Why is the biographer using this specific sort of text to present the experience or the topic?
5	In which details are the single experiences or topics presented, and why?
6	Which topics are addressed? Which biographical experiences, events, and periods are covered and which are omitted? What material comes up in subsession 2 (as a result of further questioning) that was omitted from the initial narration in subsession 1?

and

7	Which textsort, or change of speaker, or topic will occur next, if any of the above hypotheses are true? (following hypothesis)
8	What hypotheses about the whole or the current thematic field (TFH: thematic field hypotheses) suggest themselves at this stage?

FIGURE 12.27   **TFA Questions, Based on Breckner (1998: 98)**

that textsort *in the interview* – rather than (as for the BDA) later occurrences in a life.

The key immediate question is 'Why is the biographer presenting this experience or topic *now* and why is he or she using this specific sort of text to present it?' This is true of the parts and of the 'told story' as a whole. The interviewee in subsession 1 has complete freedom to introduce and ignore topics, to deal with them briefly and at length, to deal with them according to different textsorts. We are attempting to understand the state of subjectivity and intersubjectivity that produces the flow of account-giving decisions that the completed text represents.

Breckner identifies the questions to ask about each datum block of the TSS, but perhaps a note is in order. I personally find them less well organized and articulated than the questions she identified as needing to be asked at each stage of the BDA. Referring to Figure 12.27, I suggest that questions 3 and 4 – together with the following-hypotheses question 7 and question 8 which looks for 'the principle of the whole gestalt' – represent the core of the questions to be posed for each segment of the DARNE sequentialization.

In a workshop doing the TFA, each of the 'data of structure' (as presented on page 278 and following), the text segments, are presented in turn, previous following hypotheses are inspected in the light of the new datum to see which were strengthened and which weakened. Then new hypotheses answering the above questions appropriate for the TSS are developed (both particular and structural, each rendered risky and therefore useful by appropriate hypotheses about what would follow in the text). Having presented such a procedure for the BDA (with BDA questions about what follows in the life) page 260ff above, we shall not repeat the presentation since the principle of working datum by datum has been established.

Instead, on the next pages, you will find an example of a record of a detailed TFA working through some of Harold's TSS as developed during a group work-shop on the case in 1998 at the Centre for Biography in Social Policy (University of East London, UK). You may wish to compare this partial TFA of Harold's sequentialization with a more complete and more discursive TFA of the sequen-tialization of another case, Tony C, presented – with further elements of hypoth-esizing and reconstructing of the case history – by Breckner (1998: 98–103).

In the example below: 'FH' stands for 'Following hypothesis', namely an explic-it hypothesis about what will follow next or at some point in the text. Also 'TFH' stands for 'Thematic Field Hypothesis'.

> The normative model of always finding a counter and then a tangential hypothesis to complement any original hypothesis that suggests itself – a rule of three, see page 259 above – should be borne in mind.

Volante (1998) has presented a useful way of presenting a record of the TFA of a particular TSS. I have gratefully followed her format (Figure 12.28), which can include (in smaller typesize) discussion notes and contextual information. Data numbers are in roman numerals.

Please note the emergence of a 'Structural Hypothesis'. At any given point in the work, the panel should attempt to multiply possible 'structural hypotheses' and think about the way in which the work to date strengthens or weakens any that have emerged so far. Bear in mind that you need to be alert to data that refutes or at least weakens any structural hypothesis that you put forward. Don't forget to think of counter and tangential structural hypotheses to the ones that first suggest themselves and therefore to which you are personally particularly prone!

After completing the task of analysing the thematic structure of the initial nar-ration – and perhaps of other extended narrations – you will have come up with a number of structural hypotheses, thematic field hypotheses (TFHs), about the structure of the whole, and some of these will remain plausible at the end of your analysis. You will attempt to find one particular theme-statement that character-izes the initial narration as a whole. If successful, this would be a candidate for 'the principle behind the structure of the whole gestalt'.

You will probably find it useful to revisit the earlier list of some possible subject-told lifestories (Figure 12.24) and revise it, eliminating ones that bear no resemblance to your account of the actual told story as embodied in the TSS and expressed in the TFA, and its list of proved and disproved 'structural hypotheses'. How does the actual subject-told story as you have analysed it relate to the numerous possible subject-told stories you earlier imagined? You may find that it combines elements of some of your original list in a configuration you did not pre-dict, together with elements that were nowhere on your original list.

Alternatively, you may find that the initial narration as a whole is characterized not by one theme but by a contradiction: that might therefore be 'the theme' at a deeper level. The 'principle of the life as a whole' might be the struggle between two elements of a contradiction. There may be a number of different 'fields' in the

(1)   Interviewer explains about the Sostris project exploring riskier lives across Europe and asks the initial question

H1.   Harold may experience uncertainty about what to do and try
         to get more input and guidance from the interviewer.

Thematic Field Discussion: If this happened, there could be a thematic field of 'uncertainty about taking control' of a global sort, or one of 'being uncertain in unfamiliar situations such as research interviews', which would be much more local, and compatible with, say, a general thematic field of 'taking control in familiar situations'

      FH1.1. Harold may openly ask for permission to 'go ahead'
      FH1.2. Harold may ask for more information about how to proceed
              either assertively or diffidently
      FH1.3. Harold may just say 'mm' non-committally, to force the
              interviewer to carry on in some way or other

H2.   Harold may have a strong negative reaction
      FH2.1. Harold will say 'no' in a strong assertive fashion
      FH2.2. Harold will make an edgy joke 'How about another day?'

(2)   Harold: 'yeah'

H1 appears to be weakened, but it is too early to say it is refuted, though FH2.1 and 2.2 are disconfirmed.
FH1.1 and 1.2 appear to be weakened. The type of reaction predicted in FH1.3 may be operating.

No new hypotheses are put forward at this point.

(3)   Interviewer: 'but ...'

H3.   Interviewer experiences Harold's 'yeah' as requiring
         further input from him
      FH3.1. Interviewer will give some reassurance
      FH3.2. Harold will accept some reassurance
      FH3.3. Harold will ask for some reassurance about what will be done
              with the tape

**(4)   Harold: [Argumentation]   'I will aim for concision, may need to backtrack,
                     I expect to get confused and may need to correct myself'**

      FH3.2 is falsified to the extent that Harold does not wait for the interviewer
          to complete his intervention
      H2 appears to be falsified — not a negative reaction to the question
      H1 appears to be close to falsification as well

H4.   Harold is about to tell a very complicated story, with a lot of
         detail and many strands. He is a successful perfectionist.
      FH4.1. Harold will produce a Report or a Narrative of considerable
              length and/or complexity
      FH4.2. Harold will start a Report or Narrative but will break it off
              because it is too complex

counter-hypothesis

H5.   Harold is very scatty-minded and feels he has to warn the
         interviewer about himself: a completely unsuccessful perfectionist
      FH5.1. Harold will not produce a coherent Report, Narrative,
              Argument or Description throughout his response
      FH5.2. Harold will produce lots of self-deprecating self-evaluations

continued

Figure 12.28   continued

tangential hypothesis

H6.   Harold is a realist about himself, his life, and his capacity to
        give an account of himself. He wishes to warn the interviewer
        not to expect too much
        FH6.1. Harold will take care to think about the interviewer's
        understanding throughout the account he will give, trying to take
        the interviewer's 'position' into account
        FH6.2. Harold's account will be very factual

**Thematic Field Discussion: a number of implicit structural hypotheses are 'in the air' at this
point. No very strong evidence for any of them, yet, though**

(5)   Harold: [Argumentation]   'I'll start with family and family members'

*FH5.1 appears to be weakened by this systematic and conceptually complex start
H6 might be thought of as provisionally strengthened*

H9.   Harold will use a chronological reporting framework for his
        self-presentation
        FH9.1. Harold's initial narrative will be pretty chronological

H10.   Harold will report on different aspects of his life separately in
        order to avoid getting confused
        FH10.1. Harold will first report on his family life and then on some
                other aspect, for example his work life, and then on another aspect,
                say his religious life, etc.

H11.   Family is a very complicated matter for Harold and perhaps his
        most important topic
        FH11.1. Harold will report on his family at great length and reveal a very
                complex structure
        FH11.2. Harold will present narratives of very difficult family relations

**Structural Hypothesis A:
Family complexity and development will be the organizing topic of the whole TSS**

H12.   Harold distinguishes 'family' and 'family members' because
        this is an important distinction for him
        FH12.1. Harold's 'personal family' does not include all formal 'family
                members' and this will be important
        FH12.2. The individual members of the family do not exhaust the
                significance of the concept of 'the family' which will be argued as
                being more important than any particular member

H13.   Harold is taking a rather distant 'sociological approach' to his own family.
        FH13.1. He will give reports, argumentation and evaluation but keep his
                emotional distance from the events he describes. He will avoid
                narratives, especially about his own life in the family
        FH13.2. He will produce a 'genealogical tree' to help the interviewer
                understand the complexities of the large family

H.14   Harold sees himself merely as a representative of his family
        FH14.1. He will not foreground his own experience or that of any other
                particular family member.
        FH14.2. He will not tell any stories that reflect badly on 'the family'

continued

Figure 12.28   continued

> **(6)   New datum...**
> Falsifications?
> New datum-hypotheses?
> New structural hypotheses?

FIGURE 12.28   **Post-session Record of a TFA Analysis of the Harold TSS Fragment**

same text. You might find a contradiction one week, and, after two weeks more thinking and memoizing, an unexpected and unpredictable unity. Or the other way round.

After you have, relatively mechanically, done the BDA and the TFA, there are no mechanical solutions – and this includes arriving at a 'statement of theme'. You sweat and worry about getting the 'least bad solution' that you can, that makes sense of as much material as possible.[17] Sometimes you find a way of 'characterizing the whole' (of answering the CRQ), sometimes you may only be able to answer TQ4 (p. 237); I shall come to this later.

If you keep expressing and documenting your struggles and ideas in theoretical memos and free-associative writing, you will find that you will keep moving on, through the periods of 'depression and stuckness' which are inevitable in trying to develop your understanding of complex many-layered phenomena studied and recorded in depth.

Accounts of Self-presentations and Thematic Fields
A record of such a grounded theory procedure of thematic field analysing can be found in Schiebel (2000) and in Jones and Rupp (2000). An account of Harold can be found in Wengraf (2000b) and in Chamberlayne, Rupp and Wengraf (1999: 20–1). More experiential is the short biographical account of the experience of doing a Thematic Field Analysis by Volante (1998). Examples of TFAs can be found in the *Sostris Reports (1998–99) numbers* 2–7.

A Thematic Field Analysis of Harold's initial account (subsession 1) was summed up as shown in Figure 12.29.

Discursive accounts of thematic fields are long texts, and I can only cite illustrative partial quotations. First, an example of a segment from a Thematic Field Analysis of a TSS from Italy:

> 'Sasa tells his story as if it were one of pre-destination. He presents his life as a series of projects blocked by external factors: his family's poverty, the country's economic difficulties and unemployment. His story is characterized by an "I" (active and making plans) alternating with a "We" (we members of a poor family, we the unemployed, we the boys from the "Spanish District") that held back and inhibited various plans and actions.
>
> continued

---

17 By analogy to 'line-fitting' with quantitative data, you are trying out 'gestalt-fitting' to qualitative data.

I *Mother's death (tormented and broken report with argumentation)*
Family, especially father
Leaving school without qualifications
Mining, 'strong characters'
Failure of strike: divisions of NUM

II *Own life from 19 onwards (coherent story)*
Trips to America
Struggle with colliery manager
Accident
Len and his socialization as a union militant
Strike: divisions of community

III *Death of the mines: argumentation–theorizing about society
and politics*

IV *Maturity + luck (report)*
Caring and education
Handling of the post-strike disillusion, against cynicism
Luck

FIGURE 12.29   **TFA Sketch of Harold's Initial Account**

Sasa begins his self-presentation after providing a relatively long setting during which his determination to inform the interviewer of his ability to confront the required task becomes clear (*I understand … don't worry, I understand … I mean – you know – I'm ready*). He thinks the task is easy (*I can explain it in a tick*). The fact that he has to demonstrate he is up to it is the first sign of his anxiety about performance, and that the interviewer plays the role of a judge to whom he has to answer for his actions. Before starting his main narration, Sasa needs to present his extenuating circumstances, namely his origins, and make sure the judge will take them into consideration (*I'll tell you all about my life, how it began … I mean … you know, how it began. Can I go on?*) And it is only when he has been reassured (that is to say, when the interviewer says "You can start now") that he begins his story (*Well …*).

Sasa organizes his story in chronological order and focuses on the issue of work. His presentation is a long report interspersed with argumentation … [see original for details] ….

…. To sum up what we have analysed so far, there are at least three regular features. Firstly, his shift from "I" to "we" when talking about the reasons why something has not worked out (for example, he says *I'm carrying on with my shop*, but he withdraws behind a "we" when he has to explain why his work is illegal: *We haven't had an opportunity; we can't afford it yet …*). Secondly, the shift from report to argumentation when he talks about his failures. And thirdly, the "jumps" in chronology where there are events that he feels are negative; it is significant, for example, that Sasa momentarily forgets to talk about his only regular job, that is the one from which he was sacked: *when I was 20 or 21, I went to work with my brother-in-law – no, when I was 20, I went to work in the agency office.*

continued

continued

In analysing the structure of Sasa's main narration as a whole it becomes clear that such regular features are associated with three topics: dropping out of school, dismissal, and not getting married. It is reasonable to suppose that they are problematic events for him – in other words, he sees them as "mistakes" or personal failures. Such an interpretation also confirms the reason why Sasa organizes his interview as if he were standing accused of a crime or undergoing some test.' (Caniglia and Spanella, 1999)

Another example of a segment of a Thematic Field Analysis, this time from Tejero and Torrabadella (1999b) is also on an unqualified youth.

'After the interviewer contextualized the research and made introductory remarks about how the exercise would proceed, Julio immediately argued that *normally there are no opportunities to talk like this*. Julio's main narrative is short, and it is presented (in a report style) to the interviewer as a **standard life story** of a boy from El Canon, the neighbourhood from which he comes and where he still lives. His narratives are structured as follows: he firstly introduces himself by reporting where he was born. This spatial reference includes the name of the hospital and a clarifying evaluation (*everybody in Barcelona is born there*), the name of the suburb and square where he comes from and where he still lives and, finally, the village where his parents come from in Andalusia. He continues his report by introducing what he considers to be a turning-point in his life: *I started going to a private school, but my parents had to send me to a state school. From that moment onwards, my life started going down hill.* This is followed by a report on his unstable and precarious educational and professional trajectory (e.g. leaving school followed by a badly paid job) until he introduces his current employment which he evaluates as *a decent job*. Julio finishes his main narration with the following statement: *If you want to work, you have to have connections. Studying school curricula ... all the rest is pointless.* And then, *Do you want me to explain anything else, about my friends, for instance?*

... The thematical field that flows from his main narration might be as follows: "Going to the state school in El Canon means that life is preordained". In other words, he sees himself as equal with his peers in the neighbourhood.

However, if we compare the initial narrative with the rest of the interview, a much **more** complex picture emerges ... [*detailed analysis follows*]. If we take all this into consideration, we could say that Julio is presenting a world with which he cannot identify, and also the people from that world [peers of his neighbourhood] with whom he cannot identify either. This is reinforced by his insistence on presenting how the others see him: *my peers call me a puritan, and for my father and people at work, I'm a rebel ... Actually, I'm neither.* In contrast with his previous presentation, which seems to follow a more stereotypical picture, the "self" he presents here reveals more complexity. The resulting thematical field no longer complements the earlier one which we have derived from his main narration. Indeed, Julio presents himself as *someone in the middle* between two different models: the marginal / residual and the conventional / traditional. The former

continued

continued

might be structured by a past characterized by school failure and the orienting principle of "experiencing the present"; this basically includes the topics of gangs (peers) and drugs. The latter is structured by a more future-oriented and pre-established pattern that includes the topics of stable job, stable family (represented by the traditional lives of his parents and his brother) and motorcycle (symbolizing both the dominant consumption pattern and autonomy) .... To conclude, Julio is locating himself at the core of two competing or conflicting cultures which coexist in the same spatial context of the neighbourhood, yet he does not identify with any of them.' (Tejero and Torrabadella, 1999b: 10–11)

Although it is impossible to compress a full TFA into a short space, I hope that the above two quotations have given you some sense of the principles and the mode of argument characteristic of such an analysis.

A summary of a number of cases might look like Martina Schiebel's account (2000: 215) where she provides a useful comparative discussion of the biographizing strategies expressed in life-stories of "witnesses to the Nazi period":

'Our biographical analyses of ... witnesses to the Nazi period show a variety of strategies which the individuals we interviewed use to come to terms with their past. For example, one woman, who was born in 1915, de-politicizes the whole period of her life until 1945. A man, also born in 1915, limits the phenomenon of Nazism to the war years, which he characterizes as non-political. In this way he can discount politics from his military career in the Wehrmacht period. Walter Langenbach, born in 1914, was witness to Nazi crimes in the former Jugoslavia. He does not specify his actual conduct, the extent to which he personally participated, but he is still haunted even today by his memories and sense of guilt. A decisive feature of Mr Langenbach's understanding of his past is his perception of events in his life as imposed by external forces. With this biographical strategy he can avoid the question of his own role in Nazi crimes, even though he cannot escape his memories, nightmares and sense of guilt.' (Schiebel, 2000)

There is no substitute for looking at a number of examples, and the more examples that you look at, the better.[18]

With practice, you will develop your own mode of presenting the results of your thematic field analysing in a formal Thematic Field Analysis. The transition you will find yourself making is usually from a description of the 'flow' of thematic analysis, moving from beginning to the end of the told story (as characteristic of some of the above examples), to a more structural account which explains the flows at the upper level by a more constant structure (at a deeper level, as in the last example). See Figure 12.26.

---

18 At the time of writing, the most convenient source of such examples comprises numbers 2–8 of the *Sostris Working Papers*.

THE ACTUAL TOLD STORY AND THE ORIGINAL POSSIBLE TOLD STORIES

In order to further understand the significance of the actual story as told (analysed in the TFA), it is useful to compare it with the set of 'possible told stories' you developed after completing the BDA, the analysis of the biographical data.

If we were to do this for the case of Harold, a rapid sketch in respect of our original hypotheses (p. 272) might be as follows. We find (a) that he does not envisage that a smooth youthful transition to professional education might have been on the cards in any way at all; (b) his told story does have some aspects of our 'necessary informal learning and delay' second hypothesis. Although he believes that he now sees things more clearly than he did at the time of the miners' strike his actual told story contrasts with our hypothesis that he might have seen himself 'duped into militancy'. Our fourth hypothesis is partially supported, except that he does take pride in doing his best for his (ex-mining) clients – even the scabs – and does not reproach himself for 'selling out'. There is no trace in his told story of our fifth hypothesis. His story supports some elements of our sixth hypothesis insofar as much though not all of his story is told as if he were someone whose history is more determined by collective events than it is by a sustained individual project 'against the stream'.

TOWARDS CREATING A 'HISTORY' AND 'STRUCTURE' OF THE CASE

So far, the method of BNIM has been to analyse the interview material in two separate stages:

- the lived life has been reconstructed and hypotheses developed about the significance of those lived events in a BDA without reference to the way the story was told but only with reference to the bare bones of the chronology of events;
- similarly, the told story of the initial narration has been described in a DARNE/topic analysis (TFA) and hypotheses developed about the significance of the way the story was told without reference to the objective events but only with reference to the story as told.

We now move to the next stage: starting to work out *what are the best connections we can draw* between the lived-life as understood by BD analysing and the told-story as understood by TF analysing.

In my experience, after the work of developing the TFA is well started, this process of thinking about the relation of the lived-life and the told-story starts, informally anyway, inside the head of the researcher.

> As records of the BDA and the TFA were written up, you may well have found yourself writing 'theoretical memos' about what possible more general interpretations might be true or false. As always, 'don't go on without at least one memo done' might be a useful slogan!

However, after the completion of the TFA, you now proceed to address this more formally. To describe the case-history – in BNIM theory-language terms – is to describe the evolving relationship between the lived life (as analysed) and the told story (as analysed). This can be described in the form of a narration or in the form of a described structure.

We can do this in two ways: sometimes doing a microanalysis before an attempt at reconstructing the case-history (note that this is not the lived-life nor the told-story but something distinct); sometimes doing the reconstruction of the case-history first.[19]

The shift from surface flows in the sequences of the lived life and of the told story (each with indefinitely large number of data points) through a practice of condensing and abstracting that generates first life-phases and text-sequentializations and, finally, structural principles necessary if we are to stay focused through complexity.

I start – for ease of exposition – with a discussion of the case-history.

Representation of the History of the Case

The present perspective from which the told story is told is one that has emerged from the history of the individual case. The assumption is a fairly simple one: that the perspective on the past that I have now (a) is not the same as I had in the past, but (b) that it has emerged from the past in an intelligible way that I am attempting to reconstruct.

> The meaning of my first sexual kiss will have been one thing at the time that it happened; if I have stayed with that sexual partner ever since then its meaning may have stayed the same or it may have changed as my relationship with that person changed. However, if the promise of that first kiss was not fulfilled, then, when it became clear that it was not going to be fulfilled, its meaning to me later certainly would have changed. The 'meaningful future' apparently offered by the first kiss produced or enhanced a particular perspective. The non-fulfilment in the life is likely to have led the later perspective (told story) on that first kiss to change. Since then, in further retrospect, its meaning may have changed several times again (I am indebted to Susanna Rupp for this example).
>
> To take a quite different type of example, for many older people in Britain and elsewhere, their life has involved sudden disruptions: emigration, war, occupation, immigration, geographical uprooting, sudden illness or the arrival of children. Most events such as these will lead to diverse but intelligible changes in perspective on the pre-disruption past and on the post-disruption future as people struggle to cope with quite different circumstances in a now radically transformed present.

One task of the researcher into the life history is to attempt to reconstruct what may be several phases in which the retrospective perspective of the individual changed, in order to understand through what history of lived experience the present retrospective perspective came to be formed. A narrative constructed by the researcher about that evolution is called 'the (or 'a') BNIM case-history'.

---

19 The best representation of a case may be not the formalized case-structure but the narrative of the case-history. Consequently, creating a neat 'case structure verbal summary' or a 'case structure diagram' may not be possible, or produce fully satisfactory results. Case-history narratives may better convey more complexity than can be achieved by 'abstract principles' from which they can be alleged to have been generated. See below the work of Bruner and Polkinghorne; see also, Spradley and Malinowski on tacit knowledge.

An Account of the Historical Evolution of the Present
Perspective on Past, Present and Future

Breckner describes stage 3 as follows (modified):

'The function of this step is to generate hypotheses to answer the following questions:

- how is the structure of the current self-presentation connected to the experiences the interviewee had in the past, and
- how did it develop in the course of time?

1. I first look for **those events / situations which could have been important in the process of constitution** of this self-presentation structure. I **go back to the biographical data** and look at them, now with the **new perspective coming from the analysis I have just made of the interviewee's told story.**[20]
2. I collect together **those text passages from the interview which refer to events / situations / changes / turning points I consider as important** for the process of formation of the *life history* as it is presented in the *told story.*[21]

These text passages in the transcript and eventually the audio-tape are then examined with the following questions in mind for the analysis of any particular event:

First, textually for each point in the text where the event is referred to:[22]

- at what length is the event presented, and what does this pattern of length mean?
- in what thematical context is the event / situation etc. presented?
- through which textsort(s) (DARNE) is the event presented?

Eventually, constant and changing meanings of the event, given all its textual occurrences as analysed above.

- What could this event have meant for the interviewee in the past?
- What could the event mean for the interviewee in the present?
- If the meaning for the interviewee could have changed over time, what could be the reason for that change and what might be the principles with which the researcher could explain such timed change?

You will note that the procedure described above combines (i) the insistence on 'contextualization' chararacteristic of TSS analysis and (ii) the more familiar practice of 'recontextualization' which we found when extracting events for the BDC (recontextualization of events) and which we now find when extracting *all the references* to the same events (*wherever* they occur in the transcripts) and exploring possible changes of meaning, and then attempting to understand and explain such changes of meaning (recontextualization of meanings)

Harold: Comparison of Lived Life / Told Story   I can suggest what goes on here, by way of an example. In Figure 12.30, you will find a summary of the separate results of the lived life analysis (BDA) and the initial-narrative told story analysis

---

20 In the original BDA analysis of the BDC lived-life chunks, we analysed each one 'blind' to the cotext and blind to the whole of the told story. Here we do something different.

21 In the original TFA analysis of the TSS chunks, we analyed each one blind, without reference to any other point in the told story where the same event might have been referred to.

22 For example, the two different points where his mother is mentioned on p. 140.

Biographical Data Analysis	Thematic Field Analysis
Phases of the lived life	**Structure of the initial account**
• Until 9 Security in large family	I *Mother's death (tormented and broken report with argumentation)* Family, especially father Leaving school without qualifications Mining, 'strong characters' Failure of strike: divisions of NUM
• 9–11 Change of school, of village, school again and then loss of mother	
• 11–16 Housework at home for out-of-work father, bullying at school for status. Left school with no qualifications	
• 16–24 Left-wing union militant in NUM and in his colliery. Secure work-community with activist mentor. Rugby and pubs and NUM travel. Starts relation with future wife	II *Own life from 19–25 onwards (fluent narratives and reports)* Trips to America Struggles with colliery manager Accident Len and his socialization as a union militant
• 24–25 Showdown between NUM and Tory government; scabs divide the NUM nationally and locally. Miners defeated	
• 25–29 After defeat of miners, moves to non-scab other pit, continues militancy till it is shortly to close	III *Death of the mines: argumentation–theorizing about society and politics (report and much argumentation)*
• 30 'Industrial gypsy' as mobile crane operator in private sector. Starts to do 'O levels', has rugby accident, is ill and then made redundant. Short nervous crisis	IV *Maturity + Luck (report + much argumentation and evaluation)* Caring and Education – Report Handling of post-strike disillusion, against cynicism and for principle ('scab story'). 'Then I thought, now I see' … Luck for self and wife; and fear for daughter. Sadness for community
• 31–37 Career shift. Voluntary work with kids with learning disabilities, and then move into Social Work and climbing qualifications and status ladder. Thinking of going to university	
Cycle of disrupted security: first the family crisis then re-security in the mines; then divided mining community and re security in the second pit; then insecurity in private sector and re-securization in social work career	Bildungsroman (transition from the disaster years of 11–16 to naive militant 16–25 to realist for a post-mining professional new career (31–). Tortured argument around mother's death, fluent narrative around 16–25 before the strike; righteous argument around defeat of the miners, worried argument about his and especially his daughter's future in individualist Britain

FIGURE 12.30 **Harold's Life Phases and Text Structure Compared in Two Columns**

(TFA) of Harold. It is useful to attempt such a single-page sketch for your own interviewee.

In this case, there is a high degree of overlap between the two sequences; in other cases, there may be much less. Nonetheless, you can see some interesting omissions and underplayings in the initial narration told story when you look at the data from the lived life.

You will usually find that creating such a diagram of both the structured phases of the lived life, on the one hand, and the structure of the (initial) narration, on the other, is a useful mechanism. The struggle to produce such a presentation is helpful and, once you have achieved such a presentation – as on the next page – you have it in front of you to think about. It is a very condensed version of your analysis so far.

In Figure 12.30, there are some reflections at the bottom of each column which sum up the contents of that column. The eight-phase model in Figure 12.23 (p. 270) has here been 'grouped' into five that came to seem on reflection more meaningful.

The question that needs to be posed is: how could a life as lived on the left hand side lead to a story and a current self-presentation and perspective as expressed on the right hand side?

> For example, for Harold, what principle can be asserted which would explain, among other data, the virtual omission from his initial narrative of his relationship to his wife?[23]

From the point of view of your material, however, the important task is that of constructing hypotheses about any sense of previous perspectives that you think the informant may have had in the past and attempting to construe what led to the earlier adoption and later replacement of such perspectives in a sequence that leads intelligibly to the informant's current present-time perspective.

It may well be that, in some cases, previous perspectives and the life-events which led to their invention and then displacement are very clear, and that, in other cases, the attempt to reconstruct the history of the case in this way produces relatively few or no firm results. Children and young adults sometimes have very little capacity to express their 'history of perspectives'. In such cases, only the 'present perspective' is available as material to be explained by an understanding of the case-history.

Figure 12.30 suggests that there are at least two turning points in the evolution of Harold's contemporary perspective: around the death of his mother, and around the death of the mining industry.

I have little information about the perspective of Harold before the death of his mother (approximately his first decade of life) but it is clear that her death and the period around it were traumatic. We shall see (pp. 293–5 and Appendix B), in a later micro-analysis of a segment of the transcript, that Harold oscillates between his then-perspective on himself as a 'very mature eleven-year-old' who suddenly 'had to grow up quickly' and a later perspective in which he sees his development as at that point having been put back.

continued

---

23 She is strongly present in the subsession 2 follow-up material. You need to remember the intersubjective situation, before rushing to conclusions about the 'subjectivity' of the individual conceived in isolation. One hypothesis was that, Harold felt that 'private matters' (like wife and family) were of less interest to the male researcher than 'mining matters'.

continued

We also know that the death of the mining industry and the sharp division in the community between militants and scabs around the 1984–85 strike led him in the interview to sharply contrast his earlier naiveté and a later post-strike realism.

In addition, there is evidence of changes in perspective of a more minor sort in the two periods after each of the traumatic events in question.

At some point during his period in the mines and becoming a union militant, Harold shifted out of the individualistic orientation characteristic of his early adolescence and into the confident, socially outgoing collectivist miner-militant orientation of his early adulthood.

After the failure of the miners, at some point Harold shifts or is shifting from the relatively one-dimensional rage at the scabs in the community towards a more difficult understanding of the complexities of that struggle, the community and the future, and this appears to be related to his attempt to understand, to remain in communication with, and to have some influence over the future of his late teenage daughter. When he says that the rift in the community will only be healed in the generation of his daughter, but not his own, he is imaginatively placing himself now in a virtual perspective from that future time and that future person. In one sense, this is a perspective he can have; in another, he cannot experience it except as a future perspective of somebody close to him but not of him himself.

Analyses of Harold, based on more material than can be presented here, that may help to answer such a question can be found in Chamberlayne et al. (1999: 20–2, 25–6), in a paper entitled 'Stopped in their tracks: British National Report on Ex-Traditional Workers' where stress is laid on the very radical nature of the economic transformations, and the negative effects of the British welfare system are suggested.

On the basis of work summarized above, you then need to construct a formal case-history: a narrative account of present (and past) perspectives as they emerged in the course of the life.

Harold's Self-presentation: A 'Bildungsroman'

The following extract (slightly modified from Wengraf, 2000b) suggests how such a case-history can be presented. In the original text, the story of another miner, Donald, has already been described.

'While Donald's account took the form of a love story, told with speed and panache, Harold's was in the guise of a *Bildungsroman*, a personal development history, tracing through and reflecting on his experience of life, constantly (and often, though not always, very consciously) switching between past and more recent perspectives.

His interview begins with an acknowledgement of his own style:

"Obviously, when we're talking about my life-history there may be times when I may have to backtrack ... I hope I'll try and be as precise as I possibly can ... there

continued

continued

> *may be occasions when I may get slightly confused and think aha that's not quite right."*

His very long narrative continually oscillates cause-periods and effect-periods, shifting between his responses then and his judgments now. In this process the painful story of the eleven-year-old and the period between his mother's death and going into the mines only receive bare reporting, and the regression backwards is constantly forcing false starts on the attempt to go definitively forward.

"The death of our err mother" is mainly spoken of from the standpoint of his father's "burden". Note the uncertainty of tense and referent in the first sentence:

> *"er I think there were a lot of pressures on on my father indeed as there was the family and I think at such a young age of eleven even though I did consider myself and still do now consider myself a very mature eleven year old I had to grow up very quickly. (4) And I think that it taught me some it taught me a few things em my father did struggle quite a lot and I would describe him as turning into an alcoholic at at a stage not long after em which was very difficult he was never never ever abusive he was not an abusive, alcoholic em I think what it was was that he was very depressed he saw more of the negatives rather than how can I move on from here."*

Harold does not talk immediately about strong and painful events, but finds it easier to shift focus to the experience of others, taking the view of the carer concerned for others. Yet simultaneously, he is trying to tell the story of himself at the time. In a passage that significantly confuses past and present as it struggles for expression, he represents himself as:

"having had to grow up very very quickly ... I think it's just that I was kind of it it delayed my er development my em my educational development em by a number of years but I think from from ... maturity wise I think I'm far ahead of my er I was far ahead of myself."

The difference between his step-mother's previous family and the joint family of his dead mother's children is spoken of in a strong argumentation which lays stress on difference and on the lack of bonding, but which also indicates the importance of and capacity for bridging differences (even if the "I get on very very well" slightly clashes with the "no kind of bonding" assertion and may represent a slightly tricky achievement rather than a 'state of nature'):

> *'I have no kind of bonding there because we were never brought up as children that's not a problem we all get on very very well and I think that's vitally important.'*

The painful pre-history of his early adolescence and of his mother's death is a necessary 'explanation' of going into the mines, which is when he starts to narrativize beyond the bare reporting. The first day of going to the pits, standing at the bus-stop, is when his history becomes 'tellable as a continuous story'.

Despite its greater flow and narrativity, however, Harold's intended linear progression within the period 1976–85 is always interrupted by an explanatory reference back towards

continued

continued

the trauma of the mother's death or a slip forwards towards the divided community in the aftermath of the miner's strike in 1984/5, and his second betrayal, his second disillusion.[24] Thus what he thought then – *"at the time I thought you couldn't come across better characters"* – is constantly compared with his post-strike position in which he developed *"such a dislike for some people because of the deeds that they did"*, and his realizing *"how naive I was and how people can be manipulated"*.

While family relationships remain marginal in Donald's account, Harold's narrative starts with his family of origin (and his marriage gets eventually integrated into his life story). This continues in his account of the mining period, particularly through the key role of his industrial and union mentor and quasi-foster father Len. From Len, Harold gains a sense of family-like and community history, as through his sense of lineage with Len's own mentor, an uncle who was excluded from mining jobs for 13 years after the 1926 strike and defied conscription in WW2. Like the teacher at school who challenged Harold to question: *"how do you know those astronauts are really on the moon?"*, Len in the workplace and the union stimulated Harold's independence of mind, often by teasingly setting Harold and his peers against each other in argument. Travel greatly widened his horizons: *"after that first trip it em I had this em urge ... I needed to go I wanted to go other places, I want to meet other people .... I wanted to go further"*.

At the same time, and again in contrast to Donald, Harold was energetically involved in rugby and community social life:

> *"my social life was like very many others in the valleys and that was a hard drinking hard playing, rugby training (1) and generally socializing you know in pubs and clubs ... in fact if you didn't participate in that kind of social behaviour then you would be deemed perhaps as being rather strange"*.

The break in community life erupted *"overnight or certainly within a week"* with the scabbing during the miners' strike. The *"social treachery"* still, over a decade later, greatly exercises Harold's mind and impinges on his daily life and his professional work. His reaction, on passing a 'scab' in the street, is to:

> *"keep on walking and that's my immediate thought I have no other interest in them whatsoever (1) again that that may seem rather cruel and rather hard but I think what went on during that dispute I think I'm well justified in doing so ... I think I was em I was deceived by many (1) they may say the same thing about me it has to be said there's always two sides to the story and I certainly wouldn't deny that .... I still see it now you know and I (didn't) I honestly believe to the day I die you know I'll still maintain that ... not bitterness ... you know I wouldn't wish them to walk down the street I wouldn't wish anything to happen to their family you know .... I wouldn't care if it happened to them but I wouldn't wish it on them.*

continued

---

24 It may be that this resonated with two earlier 'betrayals': by his mother by dying and by his father by losing his job and temporarily being affected by alcoholism. This is speculation, which would need to be tested by further interviewing which, at the point of writing, has not been done.

continued

However, in his current professionalism as a social worker, he prides himself on managing to overcome these feelings. He tells the story of being sent to assess a former 'scab' who was *"physically and emotionally in a pitiful state"*, offering him the choice of an alternative assessment officer, the man saying *"do your bloody job"*, him doing a properly professional job, and the man's wife ringing up Harold some time later to thank him . . . .

This is not the only difficulty Harold experiences in his current position. His emphasis on his "luck" is a means of maintaining solidarity and identity with the former mining community, many of whom are now unemployed and in what he sees as being "in a very broken state". The "jolt" of going into the mines at 16 brought him from a position of individualistic bullying into values and practices of collectivist solidarity, but he sees these collectivist practices and solidarities as being already inaccessible for his daughter's post-mining generation. He also feels the precariousness of life: at any moment he or his wife could lose their job, and against that danger he regards education as an important resource.

His present perspective of the miners collectively having been betrayed by scabs but of himself personally having been very lucky emerges from a case history in which naive confidence in solidarities (family solidarity broken by his mother's death and his father's depression; community solidarity broken by the scabs within the community) is replaced by a more conscious realism.'

The above extract of a case-history analysis may suggest something of how such a narrative can be written which answers the TQ: *how has the current perspective emerged from the life-history of the individual?*[25]

Microanalysis of Selected Text Segments: Part–whole Analysis

The other method of exploring the relation of lived life to told story is that of doing a very close-up and detailed study of very small segments of text which seem particularly puzzling and/or potentially revealing. This is called the microanalysis of verbatim transcripts.

I have already discussed the practice of 'detailed analysis' of small segments of the BDC and small segments of the TSS, and their importance in promoting understanding of the lived life and of the told story. These detailed analyses were not performed on the transcript, however, but on the intermediary TSS and BDC documents. The detailed analysis called 'microanalysis' within the BNIM tradition is similarly detailed, but performed on the verbatim transcript, helped if necessary by fieldnotes and by an audio-tape copy of the original interview.

BNIM Microanalysis – Example

The principle of BNIM microanalysis is that of breaking up the verbatim text of the interview into *very small chunks* (datum bits) and performing the same activity of multiplying (then verifying) hypotheses about who is speaking, what they are

---

25 Other examples can be found in the *Sostris Working Papers*, numbers 2–8.

experiencing, and what will happen next in the interview if the hypotheses are true. It is the principle of grounded theorizing as outlined in respect of 'events in the life' (BDC) but now deployed in respect of 'events in the interview interaction' (such as change of speaker, topic, textsort, but including the prediction of the next few words).

The point, as always, is to illuminate the significance of the speaker's choice to continue his account in the way that he or she did, by exploring how other alternatives were not chosen.

I hope the partial and simplified record of a microanalysis shown in Figure 12.31 suggests the basic principles of the procedure. I have not attempted to show how contextual knowledge might be brought to bear – for example, the importance of gender roles in most mining families; the complex love-hate relations with which mining work is often regarded by those involved at the coalface – but merely to indicate the bare bones of the operation.

Scheff and Others' Principles of Close Text-analysis

In qualitative research today, close textual analysis is a practice with a very large number of procedures, all of which may produce valuable insights. It would be impossible to do more than give the barest indication in this text. I shall mention only a bare handful that have been of key interest for me.

A most detailed analysis of small text segments is that engaged in by psychiatrists and psychotherapists of therapeutic interaction. There are two lines of work that can be mentioned. The first is that of a psychiatric session which was originally made available on an LP (long-playing record) by Gill et al. (1954) who analysed it first. It was then subject to an expanded analysis by Pittenger et al. (1960) in their *First Five Minutes of a Psychiatric Interview*, an analysis which itself was criticized and taken further by Scheff (1997). The other major line of work of text-analysis is that of Labov and Fanshell (1977) which pays particular attention to intonation and the speech-act.

A semiotic approach to the study of narrative texts, integrating also the support of 'critical linguistics' (e.g. Hodge and Kress, 1979; Fairclough, 1989) has been developed by Martin (1997). A segment of Harold's transcript is dealt with in detail according to Martin's protocols of Critical Linguistics/Semiotics below in Appendix B.

The justification for such attempts to use the 'smallest things' to illuminate the 'largest issues' has been very well put by Scheff in his argument, which is very similar to the practice of the BNIM microanalysis, for parts–whole analysis (1997).

> 'Verbatim excerpts from discourse, one might argue, are *microcosms*, they contain within them, brief as they may be, intimations of the participants' origins in and relations to the institutions of the host society.' (Scheff, 1997: 48, italics added)

From Case-history and Microanalysis towards 'A Structure for the Case'

After a narrative representation of the case-history has been presented (as in Figure 12.30) and, where useful, microanalyses to test and refine hypotheses have been undertaken – using the audio-tape record where appropriate – it is then possible to move onto the final stage of the biographic-interpretive method of

Datum	Experiencing?	Prediction of (Type of) Next Words in Text	Effect on Hypotheses of Later Data
Datum 1 ... my dad worked in the mines	1.1. Pride 1.2. Concern for accuracy 1.3. Interest in Dad's subjective experience	FH1.1.1. and he did very well FH1.2.1. precise time period FH1.3.1. and he disliked it intensely	Strengthened by Datum 2
Datum 2 for, oh since he was 14 years of age	2.1. Concern for time-accuracy, embarrassment about approximation 2.2. Pride in length of time worked	FH2.1.1. I'm sorry I can't be more precise FH2.2.1. and he was very proud of this long record	Not supported by Datum 3
Datum 3 and he took early retirement	3.1. Not concerned with father's experience before early retirement 3.2. Concerned with father's subjective experience	FH3.1.1. and I was pleased by that because he had more time to spend on me FH3.1.2. but I hardly noticed because I.... FH3.2.1. and he was very happy at being able to retire early	Not supported by Datum 4 Not supported by Datum 4
Datum 4 or it was sickness	4.1. Frustrated concern for historical accuracy about real causes	FH4.1.1. No, I remember now, what it was that ...	Possibly supported by Datum 5
Datum 5 due to the death of – er	5.1. Concern for correct explanations 5.2. Unclear about causes and effects 5.3. Not clear how to 'name' to the stranger-interviewer the person who died	FH5.1.1. Will identify death and explain that FH5.1.2. Will explain how the death produced the sickness which produced the early retirement FH5.2.1. Will not attempt to clarify causal chain FH5.3.1. Will give a status-name, and not the family name	Supported by Datum 6

continued

Figure 12.31   continued

	5.4. Would be upset to give a familiar name to person who died	*FH5.4.1.* Will give a status-name, and not the family name*	Supported by Datum 6
Datum 6 of er our mother	6.1. Experiencing upset about death of mother	*FH6.1.1.* Will move to talk about something else *FH6.1.2.* Will interrupt narration about father to talk extensively about the mother	Supported by Data 7 and 8 Not supported by datum 7
Datum 7 and he really took	7.1. Concern for father's experience	*FH7.1.1....* and he really took it hard	Not supported by Datum 8
Datum 8 control of the family kind of thing	8.1. Concern for the family members in danger of lack of control 8.2. Speaker remembering some negativity – talks of 'taking control' not 'taking care'	*FH8.1.1.* and he made sure that we were all right and didn't go off the rails *FH8.2.1.* and we were difficult to control *FH8.2.2.* and he was a bit heavy-handed	

* Notice that the same following hypothesis (which is confirmed) can be explained by different experiential-hypotheses in the previous column. Similarly, the same experience might give rise to quite different next words. The relation between experiential and following hypotheses is hardly ever one-to-one.

FIGURE 12.31   **Record of a Microanalysis Segment**

analysing narrative interviews, namely that of finding *a non-narrative* representation of the structure of the case. It is to this that I now turn.

Breckner summarizes this final, fifth, stage of BNIM analysis[26] as follows:

> '... finally, based on the results of the previous four steps, a discussion of the inter-relations between the life history and the life story, contrasting the two, aims at formulating a structural hypothesis about *the principle of connection* between the lived life and the told story. This is known as "identifying the case structure".' (1998: 92, modified).

---

26 This does not mean that you cannot have conjectures about the structure of the case earlier in the research; just that this is the best moment to focus upon this aspect of the project, the answering of the CRQ.

Note that this is an attempt at formulating '*a principle of connection*' that makes sense of the *actual* connections you first drew in narrative form in the BNIM case history. By the time you have managed to get the best version of that case history clear, and have tested and possibly rectified your account by a microanalysis, you may have already had a notion of some such principle of connection itself. If not, this is the moment to do so.

Or rather, to *try your hand at doing so*. I think that there are good reasons to think that it is worth trying to see if you can detect such a principle governing the person's entire life; but there are good reasons to think that it may be quite rare that such a principle exists. Given the enormous part played by accident and chance and contingencies in most people's mostly disrupted lives, at the time of writing this, I am personally doubtful that such 'general principles of structural connection' can be derived for most people's lives. So, provided you have attempted to give a reasonable account at stage 3 of the relation between the evolution of the lived life and the perspectives likely to be held at different phases of that life and expressed in told stories, don't worry if your attempt at describing the case structure does not succeed. You will certainly learn by trying.

There are no rules for producing such an account; you have to look at various attempts to produce them. A good source of interesting attempts can be found in *Sostris Working Paper no. 4, Ethnic Minorities and Migrants* (1999). Below are two extracts from the report on ethnic minorities and migrants in Spain from that source, researched and written by Tejero and Torrabadella. The person in question is a thirty-year-old Peruvian woman who left her children in Peru and currently is living and working illegally in Barcelona (as a live-in carer for a Spanish woman with a chronic disease) while trying to regularize her situation. The first extract is that of the researchers providing three hypotheses for how the woman, Monica, might present herself; the second extract is the start of their discussion of the actual case structure.

'Assumptions for a thematic field analysis

- Monica could present herself mainly as a bad mother and wife as a result of the separation from her children through migration. Arguments and self-evaluations would be the most dominant type of text. The use of the first person could indicate that she blames herself for family problems. The topics constituting this thematic field could therefore be placed around the constellation of "me" in relation to the "family".

- "We poor Peruvians as victims of circumstances": no possibility of choice and therefore a resigned attitude. Topics: misery, poverty – of the family but in the broader context of the country (mainly narrative using epic narratives and reports) – and the migration process seen under the "sign" of injustice (use of argumentation).

- "Me as a fighter for my children and the future of the family": non-resigned attitude towards poverty and clear aspirations to improve life conditions. The topics would focus on family values and on her responsibilities towards children and parents. Her migration would be presented as the only possible option for escaping from misery and having an opportunity of social improvement. A combination of narrative and argument would be the most typical text.'

These were some logical possibilities, what did the data suggest?

> '*Case structure*
>
> The experience of migration in Monica's case structures her strategy of "fighting": but it must be regarded as a consequence of a conflictive and key situation which has its origins in the establishment of her family. In other words, **the problem of the case** is the ambivalence or contradiction that she experiences between her understanding of what a mother's role is or should be – that is, a loving mother who does not separate from her children – and her decision to migrate in order to earn enough money to improve her family's living conditions and escape from poverty. **Her response** to this problem is to prioritize the economic and material aspect of her responsibility as a mother against the emotional/cultural aspect of motherhood and, in so doing, she pays a high price. That is the reason for which she migrated, and, despite having gone through much hardship, she still considers it a good decision, because she is success-fully coping with the charges imposed by herself. **Her perception of the problem** is related to her own feeling of failure for having married too young. It is from this moment on, that she considers all her problems arose. Underlying her perception of this problem we find a subtle but clear complaint about her husband, in the sense that he has not been able to fulfill the duties of the male role as breadwinner from the beginning. In the end, she has assumed the breadwinner role, whilst her husband has not assumed the mother/caring role. It is an unresolved conflict which makes her feel uneasy and guilty regarding the abandonment of her children. Her feelings of guilt are sharpened by the psychological problems of her oldest son ....' (Tejero and Torrabadella, 1999a: 72–3 modified.)

You may wish to notice the concepts in bold face in the above extract. Notions of 'the problem of the case', the 'her response' and 'her perception of the problem' are key concepts for articulating the understanding of the case that the case-researchers have come to.[27] This conceptual framework (theory-language) represents one way in which descriptions of case structures can, in general, be organized.

Note the distinction between the 'problem of the case' as understood by the researcher, and the researcher's account of 'the subject's perception of their prob-lems' (as reconstructed from the told story and the case history).

Representations of 'the structure of the case' can also be in the form of diagrams. Figure 12.32 is an example of a draft of a diagram for Harold. This functions as a visual summary for a narrative that can be read by going down each of the columns.

I have now concluded our exposition of the five stages of the biographic-interpretive method of analysing the results of biographic-narrative interviews. It has been a lengthy one. It has, I hope, shown the stages which you must go through if you wish to eventually answer the original BNIM CRQ, namely 'What is the structure of the case?'

---

27 Compare the TQs suggested earlier (p. 87) about perceptions of reality and incorrect perceptions of reality.

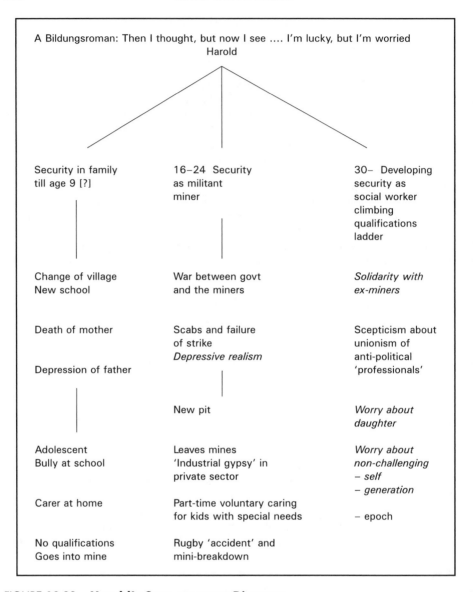

A Bildungsroman: Then I thought, but now I see .... I'm lucky, but I'm worried
Harold

Security in family till age 9 [?]	16–24 Security as militant miner	30– Developing security as social worker climbing qualifications ladder
Change of village New school	War between govt and the miners	*Solidarity with ex-miners*
Death of mother	Scabs and failure of strike *Depressive realism*	Scepticism about unionism of anti-political 'professionals'
Depression of father		
	New pit	*Worry about daughter*
Adolescent Bully at school	Leaves mines 'Industrial gypsy' in private sector	*Worry about non-challenging – self – generation*
Carer at home	Part-time voluntary caring for kids with special needs	*– epoch*
No qualifications Goes into mine	Rugby 'accident' and mini-breakdown	

FIGURE 12.32   **Harold's Case-structure Diagram**

The scope of the method of BNIM analysing stops at this point. After such an analysis has been attempted, many questions may arise which require further documentary, interview or other evidence. Even after many possible interpretations of the case are sufficiently excluded by the balance of the evidence and the argument, that may still leave a number of interpretations none of which have a decisive evidence-and-argument lead over all the others. Such indeterminacy of outcome should not be concealed but rather highlighted (and difficult data and questions stressed) in order that further research can be soundly designed and further thinking developed.

Two Theory-Questions	TQ1: 'What is the structure of the lived life?'
	TQ2: 'What is the structure of the told story?'
Third Theory-Question	TQ3: 'What is the connection between the development of the lived life and the emergence of the story as told from the interviewee's present perspective?'
The Central Research Question	CRQ: 'What is the structure of the case?'

FIGURE 12.33   **Revised CRQ–TQ for SQUIN–BNIM**

If, however, I assume that I have arrived at the best version of the case-history and/or case-structure that I can at a given moment achieve, this then – together with earlier materials and analysis – provides an answer to the CRQ with which I started off.

The third theory-question which appears in Figure 12.33 'understands' the significance of the 'told story' (the interview as a whole) by placing it within the unfinished evolution of the individual in question. In its own way, it sees the 'interview interaction as event' within a historical context of the person's life, in the way suggested by the Briggs–Wengraf anthropological-historical model. 'Given the life that X led, how come X got to tell her life-story that day in the way she did?' is one way of putting the third theory-question. Alternatively, 'Given the way she told her life-story that day to me, what do I learn from it about the life she led?' is another way.

These stages involve an understanding of the conceptual framework in which the CRQ was posed, the specification of the type of (three) interviewing sessions needed to produce the relevant material, the implications of the instrumentation theory that governed both the designing of the sessions and the questioning of the interview materials gained, and the procedure of moving in steps from the original audio-tapes and session-notes through transcripts, BDC and TSS, BDA and TFA, through microanalysis towards the attempt to construct a case-history and produce a verbal summary in the formulation of a representation of 'the structure of the case'.

Your own research purposes may call for some or all of the components of this complex methodology. Or they may use none of them. Even if the latter is true, your own different methodology – based on existing practices but also possibly innovating carefully – will need, if it is not to appear to be arbitrary and unconvincing, to have its own protocols of theorized good practice.

What can usefully be done with the results of such an analysis, beyond its value in understanding one particular individual?

TOWARDS THEORIZING THE CASE LIFE-HISTORY AND STRUCTURE IN THE LIGHT OF YOUR RESEARCH PROBLEMATIC (RP–CRQ–TQ)

Up to this point, there has been a strong – if slightly reducing – control by the procedures of the BNIM methodology on the speculations and interpretations of the researcher and his or her panel.

It should be clear that the production of the BDC and the TSS leave, in principle, relatively little to the variability of the researcher, except for the degree of detail chosen by the broadbrush and finebrush choices (pp. 245–51). The analysis of those two documents, and their elaboration by the panel into a particular BDA and a particular TFA, is rather more dependent upon the experience and the imagination of the particular panel chosen; that is why it is useful to have a comparatively large panel and one including both people psychologically and culturally similar to the case being studied and others who are as different as possible. Finally, the construction of a principle of connection between the lived life and the told story is always an uncertain task, but one where individual idiosyncrasy is subject to challenge by the panel and by fellow researchers with access to the raw data and the BDA/TSS processed-data documentation.

These limited versions of the intrinsic CRQ–TQ structure, and therefore of the intrinsic ATQ–ACRQ structure, do not exhaust the value of the materials and the understandings developed in the five steps of the SQUIN–BNIM method. Only if your overall research CRQ was that of asking for the BNIM case-history or case-structure will it be sufficient just to produce versions of these.

It is much more likely that you have your own Project CRQ around questions of social context or cultural meaning systems or psychological responses, some other key conceptual terms and the theory-language in which they are embedded (as did Sostris looking at individual and societal strategies across European societies). You may wish at this point to remind yourself of Figure 6.10, p. 151 where BNIM is based firmly within projects deploying other methods of data collection and analysis.

In order to provide material for the particular debate of the research community of which you are a part and to whom you wish to address a particular report, if you have such further theory-questions, you will have to do *further work* to interpret the significance of the outcomes of the BNIM-analysis.

You may be interested in the types of coping strategies developed within a particular societal or subcultural context; you may be interested in the historical changes of certain institutional arrangements and certain dominant meaning systems over a generation; you may be interested in interviewee's responses to certain stresses and certain anxieties, etc.

Your more general Project CRQ–TQ structure will determine the use to which you put all or part of the knowledge developed by the completed and sometimes the incompleted (e.g. King, 2000) five steps of the BNIM methodology.

Clearly, this guide cannot hope to address this problem fully, though I hope that the discussion of research method in Part I and the overall

CRQ–TQs–IIs /// IM–ATQs–ACRQ

model provides a space for thinking it through carefully.

However, in Part V, before Part VI on writing-up and representation, I shall consider the implications of comparative work for moving beyond the deep degree of historical particularity which depth-interviewing seems to produce and for the ways in which general theorizing and understanding is implicated in such particular accounts.

V

COMPARISON OF CASES: FROM CONTINGENCIES OF CASES TO TYPES OF TYPOLOGIES[1]

1 This section is a modified version of part of my chapter in Chamberlayne et al. (2000).

13

Resources for Typification and General-Models *Within* Single-Case Research

How do we understand cases, how do we compare them, and how are they related to general models in social science research?

Each of your informants has provided you with case-material. This case-material may either be about themselves as a 'case', or the 'cases' to which the material is related may be that of a 'whole family', of 'a whole family over several generations', a 'developing collective experience' or of some other unit of analysis of which you are collecting cases (Ragin and Becker, 1992).

Conventionally, the processes of comparative interpretation are supposed to start from scratch after the description and analyses of all the cases has been done (Wolcott, 1994; Wengraf, 1998). I argue, however, that it is, luckily, impossible to produce a report on a particular case – or to read such a report – without implicitly comparing other possible and actual cases and without certain universal concepts for describing and understanding cases being more or less strongly implied by the text and by the act of reading.

If this can be shown, then there is no *logical jump or discontinuity* involved in moving from single-case to multiple-case analysis. Neither is there a particular difficulty in moving from the particularities of a single case to general concepts suitable for comparative work and for generalization, since some general concepts were already employed to evoke and make sense of the particular case.

Let us look at the 'constant comparative method' as developed by Glaser and Strauss (1968; see also Strauss, 1987).[2] This involves two stages: first, the multiplication of hypotheses around any given datum until the imagination and knowledge of the researchers is exhausted; second, the consideration as to whether the next datum being examined enables any of the previous hypotheses to be eliminated. Strauss (1987) gives useful examples and Bertaux and Delcroix (2000: 87) in a footnote evoke the application of this 'guessing game' in a classroom situation.

In BNIM, this two-stage procedure is, as we saw, applied twice: (i) to the sequence of events in the lived life, and (ii) to the sequence of narrative expression,

---

2 The history of the 'grounded theory movement' cannot be considered here. See Strauss and Corbin (1994) for a disguised polemic from one (dominant) side; Glaser (1992) for an overt polemic from the (not so dominant) other.

the story as told within the interview text. The procedure was represented by Figure 12.15 (p. 257).

MULTIPLYING CONTINGENCIES FOR CASES, MULTIPLYING TYPES FOR TYPOLOGIES

Figure 13.1 shows an unpublished extract from a case-report by Astrid Segert and Irene Zierke (see their chapter in Chamberlayne et al., 2000) on an East German, 'Sophie', for which I have suggested some of the implicit comparative questions that can arise when reading it and some of the universal concepts in terms of which the description of the single case is couched.

1   The first column contains the propositions of the case report.
2   The second has to do with comparative questions that prod one to think 'What might have happened to Sophie – or to someone in some respects like Sophie – if … ?'
3   The third column identifies organizing general concepts more or less strongly implied in the case report discourse, general concepts which are necessarily available for describing all other cases.

To some of the comparative questions, the researcher-writer or the reader may have definite and well-grounded answers. However, particularly if he or she does not yet know much about East Germany and its history, the chances are that other answers may be tentative, and that to many of the questions one can only respond – like any researcher in a new field at the beginning of a research project – 'I must find out more'. Also implicit in the case-description are universal concepts being applied. Within the text, there are presumed theories of child and personal development, of family/non-family relations, of types of society and types of family and types of societal regime operating. Of any or all of these, the researcher may ask: how well-grounded are they? Again – research may be needed.

I wish to stress here that, when I suggest possible 'later particular occurrences' in the case of a particular individual, I am very close to suggesting possible *later types of occurrence* in a *typology of classes of individuals*.[3]

For example, taking an imaginary case, 'Raymond', I suggest that the biographical datum of a divorce from Mary might be followed by an affair with Suzie or by an intensification of an old friendship with Clement. This is very close to suggesting a generalization that, for some men, the breakdown of a marital relationship may be followed by the development of a new sexual relationship or by the development of an old non-sexual relationship. The 'later occurrence' diagram of branching possibilities is the same: the difference is that the names on the branches are 'abstract' rather than 'proper' names.

The closeness between multiplying *particular alternatives for particular people* and multiplying *typical alternatives for typical people* might be even greater. It may be that it was our general sense that came first. I suggest that I already have a

---

3 The same is true in relation to texts, societal contexts, told stories, subjectivities. The reader may wish to pursue this argument which I have not space to develop here.

Case report	Comparative questions to help think about the focal, and possibly other, cases	Some organizing universal societal concepts implied in the case report extract
Born at the beginning of the 1950s, she's twice married and has a son	Cohort experience of current 50-year-olds in East Germany; twice-married, why; and what are the implications of having a son (of what age?)	Birth Marriage Children – sons and non-sons
She comes from a vicar's family who experienced the political repression of both the fascist and the GDR period	What about vicars' families who don't have that experience? What is the significance of having that experience? What about those who have the experience of repression but come from non-vicar's families? What happened in that part of Germany during the fascist period? What happened during the GDR period? What is meant by repression in the two contexts?	Family of origin – types of families Father's? occupation Periods of history/types of society Repression and its absence – political and other repressions 'Non-repression' – how do you identify when it exists, in respect of what, and for whom
Belonging to a politically marginalized church, the family lived in modest circumstances	What is the significance of 'non-modest circumstances'? Were there vicar's families who lived in better/worse circumstances? What might be the different effects?	Churches Organizations – marginalized or not Circumstances – better than/worse than/modest
They preserved their high education standards, cultural values and close social connections to like-minded others	In a different location or situation, or even in the same one, similar families might not have been able to achieve such 'preservation', or at least not all of them. Implications of different patterns of non-preservation?	Family culture preserved or not Education standards – high/medium/low Cultural values – variable Social connections to like-minded and other-than-like-minded – close/distant

FIGURE 13.1 Implicit Comparisons and Universal Concepts in Sophie's Case Report

complex, many-branching, usually not very coherent, tacit typology of agents and actions and situations in my head *before* I start to make sense of a new particular case, and I use those typifications to make sense of the new particular case by applying it to the unique particular life-world of the particular person, their *idioverse*.[4] This tacit, usually not very coherent typology, like the organizing universal concepts implied in particular case descriptions, help to make up mental models that are implicit resources available for subsequent explicit comparison between cases.

If the actual sequence of agents and actions in this new particular life-world requires us to rethink our pre-existing sense of personal and historical possibilities and probabilities, then new cases are interesting to the extent that they force our previous mental models (Senge, 1990, ch. 10) into consciousness and then force us to revise and improve them.

If I take the case of Sophie, she comes from a vicar's family who experienced the political repression of both the fascist and the GDR period in East Germany. My speculations about what possible 'shapings of the biographic life experience' might be true for Sophie might include predictions that repression would demoralize the family of origin and turn her into a cynical opportunist. In terms of the 'later occurrence diagram' (Figure 12.15), this might be a dotted line hypothesis. The last cited item in the extract from the case report indicates that this hypothesis was *not* borne out in Sophie's case: the family preserved their high education standards, cultural values and close social connections to like-minded others. *Refuted for Sophie, this hypothesis remains as a potential line of development for cases other than Sophie's* that might have been analysed already or might be considered later on. Every later-occurrence hypothesis suggests a 'type of outcome' that might not be true in the case under consideration but might be true of some other case. Alternative 'particular later occurrences' suggest types of occurrence in an implicit typology that can be made explicit and thus function as a first resource for *explicit* comparative understanding.

In Wengraf (2000a), I argued that there is a connection between the implicit four components involved in the understanding of any particular biographical case – the history of the lived life and the text of the told story, the evolving context and the inferred subjectivity of the interviewee – and that these often implicit components – together with the subjectivity of the researcher – are best made explicit. This argument – which cannot be further explicated here – is summarized in the 'diamond model' shown in Figure 13.2.

DIFFERENCES/TYPOLOGIES BETWEEN THE PARTICULAR AND THE GENERAL

Typologies – implicit or explicit – lie between the general and the particular: they can be regarded as the formalization of real and imagined historical difference. I would argue that one can think more clearly if no hard epistemological line is drawn between descriptions of difference and typologies of difference, since none

---

4 A parallel argument holds true about imagining different ways of analysing the interview narration – at each point in the text (sequence) a different topic/treatment might be chosen by the speaker, and what implications might be drawn from such patterns of recurrent choices?

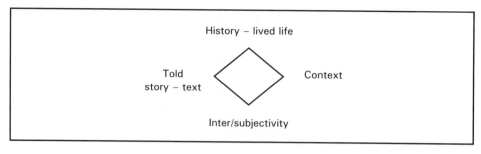

FIGURE 13.2   **The Four Implicit Components of Biographical Research – Diamond Model**

is justified. However, in any particular research process the typologies will be seen in different ways.

- Seen from 'above', from the point of view of the general and abstract orienting concepts, ideal types or typologies[5] function as *specifications of the general concepts* in their *movement downwards towards the particular*.
- However, from the point of view of the particular case descriptions, such ideal types or typologies function as *generalizations from particular cases* in their *movement upwards towards the more general*.

How can we summarize the relation between the particular and the general, and the relation between multiple possible occurrences and multiple possible types?

As regards the 'diamond' model of the four necessary components of biographical research, I argue that, even if only one component was the focus of the research effort, all the other three were implicit and should be consciously attended to. The same argument of mutual implicature can be found in Figure 1.4 (p. 14) relating discourse, inter/subjectivity and objective referents.

At the level of case description, each of the components needed to be addressed and related to each other: history – lived-life, told-story, subjectivity and context, *all of one particular person*. The model of a particular case involves (a) describing each of the four components and (b) relating them to each other in the way that they are specified for that person, at that time, producing that story, from their lived life in that context in that epoch. Each of the four components needs to be described *separately* in individually particular ways ('thick description', Geertz, 1973). In addition, how they are supposed to have *interacted* to produce the biography in the particular case must also be described in the same way.

Spradley distinguishes (1979: 210) six levels of proposition that can be found in an ethnographic text. This six-level, two column model is shown in Figure 13.8. The '4-components-interacting' particular description operates at the level of

---

5 I cannot here explore the distinction between 'collections of types' and 'typologies'. See Max Weber (1949) and Gerth and Mills (1948: 59–61) for discussion. The orientation to delivering understanding of particular historical cases is suggested by Weber's assertion that 'the goal of ideal-typical concept-construction is always to make clearly explicit not the class or average character but rather the unique individual character …' (Weber, 1949: 101, cited Mommsen, 1974: 10).

Particular model or specific case-account at level 6 or near	Each of the four components separately
	+ interaction between components

FIGURE 13.3 **The Four Components at Case-description Level (Spradley Level 6)**

concrete particulars with Spradley level-6 statements. This is summarized in Figure 13.3 about what will be found in any case-report, or model of a particular (BNIM) case, such as Sophie's excerpted above:

However, inherent in any *particular description* are *general models* of each component and their relationships.

- To have made any particular statement about Sophie's subjectivity in telling the story, I have to have had a general model of 'subjectivities in general and their possible relations to the other three components'.
- To give a particular account of evolution of the societal-historical context of Germany from, say, 1939–98, I have to have had a general model of 'societal-historical contexts and their possible relations to the other three components'; etc.

Such implicit or explicit 'four components interacting' general models of subjectivity, text, context, history are Spradley level-1 models. The third column of Figure 13.1 indicated a list of some of these.

My argument is that to describe any or all of the four components that are to be found interacting in any *particular* historical case (Spradley level 6), the researcher is obliged to be using implicit *general* models at or closer to Spradley level 1. *Without general concepts/models* of subjectivity, of context, of lived lives, of told stories, and of the possible interaction of such components, no *accounts of particular instances* could be generated. This homology is shown in Figure 13.4.

The model needs to be enriched still further. Returning to the middle zone of my modified version of Spradley, between the general and the particular lie multiple indications of difference in zones 2–5: there are contingent statements close to level 6 and relatively formalized typologies close to level 1. In this intermediate zone, too, the four components – lived life, told story, context, subjectivity – and their relations remain mutually implied to some extent or explicitly spelled out. As I have argued earlier, the description of multiple possible contingencies (as in the later-occurrence hypothesizing) is directly related to implied multiple typologizing. Statements of 'type' differences are higher in the level of abstraction than statements of 'occurrence' or contingency differences, as is suggested by Figure 13.5.

Summarizing, my argument has been, first, that the four components of the diamond model are *horizontally implicated* with each other at each level. Second, that any account of any and all of the components at the level of case description involves a model of the most general sort; consequently, there is a line of *vertical mutual implication* as well. Third, that there is no hard epistemological line but rather a spectrum between level 1 (universal) and level 6 (specific particularity).

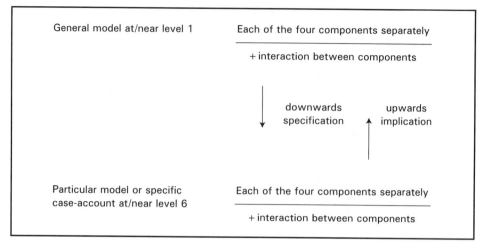

FIGURE 13.4   **The Four Interacting Components at Two Spradley Levels**

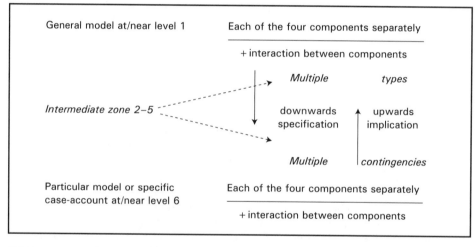

FIGURE 13.5   **The Four Interacting Components at the Six Spradley Levels**

I wish to address one further point, before considering types of typologies. The resources of conceptualized knowledge with which the multiple contingencies of later occurrences were developed in the analysis of sequences of life and sequences of text in a single case imply resources of generality and of typification that need to be made explicit and thus liable to correction and improvement. Such resources of generality and typification, as operating in the analysis of one/the first case, have the great advantage that they are part of the 'system of relevancy and thinking' of the researcher doing the work of case-description at level 6.

However confused and incoherent the cultural common-sense (Gramsci, 1971: 323–5) of the researcher may be from which these resources have been taken, emerging from his or her own individual and professional biography, the selection and utilization of such resources of generality and typification by the researcher in his or her case-description means that they are the raw materials from which *that researcher* can best develop a clearer and more coherent set of interlocking general models and particular descriptions. The stages, the necessity and difficulty of that iterative struggle are brought out by Cooper (2000). Just as the uninterrupted narrative interview enables the 'system of relevancy' of the *interviewee* to be expressed and understood, so the multiple later-occurrence arguments and descriptions of the researcher enable the *researcher's 'systems of relevancy'* to be expressed, but also improved.

14

Types of Typologies

A TYPOLOGY OF TYPOLOGIES

If typologies either determine or exist virtually within descriptions of real or imagined contingent historical differences, and if they depend upon and feed general concepts at Spradley level 1, can I develop a typology of typologies? Layder (1998) has argued strongly and persuasively for the need to develop typologies and for distinguishing between typologies of action (behaviour) and typologies of system (structure).

Typologies of Behaviour, Typologies of System

'*Action or behavioural typologies* restrict themselves largely to the depiction of lifeworld elements of society concerning subjective meaning, lived experience, motivations, attitudes and so on. The importance of *system or structural typologies* is that they concern themselves with depicting the settings and contexts of behaviour and thus provide the necessary requirements for more inclusive and powerful explanations of social life .... It is also crucial to emphasize the important role that structural or system typologies may play in research; otherwise, their influence on the behaviour or people in question will be vague and partial, or treated as an implicit, inchoate backdrop to the analysis ....' (Layder, 1998: 74–5)

Given that those drawn to biographical-interview-based research are likely to be spontaneously oriented towards action-alternatives or subjectivity-alternatives, Scheff and Layard's insistence on the importance of *context-alternatives* is salutary. Socio-biographical work such as those developed in Sostris develops our 'sense of socio-historical contexts' (Chamberlayne and Spano, 2000; Rustin, 2000; Sostris case study materials, *Working Papers* nos 2–7, 1998–99) and these lay the ground – as I have argued above – for richer typologies of context.

Other Distinctions

Three more distinctions perhaps need to be made to enrich Layder's model, an alternative to the 'diamond' model presented earlier.

1 *Individual actor characterized by states of inter/subjectivity.* First, since our concern here is with biographic research in the social sciences, I think it

important to distinguish the level of the biological 'individual'. Obviously, it would be possible to treat the individual subject as a particular type of 'system' contextualizing the text, but for convenience I think it useful to distinguish the individual actor from other features of context. By referring to 'inter/subjectivity' I am suggesting that expressions and indications of subjectivity by an individual need to be understood as part of an 'intersubjective field'.

2 *Synchronic and diachronic typologies*. Second, in addition to this important distinction, I think it necessary to add another: that between relatively *synchronic* typologies – where the typology is of different actions or systems treated in an ahistorical fashion – and relatively *diachronic* typologies – where the typology is of the historical development of a sequence of actions (like a history of community, family, or individual actions) or of the historical development of a system or structure of greater or lesser scope. A typology of BNIM case-histories would be a diachronic typology; a typology of BNIM case-structures only a synchronic one.

3 *The interview text (especially the told story) as an inter/active production*. Third, it is perhaps important to identify the 'told story' text – or even the whole of the interview text – as a distinct object for theorizing.

The net effect of these distinctions is to yield the table shown in Figure 14.1.

My argument about biographizing would be that particular accounts, typologies and general models of a synchronic nature (column 1) should always serve and lead towards accounts, typologies and generalities of a diachronic nature (column 2).

That which can be typologized (theorized)	The temporal dimension of the typology (theory)	
	Synchronic at a given 'moment'	Diachronic over a sequence of historical 'moments'
(Interview) textual product (e.g. told story)	I	V
Individual – subjectivity	II	VI
Action – behavioural	III	VII
System – structural	IV	VIII

FIGURE 14.1   **Textual, Individual, Action and System Typologies – Eight-fold Table**

CONCLUSION

I have tried to show that, in order to understand an interview text, one has to do, but go beyond, an analysis of the text itself. Naive or sophisticated recycling does not produce understanding. I have put forward a diamond model of the four interacting components of understanding.

I have tried to show that within particular accounts of real and imagined historical differences of action, context and so forth, there exist virtual types, typologies and orienting concepts (Layder) which are resources for understanding the particular cases and all other cases: these are generated in the dialogue between the interviewee's self-expression and the researcher's frame of reference.

VI

WRITING UP: STRATEGIES
OF RE/PRESENTATION

INTRODUCTION

In Part V, I tried to show how any account of any particular case can be given only by means of the use of abstractions within that general model (conceptual framework) which had allowed and helped constitute the account of particularity that was just given. I tried to show how we are usually relatively unconscious of these implicit and embedded higher-order abstractions that organize and permit our particular accounts, but that these can be made explicit and well-organized into typologies relatively rapidly once we switch our attention to them.

In Part VI, I now go on to discuss the application of this account of the relationships between the abstract and the concrete to your task of 'writing up', of producing a text for your readership or audience. Just as Part II focused on designing the research *inquiry* process, so Part VI focuses on designing the research *presentation/representation* process. In the case of putting together the design components of presentation/representation, the function to be fulfilled is that of *facilitating the reader's understanding*. This concept needs to be spelled out and I shall argue for the importance of working with two distinct modes of cognition and therefore of presentation.

I shall also argue for a framework or strategy of re/presentation which clearly distinguishes the 'voices' engaged in the dialogues that have produced the sometimes unanimous, more often contested, and invariably arguable understandings embedded in your 'findings'.[1] This 'voice-conscious' (see Wertsch, 1990, 1991; Hymes, 1996; Ribbens and Edwards, 1998) strategy is a zig-zagging one.

Although limitations of space mean that these questions of re/presentation can only be briefly addressed, I hope that the chapter provides you with a range of examples and a conceptual framework that will help you analyse, use and invent textual strategies of writing up most appropriate for your purposes and your readerships.

---

1 Which Hammersley (1990) relabels as 'knowledge-claims' in order precisely to stress and invite the conversation of contestation.

15

Conceptual Frameworks for Studying
and Re/presenting

Since we wish to 'write up' our research so that the reader 'understands' our argument and our findings, I need to address the concept of 'understanding' and how it may be fostered.

THE PROBLEM: HOW IS UNDERSTANDING HELD, CONVEYED, AND CONTESTED?

One argument has been that the researcher starts (reluctantly or enthusiastically) from the idiographic (specimen) case-study and moves 'with all due dispatch' to nomothetic general theorzing. This is a *direction-of-progression* in grounded theory (Carney, 1994 for a ladder of analytical abstraction). The idiographic detail about cases becomes less relevant once the achieved (grounded) transcendence of the myriad of details has been achieved, and the theorization has been formulated. The rocket of theory has taken off, don't worry about the now-discardable myriad of fuel-facts that were used to power it.

A strong counter-argument is that, as far as applicable knowledge is concerned, the important feature of any body of general knowledge (theory) is that it can be applied to a particular case, a form of anthropological or sociological clinical understanding. The movement is from applying generalities to the understanding of particular cases.[2] The myriad facts of particular cases need to be preserved and not discarded: the reader must be presented with some representation of the myriad of details of particular cases. I shall agree with this position, but the difficulty of 'some representation' needs to be given due weight.

I shall start from a distinction between two modes of cognition and hence of understanding, by you but especially by your eventual readers.

Polkinghorne on Conveying Understanding by Bruner's Modes of 'Paradigmatic' and 'Narrative' Exposition

Polkinghorne argues (1996) that 'narrative' is the natural way in which we construe ourselves.[3] He relies on the work of Jerome Bruner, which he summarizes as follows:

---

2 Herdt and Stoller (1990) have argued eloquently and persuasively for a 'clinical anthropology'.
3 For a definition and a discussion of 'narrative', see pp. 114–16 above and Labov and Waletsky (1967).

'Bruner (1986) holds that there are two major kinds of cognitive structuring – paradigmatic and narrative.

- Paradigmatic structuring is a mode of comprehension which produces knowledge about the kind of thing something is. In the paradigmatic mode, knowledge about something involves recognition of the category or concept of which it is an instance.
- Narrative structuring produces knowledge of something by showing how it interacts with other parts in contributing to a whole. Thus narrative understanding is a type of systemic or gestalt knowledge. Its operation requires the to and fro movement from part to whole to part, described by the term *hermeneutic circle* .... While gestalt understanding of visual objects is derived from relations in space, narrative understanding concerns the temporal relations between happenings and actions in [time] ...'.

Elsewhere (Polkinghorne, 1995), he evokes the way in which narrative cognition works. Where a 'grounded theory' model might suggest a two-step movement from (first case) to (emergent abstraction-grounded theory) to (second case), Polkinghorne suggests below a single-step model moving directly from (first case) to (second and all other-cases):

'While paradigmatic knowledge is maintained in individual words that name a concept, narrative knowledge is maintained in emplotted stories. Storied memories retain the complexity of the situation in which an action was undertaken and the emotional and motivational meaning connected with it ....

Narrative cognition configures the diverse elements of a particular action into a unified whole in which each element is connected to the central purpose of the action .... Narrative cognition produces a series of anecdotal descriptions of particular incidents. Narrative reasoning does not reduce itself to rules and generalities across stories but maintains itself at the level of the specific episode. Nor does it translate its emplotted story into a step of propositions whereby its dramatic and integrative features are forfeited .... The cumulative effect of narrative reasoning is a collection of individual cases in which thought moves from case to case instead of from case to generalization.

This collection of storied experiences provides a basis for understanding new action episodes by means of analogy. The collection of stories is searched to find one that is similar in some respects to the old one. The concern is not to identify the new episode as an instance of a general type but as similar to a specific remembered episode .... The episode is noted as similar to, but not the same as the previously selected episode. Thus, the understanding of the new action can draw on previous understandings while being open to the specific and unique elements that make the new episode different from all that have gone before. The analogical understanding recognizes the improvisation and change that make up the flexible variability of human behaviour (Lave, 1988). *The more varied and extensive one's collection of storied explanatory descriptions of previous actions, the more likely that one can draw upon a similar remembered episode for an initial understanding of the new situation and the more likely that one will appreciate and search for*

continued

continued
the elements that make the new different from the remembered instance .... [Paradigmatic] analysis of narratives moves from stories to common elements, and narrative analysis moves from elements to stories'. (Polkinghorne, 1995: 11, 12, italics added)

I think this account of the difference between 'paradigmatic' and 'narrative' understanding and presentation is in general lucid and helpful. Clearly it supports the emphasis on narrative interviewing promoted elsewhere in this book.

I have three problems with it, however. I have already argued in Part V that concepts (paradigmatic knowledge) are embedded in all particular accounts. Consequently I think his implicit downgrading of 'generalization' and 'common elements' is unhelpful. Later on, I shall take issue with Polkinghorne's implied insistence that one mode of understanding should be seen as superior to another. Here I wish to make a different point.

Forms of Collection Distinguished from Forms of Presentation

It is important to distinguish between

- the form or forms of raw materials of the (BNIM or other semi-structured) interview,
  and
- the forms of the final report-production (presentation).

One can collect narrative interviews and write a theorizing report on the basis of them. One can collect theorzing, attitude-taking, argumentative interviews, and write up the report in the form of a narrative. The form of the raw material does not dictate the form of re/presentation.

Hence the table given in Figure 15.1, where the form of the raw material and the form chosen for the communication of understanding of that material are sharply differentiated. Very tentatively, I suggest that the 'shaded boxes' are perhaps the more obvious 'echo boxes' (as on p. 173). The point that needs to be made is that 'writing up', your 'strategy of re/presentation', is likely to use a *combination* of columns I *and* IIa *and* IIb.

Though you could decide to use only one method, I would counsel against it. One key reason for choosing to 'triangulate methods of communicating understanding' has to do with their different and complementary degrees of effectiveness. The same meaning when received in three different ways is more likely to be retained by the receiver than when he or she receives the meaning by a communication in only one mode.

A second point also needs to be made that will be formalized in the next section. The researcher who derives from one interview both the transcript and his or her debriefing sessions field-notes has already, in a very common-sense way, at least two 'voices' contributing to his or her understanding: namely, the interviewer and the interviewee. The more cases, the more voices. When I include the voices of previous researchers and theorists, and the voices of those whom *they* interviewed or observed, I am getting into a serious multiplicity.

Form of the *raw interview data*	Form of *knowledge-communicating report* about those raw materials		
		Gestalt configuration	
(The initials represent the DARNE categories identified on pp. 243–5)	I	IIa	IIb
	Paradigmatic propositions	In-sequence diachronic (narrated-story) gestalt	Synchronic (spatial-visual) gestalt
A/E: theorizing argumentation and value-expression/evaluation *as in an opinion or attitude survey*			
N/R: narratives, reports *as in an account of a sequence of events or historical process*			
D: descriptions *as in an ethnographic account of the patterns of habitual practice of a community or individual case*			

FIGURE 15.1 **Interview Material and Research Reporting: Narrative and Non-narrative**

If I go beyond the assumption that each person throughout their life speaks only with one voice, and allow for the person to speak with a number of voices, sometimes quite contradictory ones, then it is clear that a serious effort has to be made to allow – in the process of knowledge production, reception, and contestation – for such multiple voices and their orderly presentation.

In addition, I am also writing for my intended readership and must therefore allow for the multiplicity of voices to be heard in the process of receiving and arguing about my research contribution.

In the light of the issues raised above, in order to facilitate understanding of this complex situation, I shall put forward a conceptual framework that I hope is useful.

A POST-SPRADLEY CONCEPTUAL FRAMEWORK FOR RE/PRESENTATION

The Six-level, Two-column Grid Derived from Spradley

A Six-level Grid for Abstraction/Specificity by Type of Informant
The model (see Figure 15.2) is derived very directly from Spradley's (1979: 210). Unlike his version, however, for the reasons of respecting the plurality of voices spelled out above, I distinguish at each level two types of source, and consequently produce two columns as well as six levels. Even though Spradley himself does not

	Spradley column 1	Spradley column 2
Spradley Level	*Informant's (theory-) language*	*Researcher's theory-language*
1. Universal statements about all societies	'You can't change human nature: everybody always wants the best for their family'	'All communications are always characterized by a sensitivity to status, even if only a sensitivity to the status of sender and receiver being equal in status'
2. Sub-universal cross-cultural descriptive statements	'In underdeveloped countries, they all want to be like us'	'In all Western cultures, men and women have different styles of communication'
3. General statements about a particular society or culture group	'I can't see the point of having a phone. You have to pay for it, even if you don't use it. Besides, people can always pop round if they want to talk to you'	'In England ... in 1948, the percentage of households owning TV sets was 0.3%. By 1958, it was 52%, while the telephone, introduced in 1877 was by the same date only installed in 16.5% of houses. Dividing the distribution according to social class, the television is very evenly spread, contrasting with the telephone which clusters thickly at the top .... By 1973, the penetration rates for television were about 90% in all social classes, and for the telephone, they were about 45% overall, with 88% in classes AB, 67% in C1, 44% in C2, and 20% in D,E (Douglas and Isherwood, 1980: 99–100)'
4. General statements about one or more specific cultural scenes	'I love weekends. I always have a special meal with all the family there ... and nobody has to do any work (English child)'	'In Australian families, the housewives said the weekend was two days of freedom away from household chores .... In England, the housewife appeared to invest as much, if not more, time in housework routines and rituals ... (adapted from Lawrence, 1982: 128)'
5. Specific statements about a cultural domain	'College stinks'	'Effects of redesign on sales suggested that redesign and refurbishing can increase the number of clients and their average level of expenditure, although most clients do not identify design as a feature in their preferences for one pub or another'
6. Specific incident statements	'On Wednesday I decided that, for our new house, I would not have a dish-washer installed. I don't think he likes the idea, though, since he's the one who does the washing-up'	'At this point in the conversation, the informant seemed to get quite agitated, screwing up her face and twisting her hands several times for about a minute'

FIGURE 15.2 **Spradley Levels and Spradley Columns**

connect his distinction of 'voices' to his distinction of 'levels', I shall do so and therefore refer to 'Spradley levels' and to 'Spradley columns'.

Notice that the writing of other expert-ethnographers (or anybody else's work you read in, for example, your research literature search) will be writing at or between or across one of these levels, and that the speech not only of your own informants but those of other researchers can also be examined in this light.

Throughout your report, you will find yourself finding, quoting, making and combining sentences and phrases which are at or between these six different Spradley levels and in one or other of the two Spradley columns. The columns should help you distinguish between your experiencing, thinking, and feeling, etc. and, in the other, that of all the other expert and informant voices with which you are dealing, and the level of proposition, question, etc. being put forward.[4]

Having such a grid in your head, should help you think through the relation between informant-evidence and your expert – argument in your presentation. It should also help you to explore the relation between 'generalities' and 'particularities' in any given text, the ones you read and the ones you produce.

These Spradley levels are another – and perhaps a more 'micro' – way of 'sorting texts' from that put forward in the chapter on biographical-interpretive method, where the sorting of text-chunks was into one or other of the DARNE categories.

Different Subsections have Different Proportions of Six-levels, Two Columns

Let us now apply the above (six by two) model to the construction of *subsections of your report.*

1 Some more pure-documentation bits of your report will consist mostly of column 1 material, interviewee-propositions at levels 3, 4 and 5 maybe.
2 Bits dominated by your own theoretical arguments will have higher proportions of your propositions (column 2 material) at levels 2 and 3, supported by informant-evidence from column 1 to demonstrate their groundedness.
3 You will find that some of your raw-data column 1 quotations will come from your own informants and your own description: others will come from other people's informants and other arguments and from theories of other experts in the field (all column 1).
4 In any literature search, your sources will be almost entirely the (column 1) statements of other researchers, relieved by a touch of their quoting from their informants (column 1 again).
5 When you are writing up and arguing your 'Findings', this will be almost entirely you as researcher (column 2) citing your informants' material as column 1 evidence and dialoguing with previous or possible counter-theorists and contrary case-material (column 1) and coming to column 2 conclusions of your own, after quite a lot of zig-zagging dialogue. You will have in mind future critics and their counter-arguments and counter-hypotheses, and will have attempted to pre-empt the objections and evidence you speculate that they might bring.

---

4 Bob Miller (personal communication) has suggested a three-fold distinction of columns, in which citing the voices of 'other researchers' is differentiated out from other 'informants'. I think this is a useful subdivision of 'other voices' but I have not retained it in Figure 15.2.

These are guides about possibilities, not instructions. Consequently, the typical structure of paragraphs in sections will vary considerably, and you should make yourself pay attention to the effects upon the reader of different proportions and sequences.[5]

Zig-zagging between Columns and Across Levels

Interviews with an interviewee may fail because of a lack of empathy, or because of an excess of it. Presentations to an audience or readership may fail for the same reasons. You have to cultivate a judicious mixture of 'empathy with objectivity'.

Keep the Languages Separate and Non-homogenized!

An excess of empathy may lead you to fail to distinguish between column 1 and column 2, and consequently between the different languages or discourses involved. You will remember the importance given in Part II to the distinction between the interview questions in the informant's language and the research questions formulated in the theory-language of the researcher. The same clarity is needed to distinguish between your theory-language in column 2 and all the other languages of all informants and of all other experts to be found in column 1.

My text-strategy for this book has been to quote lots of student researchers and their informants; I've quoted lots of writers on a variety of topics and many of the writers or speakers on whom those writers have relied. I hope that I have mostly never left you in any doubt as to what my position was vis-à-vis all those other 'voices' and 'thinkers' whom I have quoted and summarized. Referencing, putting quotations into single or double quotation marks, summarizing and making clear it is your summary of somebody else's voice and that you do not necessarily agree with what you have summarized, all these are academic practices that serve real functions.

A good research text works in a zig-zag motion between you describing and arguing in your language and all the others that you cite or summarize in theirs. The zig-zag can be repeated as often as necessary – as it is in this book, for example (Figure 15.3). You start with your intentions and your ideas and you end with your conclusions. In between, you can and you must zag over to their ideas, their language, their words, as many times as is necessary, but you must also keep the reader in no confusion when you are speaking in your voice and when you are summarizing and quoting their voices.

J.P. Spradley (1979: 74) calls this helpfully 'the language identification principle' and argues powerfully against any 'amalgamated language'. Spradley was doing fieldwork in real-life situations. Given that you have verbatim transcripts of interviews, you are less likely to run the risk of 'amalgamation' in your *raw data*. However, you have the same need to avoid what, modifying Spradley, one might call 'amalgamated thinking' in *your write-up*: researcher's thinking with unidentified mixtures of thoughts and phrases from others; or, mixtures of thoughts of others with unidentified thinking of your own mixed into it. *Your* descriptions and explanations need to be distinguished from *their* descriptions and explanations.

---

5 Just as in the design of interview schedules, the proportion and sequencing of types of question had to be carefully considered for their effect upon the interviewee.

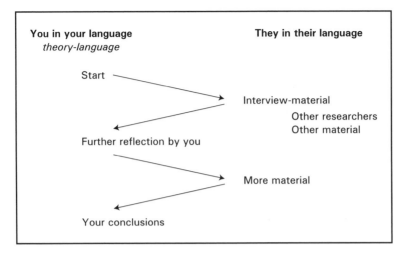

FIGURE 15.3   **The Zig-zag between You-talking and They-talking**

Some examples may be helpful to concretize these abstractions.

Don't Over-identify with the Informant's Language and Account

One fan stresses something rather implausible, but the interviewer does not notice. A rather slight factor (original type of music) is held to be a sufficient explanation of an obsession strong enough to lead to sustained unemployment.[6]

> 'John discovered that Morissey was into the same things that he was into (for example, Morissey's views on sexuality corresponded with his own) so an immediate fixation developed .... John, in particular, stressed that the reason he had chosen Morissey as the focus for his adulation was because he was front-man to the band that was playing a new style of music .... So these idols had been chosen as the object for their obsession because they provided a source of identification, were providing an original style of music, or because they were the way that the fan could pass his leisure time.'

I commented: 'You do not independently evaluate the "reasoning", the "justification", that the fan provides you with. Since you do not provide his words, the reader cannot evaluate them either. Fixation and adulation do not just arise from people being front-man to a band playing a more attractive type of music. If somebody stresses that as a justification, you need to take that with a pinch of salt. The more he stresses that, the larger the pinch of salt. The shift to "so … " recycles John's "self-explanation" again as your causal-explanation"....

Another example is from a report on students and drinking:

---

6 Later on in her text, Ruth Y wrote that "John explained how his obsession with Morissey was to lead him to give up his job and become unemployed for the next five years". Again, the self-explanation is not critically examined by the student, the two are fused: amalgamated explanation.

'For a drink to fall into the category of 'up-market' or 'glamorous' ... it seemed it was a prerequisite, or at least an important factor, for it to be expensive. There was a balance between expense and exclusivity. This is probably why most cocktails fall into the genre – most cocktails are expensive, simply because of the costly price of several spirits and fruit juices. Also cocktail bars are relatively uncommon, giving them a natural link with exclusiveness.'

I commented: 'Fine, but ... Is "exclusivity" your expert-term or is it their folk-term? You need to explore what your interviewee meant by "exclusivity" ... if indeed they used the term. If they didn't, then the reader wants to know what were the things *they* said that *you* summarize by *your* term of "exclusivity".'

Unempathetic Distancing – Too Easy a Negative Interpretation

Struggling correctly to avoid over-identification with the informant, you may fall into the opposite trap of 'excessive distancing'. If you are concerned to describe and explain an informant's point of view or experience with empathy and objectivity, this is equally unsatisfactory.

Struggling to avoid being hypnotized/engulfed by the informant/text/parent/lover, you may leap into the censorious hypercritical 'detached academic examiner' role. In this role, you 'score' by finding fault (blaming) and you 'feel safe' when emotionally distant, 'putting down'.

Censorious 'Examining' for a 'Correct'[7] Answer　As a result of doing academic work within an undergraduate 'grading' structure, students often 'identify with the oppressor' and experience the interview as a place where they, the students, are 'testing' informants for an imagined 'correct' answer.

One student wrote:

'Informant no. 2 expressed feelings of contentment and pleasure at the modular system in her wholly positive answers. Even the flaws she noted were brushed off as "can't be helped", "just the way it is". Her arguments, though, were badly structured, yet the feelings still emerged. Her answers were partially incomplete ...'

I commented: 'Show that they were, by some specified standard, "badly structured". Then try seeing if you can understand them as being, by some standard you haven't yet grasped, "well-structured"....'

Another student made a Freudian slip in the first line in the way she referred to informants and was worried about questions as if they were questions in an exam:

---

7 It could be phantasy 'academically correct' or 'I know reality' 'scientifically-correct'. It might also be 'politically correct'. In all these cases, without realizing it, you have the wrong attitude. You are no longer empathetically supporting the informant to articulate their view of reality.

'All in all, the main differences I found between the two candidates were their specific attitudes and approaches to the interview. I think this is because the interview questions were not particularly difficult and, as most first year HM101 students more or less thought the same as the other two interviews (from what I gathered), I think the answers were fairly standard and somewhat what I had expected.'

I commented: 'The interview questions were "not particularly difficult"? Maybe they should have been more probing? Why talk of the interviewees as "candidates"? How does that position you? Perhaps you think of the "candidates" as being in an "exam" and you don't want to be "too hard" on them? A mistaken stance to take up for interviewing. If the questions are not "difficult" enough, maybe they are not 'interesting' enough. If you are that confident of the answers, find more interesting questions! Or find the minority of HM101 students who you gather think "differently", and interview at least one of them ....'

Another example.

'My informants did not see themselves as part of any conventional class culture. The informants were adamant that the culture represents "a class of its own", because "you're on a different vehicle from other people".

This is an obvious distinction to make, and it represents a crude interpretation of the concept of class as a social hierarchy. The stratification of individuals according to their choice of vehicle is difficult to justify, and to make claims to be either superior or inferior to other road users causes inevitable controversy.'

I commented: 'This seems as though you are giving them "grades" for "un-crude justifiable-to-you assertions" rather than trying to understand why they make the "inevitable controversial" assertions that they do make. Failure of empathy here.'

Imposition of Evaluations on to the Informant   One student-inquirer believed that dance-theory was necessary for all dance students, and so did one of her informants, and the course insisted on it. Another informant did not, and the ethnographer then accused her of being 'contradictory':

'She didn't feel that theory subjects were essential, which I think is contradictory because she eventually wants to teach dance and theory must have some relevance for her.'

I commented: 'If she does not feel that theory is essential, then your belief in the necessity of theory is just ... your theory ... or the DA 100 teacher's ideology ... Don't foist it on to her .... Instead, explore further why she feels it to be non-essential, and what she means by *essential* anyway ....'

You will spontaneously tend to over-identify with some informants and to 'excessively distance' yourself from others. If used to academic grading, you will tend to identify with the academic aggressor and have criteria of 'correct answers' which are inappropriate for research interviewing. You are trying to find out what your informant's criteria are for adequate descriptions and explanations, not judge them by whatever your own happen to be.

Having discussed the importance of distinguishing the kinds of concrete–abstract thinking that is going on (Spradley levels) and who is doing the thinking (Spradley columns), I shall now proceed to look at the relation between three components that are likely to be found in any researcher account.

RELATING THEORIZATION, TYPOLOGY AND QUOTATION

Accounts of Accounts and going Beyond them

The Concept of 'Accounting' and 'Accounts'

In general, what I tend to get in interviews are perhaps best described as 'accounts' of some sort or other. If I ask you a question, you give me some sort of 'account'. These may include any or all of the DARNE elements of narrative interviews, they may include much justification or accusation, or description and explanation, prediction etc. 'Account' (Antaki, 1988) is a useful overarching term which does not prejudice what components one finds within the text or in what proportion one finds them nor what different functions they may perform within it.

Give, or Re/present, the Informant's Accounts, but go Beyond them

The need for the findings and conclusions to go beyond the mere recycling of the accounts given by the informants can be seen in Jane P's description of two disabled children reporting on teasing and bullying. She both gives their accounts and goes beyond them in a subtle way that repays careful consideration. D = disabled and ND = non-disabled, in the following extract.

'Teasing and bullying
Tricia (non-D) said "there's not much picking ... not much bullying at my school" compared to her primary school. But she said that, at secondary school, "some people are racist and some people just call 'your mum's a fish'". She got teased about wearing a blazer. Dominic (non-D) had his bags kicked around when he fell in a crush, and is sometimes kicked over and teased.

"Pushing and shoving" is a general problem for all the children at Mountroyal. Peter (D) said he "obviously" wouldn't go out in the playground, it's all "crowded, you can't get around". Dominic (non-D) said "there's always a crush in the corridor ... the sixth-formers ... push you out of the way and you slam against the wall".

Tricia (ND) and Dominic (ND) described some of the ways that the disabled children at Mountroyal are treated:

"When people in wheelchairs are trying to go through the door, people just slam the door in their faces ... The older children say 'Ragdoll, you can't walk' and call them some really horrible names .... Some of them are really cruel, especially to Anna."

continued

continued

But Anna (D) herself didn't want to talk about it: "I don't get teased or bullied at all". On the other hand, Peter (D) admitted "they do push us around a bit". He often falls over (he is more disabled than Anna) but he said "it doesn't bother me and the children don't laugh at me"; but when I spent a day in class with him, children sniggered when he fell over. He either genuinely doesn't notice or chooses to ignore it. The fact that the children chose to feature teasing in the playground in the video, however, is evidence that this is a time when disabled children are "picked on".'

In the above text, a lot of different data are being put together, here, to make a range of inferences and to suggest alternative explanations: answers from four children, participant observation in the class-room, choices by children about what to feature on a video.

The way in which the three paragraphs are constructed is worth noticing as an exercise in cautious grounded argument including tactics of presentation and representation, involving an interweaving of material from both Spradley columns that does not compromise the distinction between them.

I have discussed the need to fight to maintain the right balance of 'empathy and objectivity' and the desirability in principle of combining different sorts of data to 'go beyond' the accounts given of your informants. In the next section I look at the detail of 'comparative writing' about your research findings.

Examples: Vaughan, Buckingham, Liebes and Katz

As you zig-zag with empathy between yourself and the accounts of others (the others being informants and other theorists and their material), you will gradually develop a more and more trustworthy sense of the 'objective pattern' of accounts. Obviously, the longer you work with people and the more criss-crossing of the accounts with each other, the more you will get to understand the meaning of the 'shifts of accounting' that occur.

Diana Vaughan: Exemplary Chunks of Quotation   How such 'successive accounts' material might be used can be seen in the following excerpt from a study by Vaughan, *Uncoupling: How and Why Relationships Come Apart* (1987), where there seems a sort of equal balance between direct quotation and reflection.

Though the theorizing reflection may well have largely emerged from the interviewing and collecting of documentation (and the research literature quoted in her bibliography) the mode of presentation is one in which the quotations 'illustrate' a pre-stated reflection. Vaughan is interested in the way people give predictably-different accounts at different 'stages' of a supposedly fairly standard process.

'People can live apart or be divorced, and still not be uncoupled.

"I knew I was in better shape than she was because I was the one who pushed for the split. Still, even a year later, I was very vulnerable to her actions. If I saw her at the supermarket, or someone brought her name up, or if she called about something

continued

continued

which she seemed to do pretty often – like she was trying to find stuff to talk to me about, did I see the exhibit, so-and-so called, the dog got sick, you know – I was always upset by it, by talking to her, being reminded of her. I just wanted it to be over, and it just took a long time for that to happen, for that connection to be broken" (Dental Assistant, 27, separated after living together 3 years).

Uncoupling does not occur at the same minute for each partner. Both, to uncouple, make the same transition but begin and end at different times. Initiators, as I have seen, have a head start. But, ultimately, aided by the initiator's behaviour, by comparison with alternatives, and with a little help from their friends, partners begin to put the relationship behind them. They acknowledge that the relationship is unsaveable. Through the social process of mourning, they too arrive at an account that explains this unexpected denouement. "Getting over" a relationship does not mean relinquishing the part of our life that we shared with another, but rather coming to some conclusion that allows us to accept and understand its altered significance. Once we develop such an account, we can incorporate it into our lives, and go on.

Over time, the partners' accounts change from the self-blame that characterises the first attempts to understand this experience. When partners believe they are at fault, they assume that the relationship can be saved – for what they have ruined they can also fix. As they come to the conclusion that it is unsaveable, their accounts will correspondingly justify the relationship's demise on the basis of something beyond their ability to correct. Like initiators before them, partners conclude that the failure was the result of an unavoidable external circumstance, or some fatal flaw in the relationship – or perhaps the seeds of destruction were there in their beginnings.

"I didn't really feel she had left me. I felt like she was the victim of people who pulled her away from me. I think that, if she had left me for another man because she didn't love me or whatever, that I could have handled that. But it was almost like those old Shirley Temple movies. Someone kidnapped her. I felt it just wasn't fair, that she had been taken away ... that somebody took her away from me, and that was terrible, and I was just overwhelmed by this feeling that there's no chance to get her back" (Student, 24, separated after living together 4 years).

... When people have truly uncoupled – established a life confirming their independent identity – they will be again free to see both the positive and the negative qualities of the former partner and the relationship. Negative definitions are essential to transition, but they are often temporary .... They are then able to reconstruct the history of the relationship to again include the good memories of the time shared.

Each partner's account of the relationship's demise makes still another shift, as each arrives at a stable explanation that either removes them both from blame or joins them in the responsibility. As independence frees the partners to see both positive and negative aspects of the other, so eventually they are able to look back and assess their own contribution to the fall. They're aided by their discovery of who they are without the other person, for the chances are that they've learned some things about themselves that alter their view of the past.

continued

> continued
>
> "I wasn't even looking at things and evaluating things like I should have been. You know, looking at me and saying 'What were you doing, how did you get hooked up with this other person?' I really had to do all that in retrospect, after it was really over, after all the pain was gone, after all the problems were gone .... But that took time" (Student, aged 21, separated after living together 2 years).'
>
> (Vaughan, 1987: 174–8)

This is an excellent example of zig-zagging and the use of considerable direct quotation in a presentation. Vaughan uses 'illustrative quotations' to support her generalizing theory as she develops it in her text. Notice that she gives her theorizing first and then illustrative quotations (there are more in the original) afterwards.

In the Vaughan citation above, there is a roughly equal balance of combining direct quotations from others and 'interpretation' by the interviewer herself, embodying the criss-cross or zig-zag principle in fairly equal proportions. The next two extracts relate Spradley levels and columns material differently. In the first example, from Buckingham, there is a single long quotation from a 'discussion' and then a long and sophisticated 'interpretation' of what's happening in the discussion. In the example after that, an extract from Liebes and Katz, the summary has virtually no direct quotation.

The amount and placing of direct quotation and summary, the type and placing of 'theorizing reflection', the structuring of the analysis in different sorts of ways ... all these are general issues in writing-up. Think about these differences as you read the three extracts, and try to see how the text-construction determines differences in your experiencing of the texts.

David Buckingham: Perspectives on and within Fictional Texts   In the following extract from David Buckingham's excellent *Public Secrets:* Eastenders *and its Audiences*, there is a long quotation and then a long interpretation. Unlike the earlier passage from Vaughan, the interpretation in this extract explores multiple positionings and perspectives within what the girls in the group discussion say. The combination of a group interaction and the type of interpretation that Buckingham is concerned to make produces for the reader a more complex and unfinalized understanding than is delivered to the reader by the relatively completed theory and illustrative quotations of Vaughan.

> '... While the desire to be entertained by shocking and scandalous revelations was an important reason why these children watched *Eastenders*, ... for all of them, discussing the programme was also an opportunity to engage in a moral debate. The following transcript provides an extended example of such debate which illustrates a number of crucial findings. The speakers are all seventeen-year-old girls, with the exception of Rodney who speaks only once at the end.
>
> *Calista:* Michelle, in a way, is not the perfect teenager, is she? She's got her whole family round her. Not everyone's like that.
>
> continued

continued

Sandra: She's very selfish, anyway.

Calista: I think that's why she's using Lofty.

Sheila: She won't listen to anyone's advice. Her mum and her nan and her dad tried to sit down, tried to go to the clinic with her, and she just didn't want to know. She just wanted to keep herself to herself, and now she wants Lofty to take the burden off her.

Calista: When she found out she was pregnant, it was "Oh Gran, I'm pregnant" "Oh, Gran, help!" or whatever, and then, all of a sudden, it was "My baby, my life, I'm going to do what I want to" ....

Sheila: Her mum's got a lot of burden, right. She's just not taking her mum into consideration. Her mum has to go through a lot. Now suppose something happens to that baby, if it dies or whatever, who's going to look after Michelle, to try to get her out of it? Her mum. Everything falls onto the mum, I reckon. Even though it's her baby, she's got her mum, she's got her gran, she's got her dad, she's got people around her to help her. Other people haven't got that, they're just around by themselves, they usually get chucked out or something ....

Sheila: I think it was wrong that she didn't tell her parents who the father is. Any parent is going to find out. Any parent is going to drag it out of them. I mean, your parents know you better than anyone does. I think that the father should have the right to know. I mean, it would bring out more in *Eastenders*, wouldn't it?

Calista: I suppose they're saving it, really, to use later on. And if their ratings go down, then they're going to use that to pick up their ratings.

Sandra: I read somewhere that they're going to name the baby Victoria, and then everyone's going to start saying "Aha, Victoria, it must be Den" [Laughter].

Donna: That's what it said, it's going to get some tongues wagging.

Sandra: But all the time, she keeps dropping hints. Like when she heard about Jan coming down to the pub, she sat down and started crying. I mean, things like that, you would pick up these little pieces and start putting it all together. And I reckon Lofty should know who the father is, he should demand to know.

Calista: Thinking about it, though. Why did Den give him that engagement ring? All these things! If it was me, I'd start thinking, "Why is he giving me this ring?"

Rodney: But Lofty's stupid in the first place! [Laughter].

What is particularly interesting in this discussion is the way in which the speakers constantly shift back and forth between two positions .... At certain points, they seem to be judging the programme and the characters from *outside* the fictional world, while, at others, they seem to accept the reality of that world and make their judgements, as it were, from *inside*. In each case, they use different kinds of *evidence* to support their findings.

Furthermore, within each perspective, there are a range of different, but related, concerns. From the more distanced "outside" perspective, there is a concern about *representation*, in this instance, about the way teenagers (that is they themselves) are represented. Elsewhere in their discussion, this group had been critical of the "problem teenager" stereotype which they detected both in *Eastenders* and in more recent episodes

continued

continued

of *Coronation Street*. Thus they argue that Michelle is "not the perfect teenager" – unlike other pregnant teenagers who would get "chucked out". Michelle has "got all her family round her" and is therefore in a position which the girls consider untypical. Secondly, they are fully aware that the programme is a *constructed artefact* and that decisions about how particular stories develop may be determined at least partly with a view to ratings. They use evidence from their reading of the popular press to predict how in future the programme may seek to involve, if not manipulate, its audience: naming the baby "Victoria" will "get some tongues wagging" both inside *Eastenders* and outside it in every-day conversation.

From an "inside" perspective, the group is concerned to debate the moral *validity* of Michelle's behaviour. Two points are particularly notable here. Firstly, the girls are extremely critical of Michelle's selfishness, which is surprising given that they are very close to her in terms of age, gender, and class background. This would suggest that the notion that viewers automatically "identify" with characters who are like themselves is perhaps an oversimplification. Secondly, particularly in Sheila's long speech, it is clear that this criticism derives from a particular class and gender perspective, in this case, from the experience of women's roles in a working-class extended family. It is this experience which, I would argue, leads them to question Michelle's attempt to "keep herself to herself" and to take on the mother's perspective.

Cutting across this inside/outside movement is the group's concern for *plausibility*. On the one hand, for example, they argue that the other characters would have picked up the "hints" in Michelle's behaviour and would "start putting it all together". Their failure to do so is clearly regarded as implausible – though it is, by implication, something which they regard as necessary if the plot is to keep the audience guessing and its tongues wagging. On the other hand, however, this failure is seen to be the result of the charac-ters' stupidity – particularly that of Lofty who, as Rodney indicates, any regular viewer will know to be "stupid in the first place". Sheila's speech which begins "It was wrong that she didn't tell the parents ..." exemplifies the dual nature of this concern for plausibility. On the one hand she sees it as wrong on moral grounds: "her father should have the right to know". Yet it is also "wrong" because it is implausible: "any parent is going to drag it out of them". And it may also be "wrong" in terms of the development of the nar-rative, the need to reveal or to "bring out more" in the programme.

I have chosen to discuss this extract at length because it serves to introduce many of the major issues to be considered in more detail in the remainder of this chapter – in particu-lar the role of moral and ideological judgement, questions of realism and plausibility and, finally, of identification and representation.'
(David Buckingham, 1987: 171–3)

And I have chosen to quote Buckingham at length, not only as a contrast to Vaughan on the one hand (and, as we shall see to Liebes and Katz on the other) as regards the evocation in the reader of a more open and more complex under-standing, but for a different reason.

The Buckingham extract serves to provide a good example of how the 'major issues of the expert' mentioned in the last paragraph quoted are brought out in a prior well-selected 'choice quotation' which they serve to illustrate and illuminate.

The girls would never use such terms as we find in the final lines of the extract, *the role of moral and ideological judgement, questions of realism and plausibility and, finally, of identification and representation,* – all Spradley level 1 concepts – and the reader might not have been previously prepared to engage with them too well either. By the point in Buckingham's designed and unfolding text when he identifies them to us as the "major theoretical issues" that he is going to discuss later on in the (unquoted) rest of the chapter, the reader has already been brought in two steps from (lengthy quotation of group discussion) to (discursive presentation/analysis by Buckingham) to the (abstract issues to be discussed more formally later) in such a way that the future high level discussion of the abstract issues will be grounded for us *because* we have already worked through the initial and initiating lengthy quotation (Spradley column 1 mostly level 6) and the subsequent extensive middle-level discussion (Spradley column 2, level 5/6).

I consider Buckingham's sequencing of his presentation to be a very helpful mode of presentation to the reader: 'presenting a lengthy quotation' for analysis, and then analysing it in such a way to answer particular theoretical questions in relation to particular theoretical issues,[8] gradually moving from column 1 to column 2 and moving up the column 2 Spradley levels at the same time.

You may wish to consider how 'writing up' your own report might benefit from this model of sequencing and initiating. Notice that, while Vaughan theorizes first and appends an illustration, Buckingham provides transcript extract first and then appends a theorization.

Liebes and Katz Subcultural Differences in Perspectives on Fictional Texts   Similar 'theoretical issues' are represented in a fairly quotation-free abstract 'summary' of some cross-cultural research into audiences for another TV 'soap', *Dallas*.

Irrespective of the relative lack of direct quotation, Liebes and Katz's discussion seems written from a slightly more 'emotionally distant' position. I feel them to be 'less empathetic' and more 'external' to the people they write about. This does not mean that they do not have interesting 'theorizations' of the sort of material that both they and Buckingham are writing about. Unlike Buckingham's focus upon 'commonalities' within one group, Liebes and Katz are concerned above all to account for *differences* between groups. Indeed, in some ways, irrespective of the latter point, their theorizations go further than those of Buckingham. The tone of their analysis, for example of 'moral discussion', is subtly different. Like Vaughan on uncoupling, their quotations (much shorter) are illustrative rather than foundational, but where Vaughan has a theory of universal phases of experience of a longitudinal process of uncoupling, Liebes and Katz are presenting a complex theory of different modes of experiencing, a theory of difference not embedded in the ethnocentric universalism of the ahistorical sort that it seems to me that the Vaughan extract expresses. They write:

---

8 Notice how Buckingham explicitly tells the reader in advance what he is going to do with his quotation by calling it 'Inside/Outside the text'. Bear in mind that, without such 'theorizing concerns' and theory-questions, the extract would appear 'less interesting' or would serve other 'theoretical concerns' of the analyst. What you see in a text depends on the 'theorizing concerns' and the 'theorizing concepts' with which you try to look at the text, let alone guide the interview. What Buckingham does *not* do which, according to my criteria, he should do, is to distinguish between the 'folk-concerns' of the girls and his 'expert-concerns'. For example, 'plausibility' is clearly a folk-concern of the girls (though they might not use his word for it), while 'identification' seems to be merely a concern of his, and not of the girls at all.

'We have been studying the ways in which members of different ethnic group decode the world-wide hit program *Dallas* .... Our subjects are persons of some secondary schooling drawn from four different ethnic groups in Israel – Arabs, newly arrived Russian Jews, Moroccan Jews and kibbutz members – and non-ethnic Americans in Los Angeles. Groups of six persons – three couples, all friends, meeting in the home of one of them – are asked to discuss an episode of *Dallas* immediately after seeing it on the air. We have begun to conduct a parallel study in Japan but have only preliminary studies so far.

What we want to say is that to view *Dallas* overseas – perhaps even in America – is to view a program and not, as some critics say, to view moving wallpaper. It is in fact more than viewing a program: it is to become engaged with a narrative psychologically, socially and aesthetically, depending on the background of the viewer. Programs like *Dallas* appear to be able to activate very different kinds of viewers.

To analyse these different kinds of understandings and involvements, we distinguish first between the *referential* and the *metalinguistic*. In answer to our question "Why all the fuss about babies?", some viewers refer to real life and explain that families, especially rich ones, need heirs. Others, using a metalinguistic frame, say that babies are good material for conflict, and the narrative of soap operas needs conflict to keep going.

Within the referential, we distinguish between real and ludic keyings. The one makes serious equations between story and life; the other treats the program more playfully, subjunctively and interactively – turning the group discussion into a sort of psychodrama. Making a further distinction within the referential, some viewers key the program normatively, judging messages and characters moralistically; others treat the program as observers and withhold value judgements. The moralising statements seem to be couched in the language of "We": "Their women are immoral; our Arab women would not behave that way". Less moralising statements come either in the language of "they" – for those who generalise from the program to the universals of life – and in the language of "I" and "You" for those who treat the program and life more playfully.

Applying these distinctions to viewers of different education and ethnicity reveals how understanding and involvement may vary among groups.

While all groups make many more referential than metalinguistic statements, the better-educated viewers use the metalinguistic frame much more. Better educated viewers decode the program at two levels – referential and metalinguistic – thus involving themselves both in the narrative and in its construction.

Patterns of involvement vary by ethnicity as well. The more traditional groups – Moroccan Jews and Arabs – do not stray far from the referential. Even the well-educated among them make comparatively few metalinguistic statements. They accept the program as real, and deal with it seriously in relation to their own lives. The Arabs in particular discuss the program moralistically, and in terms of "them" and "us". This pattern of relating to the program is at once involving and defensive. The program is discussed referentially and seriously, but, at the same time, it is rejected as a message for "us". Even if this rejection serves as a buffer against the influence of the program, it nevertheless reflects a high degree of engagement.

The Americans and kibbutz Jews show an altogether different pattern of involvement. The rate of their metalinguistic statements is high, and their use of the referential is often in the ludic mode. Some of their dialogue reminds one of fantasy games.

continued

continued

Like the Americans and the kibbutzniks, the Russians also have a high proportion of metalinguistic statements – the highest in fact. They are critical not only of the aesthetics of the story (comparing it unfavourably with Tolstoy and other literary sagas) but about the message, which they regard as ideological manipulation. Beware, say the Russians, of the false message of the program. They tell us that the rich are unhappy because that is what they want us to think.

Curiously, however, when the Russians use the referential frame, they do seem to set aside their ideological suspicions and treat the program, as the Arabs and the Moroccans do, as if it were a documentary. Going even further than the traditional groups – who accept the program as the truth about Americans but reject the program as a portrayal of themselves – the Russians seem to be saying that entire classes of people – women, businessmen and so forth – behave as their *Dallas* counterparts do. The seriousness of their sweeping universal generalisations from the program to life are altogether different from the ludic keyings of the Americans and the kibbutzniks.

Thus we see at least three patterns of involvement in these decodings. The more traditional viewers remain in the realm of the real (and the serious) and mobilise values to defend themselves against the program. The more Western groups – the Americans and the kibbutzniks – are relatively more aware of, and more involved in, the construction of the program and deal with its reality more playfully. The Russians are also metalinguistic – most of all, in fact – but they show more awareness of the message of the program than of its structure. This concern seems to go together with the seriousness with which the Russians enter the referential, just as the more constructionist terms of the other Western groups go hand in hand with their more playful keyings of the referential.

It is clear that each pattern of involvement includes a mechanism of defence. The Arabs, accepting the program's reality, reject the values of the characters. The Russians reject the values of the producers. The Americans and the kibbutzniks reject the idea that the values – either of characters or of producers – are to be taken seriously.[9]

We cannot answer the question whether these forms of distancing – any one, or all – reduce the extent of viewer vulnerability. While it may appear at first glance that ludic keyings and metalinguistic framings are more resistant to influence, we are by no means certain that this is so. The ludic may be seductive in the sense that fantasy and subjectivity invite one to be carried away. Similarly, constructionist concerns distract one from the ideological message. Even ideological decodings are vulnerable to influence in the sense that the decoders believe their oppositional reading is the truth!'

(Liebes and Katz, 1988: 115–17)

In the above extract, a lot can be noted about method of presentation. Certain expert-terms in a particular theory-language of the two researchers (referential and metalinguistic, ludic and serious, values and defence-mechanisms) are laid out and used to analyse the interviews treated as a set of 'statements' that can decoded. Averages, or most typical patterns, are attributed to ethnic-national

---

9 Or, a 'Russian' might argue, that value-questions are questions to be taken seriously.

groups and by educational category … not by gender, age or class. The averages are compared with each other and a typology of 'patterns of involvement-defence' are laid out. A discussion of the implications of the different patterns for 'viewer vulnerability' is made at the end of the extract.

We have here a higher-order level of column 2 theorization than in the Buckingham extract – though not necessarily than that of the later Buckingham material I did not quote – and the analysis is much more concerned with differences than is the universalist model of uncoupling put forward by Vaughan or the study of one homogeneous group of girls illustrated in the Buckingham extract. For much sociological research, models that are concerned for intelligible differences are more valuable than those concerned only for universal and ahistorical constants.

The excerpts above should have sensitized you to the various ways in which you can zig-zag between your own thinking and the 'other voices' with whom you are wishing the reader to enter into a dialogue. It should have suggested ways in which discussion can move from the relatively concrete to the relatively abstract, and the ways in which the abstractions of the researcher can help make sense of the particularity of informant verbal exchanges. It should have highlighted the value of distinguishing Spradley levels and Spradley columns in the understanding of other people's presentations and in the construction of your own.

We now shift to a discussion of the types of tales from the research field that researchers can construct, as in introduction to a more formal discussion of the relationships created by text-construction between researchers' theorizations and their data.

How Researchers Construct Different Relations between their Theorizations and their Data

We will look first at the typology of 'tales from the field' of van Maanen, and then consider more formally the balance and relations constructed by researchers in their presentation of theorization, typology and quotation.

Van Maanen's Typology of 'Tales from the Research Field'

Van Maanen (1988) distinguished in ethnography between three types of reports, or 'tales from the field', which can usefully be applied more generally. He distinguished:

- the realist tale
- the confessional tale
- the impressionist tale.

The *realist* tale is one in which the author does not draw attention to himself or herself but is apparently absent from the text. The evidence is what it is, the facts are what they are, and the conclusions appear to arise by an impersonal logic. What appears is an 'objective description' of what is. The invisible author is present only in the omniscient organizing of the details by which reality shows itself.

The *confessional* tale is one in which the author is present as a personal experiencing exploring self, gradually overcoming his or her own misunderstandings in a historical report of the personal own discovery process whereby at the end some relatively objective knowledge has been achieved and can be formally presented. The reader, by identifying with the 'originally ignorant hero', follows him or her along a path of self-education and self-discovery, misunderstanding and then understanding better 'the alien scene' and the alien others, and thus acquires the current level of knowledge and uncertainty in the way that the author, by the end of the tale, confesses him or herself to have acquired.

The *impressionist* tale is one in which the reader is drawn into a succession of narrative episodes recounted by the author and in which knowledge is built up through a succession of fragmentary episodes recounted in great detail.

Quite clearly, there can be combinations and successions of such 'modes of telling' in the same overall report, and differently weighted proportions in different sequences will have different effects upon the readers.

There is perhaps some strength in combining elements of different types of tale in the same presentation. A scientific account might well include a report on the origins and evolution of the research process which included an element of the collective and personal *confessional*; it might then go on to a presentation of findings as answers to particular theory-questions in which the struggles with (inadequate) answers were presented in a *confessional-process* form and then the adequate answers could be formally presented in a more *realist-argumentative* way.

I shall now spell out these issues in terms of three basic models of theory/data presentation at points on a spectrum: integration, separation, and interplay.

Balance of Theorization, Typology and Quotation by Section

Theory–data Relationship Spectrum

I argue below that at one end of the spectrum there is full integration or assimilation of one into the other. At the other end of the spectrum, both are identified and held separately but there is no organic relation between the two. In the middle of the spectrum, both are identified separately *and* a dialectical relation of dialogue is maintained between the two.

Full Theory–data Integration/Assimilation: Two Bad Models

In this type of writing, there is no separation between theory and data and the two are fused together in a way that makes it difficult to think about the relation between the two. There are two ways in which this can happen: (a) the theory is rendered invisible and the configuration of the data appears as an effect of nature, not of the representer's artifice; (b) the theory appears as the only possible theory, given the nature of the data, and any data presented act as best to illustrate or support the theory, which also appears as an effect of nature, not of artifice. We will look at these separately.

1 *Naturalistic-empirical presentation.* This is typical of presentations for folk-audiences with low levels of concept-consciousness. The theory, the conceptual framework, is made to disappear into the presentation of 'the facts': it functions as an invisible conceptual framework that is difficult to see and therefore difficult to discuss. This is not usually a conscious operation: more often, it is that the writer is not aware of alternative theories. This might be seen as a *realist* or even an *impressionist* tale, in von Maanen's terms as discussed above.[10]

---

10 This is not an attack on 'critical realism', an approach in which theoretical debate is foregrounded; see, for example, Miller (2000: 11–12), Pawson and Tilley (1997).

2   *Super-theoretical final-theory presentation.* In such a presentation, in the extreme case, no evidence is presented at all. The data disappear into the theory. What is presented is a final version of the Conceptual Frame and Theorized Findings such that the two cannot be distinguished and any data that are presented is just those which 'illustrate' the findings. The result is that the movement of theorizing cannot be followed and the argument with evidence cannot be seen. The 'final theory' feels inescapable, no counter-arguments are mentioned, no 'difficult evidence' is presented. The reader is given the experience 'There is No (Theoretical-Conceptual) Alternative' (TINtcA). There are either no data, or no data that don't fit. This would be a *realist* tale taking the form of a final presented theorization, where no counter-evidence or counter-theory (or counter-hypotheses) are taken, or taken seriously. Vaughan would be an example of this, especially if she had not bothered to provide any illustrative quotations.

As you can guess from my tone, I don't like either of these sorts of writing. They seem designed to make critical and evaluative thinking by the reader difficult. I prefer types of writing which differentiate conceptual framework, evidence, and argued 'findings' (Hammersley, 1990 calls them 'knowledge-claims' which stresses their controversial nature even more). Such forms of writing which distinguish theory and data and respect their relative autonomy, are discussed below.

Full Theory–data Separation: A Somewhat better Model
In this type of writing, or structuring, theory and data are as far as possible separated. This at least allows for an argument about their relationship. Column 1 and column 2 are kept separate and their relation is presented as an issue. My extract from David Buckingham follows this pattern of presentation, juxtaposing a big data-chunk and a big theory-chunk.

- What you very often get is a large chunk of Spradley level 5/6 particular description.
- Then you get a chunk of (Spradley level 3 or above) Conceptual Discussion which 'frames' and purports to explain or interpret the earlier naturalistic chunk of description.

Sometimes you get the 'framing theory' before you get the 'naturalistic chunk': the crucial element is that you get both but they are held very separate indeed. The first half of Paul Willis's early *Learning to Labour* is close-to-the-data ethnography, the second half is the more theoretical analysis.

This does give you the opportunity to confront the data and the conceptual frame presented: it is therefore an improvement on the previously described model. However, full theory–data separation can have its own problems. In particular, without any specific grip on the specific data, the 'theoretical frame' can go adrift. Sometimes you feel the theoretical frame could be a frame for almost any similar chunk of data. It can become under-related theory, theory that relates very unspecifically to the specific data, and then, being equally compatible with only minor tinkering with *any* set of data, becomes a luxury option with no organic relation to the data it is merely 'framing'.

Such a juxtaposition of naturalistic description and theoretical 'interpretation' tends to be everybody's first attempt at bringing theory and practice together. It has the merit that at least you have the two of them, and not just one. Once you have them juxtaposed, you can think about the relation of that particular theorization to that particular set of data and so try to develop a more 'organic' relation between the two than just that of 'specific picture' and 'universal frame'.

Theory–data Differentiation, but Interplay: My Preferred Model

In this final type of writing, partly exemplified within David Buckingham's 'interpretive block' and more in the extract from Liebes and Katz, the conceptual frameworks, the theory-findings and the data are given their autonomy, and the presentation attempts to find a way of moving between the elements in an explicit fashion, giving 'difficult evidence', putting forward 'counter-arguments', admitting weaknesses in the research data and the current attempt at theorization, and in the attempt to relate the two. This process can be seen as a methodological-theoretical *confessional tale*, in van Maanen's terms, a 'judicial model'.

The movement is for the simultaneous 'constant inter-improvement' of data-collection and analysis on the one hand and conceptual-framing and theorizing on the other. This is an open-textured and sometimes open-ended and unfinished presentation in which the relation of data and argument is close but distinct and in which the reader is invited and enabled to join in improving and developing the articulation of better theorizations for the further understanding of data.

This is a genre of reporting in which the dominant feature is that of controversial argument. It can be seen as a *confessional tale* (capable of being audited by your peers) providing that the confession is a confession of *theoretical-conceptual struggle*. It provides material on the basis of which the reader is in a position to come to a different theoretical conclusion. It is, in its own way, a *narrative*.

In Part IV, I distinguished between different types of text to be found in a narrative interview transcript: description, argumentation, report, narrative, and evaluation – DARNE (pp. 243–5). It may be useful to think of the same *diversity of text-sorts as making up the resources for constructing your research presentation.*

What was previously understood as *the interviewee's unconscious utilization* of cultural resources for the construction of a narrative directed at you can now be understood as a basis *for your conscious and carefully planned utilization* of cultural resources for the construction of a presentation aimed at your audience, your eventual readers.

I now move to a more general discussion of questions of theorizing and narrating in writing-up.

16

Writings up: Theorizing and Narrating
in 'Presentation' Strategies

In this section, we focus first on the particular work of spelling-out how the issues and models described earlier in this part can be 'cashed' in terms of your planning your writing up.

INTRODUCTION

Disclaimer: Collect Examples and Describe Structure

You will normally be starting to work to a prescribed genre that already exists. You therefore need to study the genre of presentation product you are aiming to produce, whatever it is. Collect examples of good and bad work within the genre and sensitize yourself to the differences. We started to do this with exemplars of written-up biographic–interpretive work in Part IV and with our discussion, in the previous chapter, of the texts of Vaughan, Buckingham and Liebes and Katz.

This means sitting down, ignoring the content but studying the genre of presentation just as you would study anything else. The section below is designed to sensitize you to some differences that may be relevant, but use them only as a guide to your own research into appropriate presentations.

Answering the CRQ–TQs – Default Genre

The philosophy inspiring this writing is one of scientific research, and consequently the natural genre of presentation that I am likely to suggest is that of the scientific report, in some form or other. In particular, I stress the value of working with the CRQ–TQ–IQ/IM–ATQ–ACRQ model in order to produce specific answers to each of the theory questions and then an overall answer to the central research question (see Figure 11.1, p. 226). This may be regarded as the default mode of presentation, one which you might be expected to use if there are not strong arguments for an alternative.

Data-loss/Condensation as Emergent Condensed
Re/presentation – News of Difference

Inevitable data-loss in selection for argument – but beware biased simplification! Your presentation – I shall refer to it as a 'report' for the sake of convenience – can be expected to contain less than 10% or maybe less than 1% of your raw data. Consequently, what Miles and Huberman (1994) refer to as 'data-reduction' is crucial to your enterprise. However, you need to ensure that, though being able to present a very small amount of your data, your 'condensation' remains as true as possible to its complexities, that you 'represent' your data as well as possible. Such 'condensed representation' becomes more crucial as the proportion of 'directly presented data' has to become less.

However, the chief danger of a summary is that of losing significant indications of detail. The interesting part of a piece of basic research may lie in the small exceptions to the broad generalities, but the bad summary may just give the broad generality and neglect the more theoretically productive 'exceptions'. Learning to summarize tendencies and differences well for an audience takes time, mistakes and practice. I shall give some examples.

Loss of Factual Detail, News of Difference

Example A   A detailed discussion of sexual orientation in a population may conclude that 90% of the population are heterosexual, but 10% are bisexual or homosexual (gay/lesbian). A bad summary of that would be *Basically, the sexual orientation of the population is heterosexual*. What would a better one be?

Example B   Claudia M is discussing her informants, opinions about animal experimentation:

'Theory-Question 3: How does the informant feel about experiments being carried out on animals?

Beverley was more concerned about medical experiments on animals than cosmetic-related ones, about which she said

"Obviously, I don't like any animals being harmed, but I don't see how it can be done in any other way."

John on the other hand completely disagreed with it.

Regarding the use of animals in medical research, Beverley argued that humans are different from other animals and therefore these experiments may not tell us anything about ourselves. This is similar to what Sharpe says ....

John made a point which, although I did not come across it in my research search, I think is widely felt. He expressed the view that if he felt that animal experimentation could find a cure for a disease such as AIDS, then, if pain and discomfort were minimal, then this would give a slightly different justification to experimentation. John also said that, if science were as good "as it says", then we should find alternatives ....

[Mini-conclusion]
Basically the answer to my third theory question showed in their attitude when replying. Both felt strongly that experimentation was wrong, Beverley particularly disliking the thought of experimentation with animals that she liked. John felt that humans should be used as alternatives in research as much as possible, although he did specify against the use of humans in cosmetic research.'

The phrase in the mini-conclusion (ATQ) *Both felt strongly that animal experimentation was wrong* is inadequate.

Given that John felt it might be a lesser evil in respect of a disease like AIDS if there were no other way of conquering it, and Beverley 'could not see how (cosmetic) experiments could be done any other way', then the mini-conclusion should represent that as well.

What would be a more adequate 'representation' of the interesting detail in the passage shown? Perhaps

Both felt that animal experimentation was wrong and yet both condoned experimentation in special (but different) cases: AIDS in one case, cosmetic testing in the other.

However, the emphasis would be different if the two clauses in my version came in inverted order:

Both condoned animal experimentation in special (but different) cases (AIDS in one case, cosmetic testing in the other) but felt that in general animal experimentation was wrong.

Example C   Ruth Y is giving an account of why fans choose their idols, but gives too little information in her summary.

'She was so taken aback by his friendliness .... By seeing him so regularly, she was filling up time which she felt could not be filled in any other way.'

I commented:

'The reader needs to know what she said which you have summarized with the words that you have used. She could have been saying

(a) "My life was OK but I was a bit bored and had nothing much else to do at the time"
(b) "I was desperately lonely and had nothing and nobody to think about before he took me under his wing and became my friend that day".

The structure of feeling of these two imaginary 'direct quotations' is quite different. Both, though, are compatible with your summary. So your 'actual summary' does not enable the reader to be directly acquainted with what you are summarizing or to choose between these equally plausible 'interpretations' of the words you use to summarize ....'

Example D   Another example of an uninformative 'listing', in which there is over-theorization, with the reader given no access to the data, is the following.

'Social and cultural factors, the way that informants had been socialized by parents, the way their parents related to each other as a couple, the way the area of sex, and boyfriends and girlfriends, had been discussed between informants and their parents all had influenced the informants' ideas of how to relate to or not relate to partners and what aspects to look for eventually in a relationship with the opposite sex. Furthermore ....'

Example E Another student also had a data-empty, quotation-empty, mode of comparative reporting. Her summary had five paragraphs, of which the one below is an adequate representation.

> 'I hypothesized that society uses the media as a channel to send messages to the individual. My intuitions were that messages sent in the media reflected current social norms. Both informants stated that the media was a part of society and that, through the media, society guides and judges them ...'

I commented:

> 'This seems to be not just "personal expectations" but also "relevant findings". They are couched in a "thin description" expert-summary sort of way, which is more like experimental-method reports than like in-depth-interview reports. Where are the quotations?, I want to shout!'

Prior Research Helps you Identify Implicit Difference

However, even if you give lots of detail, you need to have researched the field of the referent. Fraser C jumped too readily to a conclusion of consensus about what being a socialist meant. He generalized too early, exacerbated by a lack of any prior knowledge beyond common-sense about the topic.

> 'TQ3. Do socialists share political priorities for future like-minded governments, or do other factors cause them to differ?
>
> My informants seemed to have a shared perception of what the ultimate aims of socialism are:
>
> *Tim*: "a classless society, with fair working conditions"
>
> *John*: "a society without conflict, no national boundaries, everybody gets a share of wealth"
>
> *Sean*: "a fair society"
>
> *Peter*: "the commune idea: all wealth shared"
>
> *Jane*: "a job, a decent wage, and a decent place to live for everybody"
>
> *Bob*: "everybody should start off with an equal chance".'

I commented:

> 'You say that your informants "seemed to have a shared perception of the ultimate aims of socialism" without specifying for the reader what you think it was. An equal wage is NOT the same thing as an equal chance. And "no national boundaries" doesn't square very well with Jane's non-welcoming approach to foreigners [you quoted her previously as complaining that "any time there's any refugees come from abroad, sling em in the East End. Everyone's entitled to live but I think it's come the time when we've got to shut our doors"].
>
> In fact, the well-developed controversy between

(i) those who just want 'an equal chance' (but have no objection to extreme inequality of final positions as long as there's an equal chance for everybody to become unequal) – a position which can be found among meritocratic anti-socialists in the Tory Party (Bob),

(ii) those who want a social minimum but are not opposed to others getting more than that (Sean, Jane),

(iii) those who want no differences of wealth and a classless society (John, Tim?, Peter?)

needs to be known by the researcher before he or she can detect unclear intimations of such positions in interview or other discourses. The notion of "sharing the wealth" is ambiguous: the "commune model" suggests egalitarian sharing, but a less stringent demand is that everybody should have some share in the wealth, a fair share even … but what criteria of fairness do the informants have in their heads? Maybe very different ones …'

I have looked at some issues involved in the inevitable loss of data generated by the need for data-condensation in presentations and representations. With these issues in mind, let's look at the question of the detailed planning of your report.

MACRO-PLANNING AND MICRO-PLANNING

Having considered earlier the questions of pure and mixed genres and of textsorts in constructing and writing a presentation, let us step back for a more structural account. We have dealt earlier with the question of 'modes of telling'. Here we are considering the basic issues of format in re/presentations. After identifying page-numbers as the working unit for planning, we consider strategies for structuring the pages, both intuitive plans and counter-intuitive plans that may often be better than the intuitive ones.

I put forward three models, and an example of a plan.

Structure in Sections and Pages for Wordage

You should start by identifying the total number of words available or required for your report. However, nobody can think or plan in terms of words, even if they have a word-processor with a word-counting facility. Therefore, you need to know how many words you get on your average page. From then on, *think and plan in terms of the number of your pages* for each section and subsection, and for the report as a whole.

Intuitive and Counter-intuitive Structuring-strategies

The way I collect evidence may give me a 'natural' or 'obvious' structuring which, if I am not careful, I automatically assume should be the dominant structure of the write-up. This may not be the best decision. Decisions about structure should be taken carefully, since taking wrong decisions about them is so easy.

Your Raw Materials
Your raw materials are likely to be

1 library search material – organized by item of writing (book, article, classified by author or title)
2 interviewee material – organized by the name of each interviewee, and structured by the sequence of questions and answers

3 notes-as-you-go-along – organized or perhaps disorganized by date or in some
   other way
4 results of the analysis – conclusions.

How might these be composed into a structure?

Three Models of Structuring-strategy
Model A:

(a) introduction, drawn from library search and notes as you go along
(b) six cases, dealing with each interviewee in turn, describing and then
     interpreting
(c) conclusions, discussing (b) material in the light of (a).

This would not *always* be a bad model, if you give a right answer to the question of how many your pages should be given to each of (a), (b) and (c), and how
to structure each of the 'six cases'. I suspect that most students would give most
pages to section (b) and just go through the question-answer transcripts for each
of the cases.

It might be more appropriate to make (b) quite short, and to make (c) much
longer than (b). This would be particularly important if the stress in reporting was
upon the drawing of theoretical conclusions from the cases and the cases were
seen only as material in a primarily theory-building, theory-testing endeavour, a
characteristic project for social science if less so perhaps for oral history.

But the model might very easily be bad in itself, irrespective of the lengths of
sections.

Counter-intuitive Structuring
Another quite different macro-structural model would be to give a large structuring priority to grouping the material by the theory-questions, as follows.

Model B:

(a) introduction: library-research and notes as you go along
(b) six cases: very short specification of sample
(c) comparison of cases by theory-answer (ATQ) differences: long main section
(d) description of the different informants, first case by case, then summarized in
     a comparative structure
(e) conclusion: discussion of case-differences (b) in the light of answers to theory-
     questions (ATQs) (c) with reference to library research that was first men-
     tioned in (a).

You might find that your six cases actually formed groups – that the answers
showed that men had more or less the same answers as each other, as did women
respondents. Or that older males had one type of answer which was quite different from all the other categories. Or whatever. In which case, your (b) or (c) groupings could be structured that way, to bring out the similarities and differences that
you found.

If your concern for theory was very strong, and the specificity of particular
informants was only a general orientation and not a primary focus, you might
even have a model in which the separate cases did not get their own section, as
follows.

Model C:

(a) introduction
(b) ATQs (answers to theory-questions)
(c) ACRQ (answer to Central Research Question) and more general conclusions.

If you compare Model A with Model C, you will see how unnatural – contrary to the research filing cabinet approach – the conscious structuring of your Findings section might need to be.

There are many different models which exist or which you can invent. You need to think out, in terms of your purposes and your findings, what is the most appropriate structure of sections and subsections and, above all, how long in terms of your pages, each of them should be. This will depend on your Research Purposes and Central Research Question and on concerns for presentation to different readerships and audiences.

A structure which would have been fine, if the proportions had been quite different, will be a disaster if the proportions are wrong. Get the right proportions!

Example of a Plan

Figure 16.1 is an example of a plan worked out by a particular student; revised further, it was accepted as a good basis for work.

Guidelines for structuring reports can be found in most books on social research method: see, for example, Arksey and Knight (1999: 180–1) who also have some useful comment on criteria for judging such reports (178–9).

Bear in mind, however, that until you have a clear number of pages for each section you do not yet have a plan.

Having discussed general issues of designing and planning reports and presentations using semi-structured depth interview material, I shall now look particularly at issues specific to presentations in which 'biographical portraiture' is a requisite of answering the TQs of the research.

PSYCHO-PORTRAITS

One of the typical products of research interviewing of a semi-structured depth interview variety is that of the portrait of the individuals interviewed. BNIM identified and described the history and structure of cases in a certain way, and Part V attempted to identify general relations between particular case-accounts (e.g. Sophie) and embedded typologies and abstractions. Here we further consider the construction of what might be called 'psycho-portraits' on the basis of interview material. Most research depends upon the comparing and contrasting of particular cases (portraits) to enable models to be suggested, supported, or falsified. Consequently, one of the tasks in the presentation of material is that of choosing between, and combining, different strategies of representation of the cases in question.

Obviously interview materials with individuals do not have to be worked-up into such 'psycho-portraits' if your CRQ and your TQs do not require this, and I do not wish to suggest that such writing-up of portraits is in any sense basically preferable to leaving them out. However, if you wish to engage in a psycho-portrait mode of 'presentation of results', then you have a wide variety of textual strategies available which this section will address.

Main body of text* needs to be 3,500–6,500 words
Average typed page is 250–300 words, say 250 words
Therefore total length of main body should be average 5,000 words ± 1,500
Therefore total length of main body should be 18 pages ± 6 pages

Major sections required		*Subsections required*	
Introduction	2	none specified, any needed?	
Research search	3	[audit trail	0.5
		[research field survey	2.5
Theory-questions and Informant-questions and sample design	2	none specified, some needed	
Brief description of informants	0.5	none specified, any needed?	
Findings	8	[introduction	0.5
		[answers to theory questions	3.5
		[description of Informants	3.5
		[project conclusions	0.5
Research conclusions	2	none specified, any needed?	
Personal Learnings:†	1		
Total	18.5 pages		

* Students were required to put working documents (principally transcripts) in an appendix, which did not count as far as the 'specified word-length' was concerned.

† In the course on depth interviewing from which this example is drawn, all students have to report on what they personally have learnt from doing the course, up to and including the writing of the report: hence the slightly odd title of this section.

FIGURE 16.1 **Example of a Plan for the Structure of a Report**

I start with the question of comparative representation, on the basis of which certain issues of single-portrait representation become clearer.

Comparative Psycho-portraits

Overview and Introduction

The metaphor that I use in the following discussion is that of the 'portrait' – an image of an overall 'visual representation' which is experienced by the viewer as being 'grasped as a whole at a given moment in time', synchronically. Using the painted 'portrait' as a metaphor is helpful, in that it suggests that no two individuals look the same in reality and also that the 'artist' (yourself in relation to your informants) has a choice as to how to 'paint' the portrait. Putting this another way, no two individuals are the same and no two portraits of the same individual even by the same artist are the same.

Psycho-portraits, biography, BNIM case descriptions, these are 'crafted products' of a skill. On the basis of the 'spoken words' of your interviews, you will be 'painting' mostly in written words – though possibly with some visual help (photos and diagrams). A 'visual painting' is 'grasped as a whole' by the viewer, but the reader of a 'verbal portrait' is led through a sequence of words and pages, and you will need to 'plan' what elements to put in what sequence, so as to produce the 'effects' that you wish to produce. You have to be as empathetic about the reader's future experience of your psycho-portraits as you were about the past and present experience of your informants.

Attitude of Analyst Towards Differences and Generalizations

If you are not concerned with variation, with differences between your informants, with contradictions within one part of an account and another part of an account, then your 'comparative account' will be weak. The difficulty of this task can be suggested by looking at examples of partial student failure. I started exploring this in our previous discussion of data-loss and data-condensation. Semioticians say that it is 'news of difference that generates meaning' (Bateson, 1972/1980; Cooper, 2000), and the value of this maxim can be seen in understanding the examples below.

Looking Only for Common Features   One student under-used her material, by just trying most of the time to find what her informants agreed upon.

> 'Further questions were centred around love and the experience of love, i.e. communicating love to partners, defining and understanding love all produced similar responses among informants.
>
> When asked to describe love, all the informants believed it to be the same thing: a feeling of fulfilment, a desire to be with someone, enjoying a person's company, strong friendship and fondness. When asked how they would communicate love to a partner based on their previous definition of it, most informants emphasized through sex, buying each other little presents, sharing things with one another, etc.'

I commented:

> 'But you don't look for any differences. For the first point, Even if they all gave identical lists – which I don't believe for a moment – did they all rank them the same? You are only looking for similarities, not looking equally hard for differences. Their descriptions seem to leave out varieties of 'passionate love'. For the second point, you say "most", but say nothing about the exceptions. You also have the bored "etc.", which suggests that to give the findings in full is what you can't be bothered to do. You're bored by it, and want to save the reader the fate of being bored by "the obvious things", because you aren't looking for differences.'

Without difference, your informants are experienced as 'homogenized'.

A student did not set up her sample to have significant differences between her 30–45-year-old women users of homeopathy. And her style of marshalling evidence did not command conviction. At one point, she said:

> 'The power-relationships between the patient and the doctor were emphasized by all the women. The GP was seen as "acting upon" the health of the patient, and "didactic".'

I remarked:

> 'Did they *all* say he was "didactic" and "acting upon"? Or just one? Which one? What would be the opposite of "acting upon" the health of the patient, which you imply would be in some way better?'

One student indicated his lack of interest in personal differences between his informants very clearly. He told the reader:

> 'There is no real necessity to distinguish the informants with ... names: they are all in the same social category (students), and the only specific divisions relevant here are sex, of which there are equal numbers. I have assumed that the largest age gap is small enough so as to render age insignificant in this study'

and in fact, throughout his findings, he just distinguishes 'an informant (male)' and 'an informant (female)'.

I commented:

> 'Doing ethnography with a sensitivity to the way that people differ from each other in their personal culture requires that the reader keep clear who is saying what. Such an indifference to personal culture may be tolerable in experimental social psychology, it is bad ethnography.'

In his findings, the same student seemed to be looking for generalizations that could characterize the group as a whole, generalizations about the uniformity of opinions or behaviour. This is not wrong in itself, though the 'flavour of the evidence' of such a 'common-group position' needs to be provided, perhaps by giving quotations to indicate both ends of the range and then a 'most common position' in the middle.

Need for Sufficient 'Direct Quotation' – Distinguishing Feature of Ethnographic Writing   It is not enough just to say, without direct quotation, in an over-theorizing way,

> 'The question of whether alcohol or alcohol advertising might influence them or their opinions and views in any way apart from intoxication was not very positively received, although not universally denied.'

I commented:

> 'Much too abstract. The reader wants more quotations to see what you mean by *"was not positively received but not universally denied"*. The words in italics are in academic-speak and give much too little flavour of the structure of feelings and of concepts of your informants, and particularly little about differences between them.'

Having suggested the importance of constructing meaning by the evocation of actual or virtual differences – usually by way of direct quotation (see earlier examples in this book by Jane Price, David Buckingham, Liebes and Katz) – at the level of the paragraph, or even the sentence, in comparative work, let us now look at larger constructions, first of all at the level of single portraits.

Psycho-biographies: from Outside or Inside?

Being able to write a 'profile', a single 'portrait', preferably with an eye to the later juxtaposition of the portraits and eventual construction of a synthetic 'group portrait', is an important task. Since our focus is the 'comparative depth interview' and the 'comparative report' I shall not give such 'individual portraiture' the weight that it would deserve elsewhere. For us, it is the necessary basis for comparative work. But constructing an 'individual portrait' is not always an easy thing to do.

An 'autobiography' is a 'psycho-portrait' written by the informant without the need for any attempt at 'objectivity'. Such a personal document[1] is a resource for ethnography, but it falls outside the realm of our discussion.

The notion of a psycho-portrait is one which refers to an attempt to distinguish the 'distinctive features' of a particular informant, their way of thinking, their way of life, their mode of experiencing their whole life or some segment thereof. It brings together material inside and outside the interview to 'make a distinctive picture'.

There could be a spectrum from (a) the apparently 'objective' and neutral 'portrait' to (b) one which explicitly requests or even requires the reader to take some distance from the preferred self-description of the informant, to (c) a completely subjective self-description by the subject him or herself. In the centre of the spectrum are portraits in which the self-preferred 'delineation' is given in a context which enables the reader to grasp the self-presentation in the terms of the interviewee but also enables or requires the reader to 'go beyond' that preferred self-presentation.[2]

Thin Summary – Caseworker Account 'From the Outside'

One student's account of drug-using mothers in a rehabilitation centre gives an account which is too 'external' by ethnographic standards; it is a mixture of apparent objectivity with evaluative subjectivity.

> 'In regard to her relations to her children, Helen was not completely oblivious of the effect it would have on them – she continued to use drugs in front of her daughter. At this stage of her life, Helen is attentive to her needs, blames herself from having missed out on Louise's childhood. Louise at times appears confused – Helen can be affectionate for a minute while the following minute she is verbally abusive. Louise comprehends her mother's experiences no doubt, but Connor is still an infant and has not had to suffer the full emotional anger of her mother. As for re-establishing herself in society, she is afraid, a natural sign of somebody going back 'outside'. She has every intention to dissociate herself from anyone involved in any form of substance abuse .... One can only admire her spunk and eagerness to make a new life for herself and her two children.'

I commented:

> 'There are not enough direct quotations. This is too much like a socialwork case-history, too "outside" a view. The reader does not get a clear idea of the structure of values, the

---

1 See Ken Plummer (1983) for a recent discussion.

2 For a typology of the way the 'presented world' and the identity of the 'narrator' interconnect, see the work of Ruthrof on narratives in fiction, to be found in Appendix A.

structure of feelings, the structure of cognitions as formulated *in her own words*. I get more of an idea of your structure of cognitions, values, feelings ... and this is the wrong proportion.'³

Richer Portrait – Half from Within, Half from Outside
Ethnographic 'portraits' of individuals need to be written with more empathy. For this, they also need direct quotation. But this can be done more or less systematically and with the direct quotation used in different ways. I shall look at three individual accounts: of Jane, of Brigid, and of Dionysos.

A Holistic Individual Portrait – No Explicit Mode of Presentation, More Use of Summary: 'Jane'   Barbara U strikes quite a nice balance in Jane Austen-like 'objectivity':

> 'Jane is the only remaining resident of the individual group who set up the housing co-operative, and regards this as a source of frustration.
>
> "People who apply are getting younger ... and I'm getting older .... You're the person that knows about the history of every single shelf or cup ... and what sort of things we ought to be doing as a co-op ... and that gets you down .... I mean I didn't choose to have a family of six people all depending on me."
>
> In spite of this she reports that it is hard to relinquish responsibility. Maybe this is because she does want a degree of control: certainly, she likes to know "what people are up to" and is irritated by "people not doing the same thing as me".
>
> Jane implies that current residents are not particularly in sympathy with her "political" work, since she now does it in her bedroom rather than in the kitchen. Also, her use of the terms "this lot" and "previous lots of people" implies a certain distancing, as does the comment "... they think I've got strange and unusual standards", and the fact that she no longer decorates the kitchen for people's birthdays.
>
> She almost invariably associates household objects in the communal area with memories of past residents and/or infringements of her personal values (her dislike of "excessive consumption" or her views of what constitutes a tidy kitchen). For instance I learn that Heather "insisted" upon a double sink and Roger "insisted" on a new chair and fridge. Jane felt these to be "unnecessary" because they would not be useful (although she admits she had been proved wrong with the fridge and sink).
>
> Usefulness often seems to mean "useful to her": Roger wanted the new chair because he had a bad back, and, although she disapproves of the TV and video, they are obviously useful to the people whom she sees as "glued" to them ....'

You might want to explore how Jane might feel she has been subtly undercut by this portrait, and how she might counter-argue. Having done that, you might think how you would evaluate the controversy about a 'fair representation' of Jane. But whatever its demerits, a 'portrait of Jane' is given and is material for a

---

3 In retrospect the 'amalgamated language' of the report makes it unclear whose descriptive and evaluative language is being used. 'Every intention to dissociate herself' sounds like the writer, 'eagerness to make a new life for herself' sounds perhaps more like Helen. It is not possible to say.

possible re-analysis perhaps by someone else to explore the degree and limits of its validity. There is a careful use both of one chunky quotation, and – embedded in the analytic description – of bit-quotations of key words and phrases.

A 'Quotational-Analytic' Style of Individual Portrait: 'Brigid'   Andrea C discusses an informant:

'[Brigid] was influenced to return to work by soap operas (i.e. Coronation Street) and Chat Shows (i.e. Oprah Winfrey). She liked the idea of "women who dominate the whole programme" and "the bread winner", "head of the household". She felt she could "take out what was relevant to me" and "relate to it", although she admits that the situations are totally different to her own.

She found dramas, such as Cagney and Lacey, "patronizing" as they "try and make women fit into a man's world" where they "go out and shoot people like the men do".

She was also not influenced to return to work by women presenters in news, documentaries or financial programmes, although she says: "It's lovely to see, I like to see, more women doing positive things on TV".

Her responses to advertisements neatly sum up the roles that women play:

"Sexual, sexual, absolutely! Sexual objects or the objects of sexual phantasies; or as a woman out to get men or men out to get women; or as housewives."

She feels that adverts reinforce the image of mothers staying at home with children and as housewives:

"It's very unrealistic: it's pandering to a view that advertisers think people want to see women like that."

The press has not influenced her decision to return to work:

"I am happy there is no particular coverage about women going back to work. People are treated as people, it's noticeable by its absence."

Finally, books. She had been influenced by the writings of Alice Walker as they were "realistic" and

"When I read a book by Alice Walker, it makes me proud and I think people can get on and do things when they want to."

Therefore, to conclude, [she agrees that] chat shows influence her to return to work ... [and that] female authoresses give her more inspiration, but, to conclude in her own words,

"I'm more influenced by people I know and my own situation. Female role models seem far too removed to be real to me. Unlike my friends who I talk to and they inspire me."'

I commented:

'Good summary, but the end-paragraph here feels as if it might lose touch with the "exceptions" to the "dominant tendency" it proposes. Don't forget what she says about Coronation Street, chat-shows, and Alice Walker's novels! You accept too uncritically, thereby recycling her theory as your own, what she says about "(not) being influenced".'

Her text goes through six informants at the same level of detail, and ends with one quotation from one of them. I remark:

> 'This is a truly excellent section in your concern for detail but I think you should end this with a conclusion. You could contrast the answers you have so carefully and usefully specified, e.g. Informant E finds Cagney and Lacey "encouraging as they play mothers who also have jobs" while Informant B found them "patronizing" as they try and make women fit into a man's world where they "go out and shoot people like men do". However short your conclusion, always have one … and make it say something across the range ….'

It should be remembered, though, that a level of detail that is supportable for just one or two informants over-burdens the reader as the number rises. In such cases, more use of data-reduction or summarization has to be made, for example, by using matrices.

A Quotation-analytic More Sociological Portrait: 'Dionysos' The *Sostris Final Report* (Chamberlayne and Rustin, 1999) presents a number of examples of theoretical discussion combined with illustrative case-studies. I cannot cite here a full example of such sociologizing discourse together with a relevant case-study but strongly recommend its consideration. From the section on 'The Early Retired', I extract the following case example.

> 'Our case example in this category, reported by Elisabeth Mestheneos and Elli Ionnanidi from Greece illustrates the informal resources available in a "traditional" society which can sometimes compensate for the absence of full-time employment. "Dionysos belongs to what may be termed a traditional life frame which is expressed and lived through the family". It is however a family without property or land; its main resources are its members' deep attachments to and support for one another. The family is more gender-balanced than one might have expected from traditional assumptions about patriarchy. Dionysos's mother is described as the family's foundation stone, and one of the informative features of Dionysos's life is
>
> > "the relationship to his father, who even though handicapped and suffering a long and debilitating illness, is a role model of a loved and loving person, someone who he describes as 'golden' in the sense of special and precious. The same image of the sweet and loving male appears to be reproduced in Dionysos's life."
>
> Dionysos deeply identifies with his family, and
>
> > "His own family becomes an almost exact social reproduction of his family of origin: e.g. a strong supportive and economically independent mother is reproduced in the same kind of life; his two sons take the place of himself and his brother even in relation to the kinds of choices of study. Even his leisure interests – fishing, gardening, helping around the neighbourhood – follow those of his father. This rather exact form of social reproduction has, as one of its consequences, that it offers emotional security and agreed goals and values … However, at the same time such exact social reproduction also acts to limit individual choice in all spheres, including the labour market."
>
> Dionysos's working life has been largely shaped by his family circumstances. He was trained as a plumber, and could probably have been successful as such. But probably

continued

continued

because of his father's long illness, and his being necessary in the family, he did not pursue his independent plumbing career after an early setback, and instead has worked all his life in the family kiosk, and in a local cooperative. He talked about his work wholly in terms of his ability to get on with others, not at all in terms of practical skills or tasks. It seems that maintaining friendly social ties is perceived as the main virtue and necessity in this family.

He is "early retired" because the cooperative failed, and because when his mother died the family lost the kiosk license. But he retains significant assets. The researchers think it likely that he will find work in another kiosk (there are visitors from the city which make little shops like these viable).

"He also has a wide network of family and friends, resources that include a pension, savings and small undeclared earnings as well as a working wife in a good job, a social position in the community, and ways of passing his time, e.g. in small jobs and hobbies, in household work and the care of his sons."

One could regard Dionysos as "entrapped" in traditional life by the circumstances of his family. A quality of sadness in his narrative makes it seem that his life has been particularly shaped by an experience of grief and mourning. However, the researchers emphasize that Dionysos does not feel deprived as a result of this entrapment. They make the point that it is impossible to perceive Dionysos as experiencing social exclusion in a society such as Greece where traditional structures are still in existence, "in particular in the context of a small area where Dionysos is a known and integrated person, belonging to the local community, who has achieved the social goal shared by the local society". This case shows how cautious one must be in applying concepts such as early retirement or social exclusion in traditional societies.' (Chamberlayne and Rustin, 1999: 52–3)

An interesting feature of this BNIM case description is that – like the original case-report on which it is based (Mestheneos and Ioannidi, 1998) – it has only one or two direct quotations from Dionysos himself. His mode of experiencing and being in the world is evoked by empathetic representation by the researchers and by Chamberlayne and Rustin's discussion of and quotation from the primary researchers and their original research report. Although the case study is strongly theorized, such theorization works well with the data to produce for and in the reader a sense of a particular case in a particular milieu. Very large quantities of direct quotation do not always have to be 'presented', but can be condensed into researcher 'representation' if the latter is sufficiently sensitive.

Comparative Portraits: Edging Beyond Juxtaposition?

We have looked so far at different practices of producing single portraits; we now turn to strategies of explicit comparison. We first give an example of 'edging beyond juxtaposition', by two long portraits organized on similar principles (Rachel D comparing two clerics). In this student example, where two cases are juxtaposed in some detail, the reader comes up against the limits of detailed comparison of a holistic sort.

Juxtaposed Portraits – Different Clerics   Rachel D gives her account of each informant under certain comparative headings: the conceptual frames, the objects of study (topics of conversation?), the methodological approach, the presentation of material, the argument put forward, any other relevant material. Her method of writing up is through large chunky 'unified portraits' of each in turn. These tend to be too long for convenient recall and synthesis by the reader, but if the number of cases is very low and the interest of the reader is very high, this method of presentation has certain advantages.

She attempts to 'systematize' the long descriptions by using a 'common grid of description' for each portrait. Unlike the previous 'quotation-analytic' description by Andrea C, which does not suggest that a grid 'usable for the next case' is in process of emergence, though Rachel C's 'common analytic grid' is not too clear, an effort is clearly being made to create comparable portraits. Rather like a semi-structured interview, a semi-structured portrait is being created!

She was interviewing two clergymen. This is her 'unified picture' of her first informant.

'A major concept that he used was *evaluation*. Things were perceived in *helpful/unhelpful* terms, and a large percentage of his argument consisted of evaluating aspects of the charismatic church as *helpful* or *unhelpful*.

For the major concepts that were important to him, he first clearly identified them, then went on to defining them, and finally broke them down into specific actions, and then evaluated them.

His own conceptual framework was organized in terms of *interpreting God's work and will*, adhering to Biblical principles: "Being as close to the Bible as I can".

He considered himself as "open" but presented a seemingly very closed argument: "I know the facts, I know these things".

These conceptual frames were also used to talk about the objects of study he presented .... These were the legitimacy of the charismatic church, the role of the Church in relation to the Christian and to the non-Christian.

There was a high regard, as an actual object of study, for the matter of interpretation, whether of a piece of literature, a Biblical reference, or an actual experience. He distinguished clearly between what he called "facts", "real issues" ("the Cross of Christ") and the "fun" (enjoyable experiences).

The terms of reference he used were Biblical references, people's work (charismatic), his own critical analysis of the Charismatics, and some reference to sociological material.

The interview came across rather as an analysis than an interview or discussion, though there was some emotional response – a rather negative feeling towards the Charismatics.

The argument he presented seemed very well thought out and complete. This was seen in the way he concisely structured his responses – including, at some stages, not really answering the questions asked. The argument was not particularly direct: a lot of inference was used along with intonation, seemingly "harmless" accusations in a joking fashion, and the use of an American accent when it came to some description or quoting.

He constantly drew me in to his argument and evaluations by appealing for my agreement. He also used a lot of inference, and hinted at quite a few things which I sometimes

continued

continued

overlooked – though there were some more obvious aspects which I did pick up during the interview, for example, his idea of "playing games".'

Rachel D went on to give a unified picture along similar lines of her second informant.

'His conceptual frames were, in terms of his view of Scripture, basing it in terms of how it relates to us personally, what response is sought for by it / required to it, the accuracy and relevancy of it, and how scripture relates to experience.

There was more of a picture of the God he knows and "relates to", along with the definition and further explanation of Man's enquiry and God's revelation. He recognized the different factors in his change of theology. It stemmed from a situational change, a different response to his ministry, a spiritual inquiry which led on to a spiritual "charismatic" experience. It was this primary situational change which he felt defined his ministry in terms of what was "acceptable" and what was "necessary".

His objects of study were founded in his beliefs (what he'd "previously been taught and believed" and what he "now believed through experiencing the Scriptures"). He made a distinction between what he calls "the limiting of God to man's reason" through "ideas, logic and understanding", on the one hand, and, on the other, "the relating", "responding to God" in "intellectual, physical, emotional and spiritual ways" and in the reciprocal nature of the relation to God.

The concept of power was used considerably: the "lacking of power" in his ministry, "the power of God", "re-empowering".

There was a focus on the specific nature of God, rather than on a theology or on specific gifts. He also focused upon his "expectation" and his "experience" or lack of experience.

His study of Christianity is achieved by looking at the World's response to God and in the nature of the Gospel and Salvation in terms of relevancy to the outside world.

He uses references from the Bible and other small quotes. With the Scriptural references, he either used them to contextualize experience ("I see it then, I see it now") or to act as an introduction to a belief or expectation he held ("It says: if I ask, I shall receive").

It didn't seem that he had a truly well thought out or defined case to bring together: this was evident in the way he had to stop and think about issues before he responded to questions, and in the way he'd lose his train of thought.

However, this made it more of a discussion-based interview and I felt I was receiving more natural, less manufactured, responses and reactions (he openly admitted that he didn't have the answers for everything and that he "wasn't right all the time").

There was some degree of inference used in regards to the Evangelical interpretation of Scripture and belief, also in terms of relating to God. Although it wasn't hostile, but more related to his own Evangelical training and experience.

His responses were more descriptive of emotions rather than critical comment.'

There is some lack of clarity about some of these formulations (e.g. the last paragraph but one). On the other hand, she is using her own experiences within the interview as well as the analysis of the interview tape to describe significant elements of the interaction which give her a sense of the contrasting personal cultures of the two informants.

To the extent to which we are engaged in researching individuals because they fall or are believed to fall into one or other 'type' (sociological, psychological, cultural, etc.), to that extent we will attempt to explore commonalities and differences. However, developing bottom-up characterizations of cases (as in the biographic-narrative interpretive method) means that there is no pre-existing typology into which they necessarily fit. This means that the way in which each case is treated just as an 'instance of a more general category' (Bruner's paradigmatic thinking and representation) is relatively weak, while the way each case is treated as characterized by a 'unique configuration' (gestalt or configuration thinking) is relatively strong.

Possible Models for a 'Synthetic Account' of Multiple Informants

In the last sub-section, I looked at ways in which 'individual portraits' of a holistic or analytic variety could be made more 'comparative'. In this section, I start at the other end of the spectrum, looking at efforts at strict comparison which then lend themselves eventually to the construction of more individualized portraits.

In this sub-section, I consider further how comparisons can be made. They can be relatively thin or abstract, or they can be enriched by adding relative personalization of the accounts. If the details become too rich, the overall comparative view is lost; if there are not enough details, then the claim to 'ethnographic density' has to be given up. Space and purpose are the deciding factors.

Thin Summary Indicating Range and Common Features

Miner (1960) did a study of a programme in which, in order to reduce the incidence of sleeping-sickness caused by tsetse flies, villagers were constrained by heavy 'ruler pressure' (fines and the removal of 'headmen') to keep local streams clear of vegetation. In the following excerpt, he briefly compares the attitudes and conceptions of the village headmen who have carried out this policy.

> 'A thorough check of the streams showed that the annual orders of the Emir have been carried out in nearly all instances, and that the area is still virtually free of fly and sleeping sickness. One may well conclude that this, the major phase of the scheme has been a success .... It comes as something of a shock, therefore, to discover that slum clearance cannot be said to have been adopted into the culture of the Hausa around Anchau.
>
> The basis of such a statement is an exhaustive study of the present attitudes and conceptions of village headmen regarding sleeping sickness and its control. The village leaders were asked why they cleared the streams every year.
>
> The common denominator of the responses was that the slashing was carried out because they were forced to do it.
>
> A quarter of the headmen literally had no idea why the work was done.
>
> continued

continued

All of the others, however, stated that clearing the brush eliminated tsetse fly, although sometimes this statement was added as an afterthought to an initial statement of ignorance of any reason for the task.

Half of those who mentioned flies also stated that they transmitted sleeping sickness. But when one pursued the subject, it became clear that this was a simple repetition of what they have been told. They saw this as the British explanation, but held firmly to their old belief that sleeping sickness was caused by spirits.

Elimination of the flies was rationalized by others as desirable because the bite was painful. Still others saw the clearing as a means of driving out crop-destroying monkeys or of improving pasturage for Fulani cattle.

Finally, the interviews produced that rare occurrence in social science data, unanimous concurrence. When asked if they would continue to clear the streams if they were not forced to do so, every headman replied "No".' (Miner, 1960)

The above extract shows how to lay out variations on a theme (and, incidentally, the importance of 'pursuing subjects' and not taking certain statements on their own at face value). However, none of the headmen come to life as individuals; there are no direct quotations.

Synthetic-montage – with Some Quotation, Alternative Pathways, Common Features

In the next example, there is some direct quotation, but one could hardly say that the quoted informants (M's with different numbers) come to life vis-à-vis each other. However, alternative pathways and common features derived from several dozens of interviews are very clearly delineated, and there is no danger of being lost in detail. Poirier et al. (1983) note of the following piece of writing that 'I have used the geographical variable as the mode of contextualizing and of differentiating the accounts'. The implication is, of course and quite correctly, that it is up to the writer to select the most appropriate 'dimensions of variation' for such comparative work as she or he goes along.

'Black Africa

When a doctor was designated for Black Africa, his "overseas" voyage started at Marseilles where he took the boat for Dakar. This was above all true before the war because, just after the war, he went to his posting by way of the convoy known as "Chanas".

M2 tells us, page 5–6: "I went overseas the first time in 1945, in April, because some comrades were being relieved who had been there 6 or 7 years because of the war. I left from Sete because Marseilles had been bombed and embarked on the 'Hoggar' with about 3–4,000 troops. I did Algiers–Brazzaville in lorry or bus. We were a dozen with a few administrators' wives who were going to rejoin their husbands and some officers in the administration. It is what we called the 'Chanas convoy', since Chanas was a transporter who had done this journey many times."

continued

continued

Professional Life

Two sorts of postings were given to these doctors:

- either a "country posting" which could itself be either fixed or itinerant (M32, 15,18) .... Medical practice in the bush involved a lot of difficulties. The doctors whom I interviewed spoke to us of their great isolation in respect of the responsibilities they had about their medical interventions.

  M.14, p. 7 "Around the dispensary, which was outside the post, a crowd waiting for me every morning at 8.30"

- or a town-posting, which, as regards medicine, always brought them a lot, given the quantity of patients and the diversity of their illnesses.

  M.9 tells of the Saint-Louis hospital in Senegal (p. 10): "There, I worked in this hospital with a terrific chirurgical auxiliary who was very helpful. I had there chirurgical work focused on the stomach, I did some 50 vasectomies with very good results."

The roles were multiple and polyvalent:

- administrative tasks: (for example, the census of the population from 1927 to 1939 in order to treat sleeping-sickness (M.15)
- construction of maternity clinics, dispensaries, bridges (very often cited)
- often in charge of the inspection of meat because of the absence of a vet
- maternal and infant protection (they all mention this)
- training of nurses so that they could help the doctors in their tasks (they all mention this)
- teaching basic hygiene.'
(Poirier et al., 1983: 193–4, my translation TW)

The above extract indicates alternative paths of the constructed entity 'the typical doctor' to start with, and then indicates universal or at least common features of most of the doctors irrespective of the path taken. You might like to think how this might be a way of bringing your accounts together.

Formal Typologies: Reality as Combinations of Analytic Variants

Clapier-Valladon's Five Scenarios of the Careers of French Colonial Doctors   In the next extract, Poirier and his collaborators present a schematic analysis in which the reports of the different doctors have been classified by S. Clapier-Valladon into a complex typology.

'An example of sequences combining the key-episodes of the corpus of medical accounts

I cite the analysis of an important theme of the return to the metropolis of the overseas doctors. The example of the lexical-thesaurus is that of the Negative Balance-Sheet of the return.

I illustrate typological analysis by the rubric "Balance Sheet of the Return". The balance-sheet is organized around three rubrics:

continued

continued

1 stability
2 life in France
3 life overseas

which I consider to be the three key-episodes of the corpus.

Episode A – Stability

A1 the longed-for stability brings, at the moment of return, satisfaction
A2 the wisdom-resignation stability
A3 the false stability – coexistence with eventual departures

Episode B – Life in France

B1 the positive aspects
B2 the negative aspects

Episode C – Life Abroad

C1 good memories of and regrets for overseas
C2 difficulties encountered overseas

The life-histories (accounts) develop according to different sequential structures which associated the episodes of the discourse in different ways, permitting a "sorting out" of narrators. In this way, I have discovered the following patterns in our researches:

- Type I – Simple Sequence A1 B1 C2
  The western migrant happy to return to his country
- Type II – Simple Sequence A1 B1 C1
  Ulysses
- Type III – Complex Sequence A2 B1 B2 C1
  The ex-migrant, man of maturity and memories
- Type IV – Complex Sequence A2 B2 B1 C1 C2
  The man of lucidity and critique
- Type V – Ambivalent Sequence A1 A3 B2 B1 C1 C2
  The man of ambivalence and acculturation
- Type VI – Complex Sequence A3 B2 C1
  Nomads

Critics who do not engage in content analysis and who carefully avoid collecting qualitative material could say that another typology is possible. There is certainly an element of truth in that, but what is important is that the narrators involved and those who have subsequently been interviewed have accepted this typology and have happily placed themselves in it.' (Poirier et al., 1983: 197–9)

A large number of 'formal aspects of all cases' are defined, and then an empirical study of the frequency of particular combination patterns can be made.

I hope the above examples have suggested how accounts of the common and the distinguishing features of several informants can be presented in an intelligible and economic fashion. They all involve some form of 'expert meta-language' which might have existed before undertaking the work or might have emerged as a result of the process of doing the work.

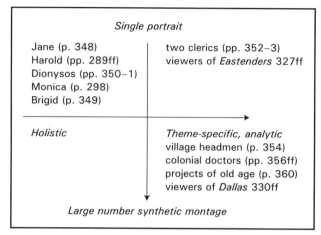

FIGURE 16.2   **Two Dimensions of Portrait Construction (Single/Multiple)**

You may have to write some sub-sections in an 'individual portrait' style; others in a firmly 'comparative analytic' style. In both cases, using or developing a systematic grid for comparison is strongly recommended, both so that you compare like with like and so that the reader can follow you.

In Figure 16.2, as the number of individual informants rises, so does the need for theme-specific contrasts, for synthetic montages, for typologies. The drive is from top-left to bottom-right as the number increases, since doing 'holistic portraits' of large numbers of informants is technically very difficult and at a certain point becomes impossible.

The firmer you are about a meta-language for comparison, the more generous you will then be able to be with 'direct quotation' without confusing the reader. Note the example from Liebes and Katz (pp. 330ff) theorizing in a complex way about members of different groups watching and commenting upon *Dallas*.

I have reached the limit of the shift from descriptive paragraphs to descriptive portraiture using implicit or explicit grids of description of a relatively concrete-holistic or a relatively partial-analytic variety. Clearly the typology of the example of French colonial doctors was on the border of leaving normal discursive writing.

In our next sub-section, I consider explicit departures from ordinary discursive paragraphs – the use of matrices and flow-charts: devices for evoking configurational gestalts to supplement discursive modes of presentation.

MATRICES AND FLOW-CHARTS

The importance of visual displays cannot be over-emphasized, particularly because most social scientists under-use such displays. For example, it would be perfectly possible to include photographs of the interviewee, of their living-arrangements, of the urban or rural milieux in which they move, of their places of work and worship and consumption, and such 'documents of life' might be a powerful support for

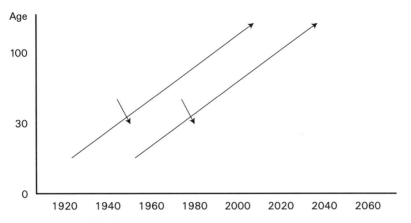

FIGURE 16.3 **Riley Life Chart**

the understanding of individual cases, just as would be the provision of video-clips of their behaviour in and out of the interview context. On the other hand, the danger of visual stereotyping might be so great that work might have to be done to counter the impressions left by such too-powerful visual images.

I am assuming that the report may have some photographs but nothing more technologically advanced than this. However, the use of matrices and flow-charts is perfectly compatible with a word-based research report.

It is a mistake – a mistake that qualitative researchers *not* trained in quantitative display devices are most likely to make – to write as if the typical flow of paragraphs across pages is the only way of presenting material. Frequently, in the presentation of statistics, the relationship of numbers is *only* rendered properly intelligible by the use of matrices and flow-charts; in qualitative presentation, as a complement to, if not a substitute for, the flow of paragraphed words, the use of images and diagrams is almost as important.

I previously argued – following Bruner and Polkinghorne – that paradigmatic presentation of concepts should be accompanied by the gestalt configuration of narrative; here I argue that both should be accompanied – as in this book – by a considerable number of visual gestalt configurations, diagrams.

The best discussion of ways of condensing and representing data for single and multiple cases can be found in Miles and Huberman (1994) which has so many examples and devices that you can get lost in them; however, browsing through their chapters is a great way of stimulating your imagination for modes of representation beyond the paragraph.

Flow-Charts

In our discussion of the biographical-interpretive method in Part IV, I had occasion to construct *flow-charts* in the elementary form of a chronologies of the sequences of biographical data, the dates of events that happened to Harold and actions by Harold, for example (see p. 238). I also created a flow-chart of the sequence of part-structures in the interview: the TSS (p. 240 for example) is an example of a flow-chart. Another example is shown in Figure 16.3. The chart (derived from

Living is achieving (4 men, 1 woman)	Living is being social (3 men)	Living is loving (3 women)	Living is family life (1 man, 2 women)	Living is struggling (2 men, 4 women)
M1 – creating a career in a thriving business – constant problems with wives – fight for physical fitness	M5 – developing, searching – learning to love after divorce		W5 – a career within the family context – coping with severe health problems	M9 – trying to overcome childhood authority figures – not shaping up until failing in school and job life
M2 – successful professor while dreaming of being an artist – difficulties in relating to women – engagement in church activities	M6 – gradually achieving career goals – living by giving	W2 – falling in love with love	W6 – marriage and family career – earning career – community career	M10 – feels imposed on by ma and important ancestors – 'playing safe' in jobs and retiring early
M3 – ever-expanding business – search for love all life	M7 – a series of jobs – involvement in: art, nature, reading – helping others out	W3 – generating love for family and husband – loving jobs, but choosing to stay at home	M8 – caring for wife, an invalid – giving kindness, generosity – receiving more than giving	W7 – struggling, with and without husband – raising boys alone, and overcoming the empty nest
M4 – life-long engagement in research – ambivalence towards students		W4 – serving God and leading His children		W8 – getting on as a woman in spite of little femininity – getting on in spite of little money

FIGURE 16.4 Projects of Old Age (in part) (Ruth et al., 1996)

Riley, 1998) indicates the actual and projected lives of two individuals: one born in 1920 and the other in 1960. The arrows indicate the dates at which they were aged 30, in 1960 and 1990 respectively. I can therefore consider what general and local conditions affected their life-courses: for example, a strong demand for coal in the period 1940–60, for the older man; a sharp decline in the coal industry 1980–2000 for the younger man, the age of Harold. Obviously, such a chart of events can be very detailed. The items on the horizonal axis might be months in a single year, or days in a week, for example.

A family history chart is another example. A large number of other examples can be gleaned from Miles and Huberman (1994: 110–22, 200–6) expositions of single-case and multiple-case 'time-order displays'.

Matrices

Figure 16.4 provides a matrix not for one case, as in the case of Harold cited previously, but for several cases. Its purpose is to enable the reader to grasp common features (in the column heads) and some summarized distinctive ones (the case-features characterized in the column below each head).

You might wish to compare it with Clapier-Valandon's representation of the French colonial doctors, above.

17

'Writing up' Biographic Sub-genres: Suggestions by way of a Conclusion

INTRODUCTION

The previous discussion of strategies of presentation and representation has been comparatively general. Starting from the work of Bruner and Polkinghorne, I identified paradigmatic theorization and gestalt configuration (whether narrative or visual gestalt) as two ways in which the reader could be helped towards understanding. I also stressed the importance of keeping a clear distinction in the text between your voice and the voices of all others, and embodied this in the revision of Spradley's six-level conceptual framework into a two-column version and the notion of the desirable zig-zag in any text between your voice and all other voices and between level-6 of specific incident statements and level-1 of universal generalization statements.

Having suggested that you needed to avoid over-identifying with anybody else's voice but also to avoid over-distancing yourself as well, I then gave examples of 'account-giving': the description of disabled children in a school, and the accounts by Vaughan (uncoupling), by David Buckingham (children discussing *EastEnders*) and by Liebes and Katz (culturally diverse responses to *Dallas*) to indicate different issues of presenting raw interview material data and conceptual interpretation to the reader. My general argument was that the separateness of each should always be recognized and that there was a good case for presenting the interplay of data and theorization in a *confessional narrative* tale of 'my/our struggle with theory and data', such that the reader follows the researcher's struggle to arrive at a matching of theory and data and is put into a position to access controversies about how the matching was finally made.

After identifying the systematic answering of each TQ separately and then the summation of these ATQs into an answer to the CRQ (ACRQ) as the default mode of writing-up, I then looked at issues of macro-planning of a final reporting portfolio (the stress was on identifying total number of pages and then creating a plan of sections and sub-sections with clear page-length targets) of which I gave an example, and discussed intuitive and counter-intuitive ideas about structuring such final reports.

I argued against any presentation in which the reader was only presented with selected theory and selected data fully integrated in a seamless *realist-naturalist* presentation or in a *finally theorized* presentation, and I argued for the differentiation of theory and data but also for their presented and developing interplay in the way described.

I then moved from this rather general discussion to the particular area of psycho-portraits, arguing for the need to indicate both common features and news of difference for the reader to understand the point of the account. The use of direct quotation was seen as crucial in distinguishing both central tendencies and types of difference and ensuring the reader's recognition of the specificity of the informant's voice. I looked at a number of student paragraphs where the attempt at presentation had not been successful. I then moved on to the area of single psycho-portraits, contrasting caseworker thin summaries from outside to richer portraits which were described as being half from inside and half from outside, and where there was a move towards a quotation-analytic mode of presentation, either on an individual basis or upon that of a comparative grid. Rachel D's account showed the tension between the common grid and the amassing of detailed description.

This led on to the need to find models for synthetic accounts of multiple informants. To do this, I moved from Miner's thin summary indicating the range and common features of those involved in the struggle against the tsetse-fly to the presentation of the careers of French colonial doctors and, finally, to the typology of Clapier-Vallandon.

By this point, the need at times to go beyond or to complement the textual paragraph presentation was clear, and the next section presented – all too briefly – flow-charts and matrices as ways of economically and powerfully summarizing data from a large number of cases. Obviously, these work well when the reader has – in the flow of your presentation – moved themselves from immersion in considerable amounts of data to the summary presentation in matrices, flow-charts, and typologies; they do not work as well when only the summary is presented.

Finally, below, I reconsider strategies of genre, this time those implied in the presentation of biographical research based primarily on the narrative interviews of a BNIM sort.

'WRITING UP HAROLD' IN MORE 'SOCIO' OR MORE 'PSYCHO' DIRECTIONS

In this final section, I start from a common base of knowledge, namely the case of Harold as analysed in Part V above. You will need to re-read certain pages, the case history (pp. 289ff onwards), in order to re-acquaint yourself with the case material.

The biographic-interpretive method (BNIM) or any other provides us with a relatively reliable understanding of a particular case: in the case of BNIM, the account of the case-history and possibly an identification of the 'structure of the case'.

At the end of Part V, I argued that once the process of describing the case had been achieved, then the case history and the case-structure needed to be theorized in the light of whatever particular research problematic your overall research project was concerned with. Another way of putting the same point is to say that you need to decide, for any particular research community audience or readership, what is the general significance of the case for the concerns of that research community.

The original SOSTRIS project in the context of which the case of Harold was originally researched and reported upon was that of exploring individual and social strategies in contemporary societies seen as risk societies. He was originally reported upon as an example of a worker in a traditional industry which had ceased operation and who consequently had to adapt to a new societal context. The British contribution to the *Sostris Working Paper on Ex-Traditional Workers* (1999) compared a number of such workers within Britain, and the volume of working papers as a whole – which had reports on people in the same category from France, Spain, Germany, Sweden, Italy and Greece – attempted to discover and describe common features and differences in the societal contexts of such ex-traditional workers and common features and differences in the way that such workers coped. Such a 'writing-up' in a national report on ex-traditional workers was then used for a cross-national synthetic account on the category of ex-traditional workers across the seven countries, each of whom had submitted comparable national reports. The case of Harold as written up for that SOSTRIS report – Chamberlayne, Rupp and Wengraf (1999) – was strongly contextualized by a historical account of social trends at the level of the national society (Britain) and at the level of the local South Wales mining communities. The flavour of such a *sociology-cum-political-economy contextualization* can be partly grasped by looking at the way the case of Dionysos was represented (pp. 350–1 above).

There are however an indefinitely large number of other research community contexts for which cases (of Harold, in our example) could be written up differently.

For example, his 'case-history' cited at length on pp. 289–92 above was written up for a collection of materials entitled *Lines of Narrative* in which the concern of the readership for the particular social reality and sociological mechanisms of South Wales miners could be considered as low. The concern of the editors and the supposed concern of the readers was held to be with the question of understanding the working of narratives, factual and fictional, and the material was written up with sets of questions about narrations and experience in mind.

The same case material could repay investigation from a more psychological viewpoint. Ted Sloan, in his *Life-Choices: Understanding Dilemmas and Decisions* argues that key life-decisions are often made not on the basis of a rational calculation of options but on the basis of psychological 'complexes' which are laid down in early childhood and then tend to persist, impinging on our would-be rational calculations or often replacing them altogether. It would be possible to explore the case-history of Harold in such a light, asking questions about the role of his biological father and then of later father-figures and then even of himself as a father. Figure 12.30 (p. 287) suggests a constant concern for security lost and security insecurely regained at certain phases of his life. Were any of these lines of writing-up and subsequent inquiry to prove fruitful, then 'the case of Harold' might be developed in a study of psychological responses to particular traumatic events of a family and/or an industrial-societal sort. In Appendix B you will find a close analysis of a text segment from Harold's transcript. This may suggest some lines for such research.

There are other possibilities. For example, one conjectured Harold-told story (p. 272) was that of the militant who had betrayed his class for a middle-class job in social work. There are some elements in Harold's argumentation late in the interviewing process which suggest such an unease on Harold's part, though they are not dominant elements in his account. Even if Harold's story indicated no such elements, this does not mean that the case of Harold could not be compared with cases of other working-class or middle-class militants or both whose militancy was constrained or reduced during the 1980s and 1990s in a variety of ways and for a variety of reasons. A research community interested in the transformation of the labour process and of the labour movement in Europe in the current period might well find relevant material in the case of Harold when compared with those of others. This would involve a differently emphasized account of the case and quite different contextual material and argument.

Similarly, somebody concerned with the development and motivation of social work action and social workers in the late 20th century might, in their sociology of occupations, take the case of Harold as an example of one type of 'transition towards a social worker identity'.

A final example: those interested in continuities in political identity in the 1980s and 1990s might find Harold's case a valuable one to study, as he shifts from the overt industrial action as a militant miner of the 1980s to the worries and uncertainties about the political socialization of his daughter, as she is formed by a completely different post-mining and post-labour-movement context. Whereas in the earlier period Harold was quite clear about the priorities and instruments of appropriate political action, now his attempt to maintain his political identity has to cope with a quite different context. This might produce a different way of writing up Harold's case and a different set of comparative cases.

In general, it is important to note that, depending on the theoretical questions / problematic with which you are concerned, you will select and combine cases differently, and you will insert discussion of their 'case' in quite different contextual material and theorizing argument. If you are concerned with mining, you will group Harold's case with that of other miners; if you are concerned with age-cohorts, you will group Harold with cases of people who may not be miners but are within five or ten years of Harold's age; if you are concerned with political or industrial activism, you may ignore age and industry and concern yourself only with differentiating cases of militants from cases of non-militants. Clearly, your research theory will be the theory that determines your theory-driven sample at the level of the use of cases examined, as it was at the earlier moment when you chose what sort of cases you wished to interview.

I hope that the above discussion has suggested the way in which your theorization of the cases you study depends upon the overall problematic or set of research questions which you and your colleagues wish to address. For some purposes, you may not need to go back to the original materials; for others a different re-analysis of the earlier materials in the light of new TQs may be necessary.

Appendix A: Ruthrof's Typology of Told-Story, Presented-World, Positions

The typology below was developed in respect of fictional narratives. It may be useful as a way of sensitizing yourself – when listening to a narration – as to how listener and narrator are invited to position themselves.

Type	Implied narrator	Presented world	Implied reader
myth	authority	dictate	minor
parable	preacher	analogue and teaching aid	believer, limited intellectual faculties
'märchen'	artist	naive moral and presence of the marvellous	naive audience
saint's legend	ecclesiastical historian	theology: process of canonization	member of medieval church
prophecy	prophet	divine vision and future truth	believer
allegorical	ideological visionary	fusion of concrete image and abstraction	naive disciple
narrative of ideas	ideologist	ideology	disciple
omniscient narration	clairvoyant	unrestricted world, especially mental processes	initiate
confession	confessor	private affairs	confidant
objective narration	observer	evidence	witness
riddle	encoder	enigma	decoder
unreliable narration 1	liar	false world	rebel
unreliable narration 2	insensitive speaker	misinterpreted world	moderator
joke	jester	incompatible realms of thought	bisociator (momentary)

continued

Figure A.1   continued

Type	Implied narrator	Presented world	Implied reader
satire	satirist	distorted world	bisociator (extended) and moral judge
metafiction	player	game	playmate
innocent narration	minor	world as discovery	adult
handicapped narration	retarded person	unmanageable task	nurse
narration as cry	persecuted person	threat	rescuer and psychiatrist
dehumanized narration	dehumanized victim	inhumanity as norm	moral judge

FIGURE A.1   **Ruthrof's 18 Positions of Narrator/Reader (Ruthrof, 1981: 137–8)**

Appendix B: Critical Linguistics / Semiotics Model

The CLS Model

Basing herself largely on the Paris School of Semiotics, but more recently on the contributions of Critical Discourse Analysis (Caldas-Courthard and Coulthard, 1996; Fairclough, 1989; Fowler, 1979; Hodge and Kress, 1979; Meinhof and Richardson, 1994), Bronwen Martin's work distinguishes three levels of text-analysis for consideration: the surface analysis of discourse; the middle level narrative structure; and the deep structure of underlying thematics.

To suggest its utility, I shall first outline the model[1] and then sketch an application of it to the segment of Harold's transcript selected for microanalysis.

I. *The **discursive** level* where figures interact – the figurative level – is itself analysed in terms of three components:

    I. A. The *figurative level as expressed in conceptual structure* of the words in play (domain-structure), especially oppositional relations. This *conceptual structure* of the relations of figures on the discursive surface is explored through surface analysis of the semantic field, distinguishing first denotation and then connotation. Such analysis of the lexical field (Spradley, 1979, calls it domain analysis) reveals isotopies, in the description of three-dimensional entities in space and time engaging in physical action and interaction.

    I. B. *Surface-grammatical features* such as active/passive voice, the concealment or exposition of agency by way of the use of nominalizations; degree of tentativeness/dogmatism (modulation) the role of cohesive markers and a variety of other surface-grammar devices.

    I. C. *Enunciative strategies: the enunciation of the speech-act enunciator:* Who is telling the story? What speaker-positions and listener-positions are implied in the text? What is the strategy of the text-producer? What degree of adherence of the speaker to their utterance is implied?

II. The *narrative structure level* – the second and deeper, more abstract, level – is analysed in terms of the theory-language of Greimas and the Paris School. This involves

continued

---

1 I am grateful to Bronwen Martin for her help in formalizing the model and checking my working through of the example.

continued

> first identifying the difference between the initial moment of the narrated history and its final moment, and identifying episodes connected to the historical *transformation* from that beginning-state to that end-state. We then apply the two narrative models devised by Greimas: (i) first, the *actantial schema* developed by Greimas on the basis of Propp's work on the folktale (Martin, 1997: 41–52); and (ii) second, a *global narrative programme of the question, the canonical narrative schema* (Martin, 1997: 52–61).
>
> III. Finally the *deep level* is arrived at which looks at fundamental oppositions and transformations. Greimas's 'semiotic square' is used to understand these constructions of meaning-systems.
>
> IV. In addition, Martin concerns herself with contextualizing the text, with questions that go beyond formal text-analysis and its craft routines: I shall not deal with this here. (Martin, 1997: 83–7)

CLS Model – Close Analysis of a Text Segment from Harold's Interview

I shall provide a summary sketch of how a CLS analysis would operate in respect of an extract from Harold's verbatim transcript. The text is as shown in Figure B.1.

I. The Surface Structures Level
This level, where figures interact – the figurative level – is itself analysed in terms of three components, as follows.

I. A. The figurative component as shown by the conceptual structure of the words in play (domain-structure), especially oppositional relations
Place: There are relatively few spatial references. They are *the mines, school, being in care, 'here', and 'there'*. There is no concrete description of any particular place. The **strong 'opposition'** is between 'being together as a family at home' and being 'taken (away) into care'.

Time: There are many references to time, both objective time (chronology) and subjective time *now, at the time, young age, 14 years old, 11 year old, 2 or 3 years, Christmas, February, three years, too long, long period, eternity, not too long, short period*. The **strong oppositions** are in the subjective length of time between 'long period, too long, an eternity' and 'short period, not too long', said from the past and the present perspectives of Harold, respectively.

Actors: Although we know that Harold's family was large and complex, the actors in this story are peculiarly few and (with the exception of 'Annie') without proper names. The siblings are not even differentiated into 'brothers' and 'sisters', though there is a 'we' which might be all the children, or some of the children, or either of these groups plus the father. Although 'my Dad' is referred to, the mother who died when Harold was 11 is only referred to rather abstractly as 'our mother'. There may be **implied oppositions** such as family/outside institutions; father/family; family/Annie.

Actor-states: There are a lot of references to 'states of being' of the actors, most referring to the father: *being anxious, being under pressures, considering oneself, being very mature, having to grow up quickly, turning into an (abusive) alcoholic, being very depressed, not seeing the wood from the trees, seeing negatives rather than how I can move*

1	... my dad worked in the mines for oh since he was fourteen years of age and he
2	took em er early retirement or it was sickness due to the death of er of er our
3	mother and he really took er he then took control of of the family kind of thing
4	because
5	I mm
6	H I think he was rather anxious at the time but if anything happened to him
7	then we would all have to go into care and perhaps the part of the family being
8	being split up and that was the main reason for for him giving up work
9	I mm
10	H er I think there were a lot of pressures on on my father indeed as there was
11	the family and I think at such a young age of eleven even though I did consider
12	myself and still do now consider myself a very mature eleven year old I had to
13	grow up very quickly
14	I mhm
15	H em (4) and I think that it taught me some it taught me a few things em
16	my father did struggle quite a lot and I would describe him as turning into an alco-
17	holic at at a stage not long after em which was very difficult he was never never
18	ever abusive he was not an abusive alcoholic em I think what it was was that he
19	was very depressed he saw more of the negatives rather than how can we move
20	on from here he couldn't see the wood from the trees basically
21	I mm
22	H and er I think this state carried on for about two or three years I think
23	which is em which is quite a short period now but for me it was quite a long
24	period and and I recognize as a child and now that when you were younger from
25	the time of Christmas until next Christmas comes round is a it would seem an
26	eternity but now at my age (laughs) we're in we're in February now (unclear) so
27	I (laughs)
28	H so three years as for me as as seeing the problems that my dad was going
29	through was quite a considerable amount of time but now reflecting on that that
30	wasn't too long and he met Annie and you know that really pulled him together
31	you know er and he doesn't touch a drop now doesn't touch a drop em the man is
32	he's quite happy you know he's he's a he's a very fit man
33	I mm
34	H Annie's relatively fit she has her she has her difficulties particularly mo
35	mobility difficulties but in in the grand scale of things about her health I think
36	she's she's quite well
37	I mm
38	H so I think er what happened then was that er er I (1) left school without
39	any qualifications whatsoever none at all and it at at the time I didn't think it was
	relevant but now I look back ....

FIGURE B.1   **Extract from Harold's Verbatim Transcript**

*on, [enduring] a considerable amount of time for me, being pulled together, being happy,
being fit, having [mobility] difficulties, being well, (not) thinking something relevant.* They
mostly are rather 'negative in tenor' (dysphoric) and suggest – with the exception
of the father and Annie's current state – that 'then' was a very unhappy time. The
strong oppositions are between such 'states of being' as anxious–depressed–seeing
negatives/happy–fit–seeing positives; being an alcoholic/not being an alcoholic;
being pulled together/[falling apart]; being mature / not being mature; having to
grow up quickly / not having to grow up quickly.

Actor-activities: Quite a few are mentioned, though mostly to do with the father.
Working in mines, giving up work, being sick due to death of mother, taking early retirement,

family being split up, (not) going into care, meeting Annie, (not) touching a drop, leaving school. There are no references to any child-like activities by Harold in or out of school, as might be expected from a story covering secondary school; the only 'meeting of any one new' is done by the father in relation to 'Annie', and none by Harold-then. Harold-then does not seem to engage in any agent-activity in this story at all. This may reflect a mode of experiencing that time of his life as a non-agent. **The strong oppositions** in this lexicon of actor-activities, mostly around the father, are to do with *being in school/leaving school; working in mines/giving up work; being dead or sick/meeting Annie and being fit and well; touching a drop/not touching a drop.*

What can I say to **summarize the tentative sense of the whole** suggested by the above exercise? Although there is a considerable sense of Harold-now as a reflector from within a present perspective on those past events of Harold-then, there is a relative suppression of any Harold-then 'I', except as an eruption into what is experienced primarily as the story of his father. References to himself are not as agent. Women are crucial – the death of his mother initiates the family crisis and his father is saved by 'meeting Annie' – but they exercise this effect just by 'being' or 'not being' (*meeting Annie pulled him together*, not 'they met and Annie pulled him together', for example). The narrator is concerned to remain as Harold-now firmly in a present perspective in which the three to four years is 'not too long', though he allows the Harold-then to erupt into the narrative and present his then-perspective that it was like 'an eternity'. He is concerned to maintain a perspective which distances the 'then' and the very painful experiences he is describing mostly in a relatively distancing way. The thymic (feeling-tone) is strongly negative and, although the father seems slightly more of an agent than does Harold-then (he *takes control of the family;* he *gives up work and takes early retirement*), both the father and Harold-then seem not to have been active players in this (segment of) story. Harold is *taught quite a lot,* he is *made to grow up very quickly,* and even his *leaving school* sounds less like an action than an involuntary happening!

I. B. *Surface-grammatical Features* such as Active/Passive Voice, the Concealment or Exposition of Agency by Way of the Use of Nominalizations; Degree of Tentativeness/Dogmatism (Modulation), the Role of Cohesive Markers and a Variety of other Surface-grammar Devices. Although Harold-now is strongly agentic in this segment as he *thinks, considers, reflects, sees, describes* and so forth, he is quite non-agentic as Harold-then. The father is slightly agentic in his response to the death of his wife but then *turns into an alcoholic* who happens to be saved by being *really pulled together meeting Annie.* The women don't act at all. There is considerable abstraction in the references to *sickness, death, pressures,* which reaches a height of abstraction in the reference to *mobility difficulties* which strongly suggests social science or social worker classifications and terminology.

I. C. *Enunciative Strategies Component: Enunciation of the Speech-act Enunciator:* Who is Telling the Story? What Speaker-positions and Listener-positions are Implied in the Text? What is the Strategy of the Text-producer? What Degree of Adherence of the Speaker to their Utterance is Implied? The text is highly tentative as Harold-now tells the story. This may be because he is genuinely uncertain about his interpretation of events – this may be particularly true in respect of the reasons why his father left the mines. It may also be a genre of 'cautious thinking-aloud and interpreting' characteristic of academic or professional discussion of tricky human realities. It may also be politeness or deference to the older and academic interviewer.

The concept of implied speaker-position and implied listener-position is a particularly fruitful one. Ruthrof's identification of some 18 such positions is helpful (see Appendix A) and one might see this narration as a mixture of the would-be objective narration by Harold-now which is concerned to show Harold-then as an 'innocent' in his own story. On the other hand, as a story of the father, there is some element of an implied 'accusee' (or is it of the mother?) and an attempt to be 'witness for the defence' of the father as possible implied 'accusee'. This struggle perhaps between the 'accusing narrator' and the 'explaining away narrator' also operates at the two deeper levels, to which I now turn.

II. The Narrative Structure Level

This second level, further down than the figurative level, is analysed in terms of the theory-language of Greimas and the Paris School. This involves first identiying the difference between the initial moment of the narrated history and its final moment, and then identifying episodes connected to the historical *transformation* from the beginning-state to the end-state. After this, we then apply the two models devised by Greimas: (i) first, the *actantial schema* developed on the basis of Propp's analysis of the folktale (Martin, 1997: 41–52); (ii) then a *global narrative programme, the canonical narrative schema*, is also applied (Martin, 1997: 52–61).

The analysis always starts by looking at the Starting-point of the story and the End-point of the story, to identify what the 'total shift' has been. In this case, the initial moment of the story is one just before the mother/wife has died; the final moment of the story is one where Harold leaves school without qualifications while his father is on his happy course to the present having 'met Annie'. For Harold, the moment of transformation is that of the death of his mother; for his father, there is a first transformation by the death of his wife and a second transformation by his meeting with Annie.

Our second task is to look at Greimas's *actantial schema*, and to see how the schema can be applied to the narrative fragment. The schema is as shown in Figure B.2. The actational schema involves those who Send a Receiver on a Quest, thereby turning him or her into a Questing Subject, Subjects on a Quest for a Quest-Object, with normally at least one Quest-Helper and at least one Quest-Opponent (some Opponents may be anti-Subjects because they are on an opposing Quest; others are not).

The 'actational schema' in our chosen text is not one but several, because there are two stories. The first is the minor and very schematic one of Harold-then; the second is that of the Father. I will look at each separately.

> **Harold-then** shifts from an implied Starting point of relative happiness and OK-ness prior to the death of his mother to an explicit End-point of leaving school without any qualifications (a comparatively negative story even if the Harold at the time did not think that 'it was relevant'). He is 'Transformed' by the death of his mother and also perhaps (more?) by the 'descent' of his father which forces him to grow up 'very rapidly'. The story presents Harold-then at the time having no 'Quest' and he neither seeks anything nor 'does' anything. He endures and his major hint of subjectivity is that it 'was a very long time, an eternity'. He has no 'Helper' at this time. His father appears as a non-Helper and maybe the father's alcoholism and depression are Opponents for Harold's virtual struggle to survive, though I have no grounds in the text for

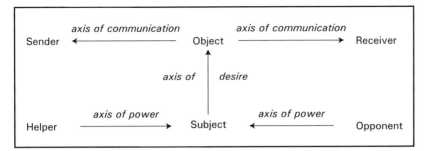

FIGURE B.2　**Greimas's Actational Schema**

attributing such a survival Quest to him. The Sender of Harold into this condition – I cannot call it a full Quest – is the death of the mother and, perhaps, the father's loss of employment and alcoholism.

Father. The father Starts from an implied position as a happy and, one imagines, fit man with wife and family and a job in the mines and Ends as a happy and fit man with a wife and family. The moment of Transformation for the father is the death of his wife, when he becomes sick, unemployed, depressed and alcoholic. He is then transformed again by the meeting with Annie. His primary Quest appears to have originally been to keep the family together – a Quest he probably inherited from his wife – and to 'struggle' for such Quest-objects perhaps as survival and happiness and non-alcoholism. It must be admitted that his Quest is not too clearly defined beyond that of keeping the family together. He may have had a Quest to stay in employment; if so, that Quest appears to have been defeated. He may have had a Quest to give up work; if so, his sickness consequent upon the death of his wife may have been a Helper. He may have had a Quest to produce happy and successful children, but this is not clear, and is merely a possibility. Annie was either the father's key Helper or, possibly, the Object of a Quest for a (new) happy marriage. The father's Opponents are perhaps the death of his wife, the social services who might separate the family, the alcoholism and depression that prevented him from doing his best. The Sender of the father on the Quest may be the (death of the) Mother.

The above sketch of schemas to cover the Questing Action of Harold-then and his father has had to be very compressed and thin. Nonetheless, I hope that it has illustrated the potential of this mode of uncovering structures within narratives.

The canonical narrative scheme is a further development. Martin's model is as shown in Figure B.3.

As for the **Father**, it seems as if a *first schema* is being suggested: in it, the mother's death means that he Has-to-Keep-the-Family-Together (in this story, though others are possible) or that his Desire-to-do-so is strengthened. Despite alcoholism and depression, he does in fact keep the family together … and should be at the end of the story Recognised by somebody as having done so.

However, this schema is never completed. I sense that a *second schema* has started where the Father seems to succeed in a story where his Quest is a more individual one, namely to find a happy New Marriage. The Narrator fully recognizes the Subject's decisive success in this implied search for non-alcoholic health, fitness and happiness.

Manipulation	Competence	Performance	Evaluative sanction
	qualifying test – can fail and be incompetent	*decisive test – can be a decisive failure*	*glorifying test – can lead to humiliation and shame*
persuasive doing of a Sender	*strengthening of a desire*		
acquisition by Receiver of a Wanting-to-do or a Having-to-do	*acquisition of a Being-Able-to-Do*	Primary Event where the Object of QuestValue is at stake	Subject is Recognized – praise and blame, moralizing 'Goodies' and 'Baddies'

FIGURE B.3   **Canonical Narrative Schema**

The non-completion of the first canonical scheme is because it is interfered with by another canonical scheme. This is a hidden normative one, never stated, but whose 'effect' (it may be the schema of the mature Harold-now) can I think be seen to be in operation.

In this *third canonical schema,* it might be argued that the Father should have the Quest of raising a set of children who are happy and successful. This is the default Quest of parents which readers will assume, unless the Narrative of a particular story particularly negates it. Having children makes all parents acquire this 'Having to raise a Happy Healthy Successful Family' Quest. However, there is no explicit reference in the text to the Father having such a Quest. The text does suggest that the Father has a successful Quest of preventing some of the children being taken into care, of keeping the family together.

After the mother's death, the Qualifying Test for the Father should lead to the acquisition of a Being-Able-to-Raise-a-Happy-Healthy Family, but in fact leads to a partial failure: the family is kept together (this is a Quest attributed by the story-teller to his Father), but Harold (and perhaps others) are unhappy (for 'an eternity') and Harold leaves school without any qualifications. He may be healthy, but he is not happy and at school he was not successful. There is a [totally suppressed] 'implicit blame for the Father' in the celebration of the Father's transformation towards happiness and, immediately after, connected by a 'next' (standing in for a bitter unthought 'as a result'?) *what happened next was that I left school without any qualifications whatsoever none at all* which 'I now' definitely regards as 'relevant'.

The first canonical schema is incomplete because of the effects on the telling of the story of the suppressed third canonical schema of Harold (at least Harold-now) for whom the eventual marriage and happiness of the Father at the end of the Father's story at the end of the segment forms a sharp 'told contrast' with the position of Harold-then at the end of the segment. 'So he became happy and I was made miserable' is the implicit contrast of oppositions of this 'Father-and-Son story', which Harold-now tells obscurely.

Let us turn to **Harold-then**. What is striking here is that Harold-then does not acquire any 'Wanting-to-do' and at most acquires the particular 'Having-to-do' of 'Having-to-grow-up-very-fast'. It is not clear that Harold-then really had a definite Object – other than the implicit one of surviving and enduring the 'quite a long period'. His 'leaving of school' is not even experienced as a positive or negative action by Harold-then. Consequently, Harold-then is on the boundary between 'being-a-Questing-Subject' and 'not being a Questing Subject'.

Whether the young Harold had really no 'wanting-to' Quests during his entire secondary school is highly dubious. However, if there were ones, this story suppresses any mention of them, perhaps so as to exculpate the Father or indeed himself from having failed to promote them.

Harold-now certainly is a Questing-Subject, and the Quest of his telling-the-story to the interviewer may include that of representing his shift from Harold-then with virtually no quest into the Harold-now *after the moment of time (adolescence)* being represented in this fragment of the longer story of Harold-now's whole life up to the point of telling.

III. The Third, Deep Level

At this level I look at fundamental oppositions and transformations. Greimas's 'semiotic square' (I prefer to think of it as a 'Square of two Transformations') is used to understand these constructions of meaning-systems.

The complete story of the father as told in the segment can be described as shown in Figure B.4. A two-triangle transition, it is a completed story within the segment. Father has a job and is married. He loses his wife, leaves his job, becomes depressed and somewhat of an alcoholic. He then meets another partner and recovers his functioning, happy, fit adult status.

However, this episode functions within Harold's story of himself. The implication of the episode with the father is that Harold is not 'completely rehabilitated' by any means by the end of the father's three years: at that point, Harold is 'without qualifications of any kind' and (what makes matters worse from the point of view of the teller of the story, the older Harold) the younger Harold doesn't even realize that this is 'relevant'. He has neither qualifications nor even the desire for qualifications at this point. See the discussion of his non-Questing, not-being-a-Subject in our account of the second narrative level.

My first version of the semiotic transition and my revised version are shown in Figure B.5 and B.6. It is clear that, in the segment, Harold's story is unfinished and so accounts of the global transformation from start-of-story to end-of-completed-story can only be tentative in the extreme.

One can tentatively ask questions as to whether the Father counts as a co-victim of the mother's death, or whether he is an Opponent or even an Anti-Subject in respect of Harold's implicit Quest, at least for a while. There may be some implication that the Mother-by-dying and the Father-by-being-depressed both function at least as Opponents for a time to Harold's Quest, provisionally identified as 'growing up normally' with a 'desire for qualifications' and with 'qualifications appropriate for age and IQ'.

It is true that Harold says, rather ambiguously, that the experience *taught me some it taught me a few things*, without specifying what, but quite unambiguously

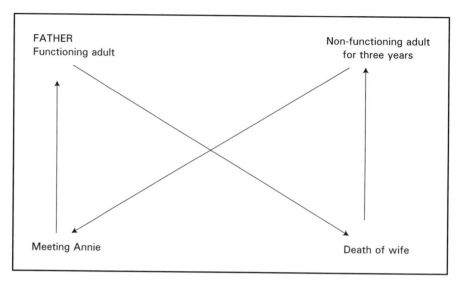

FIGURE B.4 **Harold's Father's Semiotic Transitions**

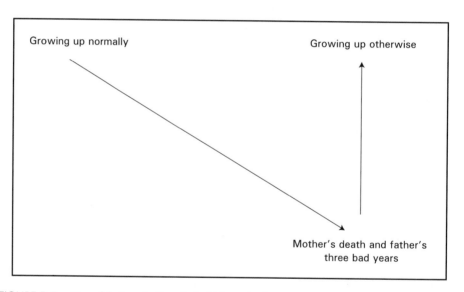

FIGURE B.5 **Harold-then's Semiotic Triangle 1**

I left school without any qualifications whatsoever none at all. He omits any cohesive statement connecting this 'what happened next' to 'the state of his father during the three years ... turning into an alcoholic at a stage not long after which was very difficult', which was the previous happening. There is no explicit theory connecting the difficulties for his father and the consequences for Harold, other than *his having to grow up very rapidly* and its feeling *three years as for me as seeing the problems that my father was going through was quite a considerable period of time*. After his father had met Annie, Harold must have been able to see it as a 'stage', but at the time, it might have felt more like 'an eternity' without a promise of coming to an

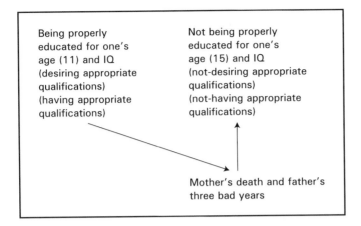

FIGURE B.6   **Harold-then's Semiotic Triangle 2**

end. He doesn't talk of 'the difficulties that he was going through', though he said 'it was very difficult', but only of those that his father was going through.

Summing up, it is possible to argue that the separate analysis of the three levels and their interconnection suggests quite strongly a 'Father and Son Story' with a strong, but strongly denied-in-story, critique of what happened and the joint failure of adequate parenting by the mother (by dying) and the father (by sliding temporarily into drink and depression), and *simultaneously* a story of 'both-Father-and-Son' being the victims of the Mother's death, being 'betrayed' by it into psychological deterioration, and, perhaps, the Father even more so. With a number of different stories (actational schemas) interfering with each other, there can be no single completely convincing 'moral of the story', and there isn't one.[2] Causality is hinted at, only to be suppressed. *What happened next was I left school without ....*

I have now completed a sketch of the three levels of a Critical Linguistics / Semiotics approach to the analysis of a narrative (segment), and I hope it has suggested its fertility. I have surveyed the ways that formal-text analysis at a surface-figurative level, at a narrative level and at a deep thematic-conceptual level can illuminate our understanding of selected texts.

What have I not done? I have not formally addressed the importance of the local co-text of the text fragment (what is the text before and after the segment?). Nor have I addressed our knowledge of the contexts of the 'produced text', bearing in mind our anthropological-historical understanding of the interview interaction as analysed in terms of the Briggs–Wengraf model (Figure 2.6). Some of this knowledge of co-text and context has been implicit in our treatment of the interview fragment, but a complete analysis would be more explicit. Despite this lack, I hope that I have shown the value of the Critical Linguistics/Semiotics approach promoted by Martin, and whetted the reader's appetite to expand their repertoire of procedures for analysing interview texts systematically. The BNIM approach and the CLS approach are only two in a large repertoire.

---

2 The Father disappears from the initial narrative completely at this point, having completed the two semiotic triangles as shown above. The story of Harold-then as recounted by Harold-now has completed one semiotic triangle, and has still a long way to go.

Appendix C: Informal Paralinguistics: A More Elaborate Example

001	Reporter	It seems to me that someone is being spanked all the time	
002	M	Not all the time	tone is indifferent and cool, dismissive as a defence
003	D	Well there are several things they haven't learnt yet	defensive
004	M	Ya I have thought about that but no better be hit now than electrocuted in the electric chair later	believes in what she is saying, looks detached, indifferent defensive, direct denial with the words "but no", looks fearful about what could happen, almost fanatical, has a warning in her voice, hard direct glaring at end, rhythm irregular
005	D	Until they get spanked they won't realize	reserved, mixed smile, appears very confident but is interrupted by Mum
006	M	NO means NO	loud, assertive challenging, eyes averted rapid condensed speech, possibly because she feels uncomfortable with having interrupted Dad, playing with hands
007	D	Most of these kids growing up who don't get spanked are uncontrollable	patiently explains, has air of superiority, mixed smile
Other material			
011	D	Let's try the time-out chair and the privileges taken away you know ... uh please give me a break [laughs] it did not work ... it seems to have gone from bad to worse	tone and expression change three times with each segment, first part eyes are darting nervously, tone is monotonous, sarcastic, stops mid sentence, changes tone, accusatorial, eyes close to emphasize frustration with the situation, third change occurs with the laughed words, authoritative tone, makes eye contact with reporter, looks to be justifying previous 'outburst', rhythm irregular, fragmented speech throughout

continued

Figure C.1   continued

012	Reporter	Why do the experts say this?	puts hands in the air
013	M	It might work for some people but it does not work for us	voice gets higher, assertive, heavy stress on word 'does not' and 'work'

FIGURE C.1 **Smith family spankings adapted from Scheff, 1997: 91–3**

Bibliography

Ackoff, R. 1953. *The Design of Social Research*. Chicago: University of Chicago Press.

Agar, M. 1986. *Speaking of Ethnography*. Thousand Oaks: Sage.

Agar, M. 1996. *The Professional Stranger: an informal introduction to ethnography*. San Diego: Academic Press.

Alheit, P. 1994. *Taking the Knocks: youth unemployment and biography: a qualitative analysis*. London: Cassell.

Andrews, M., Sclater, S., Squire, C. and Treacher, A. (eds) 2000. *Lines of Narrative*. London: Routledge.

Antaki, C. 1988. *Analysing Everyday Explanation*. London: Sage.

Arksey, H. and Knight, P. 1999. *Interviewing for Social Scientists*. London: Sage.

Bachelard, G. 1968. *The Philosophy of No*. New York: Orion Press.

Bachelard, G. 1999. *La Formation de l'Esprit Scientifique*. Paris: Vrin.

Baldamus, W. 1982. 'The role of discoveries in social science', in R. Burgess (ed.), *Field Research: a sourcebook and field manual*. London: Unwin Hyman.

Bandler, J. and Grinder, R. 1975. *The Structure of Magic* (vols 1, 2). California: Science and Behaviour Books.

Barker, C. and Renold, E. 1999. *Vignettes*. Social Research Update no. 25. <*http://www.soc.surrey.ac.uk/sru/sru.html*>.

Bar-On, D. 1995. *Fear and Hope: three generations of the Holocaust*. Cambridge, MA: Harvard University Press.

Bar-On, D. 1999. *The Indescribable and the Undiscussable: reconstructing human experience after trauma*. Budapest: Central European Press.

Bateson, G. 1972. 'Morale and National Character' in his *Steps Towards an Ecology of Mind*. London: Granada.

Bateson, G. 1980. *Mind and Nature: a necessary unity*. London: Fontana.

Bertaux, D. (ed.) 1981. *Biography and Society: the life history approach in the social sciences*. Beverley Hills: Sage.

Bertaux, D. 1997. *Les récits de vie*. Paris: Nathan (English edition in preparation).

Bertaux, D. and Delcroix, C. 2000. 'Case histories of families and social processes: enriching sociology', in Chamberlayne et al., *The Turn to Biographical Methods in Social Science*. London: Routledge.

Bertaux, D. and Kohli, M. 1984. 'The life history approach: a continental view', in *Annual Review of Sociology*, vol. 10, pp. 215–317.

Bertaux, D. and Thompson, P. (eds) 1993. *Between Generations: family models, myths and memories*. Oxford: Oxford University Press.

Bion, W.R. 1980. *Bion in New York and São Paulo*. (ed. F. Bion). Perthshire: Clunie Press.

Birren, J. 1998. 'Themes and assignments in guided autobiographies', in Schweitzer, P. (ed.), *Reminiscence in Dementia Care*. London: Age Exchange.

Black, T.R. 1993. *Evaluating Social Science Research: an introduction*. London: Sage.

Blumenthal, D. 1999. 'Representing the divided self', *Qualitative Inquiry*, 5(3): 377–92.

Bollas, C. 1987. *The Shadow of the Object: psychoanalysis of the unthought known*. London: Free Association.

Bourdieu, P. 1980. *Le sens pratique*. Paris: Editions de Minuit.

Bourdieu, P. 1999. *The Weight of the World: social suffering in contemporary society*. Cambridge: Polity Press.

Boyzatis, R.E. 1998. *Transforming Qualitative Information: thematic analysis and code development*. Thousand Oaks: Sage.

Brannen, J. 1992. *Mixing Methods: quantitative and qualitative research*. Aldershot: Avesbury.

Breckner, R. 1998. 'The Biographical-Interpretive Method – principles and procedure', in *Sostris Working Paper no. 2*, pp. 99–104.

Breckner, R., Kalekin-Fishman, D. and Miethe, I. (eds) 2000. *Biographies and the Division of Europe: experience, action and change on the 'Eastern' side*. Opalden: Leske and Budrich.

Brenner, M. 1981. 'Patterns of social structure in the research interview', in M. Brenner (ed.), *Social Method and Social Life*. New York: Academic Press.

Briggs, C. 1986. *Learning How to Ask: a socio-linguistic appraisal of the role of the interview in social science research*. Cambridge: Cambridge University Press.

British Psychological Society. 1996. *Code of Conduct, Ethical Principles and Guidelines*. Leicester: BPS Press.

British Sociological Association. 1996. *Statement of Ethical Practice*. Durham: BSA Publications.

Bromley, D.B. 1986. *The Case-Study Method in Psychology and Related Disciplines*. Chichester: Wiley.

Bruner, E. 1986. 'Ethnography as narrative', in V. Turner and E. Bruner (eds), *The Anthropology of Experience*. Chicago: University of Illinois.

Bruner, J. 1986. *Actual Minds, Possible Worlds*. Cambridge, MA: Harvard University Press.

Bryman, A. and Burgess, R.G. (eds) 1994. *Analysing Qualitative Data*. London: Routledge.

Buckingham, D. 1987. *Public Secrets: Eastenders and its audiences*. London: British Film Institute.

Burgess, R.G. (ed.) 1982. *Field Research: a sourcebook and field manual*. London: Unwin Hyman.

Burman, E. and Parker, I. (ed.) 1993. *Discourse Analytic Research*. London: Routledge.

Caldas-Coulthard, C.R. and Coulthard, M. (eds) 1996. *Texts and Practices: readings in critical discourse analysis*. London: Routledge.

Caniglia, P. and Spanò, A. 1999. 'Unqualified and unemployed youth: blaming the victims', *Sostris Working Paper No. 5 Case Study Materials: unqualified youth*. London: University of East London, Centre for Biography in Social Policy. pp. 64–75.

Carney, T.F. 1994. 'The ladder of analytical abstraction' from *Collaborative inquiry methodology*. Windsor, Ontario, Canada. University of Windsor, Division for Instructional Development, cited in Miles, M. and Huberman, M. (eds), *Qualitative Data Analysis: an expanded sourcebook* (2nd edn). p. 92.

Casement, P. 1985. *On Learning from the Patient*. London: Tavistock.

Chamberlayne, P. and King, A. 2000. *Cultures of Care: biographies of carers in Britain and the two Germanies*. Bristol: The Policy Press.

Chamberlayne, P. and King, A. 1997. 'The biographical challenge of caring', in *The Sociology of Health and Illness*, vol. 5, pp. 601–21.

Chamberlayne, P. and Rustin, M. 1999. *From Biography to Social Policy: final report of the SOSTRIS project*. Centre for Biography in Social Policy, University of East London.

Chamberlayne, P. and Spanò, A. 2000. 'Modernisation as lived experience: contrasting case studies from the SOSTRIS project', in P. Chamberlayne et al. (eds), *The Turn to Biographical Methods in Social Science*. London: Routledge.

Chamberlayne, P., Bornat, J. and Wengraf, T. (eds) 2000. *The Turn to Biographical Methods in Social Science*. London: Routledge.

Chamberlayne, P., Cooper, A., Freeman, R. and Rustin, M. 1999. *Welfare and Culture in Europe: towards a new paradigm in social policy*. London: Jessica Kingsley.

Chamberlayne, P., Rupp, S. and Wengraf, T. 1999. 'Stopped in their Tracks: British National Report on Ex-Traditional Workers', in *Sostris Working Paper no. 6*, pp. 17–27.

Chase, S. 1995. 'Taking narrative seriously: consequences for method and theory in interview studies', in R. Josselson and A. Lieblich (eds), *The Narrative Study of Lives: interpreting experience*. Thousand Oaks: Sage. pp. 1–26.

Chenitz, W.C. and Swanson, J.M. 1986. *From Practice to Grounded Theory: qualitative research in nursing*. California: Addison-Wesley.

Churchill, L. 1973. *Questioning Strategies in Sociolinguistics*. Rowley: Newbury House.

Clapier-Valladon, S. 1980. *Les médecins français d'outre-mer. Etude psychosociologique du retour des migrants*. Nice 1976. Paris: Champion.

Claxton, G. 1997. *Hare Brain, Tortoise Mind*. London: Fourth Estate.

Clifford, C. and Marcus, G. (ed.) 1986. *Writing Culture: the Politics and Poetics of Ethnography*. Berkeley: University of California Press.

Coffey, A. and Atkinson, P. 1997. *Making Sense of Qualitative Data: complementary research strategies*. Thousand Oaks: Sage.

Collingwood, R.G. 1939. *An Autobiography*. Oxford: Oxford University Press.

Cooper, A. 2000. 'The vanishing point of resemblance: comparative welfare as philosophical anthropology', in Chamberlayne et al. (eds), *The Turn to Biographical Methods in Social Science*. London: Routledge.

Csikszentmihalyi, M. and Rochberg-Halton, E. 1981. *The Meaning of Things: domestic symbols and the self*. Cambridge: Cambridge University Press.

Delcroix, C., Guyaux, A., Ramdane, A. and Rodiguez, E. 1988. 'Le Marriage mixte comme rencontre de deux cultures', *Life stories / Récit de Vie no. 5*, pp. 49–63.

Denzin, N.K. 1970. *The Research Act*. Chicago: Aldine.

de Vaus, D.A. 1996. *Surveys in Social research* (4th edn). London: UCL Press.

Devereux, G. 1967. *From Anxiety to Method in the Behavioural Sciences*. The Hague: Mouton.

de Waele, J.P. and Harré, R. 1979. 'Autobiography as a psychological method', in G.P. Ginsburg (ed.), *Emerging Strategies in Social Psychological Research*. New York: Wiley.

Dexter, L.A. 1970. *Elite and Specialised Interviewing*. Evanston: Northwestern University Press.

Dillon, J. 1990. *The Practice of Questioning*. London: Routledge.

Dohrenwend, B.S. and Richardson, S.A. 1956. 'Analysis of the interviewer's behaviour', *Human Organisation*, 15(2): 29–32.

Douglas, J.D. 1985. *Creative Interviewing*. Beverley Hills: Sage.

Douglas, M. and Isherwood, B. 1980. *The World of Things*. Harmondsworth: Penguin.

Edwards, J.A. and M.D. Lampert (eds) 1993. *Talking Data: transcription and coding in discourse research*. Hillsdale, NJ: Lawrence Erlbaum.

Eliot, T.S. 1960. *The Four Quartets*. London: Faber and Faber.

Ellen, R.F. (ed.) 1984. *Ethnographic Research: a guide to general conduct*. London: Academic Press.

Ericcson, K. and Simon, H. 1980. 'Verbal reports as data', *Psychological Review*, 87: 215–51.

Evertson, C.M. and Green, J.L. 1995. 'A framework to guide decision-making in observation', in Marshall, C. and Rossman, G. (eds), *Designing Qualitative Research* (2nd edn). Thousand Oaks: Sage.

Fairclough, N. 1989. *Language and Power*. Harlow: Longmans.

Farmer, Wei Yan. 1993. 'Attitudes towards marriage and divorce among women in modern China', in Bertaux, D. and Thompson, P. (eds), *Between Generations: family models, myths and memories*. Oxford: Oxford University Press. pp. 81–97.

Feild, R. 1976. *The Invisible Way*. New York: Harper and Row.

Field, J. [Milner, M.] 1981. *A Life of One's Own*. Los Angeles: J.P. Tarcher.

Firlej, M. and Hellens, D. 1993. *Knowledge Elicitation: a practical handbook*. London: Prentice-Hall International.

Fischer, W. 1982. *Time and Chronic Illness: a study on the social constitution of temporality*. Berkeley, CA: Habilitationschrifft.

Fischer-Rosenthal, W. 1989. 'Life-story beyond illusion and events past', in *Enquête: cahiers du cercom, 1989*, no. 5, March, Association Internationale du Sociologie, F. Godard and F. de Coninck (eds), pp. 219–25.

Fischer-Rosenthal, W. 1995. 'Biographische Methoden in der Soziologie', in Flick, U., Kardorf, E.V., Keupp, H., v. Rosenstiel, L. and Wolff, St. (eds), *Handbuch qualitativer Sozialforschung, 2. Aufl.*, München: PVU. pp. 253–6.

Fischer-Rosenthal, W. 1996. 'Strukturale Analyse biographischer Texte', in E. Brähler and C. Adler (eds), *Quantitative Einzelfallanalysen und qualitative Verfahren*. Gießen: Psychosozial-Verlag. pp. 147–209.

Fischer-Rosenthal, W. 2000. 'Biographical work and biographical structuring in present-day societies', in Bornat, J., Chamberlayne, P. and Wengraf, T. (eds), *Turn to Biographical Methods in Social Science: comparative issues and examples*. London: Routledge. pp. 109–25.

Fischer-Rosenthal, W. and Rosenthal, G. 1997a. 'Narrationsanalyse biographischer Selbstpräsentationen', in R. Hitzler and A. Honer (eds), *Sozialwissenschaftliche Hermeneutik*. Opladen: Leske & Budrich. pp. 133–64.

Fischer-Rosenthal, W. and Rosenthal, G. 1997b. 'Warum Biographieanalyse und wie man sie macht', *Zeitschrift für Soziaisationsforschung- und Erziehungssoziologie*, 17: 405–27.

Fischer-Rosenthal, W. and Rosenthal, G. 2000. 'Analyse narrativ-biographischer Interviews', in Flick, U., Kardorf, E.V. and Steinke, I. (eds), *Qualitative Sozialforschung*. Reinbek: Rowohlt (rororo Sachbuch 55 628 6).

Flick, U. 1998. *An Introduction to Qualitative Research*. London: Sage.

Foddy, W. 1993. *Constructing Questions for Interviews and Questionnaires: theory and practice in social research*. Cambridge: Cambridge University Press.

Fowler, R. 1979. *Language in the News*. London: Routledge.

Frisch, M. 1998. 'Oral history and *Hard Times*: a review essay', in Perks, R. and Thomson, A. (eds), *The Oral History Reader*. London: Routledge.

Gee, J.P. 1991. 'A linguistic approach to narrative', *Journal of Normative and Life History*, 1: 15–40.

Geertz, C. 1973. 'Thick description: toward an interpretive theory of culture', in Geertz, C., *The Interpretation of Cultures*. New York: Basic Books.

Geertz, C. 1983. 'From the native's point of view: on the nature of anthropological understanding', in his *Local Knowledge*. New York: Basic Books.

Geis, M. 1982. *The Language of Television Advertising*. New York: Academic Press.

Gelcer, E., McCabe, A. and Smith-Resnick, C. 1990. *Milan Family Therapy: variant and invariant methods*. Northvale: Aronson.

Gendlin, E. 1981. *Focusing*. New York: Bantam.

Gergen, K. and Gergen, M. 1988. 'Narratives of relationships', in R. Burnett et al. (ed.), *Accounting for Relationships*. London: Methuen.

Gerth, H. and Mills, C.W. (eds) 1948. *From Max Weber: essays in sociology*. London: Routledge and Kegan Paul.

Gill, M., Newman, R. and Redlich, F.C. 1954. *The Initial Interview in Psychiatric Practice*. New York: International Universities Press.

Gilligan, C. 1982. *In a Different Voice: psychological theory and women's development*. Harvard: Harvard University Press.

Ginsburg, G.P. (ed.) 1979. *Emerging Strategies in Social Psychological Research*. Chichester: Wiley.

Glaser, B.G. 1978. *Theoretical Sensitivity*. California: The Sociology Press.

Glaser, B.G. 1992. *Basics of Grounded Theory Analysis: emergence vs forcing*. California: The Sociology Press

Glaser, B.G. and Strauss, A. 1968. *The Discovery of Grounded Theory*. London: Weidenfeld and Nicholson.

Gluck, S.B. and Patai, D. (eds) 1991. *Women's Words: the feminist practice of oral history*. London: Routledge.

Goffmann, E. 1959. *The Presentation of Self in Everyday Life*. New York: Doubleday.

Gorden, L. 1975. *Interviewing: strategies, techniques and tactics*. Illinois: The Dorsey Press.

Gramsci, A. 1971. *Selections from the Prison Notebooks*. London: Lawrence and Wishart.

Greimas, A.J. 1990. *The Social Sciences: a semiotic view*. Minneapolis: University of Minnesota Press.

Grele, R. 1979. 'Listen to their voices: two case studies in the interpretation of oral history interviews', *Oral History no. 7*, pp. 33–42.

Gurwitsch, A. 1964. *The Field of Consciousness*. Pittsburgh: Duquesne University Press.

Gurwitsch, A. 1966. 'Phenomenology of thematics and of the pure ego: studies of the relation between gestalt theory and phenomenology', in *Studies in Phenomenology and Psychology*. Evanston: Northwestern University Press. pp. 175–286.

Hammersley, M. 1990. *Reading Ethnographic Research: a critical guide*. Harlow: Longman.

Hammersley, M. and Atkinson, P. 1983. *Ethnography: principles in practice*. London: Tavistock.

Hatch, J.A. and Wisniewski, R. (eds) 1995. *Life History and Narrative*. London: Falmer Press.

Henriques, J., Hollway, W., Urwin, C., Venn, C. and Walkerdine, V. 1984. *Changing the Subject: psychology, social regulation and subjectivity*. London: Methuen.

Herdt, G. and Stoller, R. 1990. *Intimate Communications: erotics and the study of culture*. New York: Columbia University Press.

Hertz, R. 1995. 'Separate but simultaneous interviewing of husbands and wives: making sense of their stories', *Qualitative Inquiry*, 1(4): 429–51.

Hessler, R.M. 1992. *Social Research Methods*. St Paul: West Publishing Company.

Hodge, B. and Kress, G. 1979. *Language as Ideology*. London: Routledge.

Holland, D. and Quinn, N. (eds) 1987. *Cultural Models in Language and Thought*. New York: Cambridge University Press.

Hollway, W. 1989. *Subjectivity and Method in Social Psychology*. London: Sage.

Hollway, W. and Jefferson, T. 2000. *Doing Qualitative Research Differently: free association, narrative and the interview method*. London: Sage.

Holstein, J. and Gubrium, J. 1995. *The Active Interview*. Thousand Oaks: Sage.

Holstein, J. and Gubrium, J. 1997. 'Active interviewing', in D. Silverman (ed.), *Qualitative Research: theory, method, and practice*. London: Sage.

Honigman, J.J. 1982. 'Sampling in ethnographic fieldwork', in R. Burgess (ed.), *Field Research: a sourcebook and field manual*. London: Unwin Hyman.

Hymes, D. 1996. *Ethnography, Linguistics, Narrative Inequality: towards an understanding of voice*. London: Taylor and Francis.

Jones, C. and Rupp, S. 1997. 'Coping with caring: lives of informal carers in Newham', *Rising East: the Journal of East London Studies*, 1(2): 89–110.

Jones, C. and Rupp, S. 2000. 'Understanding the carer's worlds: a biographical case study', in Chamberlayne et al. (eds), *The Turn to Biographical Methods in Social Science*. London: Routledge.

Josselson, R. (ed.) 1996. *Ethics and Process in the Narrative Study of Lives*. Thousand Oaks: Sage.

Josselson, R. and Lieblich, A. (eds) 1995. *The Narrative Study of Lives: interpreting experience*. Thousand Oaks: Sage.

Kallmeyer, W. and Schütze, F. 1977. 'Zur Konstitution von Kommunikationsschemata der Sachverhaltsdarstellung', in D. Wegner (ed.), *Gesprächsanalysen*. Hamburg: Buske. pp. 159–274.

Kiegelmann, M. 2000. 'Qualitative psychological research: using the voice approach'. *Forum Qualitative Research* [on-line-journal], vol. 1(2). Available at: http://qualitative-research.net/fqs-e/2-00inhalt-e.htm

King, A. 2000. 'Part of the system: the experience of home-based caring in West Germany', in Chamberlayne, P. et al. (eds), *The Turn to Biographical Methods in Social Science*. London: Routledge. pp. 305–20.

Kohli, M. 1986. 'Social organisation and subjective construction of the life course', in A.B. Sorensen, F.E. Weiner and L.R. Sherrod (eds), *Human Development and the Life-course*. Hillsdale, NJ: Lawrence Erlbaum.

Kosko, B. 1994. *Fuzzy Thinking: the new science of fuzzy logic*. London: HarperCollins.

Kroeber, T. 1973. *Ishi: the last of his tribe*. New York: Bantam Books.

Kuhn, D. 1991. *The Skills of Argument*. Cambridge: Cambridge University Press.

Kuhn, T. 1970. *The Structure of Scientific Revolutions* (2nd edn). Chicago: University of Chicago Press.

Kvale, S. 1996. *InterViews: an introduction to qualitative research interviewing*. Thousand Oaks: Sage.

Labov, W. and Fanshell, D. 1977. *Therapeutic Discourse: psychotherapy as conversation*. New York: Academic Press.

Labov, W. and Waletsky, J. 1967. 'Narrative analysis: oral versions of personal experience', *Journal of Narrative and Life History*, 7: 3–38.

Lakatos, I. (ed.) 1970. *Criticism and the Growth of Knowledge*. Amsterdam: North-Holland.

Lakoff, G. and Johnson, M. 1980. *Metaphors We Live By*. Chicago: University of Chicago Press.

Lave, J. 1988. *Cognition in practice: mind, mathematics and culture in everyday life*. Cambridge: Cambridge University Press.

Lawrence, R. 1982. 'Domestic space and society: a cross-cultural study', *Comparative Studies in Society and History*, 24(1): 104–30.

Layder, D. 1997. *Modern Social Theory: key debates and new directions*. London: UCL Press.

Layder, D. 1998. *Sociological Practice: linking theory and social research*. London: Sage.

Liebes, T. and Katz, E. 1988. 'Dallas and Genesis', in James W. Carey (ed.), *Media, Myths and Narratives: TV and the press*. Newbury Park: Sage.

Lieblich, A., Tuval-Maschiach, R. and Zilber, T. 1998. *Narrative Research: reading, analysis and interpretation*. Thousand Oaks: Sage.

Levy, L. 1970. *Conceptions of Personality*. New York: Random House.

Linell, P. and Jonsson, L. 1991. 'Suspect stories: on perspective-setting on an asymmetrical situation', in Ivana Markova and Klaus Foppa (eds), *Asymmetries in Dialogue*. Hemel Hempstead: Harvester Wheatsheaf.

Lofland, J. 1971. *Analysing Social Settings*. Belmont: Wadsworth.

Lummis, T. 1987. *Listening to History*. London: Hutchinson.

Malinowski, B. 1950. *Argonauts of the Western Pacific*. New York: Dutton.

Mancuso, J.C. 1986. 'The acquisition and use of narrative grammar structure', in T.R. Sarbin (ed.), *Narrative Psychology: the storied nature of human conduct*, New York: Praeger.

Mandler, J.M. 1984. *Scripts, Stories and Scenes*. Hillsdale, NJ: Lawrence Erlbaum.

Markova, I. 1990. 'A three-step process as a unit of analysis in dialogue', in I. Markova and K. Foppa (eds), *The Dynamics of Dialogue*. Hemel Hempstead: Harvester-Wheatsheaf.

Markova, I. and Foppa, K. (eds) 1990. *The Dynamics of Dialogue*. Hemel Hempstead: Harvester-Wheatsheaf.

Markova, I. and Foppa, K. (eds) 1991. *Asymmetries in Dialogue*. Hemel Hempstead: Harvester-Wheatsheaf.

Marshall, C. and Grossman, G. 1989. *Designing Qualitative Research*. Thousand Oaks: Sage.

Martin, B. 1997. *Semiotics and Story-telling*. London: Philomel-Euromyths.

Martin, R. 1995. *Oral History in Social Work: research, assessment and intervention*. London: Sage.

Mason, J. 1996. *Qualitative Researching*. London: Sage.

Massarik, F. 1981. 'The interviewing process re-examined', in Reason, P. and Rowan, J. (eds), *Human Inquiry: a casebook of new paradigm research*. Chichester: Wiley.

Mauger, G. 1991. 'Enquêter en milieu populaire', *Genèses*, vol. 6, pp. 125–43.

Maxwell, J.A. 1996. *Qualitative Research Design: an interactive approach*. Thousand Oaks: Sage.

Maykut, P. and Morehouse, R. 1994. *Beginning Qualitative Research: a philosophical and practical guide*. London: Falmer.

McCracken, G. 1988. *The Long Interview*. Thousand Oaks: Sage.

McKay, M., Davis, M. and Fanning, P. 1983. *Messages: the communication skills book*. Oakland: New Harbinger.

McLeod, J. 1997. *Narrative and Psychotherapy*. London: Sage.

McPherson, C.B. 1962. *The Political Theory of Possessive Individualism: Hobbes to Locke*. Oxford: Clarendon Press.

Meinhof, U. and Richardson, K. (eds) 1994. *Text, Discourse and Context: representations of poverty in Britain*. London: Longmans.

Mello, A. de. 1984. *The Song of the Bird*. New York: Doubleday.

Mestheneos, L. and Ioannidi, E. 1998. 'Greek National Report' in *Sostris Working Paper 2: the early retired*. Centre for Biography in Social Policy, University of East London. pp. 22–7.

Miles, M.B. and Huberman, A.M. 1994. *Qualitative Data Analysis: an expanded sourcebook* (2nd edn). Thousand Oaks: Sage.

Miller, R.L. 2000. *Researching Life Stories and Family Histories*. London: Sage.

Mills, C.W. 1959. *The Sociological Imagination*. Oxford: Oxford University Press.

Miner, H. 1960. 'The prevention of sleeping sickness in Nigeria', *Human Organisation* (Fall 1960), quoted in James Moffett (ed.) 1985. *Points of Departure: an anthology of nonfiction*. Mentor Books. pp. 278–9.

Minocha, A. 1979. 'Varied roles in the field', in Srinvas, M.N., Shah, A.M. and Ramaswamy, E.A. (eds), *The Fieldworker and the Field: problems and challenges in sociological investigation*. New Delhi: Oxford University Press. pp. 201–15.

Mishler, E. 1986. *Research Interviewing*. Cambridge, MA: Harvard University Press.

Mommsen, W. 1974. *The Age of Bureaucracy: perspectives on the political sociology of Max Weber*. Oxford: Basil Blackwell.

Moustakas, C. 1990. *Heuristic Research*. Thousand Oaks: Sage.

Oakley, A. 1981. 'Interviewing women: a contradiction in terms', in H. Roberts (ed.), *Doing Feminist Research*. London: Routledge.

Oevermann, U. et al. 1987. 'Structures of meaning and objective hermeneutics', in V. Meja, D. Misgeld and N. Stehr (eds), *Modern German Sociology*. New York: Columbia University Press.

Oevermann, U. u.a. 1979. 'Die Methodologie einer objektiven Hermeneutik und ihre allgemeine forschungslogische Bedeutung in den Sozialwissenschaften', in H.-G. Soeffner (ed.), *Interpretative Verfahren in den Sozial- und Textwissenschaften*. Stuttgart: Metzler. pp. 352–434.

Osterland, M. 1983. 'Die Mythologisierung des Lebenslaufs. Zur Problematik des Erinnerns', in Bathege, M. and Essbach, W. (eds), *Soziologie: Entdeckung im Alltägliche. Hans Paul Bahrt. Festschrift zu seinem 65. Geburtstag*. Frankfurt and New York: Campus. pp. 279–90.

Pamphilion, B. 1999. 'The Zoom Model: a dynamic framework for the analysis of life histories', *Qualitative Inquiry*, 5(3): 393–410.

Parker, I. 1992. *Discourse Dynamics*. London: Routledge.

Patton, M. 1990. *Qualitative Evaluation and Research Methods* (2nd edn). Newbury Park: Sage.

Pawson, R. 1996. 'Theorising the interview', *British Journal of Sociology*, 47(2): 295–314.

Pawson, R. and Tilley, N. 1997. *Realistic Evaluation*. London: Sage.

Payne, S. 1983. *The Art of Asking Questions*. Princeton: Princeton University Press.

Perks, R. and Thomson, A. (eds) 1998. *The Oral History Reader*. London: Routledge.

Personal Narratives Group (ed.) 1989. *Interpreting Women's Lives: feminist theory and personal narratives*. Bloomington: Indiana University Press.

Picon, M. and Picon-Charlot, M. 1997. *Voyage en grande bourgeoisie. Journal d'enquête*. Paris: PUF.

Pierret, J. 1993. 'Constructing discourses about health and their social determinants', in Radley, A. (ed.), *Worlds of Illness*. London: Routledge.

Pinney, R. 1981. *Creative Listening*. London: Children's Hour Trust.

Pittenger, R.E., Hockett, C.F. and Danehy, J.J. 1960. *The First Five Minutes of a Psychiatric Interview*. Ithaca: Paul Martineau.

Plummer, K. 1983. *Documents of Life*. London: Allen & Unwin.

Poirier, J., Clapier-Valladon, S. and Raybaut, P. 1983. *Les Récits de Vie: théorie et pratique*. Paris: Presses Universitaires.

Poland, B.D. 1995. 'Transcription quality as an aspect of rigor in qualitative research', *Qualitative Inquiry*, 1(3): 290–310.

Poland, B. and Pederson, A. 1998. 'Reading between the lines: interpreting silences in qualitative research', *Qualitative Inquiry*, 4(2): 293–312.

Polkinghorne, D.E. 1995. 'Narrative configuration in qualitative analysis', in J.A. Hatch and R. Wisniewski (eds), *Life History and Narrative*. London: Falmer Press.

Polkinghorne, D.E. 1996. 'The use of biography in the development of applicable knowledge', *Ageing and Society*, 16(6): 721–45.

Potter, J. and Weatherell, M. 1987. *Discourse and Social Psychology*. London: Sage.

Potter, W.J. 1996. *An Analysis of Thinking and Research about Qualitative Methods*. New Jersey: Erlbaum.

Progoff, I. 1975. *At a Journal Workshop*. New York: Dialogue House.

Propp, V. 1968. *Morphology of the Folktale*. Austin: University of Texas Press.

Psathas, G. and Anderson, T. 1990. 'The "practices" of transcription in conversation analysis', *Semiotica*, 78: 75–99.

Ragin, C. and Becker, H. (eds) 1992. *What is a Case? Exploring the foundations of social inquiry*. Cambridge: Cambridge University Press.

Rainer, T. 1978. *The New Diary: how to use a journal for self-guidance and expanded creativity*. Los Angeles: J.P. Tarcher.

Reason, P. (ed.) 1988. *Human Inquiry in Action*. Newbury Park: Sage.

Reason, P. and Rowan, J. (eds) 1981. *Human Inquiry: a casebook of new paradigm research*. Chichester: John Wiley.

Reinharz, S. (ed.) 1992. *Feminist Methods in Social Research*. New York: Oxford University Press.

Ribbens, J. and Edwards, R. (eds) 1998. *Feminist Dilemmas in Qualitative Research*. London: Sage.

Rickard, W. 1998. '"More dangerous than therapy"? Interviewees' reflections on recording traumatic or taboo issues', *Oral History* (autumn): 35–48.

Riessmann, C. 1989. *Narrative Analysis*. Newbury Park: Sage.

Riley, M. 1998. 'A life-course approach: autobiographical notes', in J.Z. Giele and G.H. Elder, jnr (eds), *Methods of Life Course Research: quantitative and qualitative approaches*. Thousand Oaks: Sage.

Robson, C. 1993. *Real-World Research*. Oxford: Blackwell.

Roe, E. 1994. *Narrative Policy Analysis: theory and practice*. London: Duke.

Rogers, C. 1978. *Carl Rogers on Personal Power*. London: Constable.

Rorty, R. 2000. 'Being that can be understood is language', *London Review of Books*, (16 March): 23–5.

Rose, G. 1982. *Deciphering Sociological Research*. London: Macmillan.

Rosenthal, G. 1991. 'German war memories: narratability and the biographical and social functions of remembering', *Oral History*, 19(2): 34–41.

Rosenthal, G. 1993. 'Reconstruction of life stories: principles of selection in generating stories for narrative biographical interviews', in R. Josselson and A. Lieblich (eds), *The Narrative Study of Lives*, vol. 1. Newbury Park: Sage. pp. 59–91.

Rosenthal, G. 1995. *Erlebte und erzählte Lebensgeschichte. Gestalt und Struktur biographischer Selbstbeschreibungen*. Frankfurt: Campus.

Rosenthal, G. (ed.) 1998. *The Holocaust in Three-Generations. Families of Victims and Perpetrators of the Nazi-Regime*. London: Cassell.

Rosenthal, G. and Bar-On, D. 1992. 'A biographical case study of a victimizer's daughter', *Journal of Narrative and Life History*, 2: 105–27.

Rosenwald, G.C. and Ochberg, R.L. (eds) *Stored Lives: the cultural politics of self-understanding*. New Haven: Yale University Press.

Rowe, D. 1988. *The Successful Self*. London: Fontana.

Runyan, W.M. 1984. *Life Histories and Psychobiographies: explorations in theory and method*. Oxford: Oxford University Press.

Rupp, S. and Chamberlayne, P. 1998. 'British National Report on Single Parents', *Sostris Working Paper no. 3*, pp. 52–67.

Rustin, M. 1998. 'From individual life histories to sociological understanding', *Sostris Working Paper no. 3*, pp. 112–19.

Rustin, M. 1999. 'A biographical turn in social science?', *Sostris Working Paper no. 6*, pp. 64–71.

Rustin, M. 2000. 'Reflections on the biographical turn in social science', in Chamberlayne et al. (eds), *The Turn to Biographical Methods in Social Science*. London: Routledge.

Ruth, J.E., Birren, J. and Polkinghorne, D. 1996. 'The projects of life reflected in autobiographies of old age', *Ageing and Society*, 16(6): 677–99.

Ruthrof, H. 1981. *The Reader's Construction of Narrative*. London: Routledge.

Sacks, K. 1989. 'What's a life story got to do with it?', in Personal Narratives Group (eds), *Interpreting Women's Lives: feminist theory and personal narratives*. Bloomington: Indiana University Press. pp. 85–95.

Samuel, R. and Thompson, P. (eds) 1990. *The Myths We Live By*. London: Routledge.

Sanjek, R. (ed.) 1990. *Fieldnotes: the makings of anthropology*. Ithaca: Cornell University Press.

Sarbin, T. (ed.) 1986. *Narrative Psychology: the storied nature of human conduct*. New York: Praeger.

Saville-Troike, M. 1982. *The Ethnography of Communication*. Oxford: Basil Blackwell.

Schatzman, L. and Strauss, A. 1973. *Field Research: strategies for a natural sociology*. Englewood Cliffs: Prentice-Hall.

Scheff, T. 1997. *Emotions, the Social Bond, and Human Reality: part-whole analysis*. Cambridge: Cambridge University Press.

Schiebel, M. 2000. 'Extreme right attitudes in the biographies of West German youth', in Chamberlayne et al.

Schon, D. 1983. *The Reflective Practitioner*. New York: Basic Books.

Schorn, A. 2000. 'The "Theme-Centred interview": a method to decode manifest and latent aspects of subjective realities'. *Forum Qualitative Research* [on-line-journal], vol. 1(2). Available at: http://qualitative-research.net/fqs-e/2-00inhalt-e.htm

Schuman, D. 1982. *Policy Analysis, Education and Everyday Life*. Lexington, MA: Heath.

Schutz, A. 1970. *On Phenomenology and Social Relations*. Chicago: University of Chicago Press.

Schütze, F. 1977. 'Die Technik des narrativen Interviews', in *Interaktionsfeldstudien. Arbeitsberichte und Forschungsmaterialien* Nr. 1 der Universität Bielefeld, Fakultät für Soziologie.

Schütze, F. 1982. 'Narrative Repräsentation kollektiver Schicksalsbetroffenheit', in Lämmert, E. (ed.), *Erzählforschung. Ein Symposium*. Stuttgart: Metzler. pp. 568–90.

Schütze, F. 1984. 'Kognitive Figuren des autobiographischen Stegreiferzählens', in Kohli, M. and Robert, G. (eds), *Biographie und soziale Wirklichkeit. Neue Beiträge und Forschungsperspectiven*. Stuttgart: Metzler.

Schütze, F. 1992. 'Pressure and guilt: the experience of a young German soldier in World War II and its biographical implications', *International Sociology*, 7(2, 3): 187–208, 347–67.

Schweitzer, P. (ed.) 1998. *Reminiscence in Dementia Care*. London: Age Exchange.

Segert, A. and Zierke, I. 2000. 'The metamorphosis of *habitus* among East Germans', in Chamberlayne et al. (eds), *The Turn to Biographical Methods in Social Science*. London: Routledge.

Seidman, I. 1998. *Interviewing as Qualitative Research: a guide for researchers in education and the social sciences* (2nd edn). London: Teachers College Press.

Senge, P. 1990. *The Fifth Discipline: the art and practice of the learning organization*. New York: Doubleday.

Shafer, R. 1980. 'Narration in the psychoanalytic inquiry', *Critical Inquiry*, 7: 29–53.

Shafer, R. 1983. *The Analytic Attitude*. New York: Basic Books.

Shweder, R. 1991. *Thinking Through Cultures: explorations in cultural psychology*. Cambridge, MA: Harvard University Press.

Silverman, D. 1993. *Interpreting Qualitative Data: methods for analysing talk, text and interaction*. London: Sage.

Sloan, T. 1996. *Life-Choices: understanding dilemmas and decisions*. Oxford: Westview Press.

Sluzki, C.E. 1992. 'Transformations: a blue-print for narrative changes in therapy', *Family Process*, 31(3): 217–30.

Smith, D. 1983. 'Nobody commits suicide: textual analysis of ideological practices', *Human Studies*, 6: 309–59.

Soderquist, T. 1991. 'Biography or ethnobiography or both? Embodied reflexivity and the deconstruction of knowledge/power', in F. Steier (ed.), *Research and Reflexivity*. London: Sage.

Sostris Working Paper nos 1–9. 1998–99. University of East London: Centre for Biography and Social Policy.

Sostris Working Paper no. 1: Social Exclusion in Comparative Perspective (1997)

Sostris Working Paper no. 2: Case Study Materials: the Early Retired (1998a)

Sostris Working Paper no. 3: Case Study Materials: Lone Parents (1998b)

Sostris Working Paper no. 4: Case Study Materials: Ethnic Minorities and Migrants (1999)

Sostris Working Paper no. 5: Case Study Materials: Unqualified Youth (1999)

Sostris Working Paper no. 6: Case Study Materials: Ex-traditional Workers (1999)

Sostris Working Paper no. 7: Case Study Materials: Unemployed Graduates (1999)

Sostris Working Paper no. 8: Innovative Social Agencies in Europe (1999)

Sostris Working Paper no. 9: Sostris Final Report – From Biography to Social Policy (1999)

Spanò, A. and Caniglia, P. 1999. 'Unqualified and unemployed youth: "blaming the victim"'. Italian National Report. *Sostris Working Paper no. 5*, pp. 64–75.

Spence, D. 1982. *Narrative Truth and Historical Truth: Meaning and Interpretation in Psychoanalysis*. New York: Norton.

Spradley, J.P. 1979. *The Ethnographic Interview*. New York: Holt, Rinehart and Winston.

Squire, C. 2000. 'Situated selves, the coming-out genre and equivalent citizenship in narratives of HIV', in Chamberlayne et al. (eds), *The Turn to Biographical Methods in Social Science*. London: Routledge.

Standing, K. 1998. 'Voices of the less powerful: research on lone mothers', in Ribbens, J. and Edwards, R. (eds), *Feminist Dilemmas in Qualitative Research*. London: Sage.

Steele, R. 1986. 'Deconstructing histories: towards a systematic criticism of psychological narratives', in T. Sarbin (ed.), *Narrative Psychology: the storied nature of human conduct*. New York: Praeger.

Stein, N.L. and Glenn, C.G. 1979. 'An analysis of story comprehension in elementary school children', in Freedle, R.O. (ed.), *Advances in Discourse Processes: New Directions in Discourse Processing*, vol. 2. Norwood, NJ: Ablex.

Stigler, J.W., Shweder, J.R. and Herdt, G. (eds) 1990. *Cultural Psychology: essays on comparative human development*. Cambridge: Cambridge University Press.

Strauss, A. 1987. *Qualitative Analysis for Social Scientists*. Cambridge: Cambridge University Press.

Strauss, A. and Corbin, J. 1990. *Basics of Qualitative Research: grounded theory procedures and techniques*. Newbury Park: Sage.

Swanson, J. 1986. 'The formal qualitative interview for grounded theory', in W.C. Chenitz and J.M. Swanson, *From Practice to Grounded Theory: qualitative research in nursing*. California: Addison-Wesley.

Synge, J. 1981. 'Cohort analysis in the planning and interpretation of research using life histories', in D. Bertaux (ed.), *Biography and Society: the life history approach in the social sciences*. Beverley Hills: Sage.

Tannen, D. 1990. *You Just Don't Understand: women and men in conversation*. London: Virago.

Tannen, D. 1992. *That's Not What I Meant!: how conversational style makes or breaks your relations with others*. London: Virago.

Tejero, E. and Torrabadella, L. 1999a. 'Migration and emancipation: the tension between globalisation and identity. Spanish National report', in *Sostris Working Paper no. 4*, pp. 67–86.

Tejero, E. and Torrabadella, L. 1999b. 'Unqualified youth: the biographical experience of invisibility and identity conflicts. Spanish National report', in *Sostris Working Paper no. 5*, pp. 7–22.

Thompson, P. 1988. *Voice of the Past: oral history*. Oxford: Oxford University Press.

Tremblay, M.-A. 1982. 'The key informant technique: a non-ethnographic application', in R.C. Burgess (ed.), *Field Research: a sourcebook and field manual*. London: Unwin Hyman.

Tukey, J. 1962. 'The future of data analysis', *Annals of Mathematical Statistics*, 33: 1–67.

van Maanen, J. 1988. *Tales from the Field: on writing ethnography*. Chicago: University of Chicago Press.

Vaughan, D. 1987. *Uncoupling: how and why relations come apart*. London: Methuen.

Volante, M. 1998. 'The Biographic Interpretive Method', paper presented to the 4th Postgraduate Discussion Group, *The Madness in Methodological Social Science*, Keele University, 14 November 1998.

Watzlawick, P., Beavin, J. and Jackson, D. 1986. *Pragmatics of Human Communication*. London: Faber and Faber.

Weber, M. 1949. 'Objectivity in social science and social policy', in *The Methodology of the Social Sciences*. New York: Free Press.

Wengraf, T. 1990. 'Documenting domestic culture by ethnographic interview', in T. Putnam and C. Newton (eds), *Household Choices*. Futures Publications/Middlesex Polytechnic.

Wengraf, T. 1998. 'SOSTRIS at the level of the comparative interpretation of cases', in *Sostris Working Paper no. 3*, pp. 120–7.

Wengraf, T. 1999. 'Contextualising subjectivity in the exploration and presentation of cases in biographic narrative research', in *Sostris Working Paper no. 6*, pp. 57–63.

Wengraf, T. 2000a. 'Uncovering the general from within the particular: from contingencies to typologies in the understanding of cases', in Chamberlayne et al. (eds), *The Turn to Biographical Methods in Social Science*. London: Routledge.

Wengraf, T. 2000b. 'Betrayals, trauma, and self-redemption? The meanings of "the closing of the mines" in two ex-miners' narratives', in Andrews, M., Sclater, S., Squire, C. and Treacher, A. (eds), *Lines of Narrative*. London: Routledge.

Wertsch, J.V. 1990. 'Dialogue and dialogism in a socio-cultural approach to mind', in I. Markova and K. Foppa (eds), *The Dynamics of Dialogue*. Hemel Hempstead: Harvester-Wheatsheaf.

Wertsch, J.V. 1991. *Voices of the Mind*. Hemel Hempstead: Harvester-Wheatsheaf.

Willis, P. 1977. *Learning to Labour*. Farnborough: Saxon House.

Wolcott, H. 1994. *Transforming Qualitative Data: description, analysis and interpretation*. Thousand Oaks: Sage.

Yin, R. 1993. *Applications of Case-Study Research*. Thousand Oaks: Sage.

Yow, V.R. 1994. *Recording Oral History: a practical guide for social scientists*. Thousand Oaks: Sage.

Index